SERIOUS REPERCUSSIONS

SALLIE MONTANYE

For Nicole

TABLE OF CONTENTS

Introduction		1
Chapter One	Initiative	4
Chapter Two	Bullied	11
Chapter Three	Exiled	25
Chapter Four	Deliberate and Dangerous	32
Chapter Five	Jeopardy	45
Chapter Six	Allegations	62
Chapter Seven	Loudermill	79
Chapter Eight	Directives	98
Chapter Nine	Abandoned	113
Chapter Ten	*Montanye v.*	126
Chapter Eleven	Complaint	139
Chapter Twelve	Motion to Dismiss	153
Chapter Thirteen	Dead Kids Don't Learn	165
Chapter Fourteen	Valiance or Violation	186
Chapter Fifteen	Nicole	208
Chapter Sixteen	Discovery	218
Chapter Seventeen	Depositions	231
Chapter Eighteen	Sarah	247
Chapter Nineteen	Boundaries	265

Chapter Twenty   Final Depositions   291

Chapter Twenty-One   Experts   313

Chapter Twenty-Two   Falsus Uno, Falsus Omnibus   331

Chapter Twenty-Three   Summary Judgment   347

Chapter Twenty-Four   The Appeal   363

Chapter Twenty-Five   Fraud Upon the Court   376

Chapter Twenty-Six   Writ of Certiorari   395

Chapter Twenty-Seven   Target   404

Chapter Twenty-Eight   Homecoming   429

Chapter Twenty-Nine   Birthday Arbitration   457

Chapter Thirty   Last Stand   476

Epilogue   500

Acknowledgments   503

The word *repercussion* is commonly used in the plural. Repercussions can be thought of as ripple effects occurring because of an incident or action. A decision can cause unexpected, and/or indirect, repercussions, which are more far-reaching than mere consequences. A consequence can be positive or negative, but a **repercussion is always negative**.

V2 Vocabulary Building Dictionary
http://vocabulary-vocabulary.com/dictionary/repercussion.php

INTRODUCTION

Bullycide: when unrelenting bullying and harassment combined with the lack of intervention by the responsible adults cause children to ultimately attempt or commit suicide.

Bullycide: Death at Playtime-An Exposé of Child
Suicide Caused by Bullying
Neil Marr, Tim Field; Amazon Books

Every year hundreds of school-age children make the decision to end their lives. Schools decry this carnage; the media splash gruesome details in breaking news stories. Administrators appear in tearful interviews. Politicians offer sound byte condolences, swearing to follow through with some vague legislative remedy. In spite of the hand wringing, the advice of TV psychologists, and the promises of appalled educational agencies, kids still kill themselves with frightening regularity.

So why are kids dying despite the foreseeability of these tragedies? Where are the educators who see these children daily? Why do the deeply regretful administrators have only mournful words to offer?

UGLY REALITY: Many school administrators are not motivated to do the right thing. They are motivated to cover their own rear ends, remain aloof, and to avoid the slightest suggestion of any responsibility. Their decisions are money driven.

In my experience, the superintendent and his subordinates were not fazed by a child's possible death. An independent attorney, hand chosen by the superintendent and later endorsed by the school board, emphatically stated the child's problems were of no significance. In fact, these people were only upset when a viable and legal intervention took place to save the child's life.

School districts are far more worried about extracting themselves from any shred of culpability. If they can distance themselves from a district mea culpa, the bullied, suicidal child does not enter the collective consciousness. As long as teachers do not become involved or are terrified into silence, accountability is plausibly denied.

I was the link between administrative indifference toward a bullied child, her consequential suicide attempts, and the district's steadfast refusal to take action. As stated by the upper administration: I had to be stopped and they had to insure I would never repeat any act of intervention or demonstrate concern should another persecuted, suicidal child appeal for help.

Bullying is a virulent and pervasive problem; in many cases, it's a deadly one. It thrives in the school venue. News reports of violence and premature deaths that are desperate responses to bullying are no longer uncommon. The public is familiar with the names of Phoebe Prince and Ryan Halligan. Everyone knows the story of Columbine. Bullying is the accomplice to murder and the handmaiden to suicide.

Columbine sent the government into a frenzy, which resulted in The Attorney General's Task Force Report on a Legislative Response to Bullying (2002). What the committee learned was not news to teachers. They were not surprised that the second leading cause of youth violence is bullying, which occurs in schools. There was no shock to educators that the Littleton (Columbine) and Moses Lake tragedies resulted from relentless teasing and harassing. It also came as no revelation that 71% of students reported teachers or other adults ignore bullying. **What most students and parents don't realize is that in many cases, teachers are helpless to get those in charge to take preventative or prescriptive steps.**

What may not be as well known is that bullied girls are eight times more likely to be suicidal than their peers who are not subjected to harassment. Sadly, incidences of single deaths from suicides don't rate the attention of a Columbine, even though the number of annual dead children far exceeds the grim statistics from Colorado.

Do the school boards know all of this? Articles in the archives of the National School Boards Association address bullying and the need for schools to act. A piece by Kathleen Vail, written for *The*

American School Board Journal, entitled "How Girls Hurt," discusses at length the problems associated with bullying among girls. It even has its own name-***relational aggression.***

The danger in the manner in which girls intimidate other girls is that the damage is inflicted covertly. The weapons most effectively used for relational aggression are the withholding of friendship, gossip, name-calling, and exclusion. The aggressor sets up a situation where she can hurt another girl and escape blame for the action. Teenage girls live in such fear of not being accepted; they are willing to do almost anything to obtain the friendship being denied.

The long-term consequences of social bullying are serious academic, social, and emotional problems such as: chronic absenteeism, declining grades, attempts to escape school, social withdrawal, and fear of being without adult protection.

Some sad statistics:

- Suicide is the third leading cause of death in people between the ages of fifteen and twenty-four. (The Pennsylvania Youth Suicide Prevention Initiative)
- It is estimated that 10% to 15% of all adolescents attempt suicide (Capuzzi, D. *Suicide Prevention in Schools: Guidelines for Middle School and High School Settings.* Alexandria, VA: American Counseling Association. 1994)
- The adolescent suicide rate has nearly tripled since 1950 (Firestone, R.W. *Suicide and the Inner Voice: Risk Assessment, Treatment and Case Management.* Thousand Oaks, CA: Sage. 1997)
- More teenagers and young adults die from suicide than from cancer, heart disease, AIDS, birth defects, stroke, pneumonia, influenza, and chronic lung disease combined.

Teachers can be the difference between success and failure, and in some instances, life and death. I am not advocating they replace therapists or other professionals; however, because sometimes teachers are allowed into the more private spaces of students, they can play a pivotal role in the life of a child. When it comes down to life or death, degrees and titles don't help much. What matters is showing a child she is ***valued,*** she is not alone, and death is not the answer.

CHAPTER ONE

Initiative

This maturation process can best take place in a positive learning environment...one characterized by an atmosphere of openness and mutual respect for the personal worth and dignity of each individual...one in which we communicate our belief in the *value* of every child...

The Wissahickon School Board Code of Discipline

In the spring of my eighteenth year of teaching, I was formally accused of:

- Willful neglect of duty
- Insubordination
- Incompetency
- Persistent negligence in the performance of duties
- Willful violation of school laws
- Improper conduct
- Unprofessional behavior

I was lied to.
I was lied about.
I was vilified with the intensity reserved for child molesters.

What grievous act did I commit?
I helped save the life of a suicidal child.

My work experience with troubled children was extensive. I started my career at a private school that dealt exclusively with severely emotionally disturbed children. Here, teachers were involved in therapy, behavior contracts, and weekly meetings with psychiatrists to discuss student progress.

I then worked for an Intermediate Unit, which was the conduit to Special Education in the public school system. Created by the state, IU's were considered the prime source of information regarding legal responsibility and requirements of both state and federal Special Education law. They established the guidelines, provided teacher training, and opened the Special Education classes in the schools.

When my husband changed jobs, we moved back to the Philadelphia area where I procured a job working at a highly respected suburban school district. I taught seventh, eighth, and ninth grade learning disabled students and some emotionally disturbed students. Again, I was in constant contact with psychiatrists and psychologists who were working with these children. At the request of one student's family, I accompanied him to meet his doctor and discuss his issues, which centered on him and his family.

After time off to have my children, I returned to work as a long-term Special Education substitute teacher in a neighboring district before I was hired by the Wissahickon School District. As a sub there was little time to become close with the students; however, one girl stood out in this class. She had all the indicators of a child drowning in a private agony. She was a social outcast, subjected to daily ridicule from the other students. Her face was set in a permanent look of pain. She received no services or attention from any professional in the district. When I spoke to the guidance counselor, she informed me there was "nothing they could do."

It was discovered that this girl, who was living with her mother, was not a legal resident of the district. She was instructed not to return to the school after Christmas break; she had to attend the district where her mother paid school taxes.

I called the director of Special Education at her new district. The director knew who I was, as I had completed the initial screening process to be on their Special Education sub list. My background experience lent credence to my words. I explained my concerns, provided her with as much information as I knew, including the fact that this child was self-mutilating. Now there's a red flag.

The director recited the disclaimer: "Erika is in Mrs. So and

So's class. She's an excellent teacher, and I'm sure she will make certain Erika is given everything she needs."

The director never relayed the message to the teacher. She did not tell the Child Study Team about this student who required reassessment and services. The girl's first suicide attempt and consequential hospitalization that spring were indicators that my concerns were well founded. Furthermore, a stint in a mental facility following a suicide attempt calls for a re-evaluation for a Special Ed student. But when this young lady returned to school, the same administration that ignored my warning call, ignored her. After the summer there was no need for services. The girl was dead. Fourteen years old.

How do I know the behind-the-scenes facts? I spoke with all those involved when I started my job at Wissahickon, the district where Erika was mandated to attend school. Her final stop before eternity.

I was hired to start the sixth grade Emotional Support class at the Wissahickon Middle School. Emotional Support (emotionally disturbed) is a Special Education category designated by federal law. The guiding beacon of Special Education is the federal law known as IDEA.

> The Individuals with Disabilities Education Act (IDEA) is a law ensuring services to children with disabilities...IDEA governs how states and public agencies provide early intervention, special education and related services to...youth with disabilities…

IDEA defines the categories of Special Education. According to the U.S. Government (34 C.F.R. 300.5(b)(8): Education of Handicapped children, Federal Register, Section 121.a.5, 1977), "seriously emotionally disturbed" is defined as a condition exhibiting specific characteristics which adversely affect educational performance over a period of time.

These characteristics include a "general pervasive mood of unhappiness or depression." Another qualifier is the "tendency to develop symptoms or fears associated with personal or school problems."

The nature of a viable Emotional Support program runs counter to the parameters of the public education system. My experience with these children is that they are usually bright, have difficulty fitting into the mold of "student," are overcome by problems more severe than those faced by the average kid, and are far too plagued with issues that override any or all of the demands created by standardized education. In many cases they come from broken or chaotic homes, which removes any hope of support or structure in their young lives.

Now add to this potion drugs and alcohol, suicidal ideation, bullying and personal disenfranchisement; as the Emotional Support teacher you are expected to vanquish these obstacles and convince your students of the validity of adhering to rules and getting work in on time.

The importance of the role of Emotional Support teacher cannot be overstated. For some of these children the teacher is the only stability in their lives. For some, the teacher may be the only person who takes an interest in the child. Generally, an Emotional Support pupil is intellectually able to do school work but is unable to function effectively due to a pervasive emotional overload that dominates the child's life and precludes academic success. Roughly translated: the child is too tormented to worry about learning square roots.

In the middle school it was my job to assist the students with their interactions with regular education teachers, physical therapists, speech therapists, parole officers, and any school personnel. Beside the task of teaching, the Emotional Support teacher is mother, mediator, translator, mentor, defender, and listener for her students.

The first and primary lesson Emotional Support children need to learn is how to survive in the system. They have to acquire skills on how to cope with rules and regulations, how to express their emotions in socially acceptable ways, how to deal with disappointment and failure without withdrawing or becoming self-destructive, how to avoid getting sucked into physical or verbal altercations, how to speak appropriately to adults and how to master a number of other behaviors which are assumed to have been acquired by the time they arrive in middle school.

From 1994 to 2001, I worked with sixth, seventh, and eighth grade Emotional Support students in the middle school. The last two years, when I was teaching eighth grade, my class was combined with learning disabled kids.

During my tenure in the middle school, I received excellent

7

annual ratings, with complimentary observations about my relationships with my students. At the end of my first year the director of Special Education commented on the transition the students made when the class was opened in February 1994:

> Mrs. Montanye established the 6th grade emotional support class during the Spring semester…although all students in Mrs. Montanye's class have difficulty adjusting to change and establishing interpersonal relationships, the reorganization proceeded very smoothly as a result of Mrs. Montanye's skill, sensitivity, flexibility and hard work. She is to be commended for her efforts on behalf of the students …
> (Judith D'Angelo Teacher Observation Report 4/25/94)

My annual evaluation also noted my relationships with students:

> Mrs. Montanye has successfully developed a positive, caring rapport with her students. She shows sensitivity to the needs and feelings of her students.
> Mrs. Montanye has successfully developed the 6th grade emotional support class into a positive program that allows students to grow both educationally and emotionally.
> (Snyder/J. D'Angelo/Neil Evans Annual Evaluation 1994)

My 1995 evaluation commented that I:

> maintained poise and composure in dealing with (her) students…She is concerned about them as individuals and exhibits an understanding of their situations. (Snyder/Sebulsky Annual Evaluation 1995)

In 1996 the director remarked that I:

> cared a great deal about the students…She goes out of her way to make her students feel comfortable…shows a great concern and understanding for the student...Mrs. Montanye is to be commended for doing a very good job.
> (D'Angelo/Snyder Annual Evaluation 1996-1997)

In 1998, a new director of Special Education stated:

Mrs. Montanye has developed a fine rapport with the students...She shows sensitivity to the needs and feelings of her students. Mrs. Montanye encourages and initiates two-way communication with parents. She demonstrates an active interest in her students and involves herself in their everyday lives. Mrs. Montanye demonstrates initiative to take risks and remains open to change. Mrs. Montanye displays compassion and sensitivity in working with her students. She sets high expectations for personal performance.

(Fagan/Evans Annual Evaluation 1998-1999)

The middle school assistant principal who wrote my 2000 annual evaluation also commented:

Mrs. Montanye maintains a good rapport with her students and constantly looks out for their welfare...Mrs. Montanye maintains a sincere interest and concern for her students in all aspects...

(Sebulsky/Annual Evaluation 2000)

As an Emotional Support teacher, I was available to my students both in school and out. They had my cell phone number and my home phone number in case of emergency. I received calls from kids in the hospital, terrified kids who were arrested, kids with a sudden death in the family, and sometimes kids with strange questions such as, "Does drinking bleach help you pass a drug test?"

As I pointed out before, I was involved with many professionals, including private therapists who saw my students outside school. There were instances in which this was a requirement written into the educational program. I was expected to speak with these providers on a weekly basis, reporting my observations and listening to the ones emerging from the therapy. On occasion, I met with these professionals at the request of the parents and/or student. There is no doubt that a unified support group comprised of therapist, educators, and parents is the most effective method for helping children cope with their individual agonies and the demands of their lives in school.

I did not wind up as an Emotional Support teacher by accident. It was my choice, and I spent much of my post education reading and learning about children with emotional issues. I preferred these children to all others. They were warm, honest, and complex, once they let you in. There were failures to be sure, but there were many successes. Sometimes it just takes a child understanding that she is important to someone to help turn the situation around. It is not always that simple, but children who know you genuinely care about them are responsive and willing to make an effort.

What's most interesting about troubled children is they are quite keen at figuring out who likes them and who doesn't. Lying does not work with them-they see through the phonies and pretenders. They were my harshest and most vocal critics, and they kept me honest.

There were many frustrations and limitations that prevented success within the school setting. When Special Education bumps into the daily workings of an inflexible system, Special Education goes by the wayside. There is only so much one can do.

I loved my job and I loved my kids. I considered myself to be the luckiest person because I wanted to be at work and thoroughly enjoyed what I was doing. There were moments of discouragement, but the many little victories were worth it.

Overall, the rewards were numerous. Watching your students grow and achieve was inspirational.

Making a difference in a child's life was priceless. No one told me that saving a life would end my career and change everything I valued.

CHAPTER TWO

Bullied

The **Pennsylvania Youth Suicide Prevention Initiative** is a multi-system collaboration to reduce youth suicide.

Vision: Youth suicide prevention will be embraced and incorporated into the fabric of every community in Pennsylvania to address the social and emotional development of youth at risk and survivors of suicide.

Suicide claims the lives of over 1,300 Pennsylvanians each year-an average of 3.5 lives each day. It is the third leading cause of death for young people ages 15-24. Since the 1980s, Pennsylvania has made strong efforts to prevent youth suicide through programs such as the Student Assistance Program (SAP)…

In 2001, Pennsylvania developed its own youth suicide prevention plan, based on the National Strategy for Suicide Prevention: Goals and Objectives for Action.

One of the goals in the plan is to **promote awareness that youth suicide is a public health problem that is preventable.**

© Copyright, Pennsylvania Youth Suicide Prevention Initiative

Kay's early years in school were auspicious. She enjoyed school and had a close circle of friends. In third grade Kay was evaluated for Special Education services. She had a very minor reading problem, a result of a weakness in decoding skills. She was classified as learning disabled; however, her difficulty only required minimal attention. She attended regular education classes and was given limited supplemental reading support. Sixth grade brought the beginning of a radical change in her life. Kay's friends excluded her from their activities. Along with the rejection, the more assertive girls attacked her verbally. Her wounded reactions to this excommunication served to egg on the cruelties.

By seventh grade she was ostracized completely. At the end of that year, the antagonistic behavior blossomed into overt bullying, replete with physical intimidation and degrading barbs.

The harassment reached a fevered pitch in eighth grade. Kay refused to come to school. When she did, she sought refuge in the guidance office to avoid the hallways in an effort to elude physical attacks or the loud humiliating slurs that followed her to class. The final altercation sent her to the hospital with a concussion. This occurred when she was walking in a less traveled section of the school. A group of girls jumped her and slammed her against the concrete wall.

Kay's coping response was the development of psychosomatic illnesses that resulted in numerous absences. On the days she was present she spent the majority of her time in the nurse's office or sitting in the guidance department's waiting area.

The hallways were gauntlets of terror. She would leave the classroom before the bell and go to the nurse's office to avoid the crowds. She would then return to class once she felt safe enough to move through the building.

In days past, children were able to escape emotional brutality by taking refuge in their homes. Kay did not have this luxury: the invasive nature of the Internet provided the perfect arena for cyber bullying. When she went online, she was the recipient of hate messages. There simply was no place she could find a safe haven without cutting herself off completely from the world.

Here is a sample of an online attack on Kay:

Sender: I don't need to say shit to you—you just better watch the fuck out before your face is smashed and then you cant even get girls! And im not the stupid ugly ass bitch-who the fuck can u get -your so lucky and you have soooooooo many friends but that's why the WHOLE 8th grade was standin watching you when you gonna get ur a$$ beat-but u ran…I'm just warning u.watch ur back kay

The old adage is only half true. Sticks and stones may break your bones—but words can kill you.

They killed Phoebe Prince, a Boston high school student, who on January 14, 2010, after days of harassment and taunting, committed suicide by hanging herself in the stairwell leading to the second floor of the family apartment.

They killed Ryan Halligan, a boy from Vermont, who committed suicide at the age of thirteen after being bullied by his classmates in real life and in cyber-space.

They killed Erika during her first year at Wissahickon.

They almost killed Kay.

Kay's mother was in the middle school on a daily basis begging for help. She started with the guidance department and worked her way up the administrative chain. She had meetings with Hugh Jones, the Middle School Principal, providing him with the cyber threats and notes passed to Kay during the day. Twice she had to retrieve her daughter from school after she had been attacked. During one of her visits, she heard a girl remark that the next time Kay "would go down with the first punch."

On one of the many days Kay was not in school, the middle school principal brought the girls who tormented her into his office to "discuss" their behavior. According to one of the attendees, the majority of the session was spent with the participants stating how much they disliked Kay and how she deserved what she was getting.

One of the girls present at the meeting reported to Kay what was said.

[3/21/01 email] She informed Kay that Mr. Jones started his talk with the problems that can result from teasing and name-calling. He then allowed the girls to take turns going around the table expressing their feelings toward Kay. According to this girl, all the participants, with the exception of her, openly confirmed they hated Kay.

Because the author of this email was the only one who professed any kind feelings, the principal said this girl could help Kay. He would set up a meeting with the guidance counselor about methodology. This meeting never took place. The principal then advised the girl to tell Kay the opinions of the others so it "wouldn't start an argument."

The principal's clumsy effort served no purpose other than to provide the bullies with a bitch session and to make Kay feel more isolated when she learned it had taken place. His fumbling did nothing to abate the problem; in fact, the girls upped the ante after it occurred.

Kids are crafty. They can tell how serious a matter is by gauging the response patterns of adults. None of the administrative conduct conveyed the gravity of the problem. If Kay hadn't already felt like an outcast, this meeting certainly sealed the deal.

The intimidating power of the group was the weapon being used. The principal not only reinforced the group's muscle, he fostered its energy by allowing an airing of perceived justification through the group voice. Speaking with individuals would have afforded greater information. Those who feared the group may have been more honest in private, and it certainly would have prevented the report to Kay that projected a unanimous chorus of loathing. Learning everyone was sitting around criticizing her in public while the principal tacitly gave the conversations credence, cemented Kay's feelings of alienation and lack of self-worth. The principal solidified the united front of aggression.

Kay received threatening notes on a regular basis. Some were warnings of things to come:

To Kay: Hello! Wuts Up? Are you still mad at (girl's name)? I read the email. That's a little rude! Gosh someone wants to beat you up. I would tell you who, but I don't know who.

The principal, weary of Kay's mother's concerns, refused to hold any more meetings using a number of excuses to elude her. Finally, she resorted to written communication in a letter to him, dated March 15, 2001 and referenced as "assault on Kay." The note opened with the reminder of the physical attacks on Kay. It went on to state that Kay, once again, had been attacked.

"She was assaulted again today." This act of violence involved the police and a trip to the emergency room for a concussion.

The mother referenced Kay's numerous absences due to her fear of this group, the constant visitation to doctors, and the large amount of unproductive meetings with the principal and the guidance counselor.

Her frustration was evident:

> …you have a very volatile situation at hand…my husband
> and I are outraged. We are extremely upset with the school
> administration and the lack of interest on the school's
> behalf for our daughter's safety. My husband and I find it
> difficult to believe that a child who had gone to the
> guidance office and sat there in fear, who had gone to the
> main office and sat there in fear, can be assaulted for the
> second time, been seen by the nurse, [and] dismissed to
> return to classes as if nothing had happened…
>
> I feel that the safety of my child, and maybe other
> children as well, is at stake…Please be advised that my
> husband and I plan to seek [legal] counsel with regard to
> the above request. I look forward to meeting with you to
> discuss what measures can be taken to protect my child
> and other innocent children in your school.

The letter was cc'd to a legal firm.

It was also sent to Stanley J. Durtan, Superintendent of Schools.
The district's response? They allowed Kay to move to another eighth
grade team located one hallway down, an empty gesture that did
nothing to avert the harassment or protect this child.

No parent should have to plead with a principal to ensure her
child is safe at school. Kay's mother sent another letter four days
later after her first one was ignored. This one was dated the 19th of
March; the heading read "Protection for Kay."

The letter, addressed once again to the principal, voiced the
parents' conviction: (1) their daughter was the target of harassment,
(2) their daughter had already been assaulted twice, and (3) the
parents were formally requesting

> …our daughter have surveillance from the time she
> enters school. It is our request that she is carefully
> watched when going to and coming from classes, that
> she be watched in the stairwells. We would also like her
> to be monitored during lunch period.

The first letter, asking for an administrator to take action
deterring verbal abuse and physical assaults, should not have been

necessary. Parents should not be forced to prod an administrator to take appropriate steps to protect a child who has become the focal point of virulent hostility. **It's his job!** As head of the school, the principal is responsible for making sure, to the best of his ability, that the students are safe. Ignoring a problem or demeaning its severity is not utilizing the best of one's ability.

Mr. Jones responded to the second letter with a phone call. He explained to Kay's mother that he had "1200 other students" to care for; her daughter was "not the only child in the school."

In case you're tempted to rationalize that asking for protection for Kay was over demanding, compare it to this: the same year Kay's mother's request was made, the administration took an aide from a class to sit with a Special Education student so he **could practice the violin.** His parents wanted him excused from schoolwork three times a week in order to do this. This outlandish proposition was granted by the school district. He had to have an adult with him, so they assigned an aide to babysit. Private violin lesson practice does not come under the responsibility of the public school. Although an aide was too busy to help protect a desperate child, at the instruction of the director of Special Education, one was readily available to honor an outrageous and inappropriate demand.

In a last-ditch effort to protect their child, Kay's parents asked for homebound instruction. They resorted to the only solution they were aware of: they would remove their child from the danger. Both the guidance counselor and the principal advised they would need a medical letter attesting to Kay's need to be placed outside of the school setting. Telling a parent how to remove a child from school because administrators allow a threatening situation to persist is unethical. In this case, it was also illegal.

On March 30, 2001, Kay's pediatric practice confirmed the need to have Kay removed from school. Kay's mom sent another letter, along with the doctor's recommendation for homebound instruction. She reiterated that Kay was being harassed and that her request for protective surveillance had been denied.

> It is our understanding that the school was not willing to take the measures that would protect our daughter. Under these circumstances we have taken Kay out of school and are now requesting your assistance in obtaining homebound instruction…

Kay's mother received a dismissive letter from Mr. Jones in response to her final plea: This letter dated April 4, 2001, opened with: "You stated that your daughter was 'assaulted' twice. As we discussed previously, Kay was involved in two 'fights' at Wissahickon Middle School."

Once he established that Kay's mother was "over reacting," he addressed the ever-pesky issue of protecting Kay.

You asked if a teacher could be assigned to Kay to protect her from additional harassment or fights with other students. My response was that **other students could provide this service** but I did not have a specific teacher who could provide this service. Thus, your request of assigning a teacher was denied but your understanding that the school was not willing to take measures that would "protect our daughter," is totally inaccurate. Measures are taken daily to create a safe environment for all students. Your request, however, to assign a specific teacher is not an option given a teacher's instructional responsibilities.

Shut the front door! Before addressing the second part of this letter, let's take a look at what was really going on.

Putting the words "fights" and "assault" in quotation marks was a conscious denigration of this woman's concern; the principal ridiculed the parent(s) by dismissing the problem as inconsequential. Don't forget, he had those "1200 other students" to worry about. The tone of the letter strongly pointed to his belief that the mother was making an unreasonable request when she sought safety for her child.

My favorite part in his reasoning was that Kay's mother was inaccurate when she accused the school of being unwilling to take measures to protect her daughter. Even though he had just turned her down for **any** protective measures, he assured her the school was willing to protect "all students." So, the principal cannot come up with a way to protect one child because he's supposed to be protecting all the children. And, the mother of the unprotected child is falsely claiming that the school is indifferent to her child despite the fact that the "1200" others were protected and Kay was not. How can you protect "1200" and not one? Why wasn't

Kay considered a member of the "1200"?

The principal employed the first and most revered tactic in education: he lied. Special Education assistants were employed daily to escort students to classrooms for various reasons. Kay was still a Special Education student. Surely her physical safety would warrant an escort. Secondly, they didn't have a spare aide to assure Kay didn't get bashed into the walls, but they could tap an educational assistant for three hours to **sit with a student in order for him to practice his violin?**

The most astounding aspect of this letter was the suggestion that Kay should ask her friends to protect her. To proffer that it would be the job of a student to protect another child from harassing peers is blatantly idiotic. Kids walking beside Kay would hardly deter other students from physically assaulting her. In the event a physical confrontation would develop, what should the other students do? This suggestion seemed particularly foolhardy as it invited open warfare.

The principal was precipitating a greater problem by setting up a situation where the bullies would perceive the bodyguards as a challenge and would provoke an incident. Bullying is about power and the group. Forming a secondary group-Kay's peer protectors-was adding another dimension, one that would fuel more aggression. You don't need a psych degree to figure this one out.

Most importantly, wouldn't it be the job of the adult, who was earning a substantial amount of taxpayer money as head of the school, to make sure a child was safe? Wouldn't that task be better suited to the administrator rather than to the children? This man was charged with the safety of "1200 students," and the best solution he could provide to protect one of them was to let her friends do it.

Apparently, this dangerous and irresponsible idea was acceptable to the district administration. Kay's mother had sent all correspondence to Superintendent Stanley J. Durtan; the highest-ranking school district official was aware of the events taking place in his middle school and took no steps to intervene.

Mr. Jones ended with a rejection of the reasons for homebound instruction offered by the pediatrician, instructing Kay's mother to obtain another diagnosis.

As I stated to you during our telephone conversation on April 3, your request for homebound instruction because

Kay is "fearful of attending school" is not an acceptable reason. Homebound instruction must be based on an existing medical condition as determined by a doctor...please submit a request from your doctor specifying a diagnosis for Kay's medical condition.

Kay's parents were caught between the law and Kay's safety. The law states the reasons a child may be removed from school; harassment is not one of the "legal" protocols. When Kay's parents took her out of school, they opened themselves up to charges of truancy and a multitude of fines. Without an "acceptable" reason they were in violation of the law, and yet the alternative to that was sending their child into a daily grind of abuse.

On April 10, 2001, a psychiatrist recommended that:

Kay be allowed to withdraw from class and complete her eighth grade work through homebound instruction because there has been no resolution of the animosity with those allegedly involved and there is no way to guarantee Kay's safety within the middle school...there have already been two physical confrontations between Kay and the other students, which, suggests that this situation has exceeded the more common pre-adolescent bickering among acquaintances.

Kay, according to this professional, was suffering from Posttraumatic Stress Disorder [PTSD].

PTSD is a condition resulting from extreme trauma or living in a situation where there is chronic fear of repetitious acts of physical or mental abuse. In the instance of bullying, it is the constant threat of violence and/or psychological brutality that causes emotional damage. The victim becomes hyper-vigilant, constantly assessing the possibility of an attack, which continues the vicious cycle contributing to traumatic stress. This is not paranoia; it is an intense fear resulting from a credible expectation of a personal assault.

Kay presented with the traits of a person with PTSD. She had no control over what happened to her and she had no avenue of escape. The state dictated she attend school where she was trapped for the duration of the day. The administrators would not eliminate the threats while statute forced her to relive the trauma on a daily basis.

Given the link between bullying and suicide, PTSD is an indicator of a child who, if placed on this path without intervention, may wind up dead or cause the death of others. Although those around her threatened Kay, she was in far graver danger from the feelings within.

After submitting the psychiatric evaluation, Kay's parents had a meeting with the following administrators of the Wissahickon School District to discuss the situation:

Stanley Durtan, Superintendent of Schools
Judith Clark, Assistant Superintendent
Hugh Jones, Middle School Principal
Kelle Heim-McCloskey, Supervisor of Special Education.

Would all these learned people be uneducated in the problems of harassment? They shouldn't have been. In 1999 the U.S. Department of Education Office for Civil Rights wrote a guide for schools concerning the need for safety in schools, which was endorsed by the National School Board Association:

Research indicates that creating a supportive school climate is the most important step in preventing harassment. **A school can have policies and procedures, but these alone will not prevent harassment.**

The second page of the guide is a letter from then Secretary of Education, Richard Riley:

Our schools owe students a safe environment that is conducive to learning...Harassment undermines these purposes and may cause serious harm to the development of students who are victimized by this behavior...successful prevention strategies depend on the coordinated efforts of all school employees, including individuals responsible for administration.

In Wissahickon it was the administrators who allowed Kay's daily torture; when the superintendent was confronted with the evidence of Kay's deteriorating emotional state, he elected to take the much traveled path of blaming the victim by taking away her education.

Dr. Durtan advised the parents he felt they were making the best decision in taking Kay out of school. He offered no other option. Kay's parents were operating under the incorrect assumption their only recourse was to pull her from school and place her on homebound instruction. The district did nothing to dispel this erroneous belief.

In fact, there are a number of steps to be taken before placing a child at home. The obvious was they should have done something to stop the torture. The alternative would be to place Kay in another school-either in district or out of district. Homebound instruction is the last option to be used, but it's easier than tackling the bullying issue and it's much cheaper than another placement.

The Wissahickon School District became the poster child for administrative-sanctioned bullying. Despite the fact that Kay experienced most of the symptoms of PTSD, and although it was evident she was riding the rollercoaster of self-destruction, the superintendent, the assistant superintendent, the supervisor of Special Education, and the middle school principal gave their stamp of approval for this negligence by taking no action to make Kay's school safe for her. Then, they pushed her off their horizon.

The bullies won. Kay was banished by the inactions of the administration and the actions of the kids who tormented her. Bullies are encouraged where "administrators turn a blind eye to bullying." To the bully, a blind eye is a green light. Those who were the catalysts of Kay's removal remained in school getting an education, while she was confined to her home as a social outcast.

Kay received four hours of homebound education per week. Compare four hours with the thirty-five an in-school student receives. A teacher, whom she did not know, came to the house, gave her papers to complete, and picked those up when she returned with more papers. Hardly what you would call an education.

The removal from school and the administration's deliberate neglect took its toll. Kay's disenfranchisement that began when her social circle shunned her grew with her segregation from the school community. The anguish of rejection did not melt away because she was no longer in school. Compounded by anger and despair, her condition worsened and her sense of worthlessness became more acute.

In the summer of her eighth grade year, when the pain became too much to bear, Kay tried to slit her throat with a kitchen knife.

She was placed in a psychiatric facility for three days of observation. In addition to the first diagnosis of PTSD, the second psychiatric evaluation added she was suffering from severe depression and suicidal ideation. She was now a bona fide member in the too populated ranks of children at risk.

*****

How seriously did the superintendent and his assistants view the issue of bullying? Here are a few incidents that took place in the Wissahickon School District following Kay's experience:

2002-2003: A Special Education child was badly beaten while waiting for a bus at the middle school; an ambulance was called and she was taken to the hospital. **No anti-bullying policy.**

2002-2003: Remember Mr. Jones's suggestion that Kay's friends provide protection? A high school student was punished because he protected his girlfriend who was being physically and verbally harassed. The girl reported the threats many times to her guidance counselor but nothing was done. Her boyfriend said **he had** to protect her because no one else would. The assistant principal, the parents, and a teacher met with the boy to discuss how he should handle the situation if it occurred again. It was agreed that he would seek out a teacher or administrator the next time his girlfriend was accosted. The administrators said the incident would end with this agreement. The next day; however, they reneged on the decision: they called the boy into the main office where the police were waiting. The assistant principal had called them in. The boy was arrested and taken out in handcuffs.
No anti-bullying policy.

2002-2003: Parents, who were forced to hire an attorney, won a private placement for their child because bullies

targeted him. At one of the meetings concerning this child, a district employee suggested the boy and his tormentors should be taken outside and allowed to "slug it out."
No anti-bullying policy.

2003: Middle school faculty members wrote a letter to the administrators recounting how a student violently attacked another with a pen, stabbing the victim in the temple. A teacher intervened because the attacker was continuing the assault. The aggressor, the president of student counsel, was given a three day, in-school suspension. The teachers were incensed: they were of the opinion this slap on the wrist sent a message to the rest of the student body that violence would be tolerated.

They made this known in a letter to the administration:

> The major concern beyond the incident itself is the message that this teaches our students...nothing will really happen to you if you stab another student with the intention of seriously harming them and you can still represent the student body as class president. If physical violence is not met with serious consequences, it will increase and we will fail in one of our primary functions: keeping kids safe. If the message is that you stay in school after assaulting another student and you don't immediately lose any privileges or status, then we are teaching them that violence is tolerated at WMS.
> **No anti- bullying policy.**

2006: At a school board meeting an angry mother spoke out about how her child had been forced to transfer to a different elementary school because he was relentlessly bullied. She wanted to know what the district was going to do about bullying for the rest of the kids. Dr. Durtan silenced her by saying he thought they had resolved her problem and a discussion about these concerns **"did not belong in a public forum."** [Ambler Gazette, February 2006].
No anti-bullying policy.

These are just a few of the stories that rose to the surface. Most remain safely hidden behind bureaucratic double speak.

*****

When the Wissahickon School District filed its Annual School Violence and Weapons Possession Report (July 1, 2000—June 2001/Kay's 8th grade year) it stated there were **no** incidents of assaults on students in the middle school. Under the column for children removed from school due to physical violence, there was a zero.

...we communicate our belief in the value of every child...(WSD)

CHAPTER THREE

Exiled

34 CFR §300.300 requires that public agencies provide psychological counseling services to children with disabilities who need them to benefit from Special Education.

34 CFR §300.24 (b)(9)...the term psychological services includes...information about child behavior and conditions relating to learning, planning and managing a program of psychological services including psychological counseling for children and/or children and their parents...Psychological counseling is a continuum of services...that will address an individual students' needs when behavior interferes with her learning...Such behaviors include...withdrawal, depression, and suicidal threat...

For children who are identified in the Emotional Support grouping, the law states school districts must provide some modicum of assistance because those with severe emotional troubles do not fare well in school. Tormented children do not have the focus to learn or perform to expectation; they expend most of their energy fighting their demons.

The Emotional Support group is the most neglected population in Special Education. It is the most difficult to administer: it goes against the grain of uniformity and does not always respond to cookie cutter prescriptive approaches.

Our district offers these children alternatives on paper but very little in the way of realistic support. They are provided with the label on the IEP, and they are sometimes given goals that are merely restatements of their problems in positive terms. *David will not throw objects at others more than twice a week.* How this goal is achieved is not forthcoming because, in reality, there is no program. In fact, at a Wissahickon in-service with a behavioral specialist, we were told to avoid mentioning behavior problems if at all possible because, "You don't have a program for them."

In February of 2002, the U.S. Department of Education of Special Education Programs (OSEP) released the results of a review conducted in Pennsylvania (2000) for the purpose of assessing compliance in the implementation of IDEA. One of the areas of noncompliance concerned children who needed Emotional Support. The report stated that the Pennsylvania Department of Education did not ensure that all "children … who require psychological counseling to benefit from Special Education were provided services in accordance with an appropriate IEP." [1]

The report also criticized the state because the children who should receive counseling were **only provided recommendations to outside private therapists**. The parents had to pay for the therapy. This is in contradiction to IDEA's provisions and *exactly* how it worked in our district. The upshot of the report was that children in need of Emotional Support were not getting it. Period. Their only hope was if their parents took them to outside therapists.

The essence of Special Education is distilled in the Individualized Education Program (IEP). This is a contract between the educational institution, the parents, and the child, laying out the needs of the student and the methods by which those needs will be met to achieve the stated goals. The IEP is supposed to dictate the program. The IEP is the blue print from which the teachers work, the map that guides the child through his education while providing supplementary or adapted materials to help the child overcome the deficit which defined his need for Special Education. In Pennsylvania, the IEP is revisited annually. The child is reassessed, the goals of the previous year are evaluated, and new ones are written if there has been progress.

Although couched in incomprehensible jargon, the IEP actually consists of the child's levels, the perceived strengths and weaknesses, the goals to ameliorate the weaknesses, and the techniques or programs by which these improvements can be attained.

If a child has emotional needs, this is addressed as part of the emotional component in the IEP. There are goals associated with this

---

[1] IEP = Individualized Education Program. We'll talk about this momentarily.

component, methodology provided, and timely progress checks. Of course, if the child's emotional issues are not mentioned, then nobody would be the wiser and the district can extricate itself from its legal obligations. Bottom line: the IEP's collectively should provide a thorough history of the student and what programs have been offered to help the child reach the individualized goals. Documentation is the lifeblood of Special Education.

When Kay started to self-destruct as a result of the bullying, it was the district's moral and legal responsibility to reassess her. Instead, her Special Education classification was ignored and she was denied her civil rights. The behavior of district administrators was more heinous because it was their inaction that fueled the fire of her emotional difficulties. Kay didn't enter with this baggage; she picked it up at the school door.

Because she was placed on homebound for psychiatric reasons, the law required that Kay be re-evaluated as to her disabilities and the goals to address them. This was never done. The IEP did not reflect her home placement. The IEP did not note any of the difficulties she experienced during the middle school years. The IEP did not even hint of the emotional issues plaguing her.

There were other legally required provisions omitted in Kay's educational nightmare. Special Education law mandates that all students be provided a Free Appropriate Public Education (FAPE). Kay did not get this in school (because she was constantly hiding from her tormentors), and she certainly didn't get it when she was removed from school as a result of the district's refusal to take steps to insure her safety.

There is also the requirement that Special Education students must be in the Least Restrictive Environment (LRE), meaning the student should be in regular classes as much as possible, while making academic progress. The intention of this regulation was to prevent districts from cramming Special Education children into a broom closet for the entire day. The law calls for a continuum of placements from least restrictive (regular education room with support) to the most restrictive (home placement or a hospital). Kay was tossed out of school and into the most restrictive environment.

When a student is moved from a less restrictive environment to a more restrictive environment, there must be a revision to the IEP justifying the change of placement. This is law. There were no revisions made to Kay's IEP. There was no mention of the homebound placement.

Not only was this placement illegally done in light of federal law, it was also in violation of the PA Department of Education regulations which state there are four hard and fast reasons which forbid separating a student with a disability from students who are not disabled. According to those in the Pennsylvania Department of Education, it is illegal to remove a Special Education child from school because:

1. **The district lacks an available alternative placement.**
2. **The district does not offer the appropriate programs or services.**
3. **The district lacks staff qualified to provide the services in the IEP.**

Number four, "**forbids** separating a child from her educational placement for the **administrative convenience of school officials.**" This law was designed to prevent children with problems from being exiled for the sole purpose of making life simpler for administrators. When Kay became inconvenient, both she and the law were expendable. They did not want to deal with Kay's issues; once they got rid of her, they were rid of the problem. It doesn't get more convenient than that.

If a Special Education child is assigned a homebound placement, are there any other provisions the district should provide? According to the *Cordero* decision, a Special Education child who is placed on homebound must be provided with "any supplemental services necessary." *In Cordero v. Pennsylvania Dep't of Education,* 795 F. Supp. 1352 (M.D. Pa.1992), the court stated a Special Education student is "entitled to receive intensive inter-agency services if there is an extended absence from school."

Her numerous absences and removal for part of her eighth grade year certainly qualified as an extended absence from school. Yet, Kay was provided with no services. This was especially remiss because she was placed outside of the school on a psychiatric diagnosis, which obviously necessitated therapy. In short, the district administrators could have been held accountable for Kay's first suicide attempt. They certainly took no actions to prevent further harm to her.

The refusal to follow legal requisites pales in significance to the callous manner in which this child was treated and the dereliction of duty by those who were charged with her care.

The highest placed and highest paid representatives of the Wissahickon School District ignored the requirements delineated by state and federal law. You might be inclined to offer the defense that those who attended the spring meeting that resulted in Kay's removal may not have been aware of the complexities of IDEA and PA Spec Ed Regulations. Let's review their credentials:

- **Stanley J. Durtan,** Superintendent of Schools, was a former school psychologist; he would have dealt extensively with Special Education children. Dr. Durtan was the Director of Special Education in Dallas, PA. He would have known the requirements of IDEA and the state regulations given this background.

- **Judith Clark,** Assistant Superintendent, was a former Special Education teacher. She was also the Director of Special Education in a nearby district. Ms. Clark was the head of Pupil Services when she started in the Wissahickon School District. As such, she oversaw the Special Education department. As assistant superintendent, she would be expected to know the law.

- **Hugh Jones**, the middle school principal, was the person who signed off on the middle school IEP's for the district. Mr. Jones knew the requirements.

- **Kelle Heim-McCloskey**, Supervisor of Special Education, was a former Special Education teacher. As supervisor, she was one of the persons in charge of checking all submitted IEP's to assure compliance. As supervisor, she was one of the district's experts on Special Education.

It is unnerving, given this pantheon of Special Education familiarity, that not one administrator followed the law. How is it possible that all of these experts found it acceptable to allow a five-foot-one-inch, ninety-five pound girl to be used as a punching bag by bullies and then ignored statute and civility by forcing Kay to leave school for her own safety?

Had Kay not been a Special Education student, Dr. Durtan

and the district could still be held accountable for their lack of action to resolve the problem. In *Davis v. Monroe County Board of Education* [1999 WL 320808 (US)], the Supreme Court found school districts may be liable for damages arising from student on student harassment when:

> The recipient of federal funding is deliberately indifferent to harassment of which the recipient has actual knowledge and that harassment is so severe, pervasive, and objectively offensive that it can be said to deprive the victims of access to the educational opportunities or benefits provided by the school.

Deliberate indifference is the test the courts use in determining whether a school district can be found liable for student on student harassment. The *Davis* decision found that the district's failure to act **while being aware of the circumstances** amounted to deliberate indifference.

Additionally, 18 PA Consolidated Statutes 27 says: "Pennsylvania prohibits harassment and stalking." Harassment occurs according to the statute, when:

> A person with intent to harass, annoy or alarm another, the person strikes, shoves, or threatens to do the same, follows the other person in or about a public place or places, or engages in a course of conduct or repeatedly commits acts which serve no legitimate purpose.

Even without these statutes, it would not be unreasonable to expect a superintendent, an assistant superintendent, a supervisor, and a principal to operate from a humane standpoint. Instead of exhibiting the primal urge to defend the helpless, these people refused to protect Kay, sent her home oblivious to the damage already done or the possibility of future harm.

The U.S. Department of Education Office for Civil Rights put out a guide for schools called *Protecting Students from Harassment and Hate Crimes* (1999). The National School Boards Association endorsed it. Part II is a Step-by-Step Guidance on Identifying and Responding to Incidents of Harassment. Under Emotional and Psychological Support the following is stated:

Students experiencing harassment may continue to suffer psychological problems, including impaired self-esteem, even after the harassment has ended...The target of the harassment should be offered school services, such as counseling...

Kay was diagnosed with PTSD, but those in power refused even the most basic action to insure her psychological or physical safety. They had a stable full of lawyers to argue their innocence had Kay's suicide attempt been successful, and there was no documentation (except Mom's letters) to link them to any liability.

The principal reduced Kay's problem to minor squabbles; the superintendent and his team pushed aside law and human decency by endorsing her removal from school. And yet the mantra of these administrators is, "We're here for the children."

CHAPTER FOUR

Deliberate and Dangerous

Wissahickon School District is a nurturing academic community where all students encounter challenging opportunities through which they grow, learn, prosper and discover their full personal, social and intellectual potential, and develop the skills, attitudes, and abilities necessary to become respectful, responsible, productive and contributing citizens.

Wissahickon School District Mission Statement

September came and Kay returned for her ninth grade year at the high school. The bullies who were after her in the middle school followed her across the street. When Kay walked into that building, she brought with her all the troubles that plagued her the previous year. The bullying did not abate due the change in locale; if nothing else, there was more opportunity. The harassment could operate with less surveillance in a substantially larger venue.

Kay's fragile emotional state made her a most satisfactory target. Due to her hypersensitive defense responses, she operated either in attack mode or hid somewhere quaking with fear. She was constantly developing physical ailments that granted her reprieves from coming to school. On the days when she did show up, she was late, which earned her a file drawer full of detentions.

Kay was not the only one new to the high school. I transferred from the middle school the same year. I had been unaware of Kay in the middle school as she was not in my instructional group or the team I worked with. As fate would have it, I met her the second day of the fall semester, 2001. Until that day, I had no knowledge of Kay or her problems. She was only a name on my roster.

She was assigned to my English and social studies classes. Our initial exchanges were not entirely pleasant because she should have been in a regular education English class, not my Special Education class. The first week in school, she asked her mother to remove her from my class. Her mom told her to give it some time, which Kay agreed to do. Her decision changed the course of both our lives.

*****

In October 2001, Kay asked to speak with me outside the classroom. She gave me a rundown of the previous year and the summer suicide attempt. She said the old feelings were returning. This was my **first notice** that she was in trouble. I emailed her IEP case manager about the conversation. The teacher replied she was glad Kay had found "someone to talk to."

A few days later Kay's mother called me. This was the beginning of many phone conversations. When she was describing Kay's summer, she said, "You have no idea what it's like to watch your beautiful daughter drag a knife across her throat." That picture has never left my mind.

Kay dropped a French class at her request and was assigned to my room for a study skills class. We had talks during this period. Our discussions dealt with her fear of walking in the halls, the taunts, her feelings of inadequacy, and her emotional claustrophobia. She told me about an abusive relationship she had had with her last boyfriend. She had broken it off, but she was reconsidering. This is not atypical behavior for people who have been targets for bullying; often they may place themselves in a situation that is degrading or destructive.

Kay was always late to my class or always stayed after class. I soon found out why. In order to escape the derogatory comments, she avoided the halls until they cleared. I tried to work with her to overcome their insults; however, the wounds were too deep, and she was too beaten down.

Two red flags raised from our discussions led me to believe that Kay's troubles were far greater than usual teenage angst. In late fall she told me her feelings of wanting to die were returning with greater frequency. According to almost every piece of psychological literature written about suicide, the most accurate prognostication for a successful suicide attempt is a previous one. There is no wiggle room when you are dealing with someone who has tried it.

What added to my fears was she was spending time with an older crowd, and I suspected she could be using alcohol and marijuana. Those are wild cards when dealing with someone with suicidal ideation. Both substances are depressants, and there is no predicting what an already troubled person will do under their influence.

I kept encouraging Kay to get back into therapy. She had already nixed the idea of speaking with her guidance counselor, and she did not want to share her story with the Drop-in Center counselor, a guidance counselor with a different title. Kay did not like the idea of telling more people about her problems.

I reported these conversations to Robert Anderson, the high school principal. I knew Kay's mother had also spoken with him frequently. When I was in the middle school, I was the person the students would speak with when they had personal or school problems. If the student went to a guidance counselor, with the student's permission, I was called in for a briefing.

Things were progressively worsening at home. Kay and her mother were locked in a battle over mom's attempts to control Kay's actions. From a mother's perspective, this was understandable; if Kay were kept close, she would not have the opportunity to carry out her death wish. From Kay's viewpoint she was being smothered. None of this was inexplicable given the situation. This was a family in crisis.

One night, while shopping, I received a call from Kay's mother. She was frantic; Kay had left the house saying she was going to see the former boyfriend. It was about 9:00 P.M. and her mother could not find her. She did not know what to do, and by this point, she was so beside herself with worry she could not rationalize what action to take. I told her to call Robert Anderson who advised her that her only recourse was to call the police. The problem with that is the police would not look for anyone until they had been gone for twenty-four hours. I told the mother to tell the police of the suicide factor; that way they would not wait for a day to pass. Two hours later Kay was back home.

I talked to Kay the next day. I suggested that she and her mother and I sit down and work out some form of agreement which would allow Kay a greater sense of freedom in return for her being accountable for her whereabouts. This was not an off-the-wall offer. Many times Emotional Support teachers draft behavior plans to be used at home. I had done it in years past and so had a number of other teachers.

Kay adhered to the plan for a short while; however, it was a superficial fix and quickly disintegrated. The only long term, realistic approach to Kay's turmoil was therapy.

In November of 2001, Kay's parents and I met with Mr. Anderson to discuss her regression. I felt badly for her parents who were in such crisis they were placed in the humiliating position of bearing their secrets and fears to strangers. They were grabbing at any straw they could to get help for their child.

Mr. Anderson suggested the district send Kay to a state approved alternative school that claimed to be an Emotional Support setting, but in reality was a dumping ground for the district's behavior problems. There were no therapists at this place. The "Emotional Support" label was a misnomer: without therapists the kids were not getting anything other than the offerings of the regular schools.

Understand that behavior problems are not the same as emotional problems. Kay was not comparable to kids who were attacking people or constantly in trouble with the law; nonetheless, she would be mixed in with this population. Many of the students placed there had been involved in violent altercations; putting Kay there was tantamount to throwing her to the wolves. The last thing she needed was to be surrounded by kids who were not allowed in regular schools because they were physically aggressive.

I did not see any good coming out of sending her to a place which would surround her with drug dealers, drug addicts, habitual fighters, or students who brought weapons to school. Fortunately, her parents felt the same way and vetoed the idea.

As we approached the Christmas break, I noticed Kay was not taking care of herself physically which was yet another indication she was losing ground. She looked tired and drawn. The depression and anger had her in a downward spiral, and there was no good end in sight.

In January of 2002, the classroom assistant found a note on the floor. She handed it to me with the statement, "This can't be good."

It was a note Kay had written to her friend who was also in my class. The note said:

Girl's name,

I want to kill myself! I am not staying in school today…do you have any cigs with you? If not it's cool cuz I'll probably walk home anyways. I would love to overdose on some drug!
…I can't live with my family. I need to get away from them. I called some place about being adopted. I'm going to ask my mom if I could stay with [name]. G/G Kay

The word **HELP** was written and circled at the bottom of the page.

I took the note to Mr. Anderson immediately. He referred to the "suicide check list" in his manual. He made two copies of the note, delivered one to the guidance office and the other to the nurse's office. I watched him walk down the hall and into the guidance office. When he came back to the nurse's suite, I watched through the window as he spoke to the nurse, Imelda Kormos. He placed the note on the counter in front of her.

Mr. Anderson returned to the main office and directed me to find Kay to see what her mindset was. I located her in another class and took her to the stairs next to the gym. I told her we found the note. I asked her if she would speak with her guidance counselor. She said no. I asked if she would speak with the Drop-in Center counselor. No again. I told her things could not go on like this. I insisted she consider returning to therapy. All along I maintained I did not have the qualifications to give her the help she would receive from a psychologist. I was more than happy to be a sounding board for the day-to-day issues; life and death issues were another matter.

My daughter had seen a psychologist for a maximum of three visits when she was undergoing a painful break up. I had spoken to this woman and thought Kay might feel comfortable with her. I felt confident giving Kay this psychologist's name because the guidance counselors at school were familiar with her and strongly endorsed her. I told her to talk it over with her mom. She took the therapist's card.

I reported everything to Mr. Anderson. I told him Kay had returned to her last class of the day, and I had spoken to that teacher. I informed him that I had suggested a psychologist to Kay, and she agreed to discuss this with her mother. At the close of school, I called Kay's mom to make sure Kay had gotten home safely. We talked briefly about the note.

The next day Kay said her mother was in agreement that she should try a new psychologist. Kay told me she would be willing to go. Then, she dropped a bombshell; she would only see the therapist if I went with her.

What Kay was asking was different from my usual contacts with therapists, but I understood why. She was afraid of not being taken seriously. She feared her mother would not be taken seriously. She felt a psychologist would be more inclined to believe what happened if someone other than her mother provided verification.

I told her I would go with her a few times in order to make her comfortable. After that she would have to establish a relationship with the therapist on her own. This arrangement depended on her mother's approval and agreement with the therapist.

When I spoke with Kay's mother, we agreed I would attend only a few meetings. I informed Mr. Anderson about the arrangement. My exact words were: "Kay wants me to go with her to the therapist and her mother said I could." He asked if I had this in writing. I told him I would get it.

Kay's mother called the therapist and told her about the arrangement. I also spoke with the therapist. A few days later, Kay set up her first appointment.

It is most important to point out that in Pennsylvania the law governing mental health, which is found under the PA Mental Health Procedures Act 50; Section 7210 states:

> Any person *fourteen years of age* or over who believes that he is in need of treatment and substantially understands the nature of voluntary treatment may submit himself to examination and treatment under this act, provided that the decision to do so is made voluntarily. Except as otherwise authorized in this act, all of the provisions of this act governing examination and treatment shall apply.

I bring this to your attention because Kay was fourteen and therefore was the only one who could legally make the decisions pertinent to her mental health care. In Pennsylvania, **fourteen is the age of majority** where mental health is concerned.

The law also clearly states the regulations surrounding

mental health records. Without the consent of a child fourteen years or older, the mental health records cannot be released or discussed. Unless a child is found to be not competent, she controls whom she sees, and, most importantly, who has a right to her records or any information pertaining to the therapy. The therapist is bound by confidentiality and cannot reveal anything discussed during a session. The only way a therapist can disclose information is for the child to sign a waiver of confidentiality or if the child is in danger of harming herself or others.

The therapist Kay was seeing was also an attorney; she knew the law. She knew the only person empowered to dictate who could be present in the sessions was Kay. The only person who could allow the release of any information concerning these sessions was Kay.

On the day of Kay's appointment she left school at the end of the day and went home. I spoke with her mother and told her I would be more than glad to pick Kay up after school, drive her to the therapist's, and bring her back. Her mother agreed. This was done purely for time and convenience.

The session was innocuous as all of the information Kay discussed had to do with the previous years' events. Kay spoke about the suicide attempt and told the psychologist she was presently experiencing feelings similar to those she had when she tried to kill herself in the summer. I offered only one explanation concerning a procedure in the middle school. Other than that, I just listened. We made a second appointment to take place in two weeks. I returned Kay to her home afterwards.

The following week Kay suffered a complete meltdown. It was Wednesday and she was not in school, which was not unusual. Her mom called me in tears; Kay had stormed out of the house after a huge fight. I told her to come up to school and speak with Mr. Anderson. I called him to let him know that Kay's mother was on the way.

When Kay's mom arrived, Mr. Anderson escorted her into the nurse's suite. I was called to come down. Imelda Kormos, the school nurse, was present and so was the Drop-in Center counselor. These women instructed the mother to call the police.

I knew Kay's mom had spoken to Mrs. Kormos; however, when the nurse and I were discussing Kay during this event, I got the impression her medical diagnosis was that Kay needed to be "controlled." The Drop-in Center counselor did not have any familiarity with Kay. She didn't say much, but rather deferred to the nurse. Neither one of these women ever made reference to the suicide note.

Kay called her mother on her cell phone and told her where she was. At the direct instruction of Nurse Imelda Kormos and the Drop-in Center counselor, the mother lied to her daughter saying she would pick her up. Still following their direction, Kay's mom then called the police and reported Kay's location so they could retrieve her. Kay continued to call her mother on the cell phone, but both nurse and counselor told her not to answer her daughter's calls. This poor woman just sat there listening to the phone ring with tears pouring down her cheeks.

The Drop-in Center counselor did not remain in the office once it was established that the police would pick Kay up. At no time during this episode did she speak with me about Kay, nor did she approach me any time after this incident.

The police called to say they had Kay at the station, and her mother could retrieve her. Imelda Kormos decided this was not the best procedure. She called the police back and demanded they bring Kay to school.

The police report reflected Ms. Kormos's intervention:

I had the station call Mrs.XXX and request that she meet us at the station. I was instructed to contact the school nurse at Wissahickon, as Mrs.XXX was "unable to control her daughter." It was 1040 hrs. I contacted the school nurse who stated that Mrs.XXX along with a counselor from crisis management would meet us at the high school.
(Ambler Borough Police Department Daily Log).[2]

The police were reluctant to do this. Mrs. Kormos was adamant, claiming that Kay's mom would have "trouble handling her daughter." The nurse wanted to force Kay to go to class. As she put it, Kay should not be "allowed to escape" from school.

I waited in the hallway. Imelda Kormos came out and

---

[2] There was no crisis management counselor to meet Kay. Nurse Kormos, Kay's mom and I were the only ones left there.

informed me that the police had to restrain Kay with a straight jacket. The nurse displayed no trace of empathy toward this girl.

The police pulled up directly in front of the building where everyone had a clear view of the car and Kay. Classes were changing which meant she was visible to everyone passing through the main hall. This made her extremely agitated. She already suffered from being the object of ridicule; the idea that fellow students could peer through the glass doors and see her tied up in a police vehicle pushed her over the edge.

Her mother went to speak with her, but Kay would have no parts of this conversation. Her feelings of abandonment were fueled with rage at her mother's betrayal. She did not understand this deceit was the brainchild of the nurse and the counselor. She could not know that two people, claiming to be versed in the psychological make up of human beings, subscribed to duplicity and treachery as effective tools to be used with a child in turmoil.

I asked if I could speak with her. This was a wasted effort. Kay was way beyond any reasoning by this point. Her face was streaked with mascara and tears; her small frame was wrapped in a straight jacket, and her legs were kicking rapidly against the front seat of the patrol car. Between panting sobs she kept repeating, "Can't they move the car?" I asked the policewoman if she could take the car a few feet down the drive where there were no windows. She complied.

I returned to my classroom. Robert Anderson came to tell me that Kay's parents had taken her to Montgomery County Emergency Services [MCES] at the suggestion of the police. I had been there before. It was a hellhole.

Later that evening Kay's mom came to my house. Kay was only staying for three days and then she would have a hearing to gain her release. I asked her permission to visit her daughter. She said it was fine.

The next night I went to see Kay with some gifts. I figured she needed a little cheering up. If you have never been to one of these facilities, consider that a stroke of good fortune. They are horrendous. When you go in, you have to empty your pockets and leave everything in a locker. You are frisked and questioned. You have to fill out a number of forms.

You are then escorted back into a chamber of horrors. The rooms are dingy and stink; the atmosphere is right out of

Marat/Sade and the noises make you feel as if you have just arrived in a world of the damned.

Kay was looking none too good and was particularly creeped out by some male patient who was following her around and mumbling. I told him to go away and leave us alone, which for some unknown reason he did.

We went to the empty cafeteria. While we were talking, her parents came in. The conversation was light and there was even some laughter. I thought it best they have time alone, so I left as soon as I could.

On Friday Kay had her hearing. The judge instructed her to continue therapy for three more visits. Now it was court ordered. I talked to her briefly that day assuring her no one knew where she had been and she did not have to answer any questions

The next week we attended the second therapy session. I met her at the therapist's office. I told her mother I would bring her home. The majority of the session was spent on the MCES incident. I contributed nothing. We did not make another appointment.

Afterwards, I pointed out to Kay that her mother was an extraordinary woman to be able to handle my going to the therapist with her. I admitted I did not know if I could share my daughter with someone else in that way. I also told her I would only go back one more time and then she was on her own. Kay agreed to this, but said, as she had before, she would not have gone if I had not been with her. This conversation took place the last week in February. I never went back with Kay to the psychologist's.

In March, Mr. Anderson informed me he had had a meeting with Kay's mom and Nurse Imelda Kormos. He did not say what took place at that meeting; however, he advised me not to go with Kay again to the therapist. I told him we never made another appointment and we had not talked about doing so. It was left at that. It did not make sense, however, that there was a meeting concerning Kay that did not include me. I later learned this was the nurse's doing. Kay's mother had requested my presence and remarked on my absence at the meeting. She was informed by the nurse that I was unavailable at the time.

The next week I was invited to Kay's house for a birthday dinner. Both her parents were there, and we had a pleasant time. There was no mention of the past experiences. I did have some time with mom before dinner, but I did not think to ask her about the meeting with Mrs. Kormos and Mr. Anderson.

I watched Kay during dinner. Her demeanor was so unlike the frantic, captive child in the police car or the sunken-eyed, lost girl in the psych ward. She appeared serene, but there was an aura of despair underneath. There was no spark in her eyes and her banter was forced. She was not out of the woods by a long shot.

In school I tried once again to have Kay speak with the Drop-in Center counselor. I introduced the two of them in the hallway. Kay was angry because she felt everyone was dictating that she had to speak with strangers. She said as much to this counselor. Kay told her she had a therapist and she had me; she did not feel she should have to discuss her feelings with new people.

The Drop-in Center counselor, who was only supposed to see a child a few times during the year, was no more qualified to talk to Kay than the guidance counselors. She was not a therapist. The district was forcing Kay to run in circles. The problem was no one bothered to learn her background, no one talked to Kay's mother, or me, and no one communicated with anyone else.

There was one other incident involving Kay which would come back to haunt me. In early spring her math teacher approached me and asked if we could switch the English and math periods because Kay was in a class populated by many of the bullying girls. He said Kay wilted when she walked into the room, and the few times she worked up the nerve to answer a question, she was bombarded with snide comments.

The change was made and Kay was visibly relieved. She had asked me before to do this, but honestly, I hesitated because some teachers were making negative comments to me about her and I was afraid to ask for anything. I was running into the same brick walls Kay's mom experienced.

One afternoon Kay came to my classroom extremely agitated. I was not in school that day. When the aide told her this, Kay informed her she couldn't stay in school and left to walk home. Apparently, Kay called her mother crying. Her mother called the school to see what was happening. When the assistant principal went to find her in math, he discovered she had been switched to my class. Unknown to me, the math teacher had never put through the paperwork informing the scheduling office of the change.

The math teacher had thirty years in the high school. I had been there for six months. The math teacher requested the change.

I complied. It did not enter my mind that he had not put in the proper paper work. It did not occur to me to question a senior teacher who was also the union president. Our system in the middle school was quite different.

The following week I was informed by the assistant principal that I was going to receive a letter of reprimand for this. I met with him, accompanied by a union rep. He told me I was "putting the school district and the safety of the student in jeopardy." He assured me the reprimand would be kept "in-house," meaning it would not be sent over to Central Office and placed in my file.

Outside the office the union rep told me to be careful because now "they are watching you." I didn't think much of it because I wasn't doing anything wrong. I did what I was supposed to do and more. It was the *and more* part that would be my undoing.

The math teacher also received a letter; his was written by Principal Bob Anderson and had quite a different tone. Mr. Anderson reminded the teacher of the protocol for changing schedules and the necessity of following this. He stated he was sure the teacher would adhere to the steps from hereon out. There was no mention of *allowing* the student the liberty of cutting. There was no suggestion of putting the district in harm's way. Mr. Anderson approached the episode for what it was: a clerical error.

In contrast, the letter from the assistant principal to me stated my behavior was **deliberate and dangerous:**

> You changed the student's schedule without notification from the scheduling office...You placed the student and the school district at risk...The student used this unofficial change as an opportunity to leave school early..."*(Kay didn't know the change was 'unofficial.' I didn't know the change had not been reported; therefore, she had no idea. This nullifies the theory she used this as an opportunity to leave school early).*
>
> You are to limit your requests to those students whose IEP's are your responsibility. *(He was telling me I was no longer allowed to assist Kay because I was not the IEP case manager).*

The assistant principal had no interest in why the schedule was altered. He never asked why and refused to listen when I tried to explain. He did not address this in his letter of reprimand. His solution was to place Kay back in the class with her persecutors. From that point on Kay cut math on a regular basis for the rest of the year. This matter was never brought up. Her mother stated she continued to come home early many days. Suddenly, her safety was no longer a "matter of concern" to the district or its administrators.

I wrote a letter to Robert Anderson to point out that the assistant principal's accusations were unfounded. I also noted that Kay was placed back in a harmful situation. Nothing more was said or done.

CHAPTER FIVE

Jeopardy

Child Study Team Referral Instructions[3]

When to make a referral:

- Student who is withdrawn from class activities
- Student who repeatedly cuts class
- Student who is repeatedly truant from school
- Student who is persistent in attempts to get out of class (bathroom, nurse, guidance requests)
- Student who experiences continual physical distress in regard to anxiety about school work
- Student who repeatedly discusses problems at home
- Student who indicates wanting to harm themselves [sic] or exhibits harmful behavior (cutting, substance abuse, eating disorders)

Wissahickon School District Special Education Manual

When Kay entered ninth grade, there should have been preparations made for her return.

- What plan had been put in place to catch this child? None.
- What steps were taken to make sure her return to school was smooth? None.
- What efforts were designed to help her readjust to the school setting? None.

---

[3] These are the criteria used by the district to identify children who are at risk and should be referred for Special Education evaluation and assistance if necessary.

No one acknowledged the persecution resurfacing with a vengeance. Not one of the teachers with whom Kay came in daily contact was notified of the problems preceding her ninth grade year. She was on her own.

The district will point out that it had four programs in place to provide Kay with a safety net. In fact, there were programs in place designed to identify or assist children at risk.

They were:

- **Special Education** (Child Study Team)
- **Drop-in Center counselor**
- **Guidance counselors**
- **WIN Team (SAP)**

And yet, despite this list, Kay was left twisting in the wind. How did this happen?

The faction primarily responsible for Kay was Special Education, as she was still identified as a student in the program. Kay was removed from middle school and put from the **least** restrictive environment to the **most** restrictive environment. She received a mere four hours of instruction per week, which was a denial of free appropriate public education. All of these changes were made, and laws were violated without benefit of an IEP team meeting. She had been plunked back into the high school without being re-evaluated as would be warranted by removal from school for a psychiatric diagnosis, a suicide attempt, and an institutional stay. If nothing else she should have been evaluated by the Child Study Team as she met all seven of the emotional qualifiers.

But wait! Kay, due to her status as a Special Education student, had the protection of IDEA's prescribed document—the IEP. Kelle Heim-McCloskey, the Supervisor of Special Education, did not inform anyone in the high school about Kay's traumatic seventh and eighth grade years.

The IEP, which came over from the middle school, made no note about the harassment, the removal, the placement, or the psychiatric observations. This would be the vehicle to describe her unique needs and the district's plans on how to help her. Remember, given the specifications of IDEA and PA Spec Ed law, Kay's past trauma should have been addressed in order to provide her with modifications, provisions or related services.

Ms. Heim-McCloskey did not revise the IEP, nor did she consult with the eighth grade IEP team to advise them to do so. Kay's absences, psychiatric complexities, physical altercations, eviction from the school setting, and placement in the home were all required to be written in the IEP along with the solutions or methodology used to ameliorate these difficulties. They should have been, but they weren't.

Why, you may ask, didn't Kay's mother insist the ninth grade IEP team discuss these needs? Because no one brought up Kay's problems or offered any suggestions, she assumed this was not the place for a discussion of her daughter's emotional needs.

The teacher who wrote the ninth grade IEP had no knowledge of the goings on that had taken place in eighth grade. And, although Kay's guidance counselor sat in on this meeting, no information was supplied.

No one encouraged Kay's mom to broach her fears. Sadly, there would have been no services to offer Kay had anyone bothered to listen to her mother because there was no viable Emotional Support program.

Now let's once again consider what federal law says about Emotional Support children in public schools: 34 CFR §300.300 and 300.24(a) and (b) (9) (v) require that public agencies provide psychological counseling services to children with disabilities who need them to benefit from Special Education.

That's fairly understandable. Child with problems needs counseling; school provides said counseling, which enables child to benefit from Special Education services.

The Wissahickon School District Department of Special Education also stated this was necessary for Emotional Support children:

> The learning support/emotional support classes are designed to meet the academic and social/emotional needs of eligible students. The curriculum...also addresses the needs of social skill development and behavior management systems designed to develop, improve, and increase behaviors and skills to enhance the student's opportunity to achieve within the school system.
>
> (Doc #2 WSD Board Minutes: 12/10/2001)

Do you recall the U.S. Department of Education of Special Education Programs report, (OSEP/February, 2002—hint chapter

3), which was conducted in Pennsylvania for the purpose of assessing compliance in the implementation of the IDEA?

According to this report, **Pennsylvania** public schools "...did **not** ensure that...children with disabilities who require psychological counseling...are provided [with] services in accordance with an appropriate IEP..." In other words, children who required psychological counseling in order to benefit from their education were not provided with this important aspect.

Thus, the schools were not following the dictates of IDEA. This is the explanation the schools offered for violating the law:

> ...districts reported that psychological counseling services are not considered a related service and are not included on the child's IEP, regardless of need...if children with disabilities need counseling services, they are referred to a mental health facility/agency outside of the school district.

In essence the schools were saying: this is a burdensome requirement that we refuse to provide, so we simply will consider it something other than a "related service." Then we won't have to offer it to the child, because we are not legally obligated to supplement the child's education with anything that is not "related services." Remember this argument: it is not the school's responsibility to offer counseling services, and if a student needs them, she can get them privately.

The report could have been written specifically for Wissahickon School District's denial of services to children with emotional problems. It certainly went to the heart of Kay's situation.

The OESP report stumbled upon the tried and true philosophy of *if you don't write it, you won't have to pay for it.* This is how it's done. (1) The schools eliminate any mention of an emotional component in the IEP thus avoiding the need to provide any related services such as counseling or (2) The schools consider counseling "non- related services" which puts the onus of therapy on the parents and allows the district to avoid providing this supplement.

The report makes note of this errant policy: "Counseling is not included on the IEP's regardless of individual student need." The omission of stating the need for assistance, or mentioning any service emanating from the district, eradicates the need to provide it. It's cost effective. It's legally defendable because damages are hard to prove; they are hidden within the broken child.

A month after the ninth grade IEP was written, Kay's mother spoke with the case manager who added one sentence addressing Kay's emotional issues:

> Occasionally, Kay may become overwhelmed with problems and emotions and will need to be excused so she can speak with an appropriate adult. She realizes she is responsible for making up any work that was missed.

This was prescribing a Band-Aid for cancer.

Was it possible no one knew of her history, her summer suicide attempt, and her mental anguish in eighth grade? That would be a convenient reason for the lack of attention given to this girl; it would also be untrue.

Who knew about what happened to Kay other than the Special Education supervisor? Her guidance counselor did. Kay's mom told her high school guidance counselor what had taken place at the middle school. She knew about the bullying, she knew about the homebound placement, and she knew about the suicide attempt. In addition, the local police informed the school (guidance department) of Kay's self-destructive action. Yet, in spite of this knowledge, the guidance counselor did not speak with Kay, did not broach any concerns at the IEP meeting, and did not discuss contingency plans with any professionals who came into contact with Kay.

Special Education and guidance did not follow through with their obligations. The next go-to person would be the Drop-in Center counselor who deals with incidences on a daily basis. She is not responsible for scheduling classes; her main charge is dealing with student problems. However, her services have major limitations. Her job was only part time. She was available (but only at specified times) for one or two students to drop in and discuss a problem—i.e. fighting, rumors, difficulties with teachers. The Drop-in Center counselor was a short-term fix. She was limited to six visits from a student. If more were required, the student was to be recommended for outside help or to the WIN team (SAP). Realistically, the Drop-in Center counselor could do nothing more than recommend that Kay go to a therapist.

What is the WIN team? The Student Assistance Program [SAP] was created by the state to help troubled students who otherwise might "fall through the cracks."

Let me explain, "fall through the cracks." It is assumed that Special Education programs will address disabilities, including emotional problems and social interaction; therefore, students categorized as Special Ed are assumed to be monitored by the program and would be provided an IEP that addresses their needs. However, students in regular education are not as closely monitored and do not automatically have a comprehensive yearly review. It is not hard for these children to fade into the woodwork, particularly if they are withdrawn. Drugs and alcohol wreak havoc on many kids, and suicide, as you know, is a viable response in the teen mind. Teachers have one hundred fifty to two hundred pupils on their rosters. The numbers are too daunting to assure that the lost or troubled child is found and saved. That is where the WIN team (SAP) is supposed to come in.

In the Wissahickon High School, the **Student Assistance Program** is known as the **WIN team**. (WIN team and SAP **are one in the same;** it's the same program with two names). The team is structured to do two things: (1) monitor identified at-risk students (2) refer students for outside evaluation. The members are state trained. They do not make assessments, provide therapy, or diagnose.

According to the Wissahickon School District High School Faculty Manual:

> ... the **WIN Team** is an adolescent drug, alcohol, and mental health intervention program within the Wissahickon School District. WIN has two specific purposes: (1) facilitate the educational process in the School District by creating and maintaining a chemically free academic environment and (2) identify and refer for treatment "high risk" students with chemical or mental health problems. It is considered a "helping mechanism, which works within the structure of the District's drug and alcohol policies."

The WIN team (SAP) operates as a conduit to outside services. I spoke with a number of trained SAP teachers (not from Wissahickon) who told me this was the following protocol for the team:

- Student is referred.
- The team sends out forms to the teachers requesting information.
- Intervention is done if there is enough information to warrant one.
- If the parents say *no,* the team does not move on.
- If parents agree, a meeting is held with part of the team.
- After the intervention and **IF** the parents and child (if she/he is fourteen) agree, the student will be evaluated.
- No therapy is discussed with the team.
- Their number one goal is to **help parents and troubled children find an outside provider for counseling.**
- Once the child is connected to an outside mental health provider, the WIN team's work is done.

Here is the state's explanation of SAP's purpose:

SAP is not a treatment program; it is a systematic process using effective and accountable professional techniques to mobilize school resources to remove barriers to learning, and where the problem is beyond the scope of the school, to assist the parent and the students with information as to access services within the community...the team does not provide diagnosis or treatment services, nor does it replace the parents' decision making responsibility relative to the resolution of their children's problems.

In response to the increasing suicide rate, the PA Department of Welfare, Office of Mental Health, provided the support necessary for the expansion of the SAP initiative to include intervention strategies for students at risk of suicide.

But that's not how it worked in our district.

I continued to talk with Kay on a daily basis. Some days were better than others, but she was still in danger. Sometimes she would come into the room for a study hall and just sit. She said she felt safe there.

In April the president of our local union informed me that a "letter" had been sent to the district administration making accusations concerning me. I asked him what it said, but he had not seen it so he could not give me exact information. He did know that it said I had been seen "talking to the children." He warned me to keep "a low profile" and to stop speaking with my kids. He said if *they* didn't see me in conversation with my students, *they* would leave me alone. Who were *they*?

They were the WIN team (SAP) and *they* had written this letter.

March 19, 2002

Dear Mr. Anderson:

The Wissahickon High School WIN team is concerned about the apparent inappropriate interaction between one of our high school staff members, Mrs. Montanye, and students who have been identified as high risk through the SAP process. We find Mrs. Montanye's behavior to be an impediment to the SAP process and potentially damaging to the students.

Mrs. Montanye is frequently observed outside the high school building speaking individually with these students.

She has also been seen talking with the students when she herself is scheduled to be teaching, leaving an aid [sic] with the class. Our concern is that Mrs. Montanye is unqualified to work with a student in a therapeutic way and is therefore jeopardizing the health and welfare of these students.

It has come to our attention that Mrs. Montanye has taken one of her students to three therapy sessions outside the school setting. Mrs. Montanye recommended the therapist to this students' [sic] parents and volunteered to drive the child to therapy. The parents gave her permission to drive their child to therapy and introduce her to the therapist, but Mrs. Montanye has also attended the sessions with the child. We understand that the parents have met with you and Mrs. Kormos to voice their concerns. At this point they fear their child is so enmeshed with Mrs. Montanye that there could be serious negative side effects.

As the high school WIN team we are most concerned about these behaviors and the continued lack of good judgment and professionalism Mrs. Montanye displays with students at risk. We ask that you take action before these situations become more out of control and the school district suffers serious repercussions.

The WIN Team

Their letter was addressed to High School Principal, Robert Anderson; however, it was not given to him. Before attending a night school board meeting, Mr. Anderson checked his mailbox. There was no letter.

Instead, it was sent over to Judy Clark, the Assistant Superintendent. Following the board meeting, Ms. Clark presented the letter to Mr. Anderson and asked what it was about. This was the first time the principal had seen the letter. He informed Ms. Clark that he did not have this letter and had never seen it. Mr. Anderson said there had been problems with this student. He told her I was no longer attending the therapy. The assistant superintendent put the letter away. The next morning, a copy of the letter was in Mr. Anderson's mailbox.

Robert Anderson told me he spoke to each member of the WIN team after he got the letter. These were the conversations:

- Maria Salvucci [guidance counselor] said she wrote the letter.
- Imelda Kormos [school nurse] knew about the letter but hadn't read it.
- Tom Speakman [assistant principal] said they were considering writing a letter but was unaware one had been written.
- The other members claimed they did not know of the existence of the letter.

One of the teachers on the team told Mr. Anderson she did not remember seeing a suicide note. She also remarked, "You can't trust what parents say." She added she "couldn't remember all the kids; they were just names." However, she "did not recall hearing Kay's name or what they (WIN team/SAP) did about her."

Another disturbing aspect about this letter was that it was signed only with the typed, anonymous name "WIN team." Professional letters bear the signature of the person or persons who compose them. Ascribing such a grave and deprecating letter to a generalized group is both suspect and nonprofessional. In 2001-2002 the WIN team (SAP) was comprised of:

- Two teachers
- The school nurse
- The assistant principal
- The Drop-in Center counselor
- Two guidance counselors, neither of whom was Kay's guidance counselor

A few members of the WIN team (SAP) met with Kay's parents on September 11, 2001. The police had notified the team about the summer suicide attempt. At the meeting, Kay's parents said she saw a psychiatrist after the suicide attempt; however, she did not like him and did not want to continue therapy. This was the first and last interchange between Kay's parents and the WIN team (SAP).

No member of the WIN team (SAP) discussed Kay's at-risk status with any of her teachers, the principal, or the IEP team. The school nurse, who, as a medical professional, would know the greatest predictor of a successful suicide attempt is a previously failed one, never voiced a word.

More than eight "professionals" knew this child tried to kill herself. Not one of them made an overture to help her. The Special Ed supervisor, the guidance department, the WIN team (SAP) all knew the grim statistics associated with previous suicide attempts, and yet no one demonstrated any concern. It seems there was no interest in this case for the team other than writing this letter.

It appeared the WIN team (SAP) was saying:
- I interacted inappropriately with students because I *talked* with them.
- My behavior impeded the SAP [Student Assistant Program] process because *talking* to students prevents the WIN team (SAP) from helping them.

- Talking outside the school building with teenage children endangers them.
- I kept students (plural) from attending other classes.
- I was giving unqualified therapy to children because I was *talking* with them.
- I was not qualified to give therapy; therefore, I was not qualified to *speak* with students.
- I was putting the health of the students in jeopardy by *talking* with them.
- I was putting the welfare of the students in jeopardy by *talking* with them.
- I recommended (the name of) a therapist to the student and her parents; this made me *unprofessional*.
- I drove the student in my car with parental permission and after the child had come home from school. This made me *unprofessional*.
- I attended therapy sessions, at the student's request, which made me *unprofessional*.
- I forced my way into these sessions.
- I excluded or caused the exclusion of the parents from the therapy sessions; using, I assume, the same force that got me into the sessions.
- I induced some unnamed fear in the parents.
- My helping Kay and others could cause unspecified, serious negative side effects.
- My helping Kay and others would cause the district to suffer serious repercussions.

The WIN team (SAP) was asking Mr. Anderson to stop me from the dangerous behavior of *talking* with troubled students. They wanted him to stop me from the perilous action of making sure an at risk, suicidal girl went to a state certified, professional therapist.

The WIN team (SAP) wanted Mr. Anderson to take immediate action because the district might suffer serious repercussions if someone did not put an end to the hazardous practice of helping students.

The Wissahickon High School WIN team is concerned about the apparent inappropriate interaction between one of our high school staff members, Mrs. Montanye, and students who have been identified as high risk through the SAP process. We find Mrs. Montanye's behavior to be an impediment to the SAP process and potentially damaging to the students.

- Students? The letter only referred to Kay's therapy. Who were the other students identified as high risk?
- Since when is talking to students inappropriate? Wouldn't their "high risk" category make them more needy candidates for personal attention?
- If speaking with students was so inappropriate, why didn't the Assistant Principal, Tom Speakman, discuss this with Robert Anderson, his Principal? He was on the WIN team (SAP). Why remain silent when such dangerous activity was taking place?
- If my actions impeded the SAP process, again, why didn't Tom Speakman approach me? Surely, he would not sit by while I single handedly derailed the SAP process. He most certainly was obligated to tell the principal that my actions rendered the WIN team (SAP) ineffective.
- Speaking of negligence, where was Imelda Kormos, the school nurse? If I were causing significant harm to high-risk students, why didn't the medical professional do something immediately?
- Ms. Salvucci, the alleged author of the letter, did not specify which part of the SAP process failed because of my actions.

Mrs. Montanye is frequently observed outside the high school building speaking individually with these students. She has also been seen talking with the students when she herself is scheduled to be teaching, leaving an aid [sic] with the class.

- Observed by whom?
- What is frequently?
- If I refused to speak with children who had this as a

requirement in their IEP, would I not be out of compliance with Special Education law?

- No one on the WIN team (SAP) knew my schedule; it had been changed at least five times.
- Was a specific team member assigned to watch me? They are in the monitoring business after all.
- Who are the students? She was talking about more than one child, and yet the district never addressed the other students. Why wasn't the district worried about the harm I was inflicting on them?

Our concern is that Mrs. Montanye is unqualified to work with a student in a therapeutic way and is therefore jeopardizing the health and welfare of these students.

Not one person from the WIN team (SAP) spoke with me. How did they know I was working with students in a therapeutic way? Speaking of health and welfare, how beneficial was it for Kay to be taken to MCES? It was nurse Imelda Kormos who demanded the police bring Kay to school in order to force her back into class. Kay may not have reacted in such an extreme manner and wound up in MCES had Imelda Kormos not interfered.

It has come to our attention that Mrs. Montanye has taken one of her students to three therapy sessions outside the school setting.

- I went two times, not three.
- What I did on my own time was no business of the WIN team (SAP) or Maria Salvucci.
- Did the WIN team (SAP) have a waiver signed by Kay giving them permission to discuss her private therapy? That would be a no.

Maria Salvucci, Imelda Kormos, and the rest of the WIN team (SAP) ignored the diagnosis of two psychiatrists, a child with PTSD, a suicide attempt, and a suicide note, and yet, they were incensed that I got Kay to a therapist.

Mrs. Montanye recommended the therapist to this students' [sic] parents and volunteered to drive the child to therapy.

- Emotional Support teachers were never told they may not recommend a therapist; they cannot recommend the child needs therapy.

The parents gave her permission to drive their child to therapy and introduce her to the therapist, but Mrs. Montanye has also attended the sessions with the child.

- The parents did not give me permission, Kay's mother did.
- The mother gave me permission to attend the therapy sessions and also informed the therapist this was acceptable.
- Realistically, Kay was the only one empowered to let me into her sessions.
- Ms. Salvucci never met Kay.
- Ms. Salvucci never met Kay's mom.
- Ms. Salvucci never spoke with Kay.
- Ms. Salvucci never spoke with Kay's mom.
- Wouldn't Ms. Salvucci, a guidance counselor, be aware the team was violating the state mental health laws?

The parents have been excluded from the therapy sessions.

- Was Ms. Salvucci saying I was the reason they were excluded?

We understand that the parents have met with you (Bob Anderson) and Mrs. Kormos to voice their concerns. At this point they fear their child is so enmeshed with Mrs. Montanye that there could be serious negative side effects.

- This was a complete fabrication: Kay's mom told me she never made any comment to this effect.

- The parents did not meet with Bob Anderson and Imelda Kormos; the mother did. The father could not have voiced this "fear."

As the high school WIN team, we are concerned about these behaviors and the continued lack of good judgment and professionalism Mrs. Montanye displays with students at risk.

- Again, Ms. Salvucci refers to more than one student.
- It was only Kay the district used against me.

Finally, and most importantly, once a student is in the mental health system the WIN team (SAP) is no longer involved. Again, once a student has been placed in a facility or is seeing a therapist, he or she is part of the mental health system and **is no longer a consideration for the WIN team (SAP). The WIN team's mission is to get a troubled child connected with the mental health system.**
Let's examine Kay's record up to ninth grade:

- She was assessed by a psychiatrist (2001)
- She was diagnosed with a psychiatric condition-PTSD (2001)
- She was placed in an mental facility for observation after her first suicide attempt (2001)
- She was undergoing therapy after she left the mental facility (2001)
- She started counseling with the new therapist (February, 2002)
- She was placed in a second psychiatric facility (MCES) (February, 2002)
- She was evaluated by another psychiatrist
- She was instructed by a judge to see a therapist three times, as a condition of her release from MCES (February, 2002)

Ironically, the WIN team (SAP) letter, which demanded that my "unprofessional behavior" be curtailed because it "interfered" with the SAP (WIN team) process, was written on March 19, 2002. In that case, you may wonder, why was the WIN team (SAP) writing about a child who was most obviously involved in the mental health system? Why indeed.

One viable explanation is that the WIN team (SAP) letter was written without benefit of knowledge or research into Kay's problems. It was not a chronicle of her dire history; it was a collection of baseless gossip emanating from the ill informed, nurse. The letter was not crafted out of concern for Kay; it was designed to prevent me from helping my student.

The question that trumps the first one is: why did the Wissahickon School District hire an attorney to prosecute a teacher without first researching the charges? Surely, the superintendent and assistant superintendent would have realized the WIN team (SAP) was pursuing a case in which they neglected to obtain the true facts and were negligent in their legal responsibility.

Let us not forget, the author of this missive was a guidance counselor, who knew or should have known that:

- A suicide threat or an attempt represents an important communication about the intensity of experienced despair. (Merck Manual)
- A previous suicide attempt is the best predictor of death by suicide, reflecting the concept that past behavior often predicts future behavior. (Shaffer, Garland, Fisher, and Trautman, 1988.)
- Drug and alcohol abuse is another critical factor that places children and adolescents at risk for suicidal behavior. (Achenbach, Howell, McCounaughy and Stanger, 1995; Brent, Perper, Goldstein et al, 1988.)

Mrs. Salvucci was a trained WIN team (SAP) member, a former Special Education teacher, and a guidance counselor; yet she did not take these warnings seriously. The only effort she and her team made was to stop me from helping Kay.

The WIN team's (SAP) behavior and the letter constituted a major breach in protocol, not to mention a serious violation of the PA mental health law. Mrs. Kormos had absolutely no right to reveal Kay's psychological information to the WIN team (SAP) without her permission. Kay was in charge of her mental health records and history; without her explicit consent, Imelda Kormos broke the law. It was not enough that the school nurse ignored Kay's cries for help and landed her in the psychiatric institution from hell, she was determined Kay would lose the one champion she had.

We ask you to take action before these situations become more out of control and the school district suffers serious repercussions.

You have to love this one. It is the oldest trick in the book. When an administrator, or in this case a guidance counselor, wants to prod someone into action, they raise the specter of some grim legal catastrophe befalling the district. Most of the time it's fecal hyperbole, but it gets people jumping.

In spite of the violations of law and regardless of the venom with which the letter was infused, putting aside the erroneous facts, ignoring that the team had no legitimate purpose in being involved with Kay, I have one burning question:

Doesn't anyone find it troubling that a guidance counselor did not view the possible death of a fourteen-year-old child as a serious repercussion??

CHAPTER SIX

Allegations

Confidentiality and Student Assistance Programs (SAP)

...Members of a SAP team should not participate in group, or individual treatment sessions *without the consent of the student.* Pursuant to federal and state confidentiality regulations, confidential information...*may not be released to a SAP team without the student's written consent. Written or verbal consent from the student's parent(s) will not satisfy the regulations.*

Student Assistance Program personnel receiving client information must be made aware that they are *prohibited from disclosing the information.* The information may not be used for disciplinary action or prosecution.

> Excerpted from *Student Assistance Team Development and Training Manual*
> Presented by Project Care/Policy Bulletin 1-92/Department of Health
> Office of Drug and Alcohol Programs

A week after I received warnings from the local union president (WEA), Principal Anderson took Kay and me into a deserted science room and explained to her what was happening. At least he gave it a try. He told her we could no longer be seen speaking with each other and she should consider talking with the Drop-in Center counselor. He tried his best to explain the "they" part of my problem without revealing it was the WIN team (SAP). The more he worked at getting this point across the more incredulous Kay's expression became. He wanted Kay to understand that he had to protect me from people who were angry about our relationship and who demanded it be terminated.

Kay was rightfully livid. She looked at him and said flatly, "What you are saying is now that I have found someone who is helping me and someone I can really trust, I can't talk to her anymore because some people in the school don't like it?" He could provide no response because that is exactly what he was saying. Out of the mouths of babes. She strode from the room, tears streaming, hair flying.

I was stunned. Absolutely flabbergasted. I could not believe that my superiors were telling me to abandon a suicidal student. All the more incredulous was that the leaders of the district were not concerned about a suicidal child, but rather were convulsing in a knee-jerk reaction to a letter filled with generalized, unfounded accusations, and lacking significant knowledge about the subject matter. In short, they were selling out a student to mollify gossipmongers.

Kay grew more morose with each passing day. She would come into the room and lie on the heating units in the bright afternoon sun. She did not speak with me. She was sleep walking through the day. The look in her eyes was blank. She was wrapped up in pain, and I had been told to stand by and watch her sink deeper into this unhappy, barren world. I genuinely feared we were going to lose her.

I was following the directions of the union president to not talk to students in need. I was also adhering to Mr. Anderson's instructions that Kay and I not be seen talking to each other. Both men had determined it would be for the best if I ignored Kay and my obligation as an Emotional Support teacher in order to appease the angry WIN team (SAP). Let's look at what this really was: the principal of the high school and the leader of the teacher's union were both instructing me *not* to do my job. Meanwhile, no one was doing anything to assist this lost child.

In the beginning of April, the union president came to my room clutching an email from Superintendent Stanley Durtan informing him the district was going to conduct a formal hearing for me. I would be notified of the reasons by mail.

While I waited for the letter that would elucidate my offenses, I wracked my brain for anything I did or did not do which necessitated an action of this magnitude. I had not been involved with any run-ins other than the math-English switch; and according to the assistant principal, no one at Central Office saw the letter concerning this. In addition, a clerical error hardly warranted an official hearing.

When I talked to Mr. Anderson, he was as ignorant as I, which made the situation more perplexing. The principal would certainly be privy to any action worthy of a formal hearing. No one had any idea what was taking place or the reason for it.

The email made reference to Joe, a middle school teacher, who would also be undergoing a hearing. Joe and I had worked together in the middle school. If I was having trouble figuring out the cause of my predicament, I was completely at a loss as to what serious wrong Joe had committed. His relationships with students were commendable; what's more, he worked deftly with administrators. He was a respected and highly regarded teacher. I spoke with him that afternoon; he didn't have a clue. The director of Special Education was also in the dark. This made no sense that he would have two teachers facing hearings with no knowledge of why. We had to wait for the letters.

My letter was an astonishing compilation of accusations.

May 1, 2002

RE: Notice of Allegations and of Conference

Dear Mrs. Montanye:

Allegations have been made that you engaged in willful neglect of duty, insubordination, incompetency, persistent negligence in the performance of duties, willful violations or [sic] school laws, and improper conduct growing out of the following: improperly involving yourself in situations pertaining to student K[4], making an appointment for the student with a therapist, transporting the student to the therapist, participating in the therapy session with the student, and participating in the change in schedule of the student without prior approval of the administration. It is alleged that these actions by you are unprofessional and exhibit poor judgment, that they are in violation of the rules pertaining to the procedures that are required to be followed for evaluations of students, that they are in conflict with the resources established by the school district for helping students and for scheduling students.

---

[4] We believe that you know who student K is; however, if you do not, please contact me or have your representative contact me and we will disclose that information to you. We wish to preserve the confidentiality of the student in the event this letter ever becomes a public document.

You are hereby directed to meet with us to review these allegations and for us to hear your side of the story. If any of these allegations are true, we will also want to discuss with you what the appropriate disciplinary response, if any, should be, including possible dismissal from your employment. The disciplinary response will be made in consideration of your past disciplinary and performance record.

The meeting will be conducted in the administration offices of the School District. The meeting is scheduled for Friday, May 10, 2002 at 11:30 a.m.

You have the right to legal or union representation at the meeting. These kinds of meetings are sometimes referred to as *Loudermill* hearings because they are intended to comply with the Supreme Court's requirements in a case called *Cleveland Board of Education v. Loudermill,* 470 U.S. 532 (1985)

The school district will be represented by Michael I. Levin, Esquire. *(address/phone number of Levin's practice.)*

If you or your attorney or union representative would like to contact him in advance of the meeting, please feel free to contact him directly.

At the meeting, you will be asked questions relevant to the allegations and what disciplinary action, if any, should be taken. You will be given a copy of the affidavit to insure that the summary is accurate and complete. If the affidavit is in need of correction, addition or modification, you will be able to make whatever corrections or additions you feel are appropriate before you sign the affidavit. You will be given a copy of the signed affidavit and any documents to which it refers.

Any statement that you make during the meeting (whether those statements eventually appear on the affidavit or not) can be used against you. In addition, the written statement can be used against you. However, you are required to cooperate in this investigation and/or refusal to answer any of the questions asked of you, your refusal will be considered insubordination which itself can lead to disciplinary action, including dismissal.

Sincerely,

Dr. Stanley Durtan
Superintendent of Schools

The letter was cc'd to Bill Sanni (Director Human Resources), Judith Clark (Assistant Superintendent), Bob Anderson (WHS Principal) and Kelle Heim-McCloskey (Supervisor of Spec Ed). Notably absent from this list was the **Director of Special Education**. Heim-McCloskey was only a supervisor; she answered to the director of Special Education. This meant that the top Special Education expert in the district, the person in charge of this massive educational division, was not to be part of the hearing. Why was the educator who was ultimately responsible for the district's compliance with state and federal law omitted from hearings that dealt exclusively with Special Education teachers? As director, would it not be of benefit to both district and program that he be involved with a situation that warranted an outside attorney and could possibly evolve into an event that would require public documents?

In fact, a week before the hearings the director of Special Education was in Robert Anderson's office asking what was going on. He wanted to know why two of his teachers were facing pre-termination hearings and no one would tell him anything about it. Mr. Anderson could offer no answers, as his calls were not being taken or returned by Judy Clark. They were stonewalling him as well.

The **district** hired Michael Levin of the Levin Legal Group, an outside firm reputed to have a penchant for pushing the edge of the legal envelope. It was fairly common knowledge that when a school district wanted to get rid of someone they hired Mr. Levin to build a case. Mr. Levin wrote a book with a section devoted to the ins and outs of Loudermill Hearings. He also presented in-services for administrators on the benefits of the Loudermill Hearing.

I cannot put into words what I felt when I read the charges. Given my history with my students, the excellent evaluations I received, and considering I performed these particular actions with Kay at parental request, on my own time, I could not fathom why the district would go out of its way to persecute me. Superintendent Durtan and his subordinates were punishing me for helping Kay. It seemed contrived that they would spend thousands of dollars to hire an attorney who was not the school district solicitor, to go after me because I chose to assist a child as a private citizen. This simply made no sense.

My first reaction was anger, which gave way to tears. I wound up vomiting for most of the evening. I could not sleep, I could not eat, and I could not stop shaking.

Looking closely at the letter, there were indications this hearing was merely a performance to push me into resigning or to trump up enough false charges to fire me.

The letter of allegations included a list of most of the offenses for which a teacher can be fired under Pennsylvania law. It is of no importance that these accusations were not linked to specific law or actions that violated that law. The scare factor of the pile of accusations is done deliberately to invoke terror in the teacher. It is the tried and true method of accusatory mudslinging; you throw as many charges as you can and see if anything sticks.

Here are the charges as defined by the PA Code:

Willful neglect of duty: **requires an intentional failure to perform essential duties. The major component is the intent.** A teacher can be found neglectful in duty as long as failure to perform an act is willful.

I did not fail to perform an act. I performed an act to save this child. That's why I was in trouble. As there are no laws of the Commonwealth which state a teacher cannot help a child as a private citizen, this one is out. No supervisor ever told me not to help a child outside of school. No school district regulation stated this.

Insubordination: **the refusal to follow directions or a directive.** This can be applied to almost anything an administrator wants to use it for. I did not ignore any directive or directions.

Incompetency: **want of physical, intellectual, or moral ability, inability, incapacity, lack of ability, and lack of fitness to discharge the required duties**. The charge of insubordination is a statement of negative generalities, which could be applied to anything the district chose to link it with.

The charge of incompetency must be accompanied by two unsatisfactory ratings completed not less than four months apart. I had no unsatisfactory evaluations, and my actions with Kay had no bearing on my ability to teach, nor did the district ever maintain they did.

According to Attorney Levin, incompetency also encompassed failure to maintain a proper relationship with students. (Levin Legal

Group; In-Service Presentation: Prepared for the Wissahickon School District; August 9, 2002.) Mr. Levin did not provide any examples of an improper relationship with a student; most notably he did not contend that saving a child's life would come under this section.

> **Persistent negligence in the performance of duties: continuation or constant failure or refusal to comply with directions or a violation of School Code. To be "persistent" a series of individual incidents or one incident must be carried out over a period of time.**

The kicker here is the law specifies that a teacher cannot be dismissed for persistent negligence in conduct **outside the scope of a teacher's employment.** My actions were not within the scope of my employment. They took place after school hours and off of school property.

Now that we understand the **persistence** component, let's take a look at the definition of **negligence**:

1. Duty or failure to protect others against unreasonable risk
2. Failure on the part of the teacher to exercise a standard of care commensurate with the risks involved
3. Conduct of the teacher must be proximate or legal cause of injury
4. There must exist an injury or actual loss/damage that resulted from the act

Number four is particularly intriguing. What was the actual loss/damage to Kay resulting from my actions with her? She went to a therapist. She did not make another suicide attempt. At times she felt safe in school.

Conversely, we have to ask what Kay experienced from the **negligence of** administrative actions from sixth to ninth grades.

- She avoided school with psychosomatic illnesses.
- She missed classes when she sat in the guidance office or nurse's office.
- Her grades plummeted.
- She lost her ability to concentrate.
- She suffered physical injuries.

- She had to withdraw from the track team due to the concussion she received when she was slammed into a concrete wall.
- She had to be removed from school entirely.
- She tried to slit her throat open with a kitchen knife.
- She was taken (twice) to a mental facility for observation.
- She was diagnosed with PTSD.
- She was diagnosed with clinical depression and suicidal ideation.

Whose actions would you deem to be persistently negligent and causally connected to Kay's experience?

Willful violation of school laws: "school law" refers to statutes, but it also applies to school regulations, and orders given by supervisory personnel. You can see how easily this can be used to implicate a teacher without an actual infraction.

EITHER/OR:

Either: The administration was accusing me of willful violation of school law because it was so ill defined they believed it would go unchallenged,

Or: They were claiming there was a regulation stating it was against school district policy for a teacher to help a suicidal child on her own time.

PA code says a reasonable rule or regulation should have at least an indirect relationship to the educational purposes of the school. Hard to imagine any rule forbidding a teacher from helping a suicidal child would not have a direct (let alone indirect) relationship to educational purposes.

Improper conduct: There is no part of the PA Code which states that assisting a student outside of the school day at parental request is an example of improper conduct. The code does provide a few examples of improper conduct:

- Providing alcohol to minors

- Having sex with minors
- Bringing guns to school

If a teacher is partaking in any actions which are against the law, that would be considered improper conduct. Impropriety ventures into a grey area when a teacher's behavior is considered wrong because it goes against the morals of the community. Using this undefined standard, school districts could fire teachers for being gay or for cohabitating with someone to whom they were not married.

The accusations of being unprofessional and exhibiting poor judgment were more confounding. Why would a school district, purporting to care about the students, find the action of saving a child's life unprofessional? How could a superintendent and his assistant, along with the supervisor of Special Education, justify accusing a teacher of exhibiting poor judgment because she did not want a fourteen-year-old kid to kill herself? Conversely, these people were saying that neglecting to assist a suicidal child was "professional" and the prime indicator of a person acting with "good judgment."

Remember the math-English class letter of reprimand that was "going to be kept in house?" Somehow, it made its way over to Dr. Durtan. Not much of a surprise there. The assistant principal who wrote the letter and then threw Kay back into the math class with her tormentors was Stan Durtan's protégé. Incidentally, the math teacher was never mentioned in any letter or allegations, nor did he undergo a Loudermill hearing, although he was part of the math-English switch.

The allegations letter also said my actions: "were in violation of the rules pertaining to the procedures that are required to be followed for the evaluations of students."

This was a knee-slapper. The district never evaluated Kay for therapy; they had no professional qualified to perform this evaluation. Attorney Levin's assertion that the school district had any say in evaluations performed by private practitioners was fallacious. Kay's visits to the therapist had nothing to do with the school district and came under none of their regulations. They were **private.**

My personal favorite accusation was this one: "...(my actions were)in conflict with the resources established by the school district for helping students... "

Really?

Special Education: established to help children with problems that interfere with their ability to learn.

Guidance: established to help children with problems that create conflict in their lives and interfere with their ability to learn.

Drop-in Center counselor: established to provide temporary relief for students with emotional conflicts that interfere with successful relationships/ability to learn

WIN team (SAP): tasked with identifying and monitoring students with emphasis on linking students with outside mental health services.

My actions were not in conflict with these programs. My actions were in conflict with the negligence of the people who manned these programs, the people who did not follow their moral or legal responsibilities to help this girl.

The manner of operation of these "hearings" was questionable. For example:

Any statement that you make during the meeting (whether those statements eventually appear on the affidavit or not) can be used against you. In addition, the written statement can be used against you.

Does this have a familiar ring? It should. It echoes the last part of the Miranda rights, the ones recited when police are arresting criminals.

The catch here is that any and all statements recorded are placed into the record by Michael Levin. Michael Levin was solely responsible for the "affidavit." There was no impartial court reporter. There would be no professional notes to compare with Levin's notes to insure accuracy. Even if I were provided the opportunity to correct the affidavit, it would be impossible to remember everything that was said during the time of the hearing.

In addition, "any statements made during the hearing, even if they are not recorded, can be used against you." How convenient is that? Who would vouch for what was said or not said? How could the truth of these assertions be proven or disputed? They could not. That's the beauty of it. Mr. Levin and his clients could make accusations based on what they claimed I said. There would be no way to refute this because there was no legitimate record of what was said.

The contention that this party was held for my sake "…. to hear your side of the story…" was not the truth. In the first place, I was allowed no witnesses. Secondly, at no time was any action tied to a specific statute. The hearing was held to eliminate a Special Ed teacher who was mistakenly under the impression that students who needed help should get it. More importantly, it served as a warning to any other Spec Ed teacher (or regular ed teacher) to remain silent when faced with the school district's disregard for a student's rights. You're either with us or you're out.

If any of these allegations are true, we will also want to discuss with you what the appropriate disciplinary response if any, should be, including possible dismissal.

Just to clarify: the superintendent who would do nothing to stop the incessant bullying of a student, the assistant superintendent who was in agreement with this position, the Special Education supervisor who subverted IDEA and PA regs when Kay was forced out of school, and the middle school principal who suggested that other students resolve her bullying problems were not being questioned; but, I was facing possible dismissal because I helped her as a private citizen? Suddenly, I knew exactly how Kay felt. These bullies were operating unfettered by anyone; they were determined to push me out, as they had done to Kay.

The hearing was labeled as a Loudermill. What exactly is a Loudermill hearing? It is a pre-termination hearing, which was established in the decision from *Cleveland Board of Education v. Loudermill*, 470 U.S. 532 (1985). The Loudermill decision says employees with contracts have to be given some form of pre-termination hearing before they are fired, as the firing constitutes a deprivation of property. The contract is viewed as property. The Supreme Court concluded that a pre-termination hearing required reasonable notice and the opportunity for the employee to respond to the charges.

The intent of the hearing is to provide a forum in which the employee can refute the facts that have bearing on a dismissal. Reasonable notice has to detail the charges and provide an explanation of the employer's evidence. The conference can be informal as long as the charges are explained, there is supporting evidence, and the employee is allowed to explain the reasons for the actions.

This does not play out in practice. The manner employed by the Wissahickon School District and Attorney Michael Levin is such that the Loudermill is used as a weapon against the teacher. Michael Levin makes a list of the majority of termination causes as found in Pennsylvania law. He then lists actions that were taken but have no link to the causes listed in the letter. Michael Levin claimed that by citing charges i.e. persistent negligence in duty etc., the district was fulfilling this requisite. He did not connect the accusation and the action with any law that stated such behavior was in violation of a statute.

The district requires your attendance by threatening you with dismissal if you refuse to attend; although you have the right to waive the hearing, Mr. Levin does not inform the teacher of this.

In his book, Michael Levin states:

A limitation on a school district administration's ability to question an employee is that a school district may not use an employee's refusal to answer relevant questions as a ground for dismissal if the employee's refusal was based on a constitutional right to remain silent (*Pennsylvania School Personnel Actions*; Michael I. Levin, editor. 2002)

Mr. Levin does not advise the subject of the hearing about this. Instead, the concluding line of his allegations letter says:

If you refuse to cooperate in this investigation and/or refuse to answer any of the questions asked of you, your refusal will be considered insubordination which itself can lead to disciplinary action, including dismissal.

On one hand, I had the constitutional right to refuse to

answer questions. I had the right to remain silent; on the other hand, if I remained silent, I would be out of a job and a career.

Unfortunately, for the employee, the Supreme Court did not consider how this pre-termination hearing could become an abuse of power and be incorporated as a method of illegally destroying careers.

According to Chuck Herring, (the attorney for the teacher's union) there were termination meetings previous to mine; however, these usually were for teachers charged with some criminal activity or serious breach of conduct, such as striking a student. The PSEA attorney only attended a hearing if it concerned possible criminal charges. If the information proved accurate and a board hearing for dismissal was the next step, the union attorney would advise the teacher to resign rather than be terminated. In this manner, a teacher still had the possibility of procuring employment. This struck me as ethically questionable. If a teacher was found to have violated protocol to the extent that it warranted termination, was it a legitimate action to allow him to remain in the profession and possibly go on to damage children in another district? On the other hand, if the charges were not ones that justified termination, but the union attorney advised the teacher to resign, then the union was allowing the district to coerce the teacher into resigning for false reasons. The teacher is caught between a rock and a hard place.

These hearings are also lucrative. They can circumvent the union contract, target teachers, and put a good deal of taxpayer's money into the attorney's pocket. The hearing designed to protect employee's rights is transformed into the trifecta of reprisal, combining attorney greed, administrative misuse of power, and lack of union vigilance.

There are a few distinct differences between a Loudermill hearing and an investigative hearing. In a Loudermill, the employee is not obligated to attend. In an investigative hearing this is not so; an employee is legally obliged to attend and respond to any questions put to him provided those questions are not in violation of his constitutional rights. Mr. Levin negates the Loudermill protections by calling his hearing a Loudermill/Investigative hearing. In this manner, the district is able to fire the teacher if she invokes her right to waive the hearing. When this happens, the Loudermill hearing becomes an investigative hearing where this right is not offered and where refusal to attend or answer questions is cause for dismissal.

At a Pennsylvania (PSEA) state union meeting one of the

attorneys who oversees the regional lawyers stated that Loudermill hearings and investigative hearings could not be coupled together in the manner used by Michael Levin. In fact, she asked to be notified if this practice continued. When the president of our local union (WEA) asked a question about this in relation to how it affected our district, she was told the attorney would not answer her questions and she should sit down.

EITHER/OR:

Either: It's a Loudermill hearing,

Or: It's an investigative hearing.

I called an attorney who represented Spec Ed children in due process hearings. He agreed to meet and hear my story. We had little time: the hearing was only three weeks away.

I sat in the lawyer's office shaking. I recounted the events. He listened intently. When I was through, he asked me, "What is really going on?"

I sat there speechless. Realizing that no intelligible answer was forthcoming, he elaborated on his original inquiry. He said he found it implausible that a school district was going after a teacher for helping a suicidal child. He noted that in "any other district they would be giving you a medal." Maybe so, in another district.

The attorney was at a loss to explain the district's hidden agenda. It was evident to me the Wissahickon School District was more than willing to reward employees who shirked responsibility and bypassed the law. The attorney echoed my thoughts when he asked why there was such a lack of administrative consternation over the negligence on the part of the Spec Ed supervisor, the guidance counselor, and the WIN team (SAP).

What I found most interesting was the lawyer's assessment of my situation.

He summed it up as a case of bullies picking on someone for sport. That explained a great deal. Of course, they would not have protected Kay from the bullies. Dr. Durtan and his assistants were also bullies, and they relished the idea of pushing a teacher around just because they could.

At my attorney's direction, I requested my file from the

principal. Mr. Anderson would not release the file to me because he had been instructed to tell my attorney to call Michael Levin. The president of the local union wrote to Superintendent Durtan, pointing out that I was entitled to this information.

#1
From:Warren S
To:Stan Durtan
Sent:Friday, May 17 2002 11:04 PM
Subject:Sally [sic] Montayne [sic] DISCLOSURE AND LOUDERMILL HEARING

Hi Stan,

It has come to my attention that Mr. Anderson has not given Sally [sic] Montayne [sic] copies of his file on her. She needs this to prepare for the hearing. I have been told that Mr. Anderson has been told not to give this information by Mr. Levin.

I don't believe this is legal. Delays can often be done to get around the spirit of the law.

#2
From:Stan Durtan
To:Warren S
Sent:Friday, May 17 3:04 PM
Subject:RE: Sally [sic] Montayne [sic] DISCLOSURE AND LOUDERMILL HEARING

Warren: This is a serious situation. Mrs. Montayne [sic]should have legal counsel. Her legal counsel should contact Mr. Levin to acquire any information she wishes to have. District personnel will neither be discussing this situation nor providing any written information prior to the Loudermill Hearing. Stan

#3
From:Warren S
To:Stan Durtan
Sent:Friday, May 17 2002 3:17 PM
Cc:Montanye, Sallie; Donald Atkiss (email)
Subject:Sally[sic] Montayne [sic] DISCLOSURE AND LOUDERMILL HEARING

Hi Stan,

This is dead wrong. Sally [sic] should be entitled to copies of certain materials that represent communications to her over the last year. Some recent materials that may be related to a criminal investigation, she may not be entitled to receive. I don't believe there are such materials.

I have asked our attorneys to request the material. I am told the denial of disclosure could cause the District difficulties in the future should disciplinary action be determined as warranted.

Honest people have nothing to hide. The adversarial aspect of legal proceedings should be tempered with justice and certain legal ethical values.

I have no recourse but to leave this dispute with the lawyers.

Warren

The union president was totally out of touch with the nature of the people running the district. The "spirit of the law" refers to good faith. These were not people who operated in good faith.

When I spoke with Don Atkiss, the Pennsylvania State Education Association (PSEA) Uniserv representative, the night before the hearing, he told me he had experience with the way Michael Levin conducted these hearings. He said Mr. Levin would question the teacher for long periods of time, badgering her with a barrage of accusations delivered with sarcasm and belittling remarks. The rep's interpretation was that Mr. Levin's tactics were employed to confuse the frightened teacher, thereby causing her to make a misstatement, which the attorney could then use as "proof" the teacher was lying. Mr. Levin would then recommend dismissal based on insubordination because the teacher "lied." This rendered the allegations immaterial because it was the Loudermill itself which was used to discredit the teacher and to establish a reason for discharge.

As for the union attorney (PSEA), Chuck Herring, there was no communication from him about my file. Was the attorney for the union invisible because I had already spoken to a private lawyer? No, because he did not know I had hired an attorney. The union rep only learned of this the night we spoke before the hearing. Until this discussion, the union was not aware I had private counsel.

Sallie Montanye

Although I did not know it at the time, the Loudermill hearing was based on the critical letter written by the WIN team (SAP). The district never produced the letter; I would not see it until November 2002, six months after the Loudermill hearing, when Robert Anderson gave me his copy.

Chapter Seven

Loudermill

A. Pupils:

Recognize that the school staff assumes the role of surrogate parent in matters of behavior and discipline from time of departure from home until arrival at home

B. Parents and Guardians:

Build a good working relationship between themselves, their children, and school district employees

C. Staff:

Seek to develop close relationships with parents/guardians
*Help pupils cope with negative peer pressures *(listed twice)*
***Enable pupils to discuss their problems** *(listed twice)*
Report to building administrator any pupils who jeopardize their own safety
Serve as surrogate parent in matters of behavior and discipline

D. Building Administration

Ensure that all at-risk pupils receive appropriate services

- Requirements needed to enable district to achieve goals found in the WSD Code of Discipline –

The two weeks preceding the Loudermill hearing were filled with a flurry of letters and emails. Lawyers are all about written communications. These exchanges had repeating themes: my lawyer asking for information and Michael Levin refusing to provide it; my attorney questioning the vagueness of the accusations, Michael Levin obfuscating the answers by attacking this man's professionalism.

On May 5, 2002, my attorney sent Mr. Levin a letter stating that the Wissahickon School District had made "global accusations that were impossible to address." He asked for explanations of the allegations. He also noted he could not find any information that supported the charges leveled against me. Finally, he requested Kay's educational records, all documentation leading up to the decision to hold a hearing, and names of witnesses to be called.

Mr. Levin's letter of May 13th shot back that the "factual" basis for the allegations were stated in the first paragraph of the Allegations Letter. In response to the request for Kay's records, Michael Levin lectured about the confidentiality of student records and said I had "no right to engage in a fishing expedition." He ended this with, "I would trust and assume that your client is not providing you with any student records in violation of the Family Education Rights and Privacy Act [FERPA]." The Family Educational Rights and Privacy Act (FERPA) (20 U.S.C. § 1232g; 34 CFR Part 99) is a federal law that protects the privacy of student education records. The law applies to all schools that receive funds under an applicable program of the U.S. Department of Education. FERPA states:

> Generally, schools **must have written permission from the parent or eligible student in order to release ANY information from a student's education record.**

There were a few exceptions to this rule; however, not one of the listed exceptions allowed for IEP's to be released to a private law practice for the purpose of being used as "evidence" in hearings devised by the school district against the teachers. FERPA requires that schools notify parents and eligible students annually of their rights. The actual means of notification (special letter, inclusion in a PTA bulletin, student handbook, or newspaper article) is left to the discretion of each school. Interestingly, Mr. Levin stated I would be in violation of FERPA if I provided my attorney with any student records. Oddly enough, Mr. Levin could not see any violation when the district provided him with records without parental knowledge or written consent. In essence, Mr. Levin's letter said he did not have to provide information or a legal basis for the charges. The district and their attorney decided I engaged in "wrongful acts" and our requests for materials were "simply, ridiculous."

Attorney Levin elaborated:

> With respect to student K, we will be inquiring whether your client made an appointment for the student with the therapist, whether your client transported the student to the therapist, whether your client participated in the therapy session with the student, and whether your client participated in a change in schedule of the student without the prior approval of the administration.
>
> There are really only three possible answers that she can have to such questions. Either she did it, she didn't do it, or she doesn't recall whether she did it or not. If she did it, we will be very anxious to ask why and we will be very anxious to hear whatever explanation she wishes to give and **justification for her acts.**

In what alternate universe would school district administrators need **justification** for trying to keep a kid alive? A superintendent, an assistant superintendent, the supervisor of Special Education, and their attorney wanted to know why I acted to help save a child's life. They were waiting for me to "give justification" for my acts. It seemed that those who allegedly "care" about the children were flummoxed by my behavior and wanted to know why in the world I did it. They were so befuddled they had to pay an attorney $4800 to unearth the covert and cryptic reasons that compelled me into helping save a child's life.

Our district has its own attorneys. Each year this firm submits a bid to the board. The board in turn votes to hire the firm as solicitors for the district. Years ago, the retainer was in the neighborhood of $90,000 plus per year. One of the lawyers working in this firm lists his specialties as Labor Law, Special Education Law, and teacher disciplinary issues. And yet, it's Michael Levin, not the school district attorneys, they call in. Makes you wonder.

Michael Levin ended his letter with a personal attack on my attorney:

> I have been conducting hearings like this for approximately twenty-five years, most often with skilled and knowledgeable lawyers who regularly engage in employment and labor law. They all manage to effectively represent their clients without engaging in the kind of hyper-lawyering I see in your letters.

I was bombarded with endless questions from my attorney. He wanted a blow-by-blow narrative of everything I had said and done with Kay. How long had I known her? How long had I worked with her? Did I participate in her evaluations? What was MCES? Did I have input into placing her there?

My attorney emailed me an extensive list of instructions. He told me not to discuss anything with anyone. I was specifically not allowed to speak with Kay. I was not to talk to any friends at school, adding that I had no friends anymore; everyone was my enemy.

He said we would be telling my story "in a way that it is not overwhelmed by threats or counter-threats. The story must get through." He ended by reminding me, "Also remember we are dealing with **bullies**...don't play into their hands...don't be bullied...be respectful...don't try and bully them."

*****

We sat at Central Office, waiting. Joe's hearing was to have taken place before mine. I did not see Joe come out of the room. I assumed his hearing had ended early.

Mr. Levin walked out and exchanged a few words with my lawyer. Soon we were ushered into a small, stuffy conference room. Michael Levin sat at the head of the table with his laptop in front of him. I was sandwiched between my lawyer on the right and the Uniserv rep (union representative-not a lawyer) on my left. Dr. Durtan sat next to Don Atkiss, the Uniserv rep. Judy Clark occupied the seat at the other end of the table facing Michael Levin. This struck me as odd. Wouldn't Dr. Durtan, the person who was the appointed leader of the school district, occupy this seat? Nevertheless, it was occupied by his assistant who was literally sitting on the edge of the chair throughout the entire process.

Mr. Anderson was across from Dr. Durtan; next to him sat Kelle Heim-McCloskey who, as my attorney said, "Looked like a deer caught in the headlights." Bill Sanni, the personnel director, was across from me, seated sideways staring at the floor. This position was maintained for the duration of the hearing.

Michael Levin introduced himself. He looked at me and asked, "May I call you Sallie?"

I told him, "No."

My lawyer was shifting nervously in his seat. He didn't want any challenges aimed at Mr. Levin. I felt he wanted me to grovel and show them I was afraid. He wanted to appease them.

There are two things we innately believe as human beings. One is that our mother will love us; two is that parents should not have to bury a child. Obviously both of these turn out not to be the case in many people's lives. But there was no way in hell someone would have to bury her child because I refused to respond to the child's pleas for help. I could not feign apology for helping Kay.

Michael Levin went on about how this meeting was held to "hear your side of the story." He explained he would be taking all the notes and they would be made into an affidavit. There was no stenographer; however, the affidavit could and would be used against me.

My attorney asked about the confidentiality of the information being discussed. Mr. Levin assured him that everyone there belonged to the select group permitted by law to have access to this information without a waiver of confidentiality. Well, not exactly.

No one at that table should have had access to Kay's mental health information without a waiver from her. PA Mental Health Laws concerning Confidential Communications state:

(a)   Use of a student's confidential communications to school personnel in legal proceedings is governed by statutes and regulations appropriate to the proceeding.

I lacked the status of a therapist, doctor, or minister; however, what I was forced to disclose came under Kay's mental health information. She did not give me permission to divulge this to seven strangers and at that point, she was not in immediate danger because she was seeing the therapist. Although Michael Levin said her confidential communications were not protected, the law said otherwise:

> (b) Information received in confidence from a student may be revealed to the student's parents, the principal, or other appropriate authority **where the health, welfare, or safety of the student or other persons is clearly in jeopardy.**

I was told I would be fired if I refused to answer the questions posed by Mr. Levin. I was not protecting Kay's health, safety, or welfare by revealing her private information to Dr. Durtan, Ms. Clark, Dr. Sanni, Ms. Heim-McCloskey, and Mr. Levin. In fact, I was being "tried" for protecting her health, safety, and welfare. In order to keep my job I had to violate all her confidences and expose her inner feelings to the scrutiny of those who previously refused to help her and were now determined to prevent anyone else from doing so.

The personnel director was not exempt from FERPA law. Only district personnel who have direct contact with the student or who need to know information to assist the student have access to information without the permission of the parents. The personnel director had nothing to do with Kay. Suddenly FERPA was irrelevant and dispensable.

I recited the story of what had happened. Michael Levin's eyes widened when I mentioned the suicide note. I believe this was the first time he heard about the note. It suddenly struck me that Mr. Levin hadn't been told Kay's history. He was paid to mount this attack with no information and no preparatory research. I looked over at Dr. Durtan who was intently picking at his fingers, a blank expression on his face.

Michael Levin was simply appalled that I had driven Kay in MY OWN CAR. He must have gone over this point five times. I could not understand his dismay, considering I had been instructed by an assistant principal at the middle school to drive one of my students home because she did not want him on the bus. She did not get parental permission, and she most certainly did not give me any choice as to whether I wanted to do it.

In addition, during my last year in the middle school I drove one of my students to and from school when he was suspended from the bus for two weeks. The school district had the prerogative to suspend him; however, because he was a Spec Ed student, they had to provide him with alternative transportation according to IDEA. They did not do this. They told me to get him to school and back home. No one saw this as a liability when it was for the convenience of the district. In both cases, the district would have been legally liable as I was not operating as a private citizen, and I was providing a service for the district, as dictated by its administrators.

However, as a private citizen, who helped a girl who was home from school, a child not in the district's care, and at the request and with the permission of the mother, I was suddenly in violation of a plethora of newly conjured up transportation laws.

I noticed Mr. Levin was not busy committing this information to his computer. The fact that the district did not have a transportation policy, in combination with their willingness to use a teacher to supplant services they were required to provide, lacked the relevance to be included in the investigative information.

Michael Levin's agenda was to ask me questions concerning my actions and to hear me say I had done them. These were the damning admissions. All they wanted was that I "confess" to these activities, which made me "guilty." It did not matter that my help had not constituted any violation of law, policy, or practice. It became evident early on that no one was listening to what I said. It had no bearing on the outcome.

My attorney, the Uniserv rep, and I were asked to leave the room three times. One of these times, they questioned Robert Anderson. Although I should have been permitted to hear the interrogation of the one witness present, I was not, nor was my attorney permitted to ask Mr. Anderson any questions. It was their house, their umps, and their rules.

The last time we were removed from the room, we went out to the parking lot to wait. Shortly after, Michael Levin came out and called my attorney and the Uniserv rep over to speak with them privately. Despite being the guest of honor, for some reason I was not included in this conference The Uniserv rep and my attorney bolted over to me and blurted out in unison that Michael Levin had lamented to them: "I can't get her on anything because the principal knew about it."

"I can't get her on anything…" And there friends, you have it.

We returned to the conference room for the final time. Mr.

Levin asked me if I thought I should be disciplined, and what that discipline should be. I should be disciplined for helping to keep a kid alive while the people who set her up for her first suicide attempt were sitting at the same table?

I told Michael Levin that discipline was not appropriate, as I had done the right thing. He was seriously offended by this and told me I had placed the district in a dangerous situation because Kay's mother was "considering taking action" against Wissahickon. This was definitive proof he was lying because he had not spoken to Kay's mom and I knew it. Furthermore, the mother had never thought of suing the district concerning my actions, as she would later testify.

I was curious as to what the basis of a lawsuit would be if the parents were to sue the district. Let's consider this one: what would be the cause of action? Parents sue a district because they asked for a teacher's help, the teacher complied, and the child did not kill herself. What would the damages be? They were worried about their suicidal child and their child was still alive? That would be a pretty tough sell in the legal arena.

I posed this question to Michael Levin. His response was he had "been in this business for almost thirty years and he knew about these things." He knew about these things? Not much of an answer.

Assuming the parents sued the district, the only grounds they could use would be the illegal actions of Durtan, Clark, Heim-McCloskey, and Jones. They could have gone after these people for negligence, professional malpractice, violations of federal and state Spec Ed law, and, of course, deliberate indifference resulting in Kay's emotional difficulties and the first suicide attempt. These added up to solid reasons for a lawsuit; saving her life did not.

As the hearing came to a close, Mr. Levin gathered the "exhibits" which would become part of the record. Included was a letter from the therapist Kay had seen which was a strong endorsement of my actions:

May 22, 2008

Dear Dr. Durtan:

I am writing on behalf of teacher, Ms. Sallie Montanye at her request. Ms. Montanye attended the initial two counseling sessions, when I began seeing one of my new clients. It was my understanding from Ms. Montanye and the client, that the client found it hard to talk and was reluctant to attend counseling with a psychologist that she did not know, without the teacher that she both trusted and confided in attending with her.

Further, it is my understanding that the client's mother both knew and approved of the initial arrangement. Not long into the counseling sessions, I both spoke to and met with the mother, and remember no mention of any problem with the initial arrangement being mentioned.

I am bound by the ethics of my professions, regarding confidentiality however I wanted to shed whatever light possible, upon the situation, without violating said privilege, in support of Ms. Montanye.

In my opinion, it is this type of situation that discourages teachers from mentoring and supporting students, and teaches those same teachers not to go the "extra mile," and our children lose. I work with many teachers, parents, and school professionals, and find this a sad statement for a group of professionals who are highly dedicated to helping children.

At the high school ages, children turn away from their parents and go to their peers for advice. They rarely look for, or are receptive to, much in the way of guidance from adults. Sometimes, a special bond with just one teacher can save a child's life.

The therapist had the foresight to hand deliver this to Central Office the morning of the Loudermill. She wanted to personally deliver it because she thought the possibility existed it "might get lost from the receptionist's desk to the conference office."

The exhibits also contained the letter from assistant principal about the schedule change. The Uniserv rep pointed out I had already been reprimanded for the change, and the district was subjecting me to their brand of double jeopardy. Mr. Levin agreed it should be taken out. It remained in the record.

Interestingly enough there was not a whisper about the WIN team (SAP) letter. Strange how this source of the information against me was absent when the compilation took place. It was, after all, the single accusatory item that attested to my unprofessional behavior and my continuing lack of good judgment. At this point in time, I had not seen the WIN team (SAP) letter; I knew of it only through Mr. Anderson's discussion with the union president. More importantly, the district was unaware that I knew about the letter.

There was one other letter that did not make it into Mr. Levin's pile. That would be the fax Kay's mom sent to Principal Anderson, stating she had asked for my help with her daughter and I had complied with her request. I did not know about this letter. Robert Anderson brought copies to the Loudermill hearing; Judy Clark and Bill Sanni told him to put them away. They did not want it presented. Of course, I would have no say in the matter, as I was not present when the letter was discussed. By keeping us from hearing the one witness, my lawyer and I would have no redress to any duplicity or hidden evidence because we would not have known about it.

Was this artifice relegated only to Ms. Clark and Dr. Sanni? Did the superintendent of schools also engage in this duplicity? Not only did Dr. Durtan know about this letter, so did his attorney. When I finally saw the mother's letter, it had this inscription across the bottom: "Mike, this was dropped off by Bob Anderson on 5/16/02, 4:30 PM. Bill Sanni." The letter was faxed to the Levin Legal Group.

Michael Levin knew about the letter. By not insisting that his clients hand it over or by not supplying it himself, he either suggested or approved the act of suppressing it. For people who were interested in "hearing my side of the story," they were most uninterested in information or evidence that supported "my side of the story."

At the conclusion of the hearing everyone stood up and shook hands. This had to be the most confounding moment of the entire day. Why would I want to shake hands with a man who did what Dr. Durtan did to Kay, the two women who followed his lead, and then proceeded to crucify me for helping her?

Michael Levin extended his hand to me. I refused. I told him that this was not over; it was just the beginning.

On the ride home my attorney told me he initially believed I lied to him or omitted information. He said half way through the hearing he realized I had been completely truthful. It wasn't that he thought I was dishonest; it was that he could not understand why a district would do this to a person who saved a child's life.

A few days after the Loudermill hearing Bob Anderson received a visit from Stan Durtan and Bill Sanni. They wanted to talk to him about what had taken place at the hearing. They were not pleased with his testimony. Although I did not hear what Mr. Anderson said at the hearing, he told me he made it clear to them that I had kept him informed about Kay's progress. He also supported my chronology of the events concerning the suicide note. He confirmed I did not attend a therapy session after I was instructed by him not to. In addition, he pointed out the mother had requested my assistance and had given me permission to take Kay to therapy.

Mr. Anderson claimed he did not know I was actually going in to the session with Kay. I told him Kay would not see the therapist if I did not go with her. Possibly, he did not understand what this meant. It would have made no sense for me to go with her and sit outside while she was in the session. She certainly did not need me as a taxi service.

As I was not there for the testimony, I cannot attest to what was said. I did see Mr. Anderson's notes concerning his testimony later. His main contribution was to tell them he knew what was going on, which made it trickier to fire me.

Given the collective bargaining agreement, Michael Levin knew, as did Robert Anderson, the district could not terminate me if a person in a supervisory capacity did not inform me that what I was doing was "wrong." They could hopefully prod me into quitting. With a voluntary resignation, the board would never know the laws the superintendent et al had broken; the union would have no redress against the district, and the situation concerning Kay would be swept under the carpet.

I spoke with Mr. Anderson after Dr. Durtan and Dr. Sanni left his office. They claimed they had "lost their confidence" in him. According to Bob Anderson, Dr. Durtan said, "You should have written her up for insubordination."

When Mr. Anderson pointed out that he could not have done so because I had not been insubordinate, the response was, "You should have written her up anyway." On a warm day in May, Robert Anderson was told he had to be out of the district by the first of October. He was done.

It would be unfeasible to believe the hearing was either a serious effort to establish the facts surrounding my actions with

Kay or to "hear [my] side of the story." Dr. Sanni and Ms. Clark's instructions to Bob Anderson to hide the mother's letter and Levin's knowledge of the letter and complicity to withhold it proved these administrators were not interested in facts. The displeasure voiced by Dr. Sanni and Dr. Durtan to Mr. Anderson because he did not write me up for something I did not do reinforces this. Robert Anderson was fired for not being willing to engage in their deceit. More importantly, it removed the only person who could attest to what really had taken place. Who would believe this story without someone in authority to back it up? Robert Anderson had to go.

*****

If you harbor the slightest belief that Wissahickon's Loudermill hearings had a shred of validity, let me tell you about the one held for Joe. Remember Joe? He was the middle school teacher who was charged with "infractions" the same time I was. Oddly enough, the letter complaining about Joe was dated the same day as the WIN team letter. Here is what they did to this highly respected, veteran teacher with seventeen outstanding years in this district.

On March 17, 2002, Joe emailed the director of Special Education, and forwarded a copy to Stanley Durtan, Superintendent, about a difficult IEP and his lack of time to prepare it due to district commitments.

Dr. Durtan forwarded his copy of the email to Judy Clark, Hugh Jones, and Kelle Heim-McCloskey, with this: "Please let me know how we will be addressing this issue. Stan."

On February 20, 2002, an IEP meeting was held for Joe's student. The IEP was complicated and the meeting was adjourned until March when the document would be completed. At the end of the February meeting, Kelle Heim-McCloskey sent Joe a complimentary email stating:

> You did a great job today. I know how hard it is to be such an advocate for kids but to also keep within the guidelines. If you want me to come over and help draft goals and objectives for the next meeting let me know. (email 2/20/2002)

On March 19th, the IEP meeting was held from 7:45-1:00PM.

After the meeting, the Middle School Principal, Hugh Jones, sent an email to Joe and the folks at Central Office complaining:

"A total amount of six hours were [sic] spent in the IEP meeting on February 20th and March 19th. This is an excessive amount of time to complete this task." (3/19/2002)

Understand that Kelle Heim-McCloskey chaired the meeting and there are no time limitations on IEP meetings.

Mr. Jones tried to end the IEP meeting on March 19th; however, the father insisted the IEP be completed that day. At the conclusion of the meeting, the parents expressed their gratitude to Joe.

Why then would this qualify as grounds for a $4000 plus pre-termination hearing? It wouldn't.

Joe came to his first Loudermill hearing with a complete timeline for the IEP. He had all the emails from team members proving the IEP was developed as quickly as schedules allowed. Included was Kelle Heim-McCloskey's laudatory email.

Mr. Levin glanced over the materials then declared the district would "postpone" the hearing in order to perform "further investigation."

The morning after the "postponed for further investigation" hearing, Joe walked into the middle school and was immediately approached by a highly agitated Hugh Jones. He informed Joe that a secretary from the Spec Ed department at Central Office had come to the school, gone through Joe's files in his desk, and removed five IEP folders.

Hugh Jones had "never seen a district like this. He'd never worked with people who were willing to do what they were doing." He felt Central Office's response was "over the line."

He was convinced the administrators had created an "environment of mistrust." He then informed Joe that Michael Levin had **directed** the district to take some IEP folders from Joe's desk, so he could review them. Mr. Levin's goal was to see if they could "get" Joe "for failure to properly implement" the IEP's. Hugh Jones explained to Joe they were trying "to put you in your place."

Joe discovered five student files missing from his desk. He

emailed his Supervisor (Kelle Heim-McCloskey) advising her of this. She did not respond.

The next month Joe received his **second** letter of allegations. This notice contained all the allegations from the first letter; then Mr. Levin added that Joe was guilty of a number of violations pertaining to the creating of three IEP's. In fact, the violations were so severe, that the documents "failed to comply with minimum legal requirements."

Included with the letter of allegations was a bound exhibit booklet which contained three IEP's. These were three of the five missing from Joe's files. Release waivers from the parents were **nowhere to be found.** Release waivers were never provided although they were requested. These parents had no idea their children's IEP's were being used and sent to various people for inspection.

The IEP's did not "meet legal requirements." Hmmm. Their dog don't hunt. Consider the IEP's:

- had been accepted by the district as complete (supervisor)
- were signed off on by the local educational agency rep (usually a principal)
- were reviewed by the staff at Central Office (secretaries and supervisor)
- were filed in Central Office, available for inspection by state agencies
- were sent to the parents as viable, legal documents

Suddenly, without any changes taking place, these documents **violated** laws regarding the standards of IEP's? And the only person capable of finding these gaping flaws was Michael Levin?

The mistakes were minor in nature, and Joe did not cause them. In one IEP Joe had not signed the front page. That was Heim-McCloskey's fault. She chaired the meeting. She accepted the IEP as complete.

Mr. Levin claimed one IEP lacked the present levels for reading and math. In fact, those levels were supplied from testing by the district and private testing. They were right where they should be. Kelle Heim-McCloskey was the one who wrote this section.

In another section, Mr. Levin felt the sentences did not adequately address the section. This was a drop down part of the IEP where we would choose from a selection of premade sentences. The Special Ed director and supervisors had constructed the sentences. Everyone in the district used these sentences in their IEP's.

The district accused Joe of leaving out a Behavior Management Plan. The child did not require a behavior plan. He was learning disabled. Joe, however, included **seven** goals that addressed behavior in the body of the IEP. Ms. Heim-McCloskey agreed with these goals. Michael Levin claimed they didn't exist. But there they were in black and white.

The district claimed there were no occupational therapy goals in the IEP.

Teachers do not write these. The occupational therapist writes these goals. They would have been sent by the OT to Central Office and placed in the IEP.

The second IEP lacked any highlighting. It was not possible to discern what Michael Levin considered to be wrong.

The third IEP was written under the guidance of Kelle Heim-McCloskey. According to her signature, she was present for the construction of the IEP. This would mean the district's expert completely overlooked errors so severe in nature they required the services of an outside attorney.

According to Mr. Levin and his clients, the **speech goals** and their objectives did not fulfill the requirements of the law:

> the measurable annual goal, short-term objectives/ benchmarks... so poorly written that they fail to comply with minimum legal requirements...(these goals) are so substandard they are in violation of the law.

WOW. The sticking point here was that Joe **did not write the speech goals**. Special Education teachers **DO NOT** write speech goals. The speech teacher writes them. Mr. Levin stated as much in his *Pennsylvania School Personnel Actions* book; Appendix B. The district was paying Mr. Levin to question Joe about goals he didn't write, that Mr. Levin *knew* he didn't write.

Maybe Dr. Durtan, Mr. Levin, Ms. Clark, Ms. Heim-McCloskey, and Dr. Sanni collectively forgot the speech teacher wrote the goals. The IEP program we used automatically entered the name of the person writing the section of the IEP at the bottom of the page. This is what appeared on the bottom of the speech goal pages. "Entered by: **amiller.**"

- As supervisor, Ms. Heim-McCloskey knew Ms. Miller wrote the goals.
- Judy Clark knew; she was the one who oversaw the speech department.
- Dr. Sanni, the director of personnel, would be aware of what a speech teacher's job entailed.

That leaves us with Superintendent Durtan. He knew teachers were not qualified to write speech goals. Also, he would have seen the "**amiller**" on the page. Aside from that, Dr. Durtan was well acquainted with the speech teacher in the middle school-she was his sister-in-law.

Mrs. Miller, the speech teacher, was never questioned about these "inferior goals." She was, however, promoted to Special Education Supervisor a couple of years later. Incidentally, I had never known Ms. Miller to do *anything* in an inferior manner.

According to the WSD Newsletter, Summer 2003, the following appeared under a picture of Kelle Heim-McCloskey and others from Central Office:

> ...They supervise all Special Education programs, including K-12 gifted, out of district placements, and the state IDEA funding.
> **In addition, they monitor compliance of all IEP's.**

And we know that Mr. Levin was aware that the supervisors were the end of the responsibility chain as evidenced in his article Special Education Litigation: What is Stoking the Fires? ("It's the Law"; Michael I. Levin, Esq. PSBA counsel. PSBA Bulletin: October 2003)

> Supervisors who are expected to **ensure** that IEPs are being completed properly also must be properly trained, and they must have time to review IEPs to **ensure** that the writers of the IEPs are writing them properly.

The district said the supervisors were the **final authority on the IEPs.** The attorney for the district, the one conducting the Loudermill hearing, stipulated this truth in an article he wrote for the Pennsylvania School Board Association. Yet, surprisingly, Kelle Heim-McCloskey, the supervisor, was not being questioned or accused of any infractions.

I can't count the number of times I received incomplete or poorly done IEPs. Some of them were not understandable due to poor grammar or inferior writing. Pages were missing, Sometimes the name of the child was incorrect because the pages had been cut and pasted. I had one IEP where there were three names used for one child. Children were incorrectly categorized. The year and date were incorrect. Vital information was missing. Yet, Joe was the only one to have a Loudermill hearing concerning IEP's. Out of the thousands of IEP's in the district, only three had mistakes and they all belonged to Joe. Curiouser and curiouser.

Joe had just buried his thirty nine year old wife and had three young kids to raise alone. He lacked the time or strength to continue this farce. He resigned and accepted a job in a private school at less pay than at WSD.

Speaking of breaking the law, Dr. Durtan violated FERPA law by releasing five IEP's to an outside third party without permission from the parents.

In his annual letter to the community, Superintendent Durtan assured parents:

> No individual or agency outside the school system will
> be permitted to inspect a student record without prior
> written approval from the parent.

Mr. Levin pointed out in his book that in order to de-identify an IEP, every piece of information, which would allow recognition, has to be eliminated. The IEP's used against Joe still had the student's birth date, the student's age, the student ID number, the community of residence, the student's grade level, and the complete first name and last initial of the student.

Remember Mr. Levin's comment to my first attorney: "I trust she is not violating FERPA by sharing the student's records with you…"

In Joe's situation the district was violating federal law and also School Board Policy #216.1, which states:

It will be the responsibility of the Superintendent of Schools to insure that the pupil's right to privacy is not invaded when information is gathered, maintained, released or destroyed.

The policy fails to grant the superintendent the right to send IEP's to an attorney he hired, without obtaining permission from the parents.

Finally, I would ask this most basic of questions; if the IEP's were substandard **where were the IEP's the district wrote to replace them?** Surely the district did not allow **substandard** IEP's to remain as they were. Wouldn't that leave them open to legal action?

The IEP's were never rewritten.

During the Loudermill hearing, Don Atkiss (local uniserve representative for the state union—PSEA) made a statement concerning the slanted Loudermill hearing. This was recorded in the "affidavit" written by Michael Levin:

Don believes that Joe is being singled out for this. Any remedy should not be limited to Joe. He is not doing anything out of the ordinary. This is not something that should be individualized. Don stated the union has a real concern that what occurred is for whatever the reason that Joe was identified, was for **improper reasons**.

(Affidavit of Joseph August 14, 2002)

In October, Joe contacted (WEA) the local teacher's union. He also asked the Uniserv rep (Don Atkiss) what the outcome of the Loudermill meeting was. He received the following response:

My advice to you is that you leave that issue sit. *(Results of the Loudermill hearing)* They have never formally concluded anything which means there should be no action in your personnel file. If you force their hand, knowing Levin, they may issue some sort of discipline or other conclusion with which we disagree. It is unlikely they would issue a report that absolves you. As it sits now there is no conclusion that you did anything improper. If anything you may want to wait awhile, then ask for the contents of your personnel file to make sure nothing is in there concerning this issue.

Wait a sec. This was the union—the union Joe spent many years working for. Wasn't it Don Atkiss (PSEA Uniserv representative) who expressed the "real concern" of the union that Joe was being targeted for improper reasons? This is the union that "defended the rights of teachers," telling a member to shut up and just let it be. Despite the fact that Joe was accused of nothing, that evidence proved the district was lying and everyone knew Mr. Levin was "creative" with his charges, the union was unwilling to do anything for this man.

The rep ended his email with these ironic thoughts:

Everyone in WEA *(local union)* was very disappointed at the news that you had left. The District lost a great teacher.

Let me know if I can do anything more.

(Atkiss email 10/25/2002)

More?

CHAPTER EIGHT

Directives

The state of Pennsylvania endorses the concept that the child's safety is of paramount importance. This tenet is found in the tort laws, which deal with negligence. The state has laid out the principles by which a teacher can be held negligent. However, the state has also made it clear that in the event a teacher feels a child's safety is in peril then it is the obligation of that teacher to act to prevent any perceived harm. The law also articulates that if the teacher, in the course of this preventative action, knowingly breaks a law, the teacher is not answerable to an accusation of violation of the negligence statute. **Put simply—the state resoundingly charges that a child's health and welfare hold a *value* beyond the pale of legal rhetoric.**

On the 6th of June, I received a certified letter signed by Stanley Durtan, and written by Michael Levin. By the time I got to the last page, I was having trouble breathing. Dr. Durtan and Mr. Levin were obviously disgruntled because they "couldn't get [me] on anything." Undaunted, they came up with another tactic. If I refused to quit, they would make my time in Wissahickon unbearable. This was laid out in the lengthy, restrictive, Directives Letter.

June 3, 2002

Re: Notice of Directives: **Maintaining a Proper Relationship With Students.**

Dear Mrs. Montanye:

This letter follows the Loudermill conference during which you responded to the allegations against you. As stated at the Loudermill conference we will reiterate that because the Principal had some level of knowledge about what you were doing (we should note that there are some inconsistencies between what you stated and what the principal has stated on these issues), we will not impose "discipline," but as stated to you, your conduct was inappropriate and but for the principal's acquiescence to some degree, you would have been disciplined and perhaps discharged. Your acts and omissions constituted significant wrongdoing and you are directed not to engage in such acts or omissions again either with this student or any other students.

As you know, at the Loudermill conference, you admitted that you scheduled an appointment for a student to see a psychologist and you literally drove the student to and from her first appointment and home from her second appointment. You sat in and observed and heard each of the first two sessions between the student and the therapist, you selected for her. None of those activities are related to the expectations for your position, none are required by the student's IEP, and none are required by law. In short, those activities were not part of your job as a teacher and your actions to engage in those activities illustrates [sic] that you did not demonstrate a sufficient appreciation of where to draw the line between your proper duties and acts that are not appropriate.

Because you have not demonstrated a sufficient appreciation of where to draw the line, you are being directed to attend an appropriate seminar or training session. You should contact the District's Director of Special Education to work out the details.

In addition to requiring you to obtain appropriate training, we are giving you the following directives with which you must comply.

1. Subject to the terms and conditions set forth below, you are directed not to engage in any act, conduct or activity with respect to any school district student that is not expressly required or reasonably implied by your job, any IEP of any student assigned to you, your individual contract with the school district, any applicable collective

bargaining agreement, the policies of the school district, or legal requirements.

a. Relating this directive to the allegations that were made against you, your job expectations, the student's IEP, your individual contract with school district, the applicable collective bargaining agreement, the policies of the school district, and legal requirements did not require, either expressly or reasonably by implication that you schedule this student with a psychologist under the circumstances, that you transport the student to the psychologist's session, or that you sit in and attend the psychologist's session.

2. You are directed to comply with legal processes and school district policies relating to evaluations and referrals of students and you are to be cognizant of the school district's resources and programs to address student needs, such as the student assistance program.

a. As you know, the fundamental mission of the school district is to educate students. Some students have needs that interfere with or impede their education progress. To respond to those needs, the school district has a number of programs in place, such as student assistance and special education. There are procedures and processes in place that must be complied with, indeed, some procedures and processes are mandated by law and failure to comply with legally required processes and procedures could, depending upon all of the facts of a case, lead to a violation of a student's civil rights, could lead to legal liability for the school district, and could lead to liability for you. We are sure you would not intend to violate any student's civil rights, but the failure to abide by the required procedures for such things as special education for example is a violation of civil rights. Based upon your statements at the Loudermill hearing, we are not sure that you appreciate that fact. For example, you stated several times that what you did was the "right thing" to do. Doing what you may think is the "right thing" to do may nonetheless be violative of a student's civil rights.

b. Because the school district's fundamental mission is to educate the students, the needs that the school district responds to are needs that interfere with or impede a student's education. The school district has no duty, nor even the capacity to respond to a student's needs that do not affect the student's ability to learn. Relating these concepts to the allegations against you, you stated that you engaged in the conduct you did because it was the "right thing" to do. Allow me to raise a rhetorical question-was it the right thing to do according to you, because it was necessary in terms of the student's education? Or was it the "right thing" to do in terms of issues wholly apart from the student's educational needs? If the former, then the school district policies and practices, some of which are required by law to be scrupulously followed, should have been complied with. If the alleged need to see a psychologist was wholly unrelated to education, why were you involved? You are the student's teacher. You are not the parent. You are not a social welfare agency. You were not designated by anyone to determine when a student needs the services of a psychologist, how the services will be scheduled and who [sic] the student will be transported to visit a therapist. Did the parents and student know you were acting in your capacity as teacher or were you acting in some other capacity?

3. If you engage in any conduct outside of school and outside of your capacity of your status as a teacher with any student or any parent of any student, you are to do each of the following:

a. Provide a written memorandum to the principal of your school with a copy to the personnel office stating that you will be having contact out of the school and outside of your capacity as a teacher with a student and/or parent of a student enrolled in the school district. The written memorandum must be provided in advance of such interactions.

b. You are directed to advise the student and parent/guardian prior to engaging in any such activity that you are doing so in your personal capacity only, not as a teacher or employee of the school district. You are to advise the student and parent of that fact both orally and in writing. You are required to have the student and parent sign the written statement acknowledging that they received the statement and understand that you are not engaging in such activity as a teacher or employee and that you are not acting for or on behalf of the school district. You are directed to promptly provide a copy of the written statement to your principal and supply a copy to the personnel office.

If you have any questions or concerns about these directives, please contact me promptly. If you believe that any of the directives are not sufficiently clear or are unreasonable, please contact me. If we do not hear from you, we will assume that you have no questions or concerns and that you believe that the directives are sufficiently clear and reasonable.

Sincerely,
Stanley J. Durtan, Jr. Ed.D.
Superintendent of Schools

It's difficult to know where to begin with this one. Let's start with the author. Although Dr. Durtan signed his name, Michael Levin wrote it. Dr. Durtan's style is significantly different from Mr. Levin's. Stan Durtan's letters, which I read many times as a district employee, were circuitous and comprised of long, involved sentences. Durtan would not know the boilerplate incorporated within the body of this document. Mr. Levin leans heavily on "indeed" as an introductory phrase or at the beginning of a clause. He also fills his communications with rhetorical questions.

One of Mr. Levin's legal tactics is overkill. Yes, the Directives Letter would have been enough to make me quit; however, when you saddle a teacher with a lead-in such as **"Maintaining a proper relationship with students,"** you are virtually assuring that another district will not hire her. Most school boards are reluctant to offer employment to a teacher who does not maintain a "proper relationship with students."

Consider this: if you read that a teacher did not have a proper relationship with a student, would you assume that she helped a bullied, suicidal child live through her ninth grade year or that this meant she was involved with a child in some immoral manner?

The opening line was the strongest damnation in the teaching business. Mr. Levin, who claims education as one of his areas of expertise, knew that. He didn't just want me to quit: he wanted me to never be able to work again in my profession. Mr. Levin is reputed to be the type of attorney who isn't satisfied with winning: he wants to completely obliterate his opponent. In this case, he wanted to obliterate me.

Let's look at the letter:

...because the Principal had some level of knowledge about what you were doing...we will not impose 'discipline,' but for the principal's acquiescence you would have been disciplined or perhaps discharged.

This explains why they fired Robert Anderson.

Your acts and omissions constituted significant wrong-doing and you are directed not to engage in such acts or omissions again either with this student or any other student.

By this point, I truly believed they wanted Kay dead. There was no other explanation as to why the district did not take any action against the people who were supposed to help her and did not. Not one person who let her "fall through the cracks," including the upper administrators who set the stage for her first suicide attempt, was reprimanded.

Once again, the nebulous "wrongdoing" term was applied; note there is no law or regulation provided in connection with the "serious wrongdoing."

You admitted that you scheduled an appointment for a student to see a psychologist and you literally drove the student to and from her first appointment...

This is why Mr. Levin's hearings are so effective. Kay made the appointment after school. Remember she was fourteen. She was in charge of her mental health care. Although there were no laws violated, Mr. Levin uses the word "admitted" which automatically taints the person with guilt. Admission is automatically associated with doing something wrong or illegal.

...the therapist you selected for her...

When innuendo and smear tactics fail, resort to revised history. I did not select the therapist. I provided a name. Kay and her mother could have opted for another psychologist. The only drawback with this canard was the mother's fax that stated she had asked me for my assistance in seeking psychological help for her daughter. That's why Mr. Levin and his clients made sure this contradictory information remained safely tucked away.

...None of those activities are related to the expectations for your position, none are required by the IEP, and none are required by law.

The IEP stated when Kay became overwhelmed emotionally, she should speak with an appropriate adult. What was the point of having this in the IEP if it did not mean that Kay could speak with someone she trusted? There was no definition provided as to what constituted an appropriate adult. No one ever informed me that as an Emotional Support teacher I was not appropriate. It's not as if I had no experience with at risk kids. Most of my students fell into this category. Kay was not the first suicidal child I had had in my class. Why was I appropriate in the previous years and suddenly inappropriate this year?

...your actions to engage in those activities illustrate that you did not demonstrate a sufficient appreciation of where to draw the line between your proper duties and acts that are not appropriate.

On the contrary, I knew exactly where to draw the line, and I drew it. On one side of the line was a live young lady getting help. On the other side were all the people who turned their backs on a child who wanted to kill herself.

...Because you have not demonstrated a sufficient appreciation of where to draw the line...

Michael Levin was quite attached to this phrase.

...you are being directed to attend an appropriate seminar or training session.

This would be difficult because what seminar is going to teach the most effective means on how to ignore the problems of a bullied, suicidal child? And just who would offer such a seminar? Or maybe he meant a seminar on how and where to draw lines. (?)

You should contact the District's Director of Special Education to work out the details.

Suddenly, the director of Special Education made an appearance. He was chosen to tell me where to find a course on how to let kids kill themselves. Where was he during the Loudermill hearing? Wasn't this the man who kept asking Robert Anderson what was going on? Wouldn't he be out of the loop, as he had not been invited to the Loudermill hearing and had not been consulted about what had taken place?

...you are directed not to engage in any act, conduct or activity with respect to any school district student that is not expressly required or reasonably implied by your job, an IEP of any student assigned to you...the policies of the school district, or legal requirements.

The first problem presented by this statement was that there was no conduct or activity expressed in any job description. There was no definitive job description for my position at the time. Since I had had numerous interactions with children's psychiatrists or psychologists, I would not have detected the line-crossing conundrum with this one. The only job definition any of us had acquaintance with, since I began working at WSD, was that Emotional Support teachers had to address the emotional components of the students' personalities in order to facilitate learning. This statement appeared wherever the administrators explained Special Education to the public.

The other area of confusion arose from my past experiences. As an Emotional Support teacher, I would listen to the personal problems of many students. At no time was I told this was not to be done. This is what the Wissahickon School District paid me to do. With no warning, this exploded into wrongdoing.

I would think that helping a suicidal child would be implied in the teaching profession. Not that what I did should be expected from everyone; but certainly people who truly care about children may have difficulty with the idea that listening to the outpourings of a troubled child and making it possible for her to receive help are wrong and must be discouraged. One of the staples of advice given to high school kids on a yearly basis is, if they have problems they should talk to an adult—be it guidance counselor, coach, or teacher. According to Michael Levin, *Esquire,* and Stanley Durtan, Ed.D, teachers are off limits.

> *You are directed to comply with legal processes and school district policies relating to evaluations and referrals of students...*

The school district evaluated Kay in third grade. When the district evaluates a child, it has a consent form signed. There is no consent form for having a private therapist evaluate a child. There is no form granting permission to a school district for a private evaluation performed outside of the school. You see, the school district does not have to obtain permission for an action it is not performing.

On top of that, Mr. Levin and Dr. Durtan must have realized that under the mental health laws, Kay, who was of age, was the only one legally entitled to grant me permission to accompany her or to permit a new therapist to evaluate her.

As far as "referrals" went, to whom would I refer Kay? The WIN team (SAP), which already knew about her? The WIN team (SAP) which was too busy to take any action with Kay because they were all watching every move I made?

If a police report, a suicide attempt, and a suicide note couldn't get their attention, another referral would have been of little use.

Maybe they meant I should have notified the supervisor of Special Education, who forgot to mention to the Child Study Team that an eighth grader had to be put out on a PTSD diagnosis because she was traumatized by bullies who were not curtailed by the administration. The same supervisor who did not rewrite the IEP to provide Kay with any services?

In any world, these suggestions were spurious. The school had evaluated Kay. Kay had been referred to their resources. Everyone who was supposed to help her had abandoned her.

> *...you are to be cognizant of the school district's resources and programs to address student needs, such as the student assistance program (SAP)*

I was more than cognizant of the district' s limited resources. Knowing about them was one thing; being able to coerce the professionals into performing their duties was another story.

Curiously, Mr. Levin and Dr. Durtan did not seem to grasp the concept of the WIN team (SAP), their duties, and their constraints. You would think both men would have had a full understanding of the functions of the team and the methods that were employed to achieve these goals. Had either man known Kay's background, he would have realized she was beyond the WIN team's sphere of operation. Had either man listened to what was **said** at the Loudermill he would have also been aware of this.

Some students have needs which interfere with or impede their educational progress. To respond to those needs the school district has a number of programs in place, such as student assistance and special education.

Was Mr. Levin saying that the WIN team (SAP) and Spec Ed department did not know about Kay? He is creating a picture of the caring district that was prevented from acting on behalf of a child because a teacher kept all the vital information from the "resources." The fact that Kay was in Spec Ed and known to the WIN team (SAP) contradicted this; however, when reading the Directives Letter no one would be the wiser.

With this suggestive passage Michael Levin is removing the WIN team (SAP) and the Spec Ed department from any liability; his statements imply they knew nothing about Kay's problems or past. Although they should have, Levin laid the inferential groundwork that information had been kept from the WIN team (SAP) and Spec Ed because I had not referred Kay to programs that already knew about her. In case of any real litigation, Mr. Levin could fall back on this fabrication to establish his cloudy assertions as factual proof.

Finally, Mr. Levin portrayed me as an irresponsible rogue teacher, one who pushed herself between the district's resources and the student, which could have caused great damage **if the situation had been different.** The resources of the district didn't provide help; but they were making the feeble claim that I went off like some loose cannon, making sure a suicidal child saw a licensed therapist.

> *...failure to comply with legally required processes and procedures could, depending on all of the facts of the case, lead to a violation of a student's civil rights...*

Hmmmm. "Depending on all the facts of the case could lead to a violation"; one could apply this logic to anything. If you walk into a store and leave with a pair of shoes-depending on the facts-this could lead to criminal charges. If you pay for the shoes, nothing is wrong. If you put the shoes in a bag and take them out of the store without paying for them, this could prove criminal. **Every outcome depends on the facts of the case.**

Aside from all the violations we have already addressed, does anyone find it ominous that a school district was interfering with Kay and her parents' civil rights? Didn't these parents and their child have the right to select a therapist and have a person of their choosing accompany her? Dr. Durtan and Mr. Levin thrust themselves into Kay's business, Kay's life, and the decisions of her parents. They are the ones who had no right to do so.

> *...you stated several times that what you did was the 'right thing' to do. Doing what you may think is the 'right thing' to do may nonetheless be violative of a student's civil rights.*

There's that **may** word again. Surely, Mr. Levin couldn't have gone through three years of law school without being able to recognize the difference between breaking the law and **may** be breaking the law—*depending on the facts of the case.*

It seemed to really irritate the attorney that I felt I did the right thing in saving a child's life. He took great exception to that.

> *The school district has no duty, nor even the capacity, to respond to a student's needs that do not affect the student's ability to learn.*

I know Mr. Levin wrote this, but Dr. Durtan signed it. How could a superintendent, with an Ed.D, no less, and a resumé that claims he was a school psychologist, commit his name to a letter that makes such an embarrassing statement? Didn't Dr. Durtan realize when a kid stayed home from school because she was afraid to be there, this affected her learning? Did he feel that hiding in the nurse's office during classes helped her achieve? Wouldn't anyone understand that children suffering from severe depression, as per a psychiatric evaluation, don't focus well on academic material? Here's a stumper: did the superintendent and his attorney know it's an established fact that bullied, suicidal children don't see a future; therefore, they are not really gung-ho on achieving so they can get into college? Between Mr. Levin and Dr. Durtan did neither one of them realize if a kid killed herself she probably wouldn't be making honor roll? But there it was in black and white:

*...was it necessary in terms of the student's education...
no duty to respond to a student's needs that do not affect
the student's ability to learn..*

The man running the Wissahickon School District wanted to know if being suicidal, suffering from PTSD, staying away from school out of fear of being brutalized, leaving school early, and living in constant anguish would have any impact on Kay's education?

*Or was it the right thing to do in terms of issues wholly
apart from the student's educational needs?*

I haven't the foggiest what this one means. My guess is that Michael Levin wanted to throw in some inexplicable question with hints of dirty goings on. It couldn't hurt.

*Did the parents and student know whether you were
acting in your capacity as teacher or were acting in
some other capacity?*

Another one of Mr. Levin's not so subtle innuendos. Here's the answer this question merits: In light of the fact that not one district employee would do anything to help Kay, how could her parents view me as acting in the capacity of a Wissahickon School District employee? I was doing what I could for her; they had never seen this response on the part of any Wissahickon personnel. Therefore, my behavior indicated I was not acting as an employee.

Now the letter gets better: I am to be humiliated for helping Kay.

If you engage in any conduct outside of school and outside of your capacity of your status as a teacher with any student or any parent of any student, you are to do each of the following:

a. Provide a written memorandum to the principal of your school with a copy to the personnel office stating that you will be having contact out of the school and outside of your capacity as a teacher with a student and/or parent of a student enrolled in the school district. The written memorandum must be provided in advance of such interactions.

The sounds you hear are the dying gasps of the First Amendment, at least as it pertains to teachers. Not only did Dr. Durtan not have the right to take away my freedom during my off hours, he had no right to limit my interaction within the community. But that's exactly what he was doing.

b. You are directed to advise the student and parent/ guardian prior to engaging in any such activity that you are doing so in your personal capacity only, not as a teacher or employee of the school district. You are to advise the student and parent of that fact both orally and in writing. You are required to have the student and parent sign the written statement acknowledging that they received the statement and understand that you are not engaging in such activity as a teacher or employee and that you are not acting for or on behalf of the school district. You are directed to promptly provide a copy of the written statement to your principal and supply a copy to the personnel office.

The superintendent told me what I had to do when I met a fellow community member off of school property. He told me what to say to them. Keeping in mind that a school district is considered a government entity, what statue would possibly say or imply that a school district employee could dictate to whom I spoke or what I said on my own time, in my private life?

If you have any questions or concerns about these directives, please contact me promptly. If you believe that any of the directives are not sufficiently clear or are unreasonable, please contact me. If we do not hear from you, we will assume that you have no questions or concerns and that you believe that the directives are sufficiently clear and reasonable.

Let's take a moment to assess the restrictions of the Directives Letter.

- If I attended an after school ball game and spoke with a parent without previously stating my intent, I could be fired for insubordination. Actions contrary to a directive issued by a superior **are** grounds for dismissal.
- If I did comply with the requirements, I would have to go to the supermarket armed with pad and pencil in case it was necessary for me to get signatures from any parent and/or student I spoke with over the produce counter.
- I would still be in violation of the Directives if I did not register this meeting with the district before it took place.

Aside from the impossible logistics required, think of the effect this would have on parents of my students. They would wonder why I had to go through these rituals, and many might refuse to sign the paper. If parents inquired as to why I had to perform these tasks, was I supposed to tell them I had "improper relationships" with students? This most certainly would make them uncomfortable with me as a teacher. And what about those who refused to sign the paper? Would this automatically put me in Durtan's cross hairs because I did not fulfill the demands of the Directives? How would you feel about a teacher who recited a scripted speech, recorded the conversation, and then asked you sign these notes? Would you have any faith in this professional?

There is another consideration that I am sure leant itself to this letter. I lived in this community. Both my children attended the high school. My son played sports for the high school. My daughter was in choir. I shopped at local stores. I went to a local beauty salon. I was at all of my son's games and many of my students' activities. According to this letter, any conduct outside of school would require permission and written reports.

If you engage in any conduct outside of school and outside of your capacity of your status as a teacher with any student or any parent of any student...

Dr. Durtan and his attorney were determined to make my life such a living hell, hoping that I would quit rather than being publically humiliated or fired for disobeying a directive. And in case you're thinking that this would not be enforceable because it was (1) ridiculous (2) illegal, let me remind you that they had already gotten away with accusations that had no basis in law or policy. Dr. Durtan was determined to show me that he could operate unencumbered by law or decency. He could make me a prisoner in my hometown. I was going to pay the price for stating that I had done nothing wrong.

This Directives Letter speaks for itself. It also speaks volumes about the man who wrote it and the one who signed it.

There is one important omission from the Directives. There were no people copied on the letter. Robert Anderson was not copied. He was still the principal. Wouldn't he need to know about this if I had to report to him about my activities? The personnel director was not copied either. How would he know what part he played in this if he had no knowledge of it? Letters like this are not written without delineating whom the line person in charge will be.

In addition, this final requirement would be virtually impossible to follow. What would happen during vacations and weekends, or what if I talked to someone after work hours and there was no one in personnel or at school? Should I call them at home and register my intentions with them during dinner?

I had some questions and concerns, but I knew looking for answers from these folks was bailing water out of leaky boat. The Directives were clear in their intent.

I filed a grievance.

CHAPTER NINE

Abandoned

...PSEA bargains compensation and benefits, protects members' rights, and advocates for their professions...We advocate for public education, children, and our members' professions... PSEA members are everyday heroes...PSEA members' dedication to their students benefits all of society. PSEA defends and protects members in all aspects of their working lives: compensation, working conditions and professional development.

PSEA Mission Statement

Michael Levin, the attorney for the Philadelphia schools, says these cases are typical:

"The teacher fights you and doesn't just walk away, " he told me. "The union will back them."

Hoover Digest "The Dance of the Lemons" by Peter Schweizer, 1999.

I was a card-carrying member of the National Education Association (NEA). The NEA is roughly 3.2 million strong. It is the largest teacher's union in the country. In fact, it is the largest of any union in the country. The NEA is divided into fifty uniserv entities-one per state. Our uniserv group is the Pennsylvania State Education Association (PSEA). PSEA encompasses all the local unions in the state. WEA (Wissahickon Education Alliance) is our local union.

The Uniserv groups have attorneys who represent the regional state subdivisions. When the PSEA is looking to court new members, the benefits of legal representation are stressed.

What they neglect to mention is this representation is limited by the scope of the union's interest and the willingness of the attorneys to take a case.

Union attorneys get to pick and choose their cases. If they do not want to take up your argument or if they feel they may not prevail, they do not have to represent you. There is nothing members can do about this. They cannot refuse to pay dues to force the union to do its job. In our state there is a fair share law; by statute, teachers have to pay 80% of the required yearly dues. This circumvents protesting members refusing to sign up or cancelling memberships.

Glossy brochures assure members that PSEA/NEA is "the last line of defense of the teacher's civil rights." It's only when a teacher's civil rights are violated, she may learn the union refuses to live up to this promise.

Once I had received the Directives Letter, I called Chuck Herring, the regional union attorney. He had not been present for the Loudermill hearing. The PSEA Uniserv rep who attended was not an attorney. He did not know the law; he was a contract negotiator. Despite my yearly dues, I had to pay $1800 to hire legal representation for the Loudermill, if I wanted legal advocacy.

When I spoke with Mr. Herring about the Directives Letter, he told me I had "broken no law and violated no rule or regulation." He explained, "You stuck your neck out and the district cut your head off." He then informed me what I did "was foolish." I wondered what the hell was going on. The district said preventing a suicide was "poor judgment," the union said it "was foolish," yet both organizations are forever spewing clichés about protecting the children.

KH, who had just become president of the local, (WEA), had difficulty in pinning Attorney Herring down to a time to file the grievance. There is a deadline. Miss the date, the grievance is void. KH needed the attorney's assistance in how the grievance would be worded. It was her relentless fervor which finally got him to do this.

Under the direction of the attorney, the grievance chairperson completed the form using the Directives Letter as the basis for the complaint.

Sallie Montanye's "Improvement Plan" [the quotation marks are hers] dated June 3, 2002, is a disciplinary event and violates Article VI H. The Improvement Plan is further unlawful and unconstitutional. Said plan mandates specific requirements for the grievant which violates the law of the Commonwealth of Pennsylvania and the United States. Pursuant to various case law, incorporating the external law in all collective bargaining agreements, the Improvement Plan violates the contract because of mandatory incorporation requirements. Lastly, Articles I + II are violated in their entirety.

Translation: The Directives Letter

- Was discipline without just cause
- Violated the Pennsylvania Constitution as it infringed on my private actions
- Violated the U.S. Constitution as it infringed on my private actions and dictated to whom I could speak
- Made illegal requirements for me that were not applicable to all members of the collective bargaining agreement
- Singled me out from the collective bargaining agreement

What I found to be offensive was the label *improvement plan.* Although I did not agree with this tactic, the union was trying to get Dr. Durtan to agree to modify what they were now calling the improvement plan. The Directives Letter was not an improvement plan. Improvement plans target perceived shortcomings to be corrected, have a supervisor keep track of the progress, and are finite.

The union (WEA local) tried to soften the nature of the Directives Letter, by providing what they considered to be a more aptly worded rebuke. Their version read:

Dear Mrs. Montanye:

This letter follows the Notice of Directives letter. In that letter special directives and extra training were prescribed which could be construed as disciplinary in nature; we would like to rescind that letter. We do want to make it perfectly clear that you did extend yourself past the bounds of a teacher. The legal ramifications of such an extension are ones that the Wissahickon School District is not willing to undertake

In the future, you are to conduct yourself within the guidelines of a special education teacher. If an extraordinary circumstance arises in which action must be taken you are to receive permission from your building administrator. The building administrator may be required to seek my counsel (superintendent) before such permission is given.

The death rattle you hear is 3.2 million people being collectively sold out.

Apparently, "the last line of defense of the teacher's civil rights" was perfectly comfortable with the idea that the district had a right to interfere with a teacher's private life.

A school district is not legally responsible for a private citizen's actions. And where was the PSEA attorney who said I broke no law nor violated no regulation? The district concocted accusations and the union, rather than challenging them, tried to make them palatable.

The grievance chair was the person who discussed matters with Dr. Durtan. It was her job to see if there could be any mutual ground for resolution. If they could not arrive at some form of agreement, the grievance would go to arbitration.

There were some enlightening comments made during the meeting of July 18, 2002, between the superintendent and the grievance chair. Dr. Durtan originally said he would be open to restructuring the words of the Directives Letter; however, he changed his mind and stated it would not be "altered in any fashion."

When the grievance chair brought up the subject of the mental health law granting majority rights at fourteen, Dr. Durtan, the man with the Ed.D, who headed a school district and was formerly a school psychologist, said he was not aware of this. That's upsetting. But, wouldn't this have been something his attorney should have brought to his attention? Surely he would know this.

Another strange Durtanism was made in response to the question of what kind of "course" he felt I should be looking for to fulfill this requisite of the Directives Letter. The answer was I had "displayed poor judgment," therefore he was suggesting I take a course in "making good judgments." He was at a loss when asked if he could recommend one.

In his final comment, Dr. Durtan informed the grievance chair that, "The Directives Letter doesn't really say what we meant it to say." Seriously? Between a man with at least six years of postgraduate education and an attorney with three years of law school, thirty years of experience, and someone who "knows about these things," they couldn't write a letter reflecting what they *"really meant?"*

*****

Meanwhile, KH (President of local union WEA) wanted the WIN team (SAP) letter. She also wanted to know if any other material existed which was used to justify a Loudermill hearing. She wrote to Dr. Durtan requesting any and all memos, letters, anecdotal records, and communications of any nature that pertained to the district's actions against me.

July 2, 2002

Dear Dr. Durtan:

...in order to process this grievance, the Association is requesting that the district supply all materials relied upon by the district...in the creation of the improvement plan for Sallie Montanye. This request includes any and/or all writings, memoranda, letters, emails, and SAP admissions in the district's possession that relate to this situation...

KH   WEA President

Was the union entitled to this information? Mr. Levin's book provides us with the answer: *Pennsylvania School Personnel Actions*: Chapter 5; § 5.2 pg.187:

Unions also have the right to obtain from public employers information which would enable the unions to make informed decisions about whether to pursue grievances...unions are entitled to reasonable discovery

117

of relevant materials. Moreover, the fact that a grievance may be pending does not obviate the employer's duty to provide relevant information which is requested by the union. Unions have a right to a list of witness names, but not to witness statements. Unions additionally have the right to investigative reports and to the minutes of meetings kept by the employer.

Michael Levin was not about to hand over the WIN team letter. He was equally protective of "all other materials" requested by the union president.

The union's response was to file an unfair labor practice charge. This is lodged against an employer when one of the regulations under the Public Employer Relations Act is violated. It is submitted by the union attorney to the Pennsylvania Labor Relations Board that arbitrates whether or not a violation has occurred. If the board finds the employer in violation of labor law, they will, supposedly, instruct the employer to comply with the request.

The Unfair Labor Practice charge stated:

- I was subjected to a disciplinary/improvement plan which was challenged through and by a grievance procedure.
- Despite repeated requests for the materials, the school district had failed and/or refused to respond to complainant's appropriate discovery requests.
- Respondent's conduct was designed to punish, intimidate, and harass bargaining unit members for engaging in lawfully protected union advocacy.

It ended with a statement requesting an order to compel the district to obey the law and provide the sought after information.

Mr. Levin did not want the WIN letter to be viewed by anyone. He responded to Chuck Herring, the PSEA union attorney:

October 18, 2002

Dear Chuck:

Please be advised that I will be representing the School District[5] with respect to the charge of unfair practices…Simply stated, I am disappointed that the Association would waste everybody's time and money on such a charge. The actions taken by the School District in this matter and the directive given to the employee in this case (who has not been disciplined, by the way) were based upon the conduct the employee admits she engaged in. The union and the employee were given documents at the investigative Loudermill hearing.[6] Everybody is aware of all the pertinent facts and, indeed, the facts are largely undisputed.

As you well know, public education is subject to attack from all sides. The scarce resources of school districts should not have to be wasted on nonsense like this…I suggest that if the Education Association were more interested in improving teacher performance, and ensuring that its members do not engage in the kind of inappropriate conduct that this teacher engaged in, that there would be fewer attacks on public education and on the teaching profession…This is a ridiculous request.

Very truly yours,
Michael I. Levin

According to the WIN team (SAP), I was endangering the students and would destroy the district if my behavior went unchecked. Mr. Levin saw me as a far more substantive threat because teachers like me "brought attacks on public education and the teaching profession." My pivotal importance in the destruction of troubled children and my role in the deterioration of the American Public Education system were growing by leaps and bounds.

These are the back and forth responses concerning Michael

---

[5] N.B. October 18, 2002 – Levin "representing school district"

[6] I was given no documents at the Loudermill hearing. I left empty handed.

Levin's refusal to cough up the WIN team letter. I call them *The Bite Me Letters.*

Chuck Herring's response to Michael Levin's above letter of October 18th, 2002:

> Dear Mike:
> What are you hiding?

> Michael Levin's response to Chuck Herring's question above:
> Dear Chuck:
> My disdain.

> Chuck Herring's response:
> Disdain this. [handwritten]

> Michael Levin's response:
> Say what? [handwritten]

> Chuck Herring's response:
> Hey Mikie Bite Me!! (punctuation Mr. Herring's)

During my deposition, Mr. Levin had this to offer concerning the above correspondences. He wanted to know if I was aware that they (he and union attorney Chuck Herring) had a "relationship" and that these letters were examples of how they "joked around."

- Deposition Part 2 Monday, February 21, 2005—Sallie Montanye

Levin: Mr. Herring, Mr. Charles Herring, Chuck
15 Herring ever tell you that he and I had been working
16 together as—on matters involving school districts
17 for approximately 20 years?
19 Did he ever tell you that he and I have a very good
20 working relationship with one another?

Levin: Did he (Herring) ever tell you that he and I frequently
9 joke around and clown around with one another?
Levin: Did he (Herring) ever tell you that he and I frequently

12 send to each other little short notes and cryptic
13 notes as jokes?

Levin: Did you ever talk to him (Herring) about the fact that
6 after he got my letter, (October 25, 2002) he and I had a conversation
7 and we were joking around about it?

Levin: Ever know that Mr. Herring has a father who
17 also represents the teachers union in Pennsylvania?
(Herring's father is also a lawyer.)
25 Did you know that Marty (Charles Herring's father) and I have
2 a very good relationship with one another?
4 Did you know that Marty and I frequently joke around about
items?

Ok. Let's get this straight. A child struggled through two torturous years in the middle school. She was banished from school because she "allowed" herself to be bullied. She almost died. This child was diagnosed with clinical depression and suicidal ideation. She was suffering in high school. Her desire to die had returned.

I was the recipient of career-ending charges because I extended help to this child. Michael Levin is hiding his "disdain" for me for not wanting a child to die? Or is Michael Levin hiding his "disdain" for the union because they were going through the motions of defending a teacher who didn't want a child to die? And Michael Levin and Chuck Herring are "joking around" about this? I, for one, was not laughing. I'll bet Kay's parents wouldn't find this exchange amusing, especially between a man who said it was wrong to save their child's life and one who labeled it as "foolish."

Chuck Herring sent a letter also dated October 18, 2002, which stated the Union's demands in different terminology. Again he asked for **all** materials.

October 18, 2002

Dear Mike:

On July 2, 2002, KH wrote to Dr. Durtan, a copy of which is enclosed for your easy reference.

So that there is no misunderstanding, the association

has the right to evaluate whether there is a legitimate grievance regarding the improvement plan and the discipline attached thereto. The decision to review and evaluate rests with the association...I would like for you to send...all materials that the district relied upon that is in its possession, excluding those materials that are attorney-client privileged, that the district utilized for its determination that there was a need for a Loudermill hearing as well as those materials that the district relied upon for the creation of the improvement plan. Since the allegations here involve a teacher's inaction [sic] with a student, your claim of FERPA protection arguably does not apply...You must deliver any complaints from Ms. Montanye's colleagues, co-workers, parents, and administrators that the district holds...I see no protection under FERPA for you to withhold those alleged documents.

Michael Levin's October 30, 2002 response letter to Chuck Herring was lengthy and defensive. He reiterated Chuck's requests. Then, Mr. Levin restated that the "allegations that led to the Loudermill hearing were set forth in the notice dated May 1, 2002." He recited the entire allegations letter. Attorney Levin pointed out that "admissions by your client ...coupled with her explanations and her utter lack of understanding of the inappropriate nature of those actions" were the "exclusive evidence" used by the district.

Mr. Levin had an interesting take on this matter. I displayed an "utter lack of understanding" concerning the gravity of my actions. Damned straight. I was never able to comprehend how letting a child die, by her own hand, was not a grave action. To this day, I still don't get it.

There were two reasons Mr. Levin was adamant about this request. One, as previously stated, was his desire to keep the WIN team letter buried. The second one is more intriguing. According to Mr. Levin's assertions, there was absolutely no documentation for anything that took place. Not one memo, not one note, not one scrap of paper reflecting any discussions, questions, or decisions.

Educators are avid note- takers. The standard joke in college was: A professor walks into the classroom and says "It's a beautiful morning." The science major asks what the qualifiers are for beautiful, the psychology major asks why the professor feels it is a beautiful day, and the education major writes the statement down.

Administrators' jobs are filled with endless discussions and copious writing of notes. These people are told by their legal advisors to document every decision, particularly ones that deal with teacher discipline. Mr. Levin included this admonition in his in-service for the Wissahickon school district, on how to fire teachers. Yet, Dr. Durtan, Judy Clark, Kelle Heim-McCloskey, and Bill Sanni had no written materials referring to this matter. If they had truly feared a "lawsuit," wouldn't they have backed up everything they said and did with written proof? Wouldn't Mr. Levin have asked them to do this?

Speaking of the attorney for the district. Who made the decision to hire Mr. Levin? Who decided my actions were "inappropriate?" There were no notes indicating any district employee spoke to the parents, and yet Mr. Levin said the mother was considering legal action. If this situation was as grave as they claimed, why was there not one iota of written substantiation? How does an institution hire an attorney, pay this attorney, and prosecute what is deemed dangerous teacher behavior without **any** paper references?

Think about what the attorney for the district was claiming:

- Dr. Durtan, Judy Clark, Bill Sanni, and Kelle Heim-McCloskey held no discussion about the WIN team (SAP) letter.
- These people hired an attorney, but there was no documentation to substantiate this expenditure of district funds, nor were there any minutes from an executive board meeting detailing or approving this.
- Dr. Durtan signed a contract with Michael Levin without discussing this with the school board. He had nothing in writing to show the procedures he followed to fork over $4000+ for my Loudermill; over $9000 for both Loudermills. **This is directly against school board policy.**
- Michael Levin required no documentation of any kind about Kay or what actions preceded my involvement with her. Since when do attorneys, the group morbidly addicted to documentation, go diving into something of such a "serious nature" with not one shred of information?

EITHER/OR:

Either: The district had notes they did not want to relinquish because they would impeach the claims of administrative integrity

Or: Nothing was committed to paper in the event that something would go wrong and a court would force them to produce the information.

My situation was this: the union (PSEA/WEA) would not do much except try to water down the Directives Letter. The best I could hope for was they would have it reworded. That meant nothing. The attorney was not interested in this case. He made it clear the union would not go to court for a civil rights case. There are cases where the union challenges a district in court, especially in civil rights cases, but our state union refuses to do this.

According to their literature, the union exists to defend teachers when they are innocent of the charges against them. In fact, if a teacher is found guilty of a criminal charge, he must refund the money spent by the union on his defense. The first item made known to me was that "teachers can be accused of anything without getting a defense" and the union "would not pay or be involved with any civil rights action" on my behalf.

Contrast the union's response to my predicament with their actions on behalf of teachers who cheated on an Advance Placement (AP) exam. The instructions regarding AP courses are explicit. No part of the test is to be copied. If these guidelines are not strictly adhered to, the district can lose the privilege of offering the courses.

The AP math test is changed every year with the exception of one section. This part is rotated over the course of four years. In other words, section A is given the first year, section B is given the next year and so on. In the fifth year, section A is repeated.

The Educational Testing Service people became suspicious when students from Wissahickon High School obtained perfect scores on this section. Officials were sent to investigate. It turned out the test **was** copied and the math teachers were teaching it. This is a no-no. Well, actually, it's a felony.

The high school principal was present when the ETS people questioned the students who observed when the test was copied.

A determination was made that the teachers had, in fact, violated copyright law.

The Educational Testing Service filed charges for violation of copyright law. [US District Court Eastern Division 97-CV-7051] *Educational Testing Service v. G, S, and G.*

Strangely enough, the case never went to court. It was settled. PSEA doled out a hefty amount of money (supposedly thousands) to pay the fines and squash the case. A few years later, one of the teachers involved with this illegality was cited as teacher of the year and honored at a Wissahickon public school board meeting.

So the union (PSEA) was willing to buy off the testing agency from prosecuting teachers who allegedly violated the law, but they could not be bothered defending the rights of teachers even "if they had broken no law and violated no rule or regulation."

The union attorney told me if I elected to pursue this legally, he would help me evaluate an attorney to make sure I wasn't "swindled" by a charlatan who would take my money and do nothing for me. Right. I was on my own.

I went looking for a lawyer. Michael Levin claimed the district feared a lawsuit.

I was going to give them one.

CHAPTER TEN

Montanye v.

One of the reasons why Wissahickon School District is a leader in education is because we *value* the importance of our staff. We believe in attracting and investing in the best and the brightest people, who show energy, compassion and dedication to improving the lives of our students by facilitating their academic achievement and individual well being.

Wissahickon School District website 2009

You may wonder what my Loudermill attorney had to say about the Directives Letter. Initially, he took the astonished approach. I read him the letter and he wondered aloud if the superintendent had been "sleeping through the hearing."

When I suggested that I sue the district, he raised his voice and berated me about the silliness of this notion. First, he claimed that a person could not sue the state, or in this case, a state operated institution. This simply is not so. You most certainly can sue a school district. It's difficult, your chance of success is severely limited, but it is possible. Keep in mind school districts are constantly crying about how often they get sued.

I finally stemmed his speech by reminding him that I had not asked for this, I had done nothing wrong, and I deserved to be left alone, rather than punished for the simple act of helping a student. After he regained his composure, he said if I did pursue a legal course, I would cut myself off from my social world. I would become a pariah in my own community. It would be a long, drawn-out action, and I would be completely on my own. He warned I could also wind up in horrendous debt with nothing to show for my efforts. He was correct on all counts.

****

I did not return to school in the fall of 2002 because I could not live under the oppressive demands of the Directives Letter. I developed hypertension, chronic depression, anxiety, sleeplessness, and all the physical manifestations of extreme duress. The strain of the Loudermill, the Directives Letter, the threat of termination, and the administration's overt animosity had taken its toll. On the advice of the local union president (WEA), I applied for disability based on the medical problems bequeathed to me by the administration. Although I believed in my heart I had done nothing wrong, I also knew I would be a social leper in the school. Everyone would be wary about interacting with me for fear this association would mark them as targets. I was not wrong in this assumption. This was proven when a Special Education aide, who was related to someone in the administration, stated at a faculty meeting that I was "a marked woman."

You have to understand what this did to me. I thoroughly enjoyed my students and was happy being with them. I always considered myself exceptionally lucky because I loved my job. I could put up with all the administrative shenanigans because my students meant so much to me. I knew the system was failing them, and I did what I could. If I couldn't change their world, I could help them deal with it more productively. There is a lot to be said when you are able to build up a child's self-esteem and effect a beneficial change in his life. The students were the greatest payoff of the profession.

Then one morning, without warning, I woke up to find my whole life had been blown apart. I was physically and emotionally devastated by their accusations. I was at a loss to explain the antagonism on the part of Dr. Durtan, Judy Clark, Kelle Heim-McCloskey, Bill Sanni, and the WIN team. They did not have to like me, but the extent of their vengeance upset me considerably. At this point, how I was viewed as a professional still mattered. I didn't care if these people liked me, but I wanted acknowledgement that I was a decent human being and a decent teacher. This was never going to happen.

*****

If you think job interviews are demeaning, they pale in comparison to finding a lawyer to represent you. First, you have to convince a professional who is prone to cynicism that you have been placed in your unfavorable position because you cared about a child's life. Many attorneys I spoke with shared the opinion of the union attorney: Putting yourself out for a bullied, suicidal child was "foolish." Then there's the "it's got to be more than what she's telling" response. This case was a hard sell because it was so unbelievable.

Getting in to see an attorney is no small matter. They are busy and not inclined to waste time on your case if it doesn't promise an easy win or a boatload of money. Suing a school district bodes neither. It's an uphill battle with limited chance of victory.

In order to get a face to face with the lawyer, you have to get past the secretary/receptionist. This entails going through the whole saga. It is not an uplifting experience. Naturally, in my mind I was in the right; after all, everyone would see the virtue of saving a child's life. Not necessarily. I found that many people, when first hearing this story, assumed I was lying, insane, omitting pertinent details, or all of the above. It simply does not compute on the opening recitation. Depending on how your story is received, you might actually get to speak with the lawyer. The likely outcome is a dismissive letter or the attorney plays hide and seek when you make a follow-up call.

Legal people are by nature skeptical creatures. Realistically, you cannot blame them; if they jump into a case based solely on the client's rendition, they can find themselves in a losing battle as detrimental information comes to light. If an attorney does not ask the right questions, she can invest hours of her time before uncovering damaging evidence that hurts the case. An attorney won't stay in business for long if this happens with any frequency.

I spoke on the phone with many attorneys. Some patiently listened and then politely told me I did not have a case. Some were not so polite; they literally laughed in my face. A few said they would take the case if I provided anywhere from $30,000 to $60,000 up front. I did not have that kind of money stashed away for a rainy day or a civil lawsuit. I moved on.

One attorney was willing to see me in person. He read over the Directives Letter and asked me if the superintendent ever heard of a trial held in Nuremberg. His reference was to the argument that I could not be punished because the "principal knew about it." His contention, like the decision at the famous trial of Nazi criminals, was if the action I had taken was illegal, then the principal's knowledge of this action could not be used to negate its illegality.

The attorney said I should write a rebuttal. He wanted it to be in my own words, but he would read over what I wrote and advise me on any needed corrections. I left his office feeling I was on my way. I was about to get my first lesson on attorneys and how they get out from undertaking a case when they have a change of heart.

I went home and diligently worked on my reply. A few days later I phoned my legal editor. He was not in the office. He would call me when he returned. I called the next day. He was on the phone and would return my call when he was free. The next day he was with a client, but he would be given my message. This went on for two weeks. It took me a while, but the light bulb finally went off.

The next attorney was someone who was one of my husband's clients. He agreed to see me, I assume, as a favor. I took all my carefully organized papers and left them to be evaluated for their worthiness. After a week of unreciprocated phone calls, I got the hint. I was getting more astute at rejection by now. I retrieved my binders and went back to the drawing board.

One lawyer was very interested in the case. He told me how much he admired me and how these people deserved to be taken to court. He instructed me to call him the next week to set up an appointment and bring all my paper work. I phoned him a number of times. Strangely, he was never in the office when I called; he had just stepped out or he was on an important conference call. I really liked this man and he had been so enthusiastic when we met. Finally, I decided to wait for him on his office steps. I sat there for two hours until he arrived at work. He was "impressed" with my determination. We spoke a number of times after that. He was friendly and encouraging. Finally, he told me he was afraid of the IDEA component of the case and he couldn't represent me. It was not his sandbox, and he didn't want to be in a strange one. He wished me the best of luck.

During my search I also contacted the ACLU. I sent them a detailed letter including some pointers to the First Amendment violations. The ACLU claims to be a stalwart defender of the First Amendment, at least that is what their printed propaganda says.

There is no higher calling, nor greater reward, that a democracy can offer an individual than the opportunity to stand up for fundamental freedoms in trying times. These are indeed trying times for civil liberties.

The gist of the pamphlet is to win membership and money by painting a picture of the ACLU going into battle for the rights of the little people. Yes and no. The ACLU chooses its cases; many times their choice is a trifling legal matter which reflects the political views of those doing the choosing. An example of a case the ACLU took on during this time period: they fought to have a cross removed from a cemetery located in a rural, remote area of the country. Without a map, no one could find this place. Banning a pipe-cross in a place where no one other than the family, who are most likely Christians, will see it is a waste of money and effort. In addition, why is a cross an offensive image in a cemetery? Why does this insignificant issue captivate the attention of civil rights "warriors?" Is this worth thousands of dollars for litigation? In case you don't know, when the ACLU wins a case like this, the government pays their legal expenses. Actually, we, the taxpayers, shelled out the money to stamp out the presence of a cross, which no one cares about, in a place that most people will never see.

I received my official rebuff in the mail a few weeks later. The ACLU informed me that they could only take "cases of importance." Mine was not one of those. The organization that championed Nazis' rights to march through a Jewish neighborhood populated by concentration camp survivors could live with allowing a school district to annihilate a teacher's First Amendment rights by punishing her for her private actions and restricting her life with the threat of dismissal for violation of unconstitutional directives.

Surely, there would be advocacy groups that would help me. With all the verbalized concern in this country about children and issues surrounding their security, there must have been someone who would listen, if not offer tangible support. I wrote to a myriad of concerned factions but found that no one was particularly upset about a teacher who was punished for helping a bullied, suicidal student.

My first letter was to The Council for Exceptional Children (CEC). This is the organization that fights for the rights of exceptional children. These are the people who exist to defend and advocate for children in Special Education. The letter was addressed to the executive director of CEC at the time. I sent a rendition of my experience with a cover letter. I told her what was done to me for helping Kay. I warned her that the district and their attorney were bastardizing IDEA in order to deny children necessary services and to escape accountability for not educating these children. There was no response.

I wrote to *Dateline* after I had seen one of their shows exposing school corruption. There was no response.

I wrote to Oprah three separate times. I submitted the information on line as directed. There was a response that my letter had been received. My high school daughter wrote to Oprah also. Nothing.

Some time after this, Oprah had a segment showcasing an older, male teacher who mentored a female, suicidal high school student. This man became involved in the girl's life when he learned she was depressed and thinking about ending her life. They had a strong relationship throughout her high school career. The teacher would also participate in outside activities with the student. The girl said he was "like a grandfather" to her and without his interest and concern, she would not have lived through high school. Go Oprah! A friend explained that Oprah was interested in stories with happy endings. Mine didn't fit this category.

I wrote to the *Montel Show*. After all, he is the one who is indignant about the offenses in society that demand to be addressed. There was no response.

I sent a letter to the reporter who wrote an article about the Camden, New Jersey testing scandal. Refusing to help a child and targeting a teacher who did should make a good read. There was no response.

I talked to a reporter for a Bucks County paper. She listened and couldn't believe the district would do something like this, especially considering the parents were supporting me. She did not feel she should write the story because I lived in Montgomery County.

A friend of mine who worked for a TV station tried to interest the reporters in the story, but she had trouble coming up with a "hook." The story wasn't enough. I needed an "angle."

I wrote to the school reporter at the *Philadelphia Inquirer*. I received a response expressing interest. I spoke twice with the reporter. That was the last I heard from the woman. I called her a few times but she never took my calls or returned them. I knew what that meant. I was a pro by now.

I sent a letter to Vicky Phillips, the then Secretary of Education for Pennsylvania. I received a letter from her secretary stating that Secretary Philips was "interested in learning about issues and concerns that affect school districts and their employees." Nothing ever came of this. Phillips left shortly thereafter to take a position in Oregon.

My friends were stalwarts; they encouraged me to keep looking. Their belief in the importance of what I was fighting for kept me going. When discouraged, I would get a pep talk from someone and start calling from my list of people who had yet to turn down my case.

One of the most memorable conversations was with Joe the district's other Loudermill subject. I was recounting my list of personal indignities; I cried that I would never find anyone to listen to my side and the district would be victorious in its depraved message. His words were comforting. He said, "Don't you see that you have already won?" He reminded me that nothing the district could say or do would change the fact that I had helped Kay through her darkest hour. My victory was a breathing human being who would live to blow out the candles on her next birthday cake because I helped her. Whenever I was in a dark place, there were so many of them, I would comfort myself with the knowledge that I did not have to go to sleep with the face of a dead child looking at me.

*****

A few weeks into the new 2002 school year, I ran into Kay's mother at a local convenience store. She asked me why I had not returned to school and if this decision had anything to do with Kay. I told her what had taken place. She was horrified. She said she suspected that Imelda Kormos was at the core of all of this. She made reference to the meeting held with Nurse Kormos and Robert Anderson. She stated that she did not want Mrs. Kormos at the meeting; she had wanted to speak with Bob Anderson and me alone. Her reason for this was she distrusted the nurse. When she was notified of the meeting, she thought I chose not to attend and that Robert Anderson requested the presence of the nurse. In fact, the nurse set up the meeting, which explained her presence and my absence.

Kay's mom was angry that Ms. Kormos repeated to the WIN team (SAP) the discussion that had taken place in the meeting. She thought her concerns would be kept confidential and would not be fodder for gossip at a WIN team (SAP) meeting. She ended our meeting by apologizing for what had happened to me. She said she believed in her heart that I was the only reason Kay lived through the year.

Kay was another aspect I had to consider. I was worried about the effect a lawsuit would have on her. She would have to testify. In addition, she would have to revisit the emotional traumas of middle school. She was still depressed and self-destructive. I did not want to push her backwards by forcing her to relive the hurt and humiliation. Despite my feelings that the district should not be able to persecute teachers, and although I firmly believed those who ignored Kay should have been held answerable, I had to weigh the cost of exposing her to the invasive scrutiny of a possible trial.

We met for lunch and talked about her school days before she met me. The conversation turned to our time during her ninth grade year. I told her what had happened. Although her mother gave me permission to tell Kay everything, I did not want her to feel any guilt, so I held back on my feelings and stuck with the basic facts.

I told Kay I had two options. The first was to let the past stay buried and to find another career. I downplayed my reservations by assuring her I could get a job elsewhere. The alternative was to file a civil rights lawsuit. I did not want to paint a rosy picture for her only to have her fall apart for my sake. There was no point in pulling her back together, then destroying her with the process of fighting my battle.

I listed the negatives. If the case went to trial, she would have to testify in front of an open courtroom. We might be able to get the judge to agree to have her testify in chambers, but that was a long shot. After all, she was already fifteen and would be at least sixteen by the time we went to court. I pointed out that there would be many people listening to her. The defense attorney would pry into the intimate details of her life. He would try to create the picture of a mentally unstable girl, far too troubled to be helped by anyone in the school district. His goal would be to prevent any sympathetic leanings on the part of the jurors. Mr. Levin could not afford for the jury to see the district personnel as professionals who were too indifferent to help a needy child. It would be up to him to paint a picture of Kay that the jurors would not like or be sympathetic toward.

I gave her examples of questions she might be asked. She would have to answer them if the judge instructed her to do so. I said it would be a long and tiring day; possibly she might be on the stand for a couple of days. She had to understand I could not protect her.

She didn't have to make the decision at that moment. She could take a few days and talk it over with her mom. I already discussed this with her mom. Kay looked straight at me and said, "I want you to get them for what they did to us." I took that as a yes.

*****

I was not making great headway finding an attorney. Most of the rejections centered around my inability to hand over thousands of dollars or the fear of taking on a school district. I would call at least three attorneys per day, if not more. At the end of the conversations, I was humiliated and frustrated. It's truly difficult to sell a story as unlikely as mine.

I decided to go to a source already familiar with my story, the therapist who saw Kay. Remember, she was not only a psychologist, she was also an attorney. Aside from the obvious advantage of her legal background, I would not have to recount the events nor would I have to present all the arguments that the district had no legitimate justifications for its actions.

She could not take my case because she did not have the experience with civil rights matters. She suggested an established civil rights attorney who had a sense of decorum she felt would be beneficial to my case. Her name was Anita Alberts.

Ms. Alberts agreed to see me that week. I asked Robert Anderson if he would go with me to support my story. By this point, I felt the backing of an administrator would carry more weight than the lone assertions of a teacher. Mr. Anderson's presence would lend credibility to my tale.

At our first meeting Anita Alberts let me talk uninterrupted. Unlike the other attorneys, she did not appear distracted. I had her undivided attention. When I completed my lengthy story, she looked at me across her massive desk and said, "You realize if you don't stop this man he will run through every district spreading this disease." She was referring to Michael Levin. Not only did she believe what I told her, she validated my position. For the first time since this whole matter started, I felt someone was on my side. Anita took the case on a contingency basis. I would have to pay for depositions and filing costs. I was no longer a teacher with a sad story; I was a plaintiff.

At our next meeting, Attorney Alberts told me she dealt with many cases where Special Educators were drummed out of their profession due to their active support for the students. She said she had clients where districts presented tortuous reasons to avoid delivering the educational programs required by law, then found the teacher or principal "guilty" of some infraction if he or she questioned this practice. These people were victims of counterfeit accusations; they were also defenders of the children who were in Special Education.

Anita wanted to know if I had been marked down in my yearly evaluation. She said this was usually the first step. In fact, this **had** happened to me.

I had been observed twice during the 01-02 school year. Jeff M was the assistant principal assigned to this task. Right after the Loudermill hearing he and I had an evaluation meeting. He went over the observations, which were complimentary; however, he lowered my rating from "very good" to "good." The district's guidelines state that a drop in a rating level has to be justified by a "noticeable deficiency in one of the areas observed." Mr. M had not met this qualifier. He made only two recommendations at the bottom of the page:

1. Keep students in their assigned classes.
2. Hold more IEP meetings.

Keep students in their assigned classes? When Jeff M observed me no student was in the class other than the ones assigned to it. No student came into the class during the period. Not one student left during the class period. What basis would he have to make this recommendation? Ah, the WIN team letter. When I questioned why he had written this, he had no answer. He just stared at me.

I then asked him what "hold more IEP meetings," meant. I held all the meetings for the IEP's for which I was responsible. How could I hold more meetings? His response was that Kelle Heim-McCloskey told him she was not invited to any of my IEP meetings.

Supervisors are not invited to run-of-the mill IEP meetings.

They only attend when the IEP is difficult. Ms. Heim-McCloskey announced to all the Special Education teachers, at the beginning of the 01-02 year, that she was too busy to attend IEP meetings. Unless the meeting dealt with exceptional issues, we were to have the assistant principals as the local education agency representative (LEA). Now, I was being penalized for following Kelle Heim-McCloskey's directions. I was dropped a level in my rating for an unsubstantiated rumor and for following the instructions of the supervisor of Special Education. I pointed this out to Mr. Madden; however, he had his orders and no answers. I ended by asking the assistant principal what I could do to return to my former rating. He answered with three words. "***Be more involved.***" (*more involved??*)

Even though the district had ignored its own procedures, I knew the union would not address this. These people were sending me a message. They wanted me to come to school, go through the motions, and leave at the last bell. As long as I would cover their indiscretions, I would be considered a good teacher. If I went against their policy of malignant neglect, I would pay for it with my career.

I wrote a rebuttal letter to Jeff M stating that the Special Ed program needed better structure. I pointed out we did not have consistent leadership; we had already gone through three directors in one year. I told him I held all my IEP meetings and had done so with the appropriate personnel present. I stated I did not take students out of their classes, but I did allow them to come for study halls where they would receive help.

> I am sorry if this does not fit into the neat package that educators prefer. However, we are Special Education and that means we have to make exceptions in order to meet the needs of these special children.
>
> Unfortunately, Special Education is asked to serve two masters: the structured program of the school and the needs of the students. Neither this administration nor our department had specifically defined what course we have to follow…

By this point I was tired of being punished for helping my students.

If I had not been willing to extend myself, there would have been far more students who would have been brushed aside, once again, by a system that only tolerates their existence under duress of legal action.

The long and short of this is you cannot mandate love or acceptance through legislation. If this were possible, we would not have racial inequities despite definitive civil rights law. Special Education is no exception.

*****

Attorney Alberts wanted to file a claim with the Equal Employment Opportunity Committee (EEOC) based on a charge of discrimination. She maintained my case was proof that the district was going after Spec Ed teachers. I felt uneasy about this because, although I knew of Special Education teachers who had been singled out for retribution, it would be difficult to prove. The Spec Ed teachers who were compliant with the district's deceits were left alone. It was the vocal ones who walked around with bull's eyes on their backs.

We met at the EEOC office in October 2002. The woman taking my history asked for a list of teachers who had undergone discriminatory behavior. My information about other teachers was not as cut and dry as the EEOC wanted. The woman said she had no doubt that what had happened to me was an expression of discrimination; but without a substantial list of names, she was unable to go forward.

Ms. Alberts was upset with my inability to produce the necessary evidence. I was confused as to why she expected anything else. I had always maintained that Joe and I were used as examples for the rest of the staff. We were the warning shots fired across the bow. There was no need to go after all the teachers; they would fall into line once they got the message of what was in store for anyone who was on the wrong side of the administration.

Regardless of the discrimination dilemma, Anita believed my case rested strongly on violations of First Amendment rights. When I accompanied Kay to the therapist, I was a private citizen; therefore, the district had no legal right to punish me through the employer-employee relationship. What I did own my own time was supposed to be my own business.

Ms. Alberts explained, as best she could, what a lawsuit would bring. Having never experienced one, it is impossible for the layperson to comprehend all that is involved in the legal process. She emphasized two features that were the standard defense practices: delay and deceit. Michael Levin would take every possible opportunity to keep the case going nowhere in an effort to bankrupt me. Defense attorneys play the odds that the plaintiff will run out of money or determination, and the case will wither away. Misrepresenting facts was another staple of a good defense.

Anita advised that once we set this into motion it could take a long time to resolve; she also made it clear that plaintiffs undergo great stress and emotional upheaval. Lawsuits take over your life; they consume you. She ended by saying:

> The basis of a society is the law it creates; when the law is
> ignored or violated and these infractions go unchallenged,
> the society begins to decay. The adherence to law is what
> makes us civilized.

She told me to think long and hard about the emotional and physical costs of continuing. I had no choice. This was about letting a child die. These people were trying to bully me into allowing a girl to suffer until she took an unacceptable out. They let her be victimized by bullies and they were doing the same to me with their kangaroo court and vindictive Directives Letter.

On November 19th 2002, *Montanye v. Wissahickon School District* (No. 02-cv-8537) was filed with the Clerk of the United States District Court for the Eastern District of Pennsylvania.

CHAPTER ELEVEN

Complaint

Who is the "client"...*conflicts of interest*...can arise when one attorney represents more than one party in the same matter, even if both parties are part of the same entity, such as a superintendent and a board of education who are both named as defendants in a lawsuit.

Nancy Fredman Krent from Chapter 11, Legal Ethics:
Some Important Aspects of the Attorney Client
Relationship

The roles of the school attorney include ethical considerations, knowing "who is the client," ...The attorney's best service to the school district may be keeping the school district out of legal difficulties.

Edgar H. Bittle from Chapter 5,
What to Expect of a School Attorney
Excerpts from *About School Lawyers* for the National School Boards
Association (www.nsba.org/site/doc.asp)

Mr. Levin: I am not her attorney personally (Judith Clark), I am the school district attorney, she's a representative of the managerial team of the school district.

Judith Clark Deposition 2/23/2005

Michael Ira Levin, *Esquire*, filed his notice of entry December 11, 2002, as representative of the Wissahickon School District. Let's become more familiar with Attorney Levin.

This was his firm's mission statement:

> It is the mission of Levin Legal Group P.C. to improve the legal affairs of those it serves with a commitment to excellence in all we do. Our goal is to offer quality services and exceed clients' expectations in a professional, convenient, cost-effective and accessible manner. To accomplish our mission and to meet our goal, we believe that we have a duty to our clients to be well informed, to think, to listen and to ask questions...

Yet, Mr. Levin had no idea about Kay or her troubles.
Returning to the write up:

> The firm's lawyers regularly appear in federal and state courts defending a multitude of actions ...in *Gaudiello v. Delaware County Intermediate Unit,* attorneys in the firm defended a decision not to allow a disabled child to bring a support dog to school.

Now there's a feather in your legal cap!
The blurb adds this assurance:

> The efforts of the firm's attorneys in these cases, illustrate the kind of **creativity** that will be applied to a situation to defend individuals and entities from novel and unique claims.

The Levin Legal Group used its creativity to separate a disabled child from the dog who assisted her. In Kay's case, Michael Levin used his creative talents to minimize the *value* of a child's life.

Mr. Levin had written numerous articles on various aspects of public schools. One such article enumerates the legal problems inherent in "hazing." [Hazing- Debunking the Myths About This "Right" of Passage. Michael I. Levin. PSBA Bulletin. PSBA. October 1999.]

Mr. Levin points out aspects of this ritual result in school liability. Although the article focuses on the practice of hazing, many of the problems have a familiar ring, as Mr. Levin states: "hazing includes, but is not limited to, physical and mental abuse."

According to Attorney Levin, hazing has been made illegal in institutions of higher education in Pennsylvania. Hazing is defined as follows:

- Any action or situation which recklessly or intentionally endangers the mental or physical health or safety of a student
- Any brutality of a physical nature
- Any activity which would subject the individual to extreme mental stress
- Any activity which could adversely affect the mental health or dignity of an individual

Where have we heard that before? Kay was not undergoing hazing per se, but she was subjected to all the components that defined it under Pennsylvania law. Mr. Levin points out schools can be liable for hazing even if the students willingly participate in the process. Kay was not a willing participant. The schools are not to allow such conduct. It is immaterial if the students who engage in the hazing process do so of their own free will. But what if the cruelty was against the will of the victim?

Let's look at these commentaries in respect to Kay and the actions on the part of the Wissahickon School District. Kay was not undergoing abuse to gain acceptance in a group. She was not a willing volunteer. She was a victim of the same type of abuse described above: endangered mental and physical health, brutality, extreme mental stress, and adverse activities that affected her mental health and dignity.

Michael Levin states in his article that allowing a student to participate in abusive behavior makes the district liable because it is indicative of an administration that **approves practices that cause harm to the student.**

Mr. Levin as a defense attorney provides arguments as to why school districts and their administrators should not be found liable for certain actions when another party brings charges against them. With all of the violations on the part of the district administrators, it was Michael Levin and Stanley Durtan, **not** Kay's parents, who accused me of wrongdoing. Michael Levin was not defending the errant school district against angry parents. He was manufacturing a case where there was none. He was beclouding Wissahickon's liability by creating accusations against me.

The Wissahickon School district did not have an anti-abuse or anti-bullying policy in place during Kay's tribulations. They also did not bother to put one in place afterwards. Wouldn't an attorney, who was so adamant about how awful it was that a teacher had privately helped a child point out to his clients that it would be of benefit to have such a policy? Mr. Levin also says in his article that, "school district officials must take at least that action which is reasonably calculated to stop hazing from recurring." Should Wissahickon have taken immediate action to stop the bullying that drove Kay out of school, or was being beaten up for no reason acceptable?

In addition to his creative talents, Mr. Levin also had the ability to defend many people with different stakes in my lawsuit. An attorney has to be cautious in this area. He should not represent clients where there may be conflicting interests, as one of them can be short changed. Look at Mr. Levin's client list in *Montanye v. Wissahickon*:

The School Board
Stanley Durtan
Maria Salvucci
The school district's insurance company

Do you sense a possible conflict of interest?

- The School Board has differing considerations from its employee, the superintendent.
- Stanley Durtan was an employee of the school district. His interests may not necessarily have been the same as his employer's.

Let's see what *School Law in Review 2003* suggests in the article, "What Boards and Superintendents Should Know About School Attorneys." (Martin Semple: Semple, Miller and Mooney, P.C. Denver, CO)[7]
First and foremost:

---

[7] The author cites Michael I. Levin ed, 2002 U.S. School Laws and Rules.

Model Rule 1.13 is the most critical ethical guideline…It provides that (a) The lawyer employed or retained by an organization represents the organization through its duly authorized constituents.

In practical terms, this means that the school district and its board of directors, as a board of directors, not as individuals is the client…the superintendent and the board should clearly recognize that the attorney's responsibility is to the school board and not the superintendent…

Ms. Salvucci was an individual. Not only that, she was represented by the union (PSEA), which was supposed to defend her. Suddenly, the school district was spending its money to supply her with legal representation. She did not pay dues to the school district; she paid them to the union with the agreement they would provide an attorney in her hour of need. Now Mr. Levin, a man employed by the superintendent, not the school board, was her counselor.

Michael Levin was also the attorney for the insurance carrier, who had to shell out money for the lawsuit he and Dr. Durtan spawned. The company's focal point would be to avoid any outlay of money. And then there's that ever- vexing issue of conflict of interests.

Conflict issues can also arise when the school district is represented through the attorney hired by the insurance company. Regardless of who actually hires or pays for the attorney, the attorney owes his primary duty of loyalty to the client he is representing, namely the school district…The interest of the insurance company…may be in conflict with the interest of the district. "What Boards and Superintendents Should Know About School Attorneys" (Martin Semple: Semple, Miller and Mooney, P.C. Denver, CO)

In a sense, Michael Levin was also defending himself. He had not been hired to get the district into this pickle; but now he had to get them out of it.

The democratic concept of the right to redress wrongs is basic to a free society. Occasionally, the law may serve the purpose of protecting those it was originally designed to serve; in many cases, it does not. Often, the law is designed to protect those who occupy a position of power. This is particularly true for public figures. They are shielded by immunity. This provides them with flexibility in their job; it also permits them the luxury of abusing power without fear of reprisal.

We are first introduced to civil rights in school. Schools are government entities and are considered the arm of the government. As students we are indoctrinated with a governmental perspective, promising rights and the ability to redress the violation of those rights. Everyone is entitled to her day in court. In reality, you have rights if you have money. Your rights are proportionately linked to your bank account.

Courts are not concerned with finding the truth. Neither are many lawyers. Attorneys who represent cases that are not profitable or go against the legal grain are rare. Oh, and judges? Their clerks write many or all of the decisions. That's assuming the judge will agree to hear the case. Cases may be dismissed if the judge does not want to hear it, because it is too long, too involved, or just not to the judge's liking. Judges have judicial prerogative. Federal judges are set for life and nothing short of committing some heinous crime can unseat them. But you say, what about the appeal process? You'll see how effective that is later on.

Understand the legal system is not truly a system. It is an industry. Self-perpetuating. Self-serving. The best analogy? It's the equivalent to doctors injecting patients with diseases, then treating them for the illness. An industry.

A lawsuit is filed in the state or federal court depending on the area of jurisdiction. In my case, because the claimed violations were constitutional, we had the option of filing in either venue. Ms. Alberts said we had a better chance in federal court, plus cases did not languish there for extended periods of time.

The federal court is known as the *rocket docket*; federal judges want cases that move through quickly. If a case is not short and sweet, there is the possibility a judge will dismiss it because he does not want his docket clogged up. Can he/she do that? You betcha'.

The initial filing (the Complaint) lists the offenses the plaintiff believes have been committed and the laws that are violated by these offenses. This is where the plaintiff and defendants are listed. Mine was quite populated because there were many defendants.

SALLIE K. MONTANYE v. WISSAHICKON SCHOOL DISTRICT and WISSAHICKON SCHOOL BOARD OF DIRECTORS, DONNA LEADBEATER, President; BARBARA MOYER, MARJORIE BROWN, BETSY CORNISH, WILLIAM McKERMAN, III, ROBERT McQUADE, YOUNG PARK, PAUL REIBACH, and TERESA WILLIAMS, Members of the Board; and STANLEY J. DURTAN, Supt. of Schools; and MARIA SALVUCCI, Guidance Counselor, Defendants

The initial complaint is known as a prima facie case. As the plaintiff, I had to present enough evidence and information to establish that my complaint was legitimate. The law supports the plaintiff's initial argument; the judge is supposed to view the facts in the light most favorable to the plaintiff. As the case evolves, the burden of proof becomes greater for the plaintiff.

The complaint is divided in sections.

Part I deals with the jurisdiction of the court. The attorney explains why this particular court should be hearing the case. If the subject matter is not within the jurisdiction of the court to which the complaint is submitted, it will be dismissed.

Part II provides information on the parties. This is the cast of characters involved in the action. The players are defined, addresses are supplied, and in this instance, how they were being sued.

When you sue a school district, you are technically suing the school board, which is the embodiment of this public entity. Public employees make decisions that will be unpopular with a given sector of people. Hence, the immunity laws. Immunity allows public officials great leeway; because they are usually sued in their public capacity, which means none of the defense money is coming out of their pockets.

In my complaint, I was suing all of the defendants in their capacity as public officials and as individuals. I was suing Stanley Durtan, the Superintendent of Schools and Stanley Durtan as a private citizen. Most public officials can be sued in this manner if they have violated a person's civil rights and if it can be proven they have done so by acting beyond the scope of their position. We were asserting that Dr. Durtan and the defendants did not have the official authority to insert themselves into my private life or to take steps to punish me for activity done outside my professional responsibilities.

I was suing the members of the board, Stanley Durtan, and Maria Salvucci in their public and private capacity. You may be wondering why Judy Clark (Assistant Superintendent) and Imelda Kormos (high school nurse) were not named. Believe me, this was not my choice. I felt both these women should be defendants. Judy Clark was obviously involved in the decision to have the Loudermill hearing and was part of the conspiracy to withhold Kay's mom's letter. Imelda Kormos had violated a ton of Kay's rights and mine. In addition, she was the source of the WIN team (SAP) letter and caused actual harm to Kay by interfering in her personal mental health issues.

Anita Alberts felt I would "look petty" by naming these two. A lot of what is done in legal proceedings has to do with how it looks. God forbid a judge might think a teacher is angry because a group of narrow-minded, malicious bullies blew apart her life and denied a suicidal child a champion. Attorney Alberts was the expert. I relented.

Part III contained the factual background. It discussed the WIN team (SAP) and its purported purpose. My teaching history was presented, along with the contention that I provided Emotional Support to students at risk during my years in Wissahickon School District. The events concerning Kay were recounted including the math class switch.

Anita introduced the WIN team (SAP) letter at this point. How, you may ask, did I get the letter? Well, Mr. Levin certainly didn't provide it, but Robert Anderson did.

A week before we filed, I called Mr. Anderson for the letter. I could not wait for the union to get it through the Unfair Labor Practice Charge. That was going to take forever. Also, I had not told Chuck Herring or anyone in PSEA about the suit. I did not want Michael Levin or the district to be forewarned. There were some instances where Michael Levin had procured information that could only have originated from PSEA personnel. The Unfair Labor Charge was dropped when Herring learned I had the WIN team letter. Of course, the district had been asked for *all* materials used. These were never obtained. Every Unfair Labor Charge filed on my behalf was dropped. No follow through.

Ms. Alberts numbered each new entry of the history.

Number forty-one concerned a memo written by Robert Anderson, dated March 22, 2002. I had never seen this memo. Robert Anderson's memorandum was directed to the WIN team (SAP). It was written in response to their letter.

CONCERNS—FACULTY MEMBER:

I want to thank you for your note and your concerns over the situation with Mrs. Montanye. The high school administration as well as the central office staff have been apprised of this situation and have already taken steps to rectify this potentially explosive situation.

As always our primary concern must be the health, safety and well being of the child. We will keep this in mind as we help Mrs. Montanye create appropriate professional space between she, [sic] the child, the family, and the child's treatment plan.

Please, if you hear of any further entanglements or any perceived breach of professionalism, let me know.

This memo served two purposes: it was an attempt to establish the situation was now under control and there was no need for any further action from Central Office. In this light, Mr. Anderson was trying to put an end to the matter.

The principal was tacitly agreeing I had breached my professionalism, that I needed help in creating appropriate professional space between Kay and her family, and her treatment plan. My effort to keep Kay breathing was an "entanglement." My desire to see a child get much needed psychological help to deal with her inner turmoil was a "potentially explosive situation."

You have to love administrative doublespeak. In an attempt to protect me from the administration, he was thanking the group who did nothing for Kay; he was thanking the nurse who got her a three-night stay in that pandemonium of a mental facility, and he was appreciative of the stoic silence on the part of the assistant principal (Tom Speakman, WIN team member) who never mentioned the "potentially explosive situation."

He was expressing gratitude to the people who ignored the suicide note he personally delivered. He was praising these folks for not doing their jobs or taking any responsibility in a potential life or death situation, while assuring them that I would be kept in line and shown the neglectful path of the true professional.

He was doing this because, "as always our primary concern

must be the health, safety and well being of the child." Which action on the part of the WIN team (SAP) or the district administration demonstrated that the "primary concern must be the health, safety and well being of the child?" Of course, this assertion would have been even less convincing had Kay killed herself.

In all fairness, Mr. Anderson had no choice. Had he sided with me he would have been fired on the spot. He was not being paid to be honest or protective of the children. He was paid to do the bidding of the upper administration, no matter how deceitful or unethical they were.

Anita then went after the Directives Letter, stating its purpose was "to intimidate Plaintiff from supporting Special Education students, in accordance with WSD's official policy of discouraging at risk students from finding help and advancing in public school, therefore in life."

> **Entry number fifty-two said:**
> No defendant has, at any time, told plaintiff specifically how her teaching ability objectively dropped a level (the evaluation which went from very good to good), what law she has broken, what rule she violated, what 'wrongdoing' she did, what procedure she ignored, what 'line' she crossed, or what harm she caused. Nonetheless, she has been targeted for termination, simply to create an appearance of legitimacy for Defendant's arbitrary, willful, malicious and illegal misconduct.

Ms. Alberts pointed out that I had run into Kay's mom at a local convenience store in September 2002. My attorney observed: "Plaintiff did not obtain prior written approval for this conversation and is therefore subject to immediate termination in retaliation for engaging in truthful and protected speech."

> **Number sixty-four** went to the heart of Anita's argument: Defendants' actions against Plaintiff are part of a continuing official but unwritten policy and practice of maintaining the least possible involvement with at risk children, providing the least possible services for Special Education, persecuting and denigrating Special Education teachers...denying "Special Ed" children the attention and help they need to cope with

psychological, family, and other difficulties, and to deny them a proper education... Any WSD Special Ed teacher who goes out of her way to help a Special Education student will be treated as Plaintiff has been.

I agreed with Anita's take on how we conducted our Special Ed program, especially when it came to the Emotional Support students. As stated previously, they were the most neglected group in the schools. The difficulty would lie in proving the unwritten policy of neglect. Schools know how to cover their deficiencies with all kinds of protocols, programs that operate in theory, and testimonials from administrators. The education business is well versed on how to present itself in the most flattering light. Just don't draw back the curtain.

The pleading then explained what laws we claimed were violated and the actions on the part of the district that caused them to be violated.

Count I: U.S. Constitution 42 U.S.C. § 1983

We were claiming that Dr. Durtan and the school board, as public officials, took actions that deprived me of my rights or privileges:

(1) Undeserved mark down in evaluation
(2) Ongoing campaign to terminate my job in retaliation for helping an at risk student
(3) Violation of First Amendment right to free speech and association
(4) Defendants' retaliatory misconduct [which] effectively ended my career, chilled my right to freedom of speech, and limited my actions as a private citizen.

The complaint asserted that my speech and conduct were protected because I was "helping Kay by giving her Emotional Support and this support was constitutionally protected speech concerning matters of public importance i.e. Special Education in public schools."

Anita opined:

> WSD is determined these students will be graduated without having gotten educated, rather being pushed through school with minimal effort, because administrators seek to protect themselves and the district from fear of 'being sued' if Special Education teachers were allowed to actually help at risk students.

Count II: §504 of the Rehabilitation Act of 1973 prohibits retaliation against any individual who provides special assistance, advocacy, and support for children at risk within a program receiving federal funds. The Rehab act says if a person provides specific assistance or advocates on behalf of someone in a program that is subsidized with money from the federal government, it is unlawful to punish or "get" someone for helping the individual under the protection of the program. Kay was in a Special Ed program. The program exists through federal dollars. I provided special assistance to Kay. Wissahickon School District, the provider of services and the recipient of tax money, hired Michael Levin to conduct a retaliatory hearing and write a punitive Directives Letter because I helped Kay.

Unfortunately, just because a law exists does not mean it has to be obeyed. It's like speeding. If you don't get caught, you can do it. If you do get caught and you know someone on the police force, you still can do it. Laws are only viable if the judges or officials who enforce them are honest.

Anita ended Count II with a recitation of what they did to me and why:

> Plaintiff was vilified, punished, harassed, unfairly evaluated, unfairly disciplined, persecuted and suffers ongoing retaliation for saving a child's life. She will not get recommendations from her WSD supervisors should she attempt to get another teaching job and her career as a Special Education teacher is destroyed. She has suffered wage loss by having to live on accumulated sick pay, loss of future earning capacity, pension loss, incurred legal fees in a vain attempt to protect her reputation, job and career, and suffered physical and mental anxiety, depression, humiliation and disgrace, for helping to save a child's life.

Count III: Violation of Plaintiff's Rights Under §7 and §26 of the Pennsylvania Constitution. This in essence was a repeat of the violations under the U. S. Constitution.

Count IV: Defamation 42 Pa. C.S.A. § 8341

This was directed specifically at the WIN team (SAP) letter and the Directives Letter. Because Maria Salvucci told Robert Anderson she had written the letter; because the rest of the team said they had not read the letter nor did they know one was written, the assumption was that Ms. Salvucci wrote the letter and sent it to Judy Clark. From the information Robert Anderson gathered, it appeared that Ms. Salvucci typed the letter and put *WIN Team* at the conclusion. Although Ms. Salvucci would later re-structure her account of what took place, it seemed unlikely the team had written the letter because the members did not sign it.

A document as significant as a request to stop a teacher from bringing down a district would have warranted signatures of the teachers, the administrator, the guidance counselor, the Drop-in Center counselor, and of course, Nurse Kormos. The team was so frantic that they by-passed all the chain of command protocol, but they were not committed enough to prove validity by putting names on a letter?

Defamation is defined as an injury to one's reputation caused by false statements of fact; defamation includes both libel (written) and slander (spoken). In order to establish a case of defamation in Pennsylvania, the Plaintiff has to prove the communication was defamatory, it was published by the writer, it applied to the plaintiff, and harm resulted from the publication.

Conversely, in order to prove innocence if one is accused of defamation, the defendant must show that the statements were truthful and the subject matter of the defamatory comments was of public concern.

It would be up to me to show how the defamatory material hurt my reputation. A teacher's reputation is easily tarnished. Given the climate in today's world, a teacher who is accused of being unprofessional and displaying poor judgment by becoming "enmeshed" with a student will not find employment. The WIN team (SAP) and the district made certain no other district would hire me.

Maria Salvucci and Stanley Durtan were the defendants

accused of defamation; Ms. Salvucci's WIN Team (SAP) letter was named, and Durtan's Notice of Allegations and Directives Letter were his contributions.

At the time defendants prepared these documents, they knew them to be false and defamatory. Nonetheless, the School Board and School District adopted these documents and imbued them with the power of official policy and practice in order to target and punish Plaintiff.

Attorney Alberts ended with the statement that what was done to me was performed in an:

...effort to cover up WSD's illegal and improper policy of providing the least possible, most minimal level of service and support to Special Education teachers and children in order to simply push the children through school and collect federal funds with as little effort as possible.

Everything Anita said was true. We were pushing the kids through with a minimal education. Emotional Support kids received no services. Teachers were afraid to speak up because the atmosphere in the district was vengeful toward those who raised objections. People were so paranoid, they said nothing. We were always looking over our shoulders.

I was troubled because there was no mention that what I did was on my own time as a private citizen. I was not a lawyer, so I assumed this would come later. When I mentioned this to Anita, she gave me some legal explanation that didn't convince me, but I was in no position to argue. I had to trust the woman who was fighting my battle.

The local union president, KH, informed me that the attorney for PSEA (state union), Chuck Herring, had put the grievance in abeyance. The attorney said he didn't want to influence the Federal court decision. Anita said that was "ridiculous." Attorney Herring assured the local president that if and when I came back to work, the grievance would be re-filed.

KH believed this would happen. I felt badly for her. KH believed in the sanctity of the values of the union and she believed they shaped the actions of those who represented the union. Unfortunately, trusting in PSEA was, in Mr. Herring's words, "foolish."

CHAPTER TWELVE

Motion to Dismiss

Mr. Levin explained to me that the answers my attorney (Anita Alberts) wrote in the *Admissions* would be the same as if I had answered them myself, in my own words. According to Mr. Levin, the lawyer speaks for the client. The lawyer's words **are** the client's words. Therefore, the client is answerable for all the statements of the attorney.

Montanye: When you say what are *you* referring to, I mean, obviously these (answers) were prepared with my attorney.
Levin: Well, they are your answers.
Montanye: So I am responsible for these answers?
Levin: Absolutely.
Deposition Sallie Montanye February 21, 2005

Think of a lawsuit as a tennis match; you are forever lobbing legal pages back and forth, using multi-word titles and tortured grammar, while decimating acres of forests to bury your adversary under mountains of endless papers. I cannot conjure up anything in existence that wastes more time, wood pulp, and words than the legal industry. Although, I will admit academia runs a strong second.

The plaintiff files the complaint; the defendants return the serve with a Motion to Dismiss. On both sides what the attorney says is considered **the spoken words of the client**(s). If you have an attorney who does not listen well or interprets your responses differently from what you meant, this can cause a great deal of confusion.

Mr. Levin would provide the court with all the reasons why my case had no grounds. His basic argument was that the district held an "investigation," I was not "disciplined," and I was merely given a letter instructing me how to purport myself *appropriately* as a Special Education teacher. End of story.

Attorney Levin's situational summation:

> K has serious emotional and psychological problems and had made threats and attempts at suicide in the past. These emotional problems continued throughout the school year. Montanye, although not a certified school psychologist, counselor or member of the "WIN" or "SAP" teams began (on her own and without any legitimate authority, as well as in violation of the special education laws) mediating disputes between K and her mother concerning attendance at therapy and rules at home.

This rendition was not particularly accurate.

- Mr. Levin either believed or claimed the WIN team and SAP were separate entities. As you know this was not the case.
- I did not lack legitimate authority. I was an Emotional Support teacher.
- I did not lack legitimate authority. I responded to the request of the mother, the child's legal guardian.
- There are no laws which state teachers are not allowed to speak with Special Education students or their parents.
- I was not mediating disputes. We were working out a behavior plan for home. Standard operating procedure for Emotional Support teachers.
- Kay and her mother were not arguing about "attendance in therapy." This topic was not discussed or included in the behavior plan.
- There are no Special Education laws governing what parents can discuss with teachers or forbidding them from requesting assistance.

Levin Footnote:

> K is a disabled child as defined by the IDEA. Any and all evaluations and services she receives must be pursuant to her IEP and the IEP process. Failing to appropriately

follow this process for the evaluation, transportation and therapy is a violation of students rights under the IDEA 20 U.S.C. §1400 et seq.

Well, not exactly.

- Any and all evaluations and services received **FROM THE SCHOOL DISTRICT** are pursuant to the IEP process.
- IEP's are not applicable to private services outside of school, which are contracted and paid for by the parents.
- IDEA has nothing to do with private evaluations or services received outside school and paid for by the parents.

But! If we are to follow Mr. Levin's logic, IDEA places restrictions on *all* activities of Spec Ed students, including those that take place in their private lives. Ergo, if IDEA holds authority over private evaluations and services, school districts should be required to *pay* for all private evaluations and therapies. If IDEA governs it, then the district is financially responsible for it. I challenge anyone to find a school district that would endorse Mr. Levin's claim.

It also would be interesting to hear the argument about how helping a fourteen-year-old get into private therapy was a violation of her civil rights. Speaking of civil rights, which liberty was it that promised a child can be pummeled and persecuted daily in school?

Pursuant to the IEP process? Where was the IEP process when Kay was hiding in the nurse's office, missing class? Where was the process when Kay was being brutalized in the hallways? Where was the IEP process when Kay was forced out of school, placed in the most restrictive environment, and denied FAPE (free appropriate public education)? These were all events that took place during the school day, under the administration of the school district, governed directly by, you guessed it, IDEA.

We also were charging that Dr. Durtan and Ms. Salvucci were guilty of defamation. We maintained that the WIN team letter and the Directives Letter contained untruths that were damaging to my reputation. It is interesting to note that Mr. Levin referred to the WIN team letter as "Salvucci's letter." He never postulated that anyone other than Maria Salvucci wrote the letter. This story underwent a major revision down the line.

Arguing against defamation, Mr. Levin proffered:

> Montanye has not been stigmatized by Defendants' alleged actions such that she has been made unemployable.

Which one of these made me a prime choice for employment?

WIN team (SAP) letter:

- Apparent inappropriate relationship between…Mrs. Montanye and students who have been identified as high risk…
- We find Mrs. Montanye's behavior to be an impediment to the SAP process
- We find Mrs. Montanye's behavior to be…potentially damaging to the students
- Mrs. Montanye is…jeopardizing the health and welfare of these students.
- …(the parents) fear their child is so enmeshed with Mrs. Montanye
- …there could be serious negative side effects.
- …most concerned with the continued lack of good judgment and professionalism Mrs. Montanye displays with students at risk…
- … the school district suffers serious repercussions

Allegations Letter:

- …you engaged in willful neglect of duty, insubordination, incompetency, persistent negligence in the performance of duties, willful violations of school laws
- improper conduct growing out of the following: improperly involving yourself in situations pertaining to student K
- these actions by you are unprofessional and exhibit poor judgment
- they are in violation of the rules pertaining to the procedures that are required to be followed for evaluations of students
- they are in conflict with the resources established by the school district for helping students and for scheduling students

Directives Letter: maintaining appropriate relationships with students

- your conduct was inappropriate
- we will not impose "discipline,"…but for the principal's acquiescence to some degree, you would have been disciplined and perhaps discharged
- your acts and omissions constituted significant wrongdoing
- you did not demonstrate a sufficient appreciation of where to draw the line between your proper duties and acts that are not appropriate
- you are being directed to attend an appropriate seminar or training session
- failure to abide by the required procedures…is a violation of civil rights
- you are to be cognizant of the school district's resource… such as the student assistance program
- failure to comply with legally required processes and procedures could lead to a violation of a student's civil rights
- could lead to legal liability for the school district
- could lead to liability for you

By Attorney Levin's accounting, all these accusations wouldn't faze a school board. Indeed, they would jump at the chance to snag me. Aside from being a danger to children, the fact that I was a legal liability to a district definitely made me a keeper. Remember these letters would be in my file, which would follow me wherever I went. But, Mr. Levin assured the court that:

> …the directive fails to state any activity by Montanye that would rise to the level of implicating her integrity or morality…
> No statements have been made by any Defendant that implicates her integrity such that she has become unemployable.

Mr. Levin's next defense of the Directives Letter was that it was not "published," meaning that no one else saw the letter but me. "Publishing" is one of the requisites to meet the charge of defamation.

Again, one would wonder how these directives would be put into play without the knowledge of the personnel director and the high school principal. If no one knew about the Directives Letter, what was its point? How was it going to be enforced? It made no sense.

Neither did this statement:

> Montanye was investigated for possibly unprofessional behavior. She admitted her behavior but, in this case, she was not even subject to discipline.

Why would Dr. Durtan, after finding out that I was guilty of "unprofessional behavior," not discipline me?

Let's examine Dr. Durtan's activities:

- Dr. Durtan hired an attorney without approval from the board.
- Dr. Durtan paid the attorney without board approval.
- Dr. Durtan took part in two costly pre-termination hearings while keeping these secret from the board.
- Dr. Durtan found me guilty of "serious wrongdoing" but did not discipline me.
- Dr. Durtan found me guilty of "serious wrongdoing" but did not inform the board of my "infractions."
- Dr. Durtan issued a Directives Letter with instructions that would include the cooperation of personnel and the high school principal, but he never let either know about the letter or its conditions.
- Dr. Durtan issued a Directives Letter restricting my personal actions but never told the board about this, even though they were the governing body of the district.

Mr. Levin makes sure to state the board's ignorance in a footnote:

> Because of the generally confusing nature of the complaint, including assertions that will be shown to be totally frivolous (**such as the School Board Defendants had anything to do with the events in this case**)...

Hmm. I wonder if Mr. Levin knew that:

> …when the attorney is initially retained the issue of access needs to be clearly defined and those who are authorized to deal with the school attorney need to understand that the attorney does not represent any individual, the superintendent, the administrator, the director of Special Education, or an individual board member. Rather, the attorney's loyalty and responsibility is to the **school board**. "What Boards and Superintendents Should Know About School Attorneys" (Martin Semple: Semple, Miller and Mooney, P.C. Denver, CO)

It would be difficult for Mr. Levin to keep the board apprised of what was taking place, especially if they didn't know they had hired him. When I was found guilty of "serious wrongdoing," would it not have been incumbent upon the attorney to inform the board that they were harboring a teacher guilty of all his accusations?

I'm certain the board never found out about Joe Loudermill hearing. He never filed a grievance. The only thing the board knew was that he resigned. Thus, Dr. Durtan effectively got rid of a teacher without the employer's knowledge, and he used the taxpayer's money without the board's permission.

Mr. Levin also did some fancy dancing with immunity by claiming that Dr. Durtan and the school board were covered by "High Public Official Immunity."

Public officials have a higher level of immunity than the general population. If they are operating within the scope of their employment, they are exempt from certain legal actions. Close, but no cigar. For one thing, Dr. Durtan was not acting within his scope. Secondly, high public official immunity is reserved for people like district attorneys. Dr. Durtan was entitled to "qualified immunity" which has a lower standard and allows greater leeway for private lawsuits.

I sued the school board members as individuals and collectively. I didn't understand why, but Anita said that was the way to do it. Now this is where it gets interesting. Mr. Levin stated:

The school district as an entity cannot be liable for isolated acts that were not taken pursuant to a policy, practice or custom of the School District.

and

The Individual Defendants are not recipients of federal financial assistance and cannot be liable for violations of §504 (The Rehab Act).

But wait! Wasn't it Mr. Levin who said Kay's mother was considering taking legal action against the district because I had helped her daughter? When asked what the grounds for such a suit would be, remember what he said? He "knew about these things." Here he says a school district **cannot** be sued for isolated acts that are not "policy, practice or custom." Therefore, my actions could not have resulted in a lawsuit because what I did was most certainly an isolated act and most definitely not policy or practice. So when Mr. Levin said at the Loudermill hearing, he "knew about these things," what exactly did he mean?

Mr. Levin also said the school board members could not be held responsible for violation of the Rehab Act, because they, as individuals, did not receive federal funding and were therefore not accountable for violations of this statute. The school board members were not suable, but I was, even though I too did not receive any federal funding. Although my actions were on my own time, after school hours, **I** alone could be the catalyst for a lawsuit against the district and against me!

...depending upon all of the facts of a case...could lead to legal liability for the school district, and could lead to liability for you. (Directives Letter)

Either they were suable or they were not. If they were not suable, neither was I.

In addition, Mr. Levin pointed out in a footnote (#11): To satisfy the "case or controversy" requirement for Federal jurisdiction I would have to establish a legal controversy, not a hypothetical one. I could not argue that I would not get a good recommendation from the district, as I had not yet asked for one.

Wasn't it Mr. Levin who said, "depending upon all the facts of the case," I **could have** violated Kay's rights? I believe it was.

These were a few of the phrases Mr. Levin used to describe what I did.

> Montanye *insinuated* herself into the personal and family life of a very troubled and emotionally disturbed youth.

> Montanye engaged in *officious intermeddling* in violation of her professional and legal responsibilities.

Mr. Levin also mischaracterized my job.

> Montanye received a letter addressed only to her, directing her to act within the scope of her employment as an English teacher.

A regular education English teacher is a far cry from a Special Education Emotional Support teacher. Mr. Levin was well aware of this. Certainly Dr. Durtan would have known this was not accurate.

The attorney for the school district also attacked me for accepting a birthday gift from the family:

> a professional educator may not accept gratuities, gifts or favors that might impair or appear to impair professional judgment (22 Pa. Code 235.8(2))

This is patently ridiculous. Kay gave me a picture frame. She was not bribing me with season box seat baseball tickets. And of course, her favor could not impair my judgment because I received this bias-inducing gift well after the therapy sessions.

Mr. Levin had a definitive game plan. His first tactic was to invoke the specter of IDEA to create confusion about the facts of the case and to cause attorneys unfamiliar with this law to make mistakes. He would use IDEA and all its intricate facets to blur the facts. In reality, IDEA really had little to do with this case. In fact, it was the district's illegal behavior and denial of services which were in violation of IDEA. My actions were not.

The next red herring was the Procedural Safeguards notice.

Procedural safeguards only apply to the **school district**.[8] They guarantee rights to the child and the parents concerning testing, placement and programs for Special Education. They do not apply to outside services. They were irrelevant in this case.

Next, Mr. Levin went after the case upon which we based much of our argument. I have to give you a brief explanation of *Pickering v. Board of Education,* 391 U.S. 563 (1968), so you understand the premise.

Background: *Pickering* involved a teacher who was dismissed after writing a letter to a local newspaper that was critical of how the board of education and the district superintendent had handled past proposals to raise new revenue for the schools. He was fired by the district for writing the letter. Pickering claimed his action was protected by the First and Fourteenth Amendments. This notion was rejected by the board of education. He appealed the board's action to the Circuit Court and then to the Supreme Court of Illinois, which both affirmed his dismissal. However, the Supreme Court of the United States agreed the teacher's First Amendment right to free speech was violated and reversed the decision of the Illinois Supreme Court. In its decision, the court said that a government employee (teacher) has First Amendment protection if his speech, which is critical of a government entity (school district), addresses matters of public concern. In other words, a teacher is not protected if he publically criticizes the district for giving him difficult classes, but he is protected if he is critical of poor use of taxpayer's money.

Even though I did not openly criticize the district's neglect and indifference toward Kay, they chose to put me through a pre-termination hearing and saddle me with baseless charges and the Directive Letter.

Not to worry. Mr. Levin had the answer to *Pickering.* It was simple. It was also in keeping with the district's behavior toward this child. Mr. Levin and the Wissahickon School District did not feel my actions involved "matters of concern."

The district stated I was acting in my own interests. Although I was working fulltime, running a household, and raising two

---

[8] Procedural Safeguards will be discussed with Judy Clark's deposition.

children, I selfishly spent all my extra time between batting lessons and singing lessons helping Kay and accompanying her to the therapist's.

> Matters concerning one's personal interest only are not matters of public concern...Montanye's speech does not concern the **community...**

I guess the Wissahickon School Board, the superintendent of the district, and their attorney did not subscribe to the theory that it takes a village to raise a child. Also remember that it was Michael Levin who argued the WIN team letter was not defamatory and yet one of the qualifiers which made it defamatory was the subject matter was not of public importance. If you were arguing that you are innocent of defamation, you would want to put forth the idea that the subject matter of the letter was of importance to the community. Here was the attorney for the district, stating unequivocally, that K's problems were NOT of interest to anyone; they were only her personal problems. Following his reasoning, Mr. Levin was declaring the topic of the WIN team letter as defamatory. It only dealt with private problems. Like Kay's, these problems were not of concern to the public.

In the event that the above statement is misunderstood, further on in the motion, Mr. Levin declares again:

> Montanye's alleged speech or expressive conduct concerned only K and her emotional issues. These issues are not matters of public concern as they only relate to the treatment of a single student.

This from the district that defined the learning environment as one

> ...characterized by an atmosphere of openness and mutual respect for the personal worth and dignity of each individual...

and then cut a check for $10,000 (January 2003) to pay their legal advisor to state what they believed.

The district that claimed the learning community was

> **...one in which we communicate our belief in the value of every child...**

now offered to the court and the world, in writing, its admission that a bullied, suicidal child was not *its* problem. In his Motion to Dismiss and Request for a More Definitive Statement, Mr. Levin charged that I accused the district of having an "official but unwritten policy and practice" against Special Education children, but (I) "failed to allege who enacted this policy or when it was enacted."

The attorney for the school district provided the philosophy that was the underpinning for this policy:

> **K's emotional and psychological issues are not matters of public concern...**

Now it was committed to paper.

Chapter Thirteen

Dead Kids Don't Learn

Generally speaking, the government is immune from liability…the school district…viewed as an arm of the state it is protected by this immunity…One of the difficulties in sifting through school law, is so much of it is based on individual interpretation…The definitions are murky…Add to this…the convoluted arguments of lawyers and administrators who in an effort to protect themselves spew forth deliberately distorted translations designed to obfuscate the intent and the spirit of these laws. The vagueness …of these statutes lends itself to supporting those who are corrupt and in violation of the very laws they hide behind.

Administrators twist the truth in order to keep up appearances. Lower administration is forced into collusion with whatever upper administrators are saying. If they openly challenge a falsehood they are not team players and are looking for another job in a remote part of the country

The bottom line…when you give people a whole bunch of money, allow them to ignore the will of the community, have a solicitor counter questions concerning the school board actions…tell them they are shielded from litigation—you have the perfect recipe for corruption. Court systems are loath to get involved, thereby assuring the misdeeds will not only flourish but also grow in scope. People are afraid, uneducated about school law, or just downright disinterested. **There is no one to speak up for the community. If teachers are silenced into submission, who will speak up for children who are voiceless?**

Tort Law: The Heart of the Liability Matter
(author unknown)

Nestled at the end of the seventy-one-page Motion to Dismiss were two affidavits; these are used to refute or assert ideas without benefit of challenge. In other words, you can pretty much say what you want without fear of flames shooting from your pants or your nose growing ten inches longer. According to Anita Alberts, affidavits carry little credence as far as testimony goes.

Superintendent Durtan's affidavit had some interesting points:

- Ms. Montanye was investigated by the WSD for possible inappropriate behavior concerning the counseling, therapy, and transportation of a Special Education student.
- I did not contact the School Board or any members of the school board…concerning the investigation until **after the grievance was filed…**
- The school board members did not have any input into the decisions made concerning the investigation or the issuance of the directive…
- If Sallie Montanye believed that a student's behavioral needs were not being met, the proper procedure would have been to complete a referral form to the WIN team…

Dr. Durtan's investigation didn't produce much useful evidence. Apparently, he did not probe too deeply into the facts, or he would have known that the WIN team (SAP) already knew about Kay and had already performed an intervention. A referral would have been redundant, particularly in light of the fact that the team took no notice after they were given the suicide note.

Of greater concern is that Dr. Durtan admitted that he hired and paid Michael Levin without the approval of the school board. School Board Policy makes it quite clear that a superintendent does not have that power.

No. 003
SECTION: Local Board Procedures
TITLE: Functions
March 2000

The Superintendent shall be delegated the authority to take necessary action in circumstances not provided for in Board policy, provided that **such action shall be reported to the Board at the next meeting.**

No. 006
SECTION: LOCAL BOARD PROCEDURES
TITLE: MEETINGS
March 2000

Section 2. Quorum
- A. quorum shall be five (5) school directors present at a meeting. No business shall be transacted at a meeting without a quorum…
- B. The following actions require the recorded affirmative votes of two-thirds of the full number of school directors:
  - 3. Incur a temporary debt or borrow money upon such obligation…
- C. The following actions require the recorded affirmative votes of a majority of the full number of school directors:
  - 13. Expending district funds
  - 14. Entering into contracts of **any kind**, including contracts for the purchase of fuel or contracts for any supplies where the amount involved **exceeds $100**…

The Board may discuss the following matters in executive session:

- a. Employment issues
- d. Consultation with an attorney or other professional advisor regarding potential litigation or identifiable complaints which may lead to litigation
- e. Matters which must be conducted in private to protect a lawful privilege or confidentiality

Official actions based on discussions held in executive session shall be taken at a public meeting.

No. 302
Section: Administrative Employees
Title: Employment of Superintendent
March 2002

PURPOSE

...The Board holds the Superintendent responsible for the administration of its policies, the execution of Board decisions, the operation of the internal machinery designed to serve the District program and **keeping the Board informed about district operations and problems...**

What makes all of this more curious is the history of theft in Wissahickon School District. Prior to Dr. Durtan's tenure, WSD had a superintendent who was found guilty of "unsanctioned" expenditures of district funds. In January of 1999, the board was going to pass a ruling requiring more than one signature on purchases. This would be done to prevent a repetition of misspent money. Two board members spoke of this in a local paper:

> Board member **Barbara Moyer** said she has been doing spot checks of purchases made by the district, and over the years there have been some problems with purchasing and reimbursement procedures.
> "I've seen enough to know that we need to tighten the procedure," said Moyer.
> School Board Vice President **Donna Leadbeater** said that she would like to see a written policy establishing formal purchasing and business expense reimbursement guidelines so that everyone, including district employees and the public understands what the district expects.
> "I would like to see something in writing...For example, sometimes descriptions of what was purchased are too vague," said Leadbeater. (The Reporter; Local/Region January 29, 1999 p. A4)

A private audit, conducted for the WSD board, indicated that close to $200,000 had disappeared from the coffers. When the state audit was conducted, the amount missing was less. The point here is this district and its taxpayers had been "victimized" by illegal purchases and shady expenditures. The board claimed innocence through ignorance.

A little over three years after the above article appeared in the paper, the school board was accepting of the fact that this superintendent had purchased services and brought on expensive litigation without their knowledge. What defies explanation is that both Ms. Moyer and Ms. Leadbeater, champions of tighter spending patterns, served on the board that was bilked out of a lot of money and were also on this board when Mr. Levin was hired and a lawsuit was begun without any input from them. Fool me once, shame on you...

Here's what I wonder: Did Dr. Durtan's attorney, Michael Levin, ask if the superintendent was authorized to hire him, and did Mr. Levin inquire as to whether this was ratified by the school board? That's quite an oversight for a seasoned attorney and respected author of school law. According to Dr. Durtan's affidavit, the school board knew **nothing** about Attorney Levin's hiring.

The second affidavit was from the assistant principal who dropped my rating. He swore that he had no knowledge of the Loudermill hearing or the WIN team letter. Right. Things like that are always kept under wraps.

You also might wonder why a teacher who commanded an alleged school-wide investigation, a contract with an outside attorney, a pricey Loudermill hearing, a four page directive, and a requirement for special course work, would be given a "good" rating. Why would a teacher who was unprofessional, showed poor judgment, and had inappropriate relationships with students be given any rating other than unsatisfactory? Why didn't Dr. Durtan let his employers know they were harboring such a problematic teacher?

The ball was in our court now. Our next opus was an Amended Complaint. We were adding onto the first complaint.

The most notable addition was the charge that I had been **constructively discharged**. A constructive discharge is where the working conditions have been made so intolerable an employee is forced to resign. If the action on the part of the employer is an official act and it can be proven the employee's resignation was a response to this official act, the court could view the resignation as a constructive discharge. It is up to the plaintiff to convince a jury that other employees would be inclined to quit if they too were forced to work under the conditions imposed by the employer.

Unfortunately, I was given contradictory advice concerning this. Initially, I was told not to resign. During the suit, I was advised I should resign. This went back and forth. If I quit, I knew I would never work again as a teacher. If I returned to work, I would be harassed, or worse, I would have such restrictions put on me that I would no longer be of any help to the children I served. I just wanted the Directives to be nullified so I could get back to my class and kids.

Anita Alberts talked more about the Directives Letter:

Durtan issued the malicious letter constructively discharging Plaintiff. The letter states that Plaintiff is guilty of significant wrongdoing. The letter creates mandatory limitations on her personal ability to communicate with others, which Plaintiff cannot meet. If she returned to work she faces immediate discharge based on Durtan's letter.

The Amended Complaint raised the use of Kay's records, the district's violation of her mental health rights, and her confidential information for the first time. In a footnote, Anita stated:

The use of K's records and personal file information to discharge her teacher is apparent on the face of Durtan's May 1, 2002 letter. At no time did Durtan obtain K's consent for disclosure of her private information or its use against her teacher. At age 14 K has legal control over release of her own mental health records and is entitled to know the purpose for which they are to be used. See 55 Pa. Code §5100.330

Anita wrote that I was the first to undergo a Loudermill hearing in the district. That was not what I said. This troubled me because I knew they could attack it as untrue. I maintained I was the first to have a hearing with the Loudermill label. There were other disciplinary hearings; however, there had not been any formal ones for years.

The arbitrariness of these hearings was what made them so questionable.

- Bill Sanni, the personnel director, allowed a teacher to work without certification for four years. When the state discovered this in an audit, the teacher was let go. The district lost a hefty amount of money in state funding as a penalty. Bill Sanni did not have a pre-termination hearing. Instead, a new job was created for him at the same salary level. When Dr. Sanni retired, Stanley Durtan recognized him at a board meeting "for his diligent efforts in the many roles he has portrayed over the years." (Report on Personnel/WSD Board minutes/#10-30/5/28/03)
- Another example of a lack of appropriate discipline: In a spring meeting with Stanley Durtan, the swim team parents informed the superintendent the coach was getting high with the students and providing the children with alcohol. Dr. Durtan assured the parents he would look into this. The following September the coach's name was on the board agenda to be rehired. Dr. Durtan, who was so worried about "liability" in my case, was willing to overlook criminal activity on the part of this employee. The enraged parents called Durtan about this and the coach's name was removed from the hiring list.

Ms. Alberts again addressed Michael Levin's employment, which had not been disclosed to the community. She stressed that the Sunshine laws were in place to assure that public spending was done in an open and honest manner. Question: Who had the idea to keep the board in the dark? There had to be some form of agreement to keep all this secret. The superintendent, the assistant superintendent, the supervisor of Special Education, the head of personnel, and the attorney for the district never breathed a word to the board members. Someone made the decision to keep these events hidden from the governing body of the district.

*****

It was the district's turn in the "did to—did not" argument. The Levin Legal Group relied on a great deal of cut and paste for their responses. This one was a reproduction of the initial Motion to Dismiss. In many parts it was the same wording pasted behind a new lead sentence. They made a few stronger statements about counseling.

171

Specifically she admitted that she counseled a student K and her family.

I never did anything of the kind. I never said I counseled, nor did I counsel Kay or her family.

The next defense of the Directives Letter said:

The letter further provides instructions concerning what to do if her [sic] intends on engaging in conduct **outside of school** and outside her status as a teacher.

Did Dr. Durtan truly believe my actions as a private citizen presented liability problems for the district? Let's see what he said about other actions that took place after school hours, off of school property.

- In 2004, a Wissahickon School District bus driver was accused of sexually molesting a twelve-year-old girl. Stanley Durtan was quoted in the paper stating the **district could not be held accountable for behavior that took place outside of school;** the district had no authority or responsibility for what the driver did after school hours.
- In 2006, a teacher pled guilty to charges of sexual relations with a student. In addition, he provided her with alcohol. When the story hit the press, Dr. Durtan confirmed that the district was not responsible for any of this because it happened **after school hours and/or off of school property.** He had to specify after school hours, as it was rumored that some of the acts had taken place on school property. Dr. Durtan made sure that after school hours qualified the district as non-liable because it was done after the school day had ended.

The superintendent of schools relieved the district of any legal responsibility for two men accused of **criminal activity** because it happened *after school.* Yet, this same man hired an attorney to investigate my acts of **helping** a student after the school day and off of school property because he feared "liability" for the district.

One last example of Dr. Durtan's haphazard approach to discipline:

A high school employee who had a large codified binder of various forms of pornography, an illegal lock on his door, and a dildo in his desk was reported to the superintendent (Durtan) in the fall of 2003. Nothing was done until late spring when the employee was reported *again* to the head of personnel.

The authorities should have been notified immediately. The man's computer, the binder, and any other materials should have been turned over to the district attorney. Possession of child pornography is a **felony.** There might have been criminal charges with this situation.

> The improper possession in a work location of such materials negatively impacts the efficient operation of our school district, has an adverse impact on your working relationship with other district employees, and also has the potential to negatively impact staff and students. (WSD letter 5/5/2004)

What did the district that quaked at lawsuits do? The employee was suspended for **three days without pay.** They told him to take his dirty pictures and dildo home. He worked in the high school until he retired.

Returning to the Motion to Dismiss, Stacy G. Smith, the Levin Legal Group attorney who wrote this response, supplied this analogy to justify the WIN team letter:

> If a teacher observed another teacher physically assaulting a student, wouldn't the teacher be acting within the scope of her employment by informing school administrators of what she witnessed?

Did this argument indicate that the Wissahickon School Board and the superintendent of the Wissahickon School District believed that physically attacking a student was equivalent to keeping her alive?

Ms. Smith provided a new slant on my actions: I was not

authorized to do this on **behalf** of the school district. Who said I did this on behalf of the school district? During the day, I adhered to the IEP. After school hours, I was a private citizen acting in the belief that we owe our fellow humans assistance when they are in trouble. I could not be acting on behalf of the school district, as my belief was obviously counter to the practice and philosophy of those in charge.

During the course of the litigation, I was not working. I was out on disability because of hypertension and related problems with stress. Ms. Alberts could not decide if I should quit or continue to be on medical leave. In this case, Anita was concerned with my not being at work without benefit of treating my condition with therapy.

In March 2003, she wrote me a letter starting out with, "I think you are a great person." She went on to say she was impressed with my sense of character. An incident that occurred at her office caused her to reconsider my situation. We had been discussing the case when tears started streaming down my face. Anita was taken aback, as I had never cried in her presence. She said she did not realize how deep the wounds were. How could she? I tried to keep a stoic persona, but in truth, my heart was broken. I missed my kids. I missed the energy of the school. I missed everything about being a teacher. By definition, I was an Emotional Support teacher. Now that was gone. It had been ripped away from me.

Her letter continued, claiming we had Durtan "just where we want him. Whining, falling on his sword to protect the school board, trying to save his job while rumors say he's on his way out."

I don't know where she was getting her rumors from, but her mill was not grinding full tilt. Contrary to Anita's hearsay, the board went out of its way to make sure Durtan would be around for a long time. At a board meeting in December 2003, Dr. Durtan resigned and then was rehired for five years. Board President Donna Leadbeater explained the unusual practice:

> The superintendent can only be reappointed in the last year of his term or if there is a vacancy...Dr. Durtan has two years remaining in his contract, so the resignation was necessary to create a vacancy.

Ms. Leadbeater continued:

> The Board decided it wanted to extend Durtan's time with the district during his annual performance evaluation this fall. Based on his outstanding performance over the past few years, we believe it is in the school district's best interest to secure (Durtan's) involvement for the maximum term.

This indicated to me that Anita's supposition was way off course. In fact, it was apparent that the board, now in full knowledge of Durtan's illegal actions and the resulting lawsuit, felt the most appropriate response was to reward him with a longer contract. They were not even willing to wait out the two years on his existing contract. Instead, they sidestepped the law in order to insure that Stan Durtan would be superintendent, despite his actions and the liability he brought on the district.

Attorney Alberts ended her letter saying, "This blip does not have to be the end of a distinguished teaching career." She was referring to the persecution I was undergoing as a "blip." "You've got too much to give, and the kids need you." She refused to accept this was the beginning of the end of my career. I felt like a visitor in the twilight zone.

I started therapy the next week.

*****

The lawsuit dragged on with the eternal continuum of accusations and retorts. It was once again our turn. As you may have guessed, there was a certain amount of repetition to these writings. With each motion there were a few different cases cited; however, there were standard cases that appeared in most of the pleadings.

A good defense lawyer wants to "establish facts" most favorable to his case, especially before testimony is taken which might contradict these assertions. How is this done? It's easy. First, you state facts. Then you imply from assumed premises invalid meanings which appear to be derived from those facts. Let's see how this is done.

1. Michael Levin says that I went with Kay to the therapist. [fact]

2. Michael Levin accuses me of willful negligence and connects it with my accompanying Kay to the therapist. Implying that my act was negligent and there is a law associated with it.

3. Michael Levin recites IDEA, which is only applicable to the school district. He says the district will be in trouble for violating IDEA. True, the district can be held accountable for violating IDEA. A private citizen cannot. But, he has coupled the accusation with recitations of what happens when the district is out of compliance with IDEA. Thus, he links my private actions with a law that has no bearing on them.

Anita went after the idea that Kay's problems were of no import to the community in her opening of Plaintiff's Answer Opposing Motion to Dismiss Amended Complaint.

It is not possible that the school district and the entire community would consider a troubled adolescent's suicide of no public moment. It would be one less troubled student to deal with, true, but Wissahickon School District is supposed to help troubled students, not look away when they write suicide notes about killing themselves. If school children kill themselves, they can't learn.

She continued in this vein:

It is hard to believe WSD would have its Special Education teachers ignore suicide notes. It is hard to believe WSD requires Special Ed teachers to do nothing after having urged troubled students to speak with a Drop-in Center counselor and having the school principal give a student's suicide note to the WIN team without anything happening. Yet that is precisely what defendants argue.

For the first time Anita talked about K's parents.

Perhaps the most important fact in this case, significantly ignored in the Motion to Dismiss, is that K's parents made no complaint against Montanye, and indeed were grateful for her help. They are potential witnesses for Montanye.

Anita included the fax from K's mother. She stated that Principal Anderson was "not permitted to place the supportive message into evidence at the Loudermill."

Ms. Alberts pointed out that the argument as to whether my actions interfered with the operation of the school was never in question; Dr. Durtan stated that nobody "knew about anything Plaintiff did or said, especially the school board."

When she discussed the evaluation, she noted that my first observation contained several more positive comments, while the second evaluation was not as complimentary. Although there were no deficiencies noted in either observation, the vice principal dropped my rating.

In order to prove retaliation, we had to show that my actions were the motivating factor in the district's behavior toward me. This was not difficult as both the Letter of Allegations and the Directives Letter stated clearly that what I did for Kay was the reason the superintendent moved to prosecute me.

Anita once again addressed the Directives Letter:

Durtan has no right to regulate any employee's private life, but clearly he limits Montanye's personal freedom on her own time, restricting who she may communicate with, and requiring her to say demeaning, unprofessional things about herself. No one asked to sign one of the statements required could respect such a teacher...Durtan stripped Montanye of her professional status. She is constructively discharged.

In the defendants' brief, they attempted to counter this by saying the Directives Letter only stated conditions required of *all* Special Education teachers in the district. Anita asked if such a letter were applicable to all the teachers, did Dr. Durtan have the signed papers they would have turned in when they spoke to parents outside of their jobs and on their own time?

I was never able to find any dismissal or even disciplinary action based on a teacher's activities that were done outside of school in an effort to help a student. Unless there is an immoral implication in the activity and lacking proof that the activity causes the teacher to be ineffective in her teaching duties, the school does not have any authority to inject itself into the teacher's personal life. In all my research, which was extensive, I was unable to locate any disciplinary or termination actions against a teacher for helping a suicidal child on her own time.

As Anita pointed out, the most extraordinary aspect of the school district's behavior was that it was not generated by the parents, but rather by the district itself. The defendants had neither the authority nor any legitimate invested interest in taking action against me. The negligence of the administrators, on the other hand, could be grounds had the parents sought legal action against the district.

SIDEBAR: Let's take a quick look at why a district that turned a blind eye to a possible felon (worker with porn, illegal lock and dildo), a teacher who was rumored to be sleeping with students (and was), a swim coach who got high with the students and supplied them with liquor, a personnel director who allowed an uncertified teacher to work with children, supervisors who did not provide services required by law, supervisors who accepted "inferior" paperwork, and administrators who violated a student's civil rights with an illegal placement/program, would target a teacher who did nothing but help a child in trouble.

Simple. Who was the one person aware of all the illegal machinations that the administration could not trust to help with a cover up? The administrators would cover for each other; that is the standard practice. But what if the parents decided to sue the district? What if (God forbid) Kay had had a successful suicide attempt? I was not part of the administration's select club. In addition, I had established myself as a strong advocate for my students. That combination is a potential for disaster in the eyes of those who ply their trade in deception and paperwork shell games. The last thing this district needed was someone with information and integrity.

Those in power could not risk my close association with the parents in the event that I would point them toward a legal resolution for their daughter. A year before, when I taught in the middle school, a parent of a seriously troubled child asked for a private placement. After the meeting, Kelle Heim-McCloskey said she was going to drag me "in front of Judy Clark on charges of insubordination" because I had not talked this mother out of asking for this change.

The only safe teacher is a frightened, silent one.

Stacy Smith fired back to our assertions with the Defendants' Response to Plaintiff's Answer Opposing Motion to Dismiss Amended Complaint. It was a catchy new title, but basically the same old, same old.

The already worn out argument that I did not criticize the district was reiterated. Remember *Pickering?* The teacher was protected because he spoke out for the good of the public. Unlike *Pickering,* I did NOT "speak against anything, including the school district's handling of suicidal students." Therefore, it made no sense that the district would even take note of my actions. The district was claiming if I had publically accused them of not having programs or providing support for Kay, **then** I would have First Amendment protection. If I thought the school district's handling of suicidal children was adequate, I would not have taken any action. If Kay had been in good hands, or for that matter, any hands, I would have encouraged her to continue on that course.

In a footnote, defense counsel stated that:

Montanye's counseling of K and her family concerning rules and behavior at home was unrelated to K's educational needs.

This is just plain stupid. Didn't anyone tell Ms. Smith and Mr. Levin what happens at home can substantially influence a child's education? What did they think all the chatter about strong ties between school and home meant? Or worse—did their client, the school board, not recognize the relationship between home and education?

Ms. Smith had an interesting take on suicide.

Montanye chastises the Superintendent and defense counsel for "knowing better" than arguing that suicide is not an issue of public importance. (Pl's Brief at 3). Montanye, however, cites no cases to support her **notions.**

Notions? These people needed case law to prove to them that teenage suicide was an issue of public concern. I realize that arguments have to be substantiated by previously decided cases, but to claim that suicide was not an issue of public importance because some judge didn't say so is frightening.[9]

My arguments concerning the constructive discharge,

---

[9]An appellate court did state that suicide was an issue of public importance. We'll see that in *EISEL v.*
BOARD OF EDUCATION OF MONTGOMERY COUNTY, MARYLAND, ET AL. (1991)

according to Attorney Smith, were "confusing, misleading and paranoid." They were also "unfounded, and unprofessional." After all, as defense counsel pointed out, the Directives Letter asked (me) to "follow the laws concerning Special Education and the policies of the school district when doing (my) job as a Special Education teacher." But wait; didn't the Directives Letter give me instructions to follow when I was *outside my job as a* teacher? Didn't the letter state I was guilty of wrongdoing because my actions *were not* part of my job responsibilities? And the Levin Legal Group felt **our** arguments were "confusing, misleading, and paranoid?"

*****

Michael Levin, Anita Alberts, and Judge DuBois had a phone conference to discuss the case management plan. The judge wanted a settlement discussion between the parties. This is done in an effort to avoid trial. Only about fifty percent of filed and accepted suits ever make it to trial. Settlement is always encouraged. Most lawyers prefer settlements because trials consume an inordinate amount of time and you never know what the outcome will be. It is a safer bet to get a solid settlement, rather than take chances with a jury. Juries can be fickle. Lawyers have a strong aversion to fickle.

In a March 2003 letter, Anita wrote to Michael Levin with a settlement offer:

- restoration of my "very good" rating
- withdrawal in writing of Durtan's June 2002 Directives Letter
- the Loudermill charges and any records concerning the hearing were to be removed from my file
- the unsigned WIN team letter was to be expunged from my records
- $150,000 for emotional distress and counsel fees (most of this would be counsel fees)

Had the district been willing to expunge my record and scrap the Directives Letter, which the grievance chair first proposed, I would have returned to school. There would have been no reason to discuss the cost of future wages or attorney's fees. All I was asking was to return to my job without the labels from the Allegations letter and without the threat of being fired.

If Dr. Durtan had been willing to eliminate the Directives Letter in the first place, I never would have filed the lawsuit. If Dr. Durtan would have written a follow up to the allegations stating that I had parental permission and that my actions took place as a private citizen therefore the charges were not applicable, I would have happily returned.

If the board had been willing to discuss this settlement, the outlay of money would have been minimal. Instead, the school board refused to hold any discussion and chose to pursue a costly lawsuit, which would eat up substantial amounts of funds and time. I have to assume the Wissahickon School Board was so determined to convey the message that helping a suicidal child was such a serious breach of conduct that it was willing to sink thousands of dollars to prove its point.

EITHER/OR/OR:

Either: the board wanted to establish the precedent that it had the power to discipline teachers for what they did in their private lives

Or: Michael Levin advised the district to reject any settlement offer (billable hours!).

Or: There is a third option. It's possible Dr. Durtan and Michael Levin did not advise the board of our settlement offer.

If this were the case, Mr. Levin was in violation of his professional ethics by not informing his clients of the offer. Stanley Durtan did not have the authority to encumber the board with a costly lawsuit. As named defendants and administrators of the district's funds, the board would have a say in a settlement agreement. If Dr. Durtan or Mr. Levin kept this information from the board, they were both guilty of serious ethical infractions.

Mr. Levin's response letter to the settlement offer: I had a job. The Directives Letter stood. The allegations would not be removed from my file. Period.

Attorney Alberts wrote that I wished I could return to my job. I missed my students (terribly) and they missed me. She repeated the settlement offer. She ended by stating that Mr. Levin, Stanley Durtan, and the WHS administration "collectively mounted an unprecedented campaign of attack against this teacher."

Letters flew back and forth. Anita told Michael Levin that the offer of "unqualified" right to return to work was meaningless and self-serving.

> There can be no 'unqualified' right to return to work where the intolerable directives have not been rescinded, the unfair and improper lowered performance evaluation had not been corrected, and (she) would again face discharge or forced resignation.

Michael Levin went into his condescending mode. The comments Anita made, led him:

> to believe that either you or your client don't necessarily understand the facts. To the extent that you and/or your client may not understand the directives, for example, we would be happy to sit down with you and your client to review them to make sure that they are understood by your client. We feel rather confident that any reasonably objective individual would realize the reasonableness of the directives assuming the directives are properly understood.

Dr. Durtan stated to the union rep that filed the grievance, the Directives Letter "didn't say what we meant it to say." Now, Michael Levin was proposing that we lacked the smarts to interpret this letter. The people who wrote the letter that "didn't say what they meant it to say" were willing to sit down and explain it to us.

Mr. Levin said he was "not exactly sure" what Anita meant when she said I was "threatened with discharge." Neither Mr. Levin nor his clients could "recall any threat of discharge." That amnesia thing was contagious. Maybe, he posited, she was referring to the Loudermill hearing notice where it stated that "possible dismissal" could be a result of the hearing. "With all due respect," Mr. Levin offered, "we do not believe this is a threat of discharge." If it looks like a duck, walks like a duck, and quacks like a duck…

Mr. Levin supplied this take on the Allegations letter:

I suggest that a notice of the topics for discussion at a meeting between employer and employee is not a threat, but instead is proper notice so that the employee can prepare.

Maybe Mr. Levin overlooked that Stan Durtan referred to this "meeting" as a "serious matter" and advised me to seek legal counsel. That sounds like more than a conversational sit down. Mr. Levin suggested the Allegations letter was sent to allow me time to prepare? Was this the same Mr. Levin, or was it his doppelganger, who refused to supply any information and instructed school district employees to do likewise?

This letter was copied to Michael Peale, Jr. one of the attorneys in the firm that represented Wissahickon School District. This was the first (and last) time *any* communication was cc'd to the district's solicitors.

Anita would not let this one go. She zapped back a terse answer instructing Mr. Levin to re-read the Allegations letter, which "tracked School Code provisions for discharge of a teacher." She also recommended that Mr. Levin read the last paragraph of the letter which "tracks the Miranda warning required in custodial interrogation of a suspected perpetrator of crime." The Directives Letter, she said, was "no less threatening; it states my client committed 'significant wrongdoing' and again referred to 'discharge.'"

Michael Levin claimed that in his view I:

was never threatened with discharge…Your (Anita's) tortured and frivolous view of the facts of this case would be laughable if this litigation were not so costly to the School District, the defendants, and their insurance company.

Who took the actions that created the "costly" litigation? Who fueled the "costly litigation?" And while we're on the topic of costly, who was bankrolling Dr. Durtan, Mr. Levin, and the board members? The money certainly wasn't coming out of their bank accounts. You don't think these people would have done this or kept it going if they were forced to make it fly using bundles of their favorite dollars?

Michael Levin offered that the school district was *helping* me out by showing me that failure to comply with "legally required processes, could lead to legal liability" for me.

He chided Anita, saying she should realize that this view was "based upon the many cases where individual school district employees were sued where they failed to follow the rules required by Special Education laws."

First of all, the "individuals" who are sued for not following procedures are the administrators. Generally, it's the school district, the superintendent, and whoever is responsible for the Special Education program. Teachers are rarely sued unless they openly refuse to follow the IEP. In all the cases I read concerning Special Education lawsuits and due process hearings (which took place across the nation), I only ran across **one** where only a teacher was sued. Teachers don't have decision making power; therefore, they can't be sued for policies they don't make.

Mr. Levin ended his letter by refuting Anita's reference to a settlement. "I have no idea what you are talking about." Mr. Levin did not want to settle. Mr. Levin wanted to go to war.

This letter was not copied to the district solicitor or the superintendent. Why would Mr. Levin not send this to the solicitor? Did he want to keep him from knowing that we had made a settlement offer? Was he afraid the attorney might suggest this to the board? Why no copy to Dr. Durtan?

Why was an attorney who was appalled at the cost of litigation not making every attempt possible at finding a reasonable and financially practical settlement?

Mr. Levin was no stranger to spending large amounts of school district money. Let's take a quick look at the Hanover case. (*Hanover School District v. Hanover Education Association.* 829 A.2d 308 (2003).

A teacher in the Hanover School District smacked a computer mouse out of a student's hand. The district suspended the teacher for three days without pay. The union filed a grievance alleging contract violation because the district suspended the teacher **without just cause.**

Michael Levin, *Esquire*, argued two points: (1) the merits of the suspension (2) the issue was not subject to the grievance procedure because the collective bargaining agreement (CBA) did not contain any provision governing employee discipline. The arbitrator determined that the grievance was arbitrable based on the "generally accepted principal of **implied just cause."**

An arbitrator's authority is drawn from the contract. Mr. Levin asserted that because the contract did not contain specific language dealing with discipline, the arbitrator had no say in this matter.

The arbitrator found in favor of the school district upholding the suspension. However, he determined the grievance came under the domain of arbitration.

Mr. Levin took the case all the way to the Pennsylvania Supreme Court. All the courts decided in favor of the district's discipline; however, they **all** found against the claim that the lack of wording in the contract disallowed arbitration. Rats!

Translation: If the contract specifically removed employee discipline with specific language, then discipline would **not** require just cause. Lacking specific wording to that effect, implied just cause was present. Double Rats!

Mr. Levin, the anti-hero of the Hanover decision, was back peddling as fast as possible to establish that I **had not been** disciplined. The last thing he needed was to provide grounds that found the district out of compliance based on a precedential case he lost.

Meanwhile, the taxpayers of the Wissahickon School District had paid for:

- a pre-termination hearing which was really only a "meeting between employer and employee"
- a disciplinary letter that was not disciplinary
- a lawsuit which could have been avoided/squelched easily/resolved cheaply with a settlement

For a man so concerned with financial expenditure, Mr. Levin was quite content to use up hard-earned taxpayers funds.

EITHER/OR:

Either: Levin and the district were terrified that the parents would wise up and sue them,

Or: the Wissahickon School District had enough collateral money to financially promote their message that children with emotional troubles were not important to the community.

CHAPTER FOURTEEN

Valiance or Violation

Sallie Montanye's simple, quiet acts of helping a troubled student who had threatened suicide do not have to be *publicized* to have First Amendment protection against punishment by a public school board, a government entity. She did the right thing. She broke no rule. She violated no law. She helped a child. She has lost her teaching career. This is "unworthy" of Constitutional protection? For crying out loud, what is wrong with this district?

Anita Alberts-Counsel for Plaintiff
Plaintiff's Sur Reply Opposing Defendants' Motion to
Dismiss (2003)

Judges have a great deal of leeway in deciding the nature of a case and if it will see the light of day in a courtroom. These decisions are supposed to be based on precedent and law; however, that is not always followed. If a judge does not want to hear a case, he can instruct the parties to arrive at a settlement. He simply refuses to allow the case to progress. Using another approach, if a judge does not want a case to survive, he can grant the Motion to Dismiss without providing substantive reason.

The point is the illusion of being able to take legal actions for the infringement of civil rights is just that-an illusion. Your day in court depends on the temperament of the person presiding over the case, the political entanglements of the adjudicator, the power of those you sue, and any inconvenience the case may present. Then there's the money. You better have a small fortune saved up for legal fees or be willing to dive into massive debt which will cripple your economic life for years.

This may sound like sour grapes; but, as my case progressed, it became more evident that this judge, Jan E. DuBois, was violating federal rules of court, ignoring blatantly unethical tactics on the part of the defense counsel, and disregarding concrete evidence in favor of illogical, unsupported arguments.

On August 11, 2003, Anita Alberts received the decision from the judge concerning the disposition of the Amended Complaint. She was elated and wanted me to come to her office. Thirty minutes later when I walked in, I found her sitting at her secretary's desk; her eyes welled up with tears. She looked up and said to me, "This is awful." She had a yellow highlighter in her hand. She was marking line after line.

Before I tell you the decision, it is important to understand that, under Rule 12(b)(6), when the court is considering a Motion to Dismiss, the **plaintiff's** argument **carries more weight than the defendant's reasons** as to why the case should be dropped.

In considering a Motion to Dismiss, "The court must take all well pleaded facts in the complaint as true and view them in the light most favorable to the **plaintiff.**" The judge stated, "Therefore, the facts in plaintiff's Amended Complaint are accepted as true in deciding this motion." And yet, Jan DuBois chose to ignore the facts we presented.

The opening section of a decision is a recitation of the case. The background information of the case is supplied to establish the claims. Judge DuBois made some interesting errors.

The Win team is one of the two school programs, the other being the Special Assistance Program, (SAP), specifically designed to assist at-risk students.

We made it perfectly clear that SAP and the WIN team were one and the same. The judge was quoting Michael Levin, who stated SAP and WIN were two entities.

In February 2002, plaintiff scheduled a session with the therapist, drove K to that first session, and attended it with her.

I did not schedule an appointment with the therapist. After school was dismissed, Kay called the therapist to set up the appointment. Michael Levin created this myth. He was told repeatedly that Kay had made the appointment. The judge also neglected to note that Kay had gone home before the therapy session.

> Plaintiff met K and her mother at the next scheduled session, with the therapist, but K refused to permit her mother in the room with the therapist and insisted that only plaintiff attend. This upset K's mother and she 'temporarily withdrew' K as a client of the therapist.

This was news to me. Kay was not withdrawn from seeing the therapist. She had to see her at least three more times to fulfill the court's release agreement. The judge made this up on his own.

> Because Principal Anderson was to some extent aware of plaintiff's actions with K, Superintendent Durtan decided against disciplining plaintiff.

It was Mr. Levin and the district that proposed Mr. Anderson's "knowledge" was the reason I was not "disciplined." It was also defendants' argument that viewed the Directives Letter as a non-disciplinary action. It would be impossible to evaluate my side as true when the judge was only considering the defendants' version. Michael Levin was the ventriloquist for this jurist.

Discussion

It is here where the judge reviews the facets of the complaint and applies law and precedent to support his conclusions.

Claims against the individual defendants as individuals.

These were dismissed based on the reasoning from previous cases that the party of interest was the government entity, not the "named officials." The school board members and Stanley Durtan were off the hook as individuals.

The defamation claim against Maria Salvucci and Stanley Durtan in their *official* capacities.

The judge concluded a local agency could not be held liable on account of injury to a person caused by an act of that local agency. The school district could not be held accountable for any acts of defamation committed by its employees.

42 U.S.C. §1983.

This is the claim that someone acting under the color of state law deprived another of rights guaranteed by the Constitution or federal statutes.

The court did not agree that my First Amendment rights had been violated. The reasoning being my action with Kay did not "send a message"; therefore, it was not protected. Although there exists a "kernel of expression" in all activities, my activity did not have a big enough kernel. The judge likened my assistance to Kay as having the expression of nothing more than "walking down the street."

There were few flaws in this logic. As you know, under the *Pickering* case the Supreme Court ruled that a public employee speaking critically, as a private citizen, has First Amendment protection if the employee is addressing a matter of public importance. If the employee does not criticize, she has the protection of the First Amendment like anyone else. The *Pickering* case applies to ensure government employees the same rights as others when criticizing the government entity.

Pickering does not address protection of speech that is not derogatory, because why would anyone attack an employee who was not critical? The First Amendment does not require a private citizen speak negatively about something in order to have protection in her private life. In fact, in light of *Pickering*, it makes even less legal sense that the district went after me, considering they asserted I made no public complaints.

More importantly, by applying *Pickering,* the judge was admitting my actions were **taken as a private citizen**. In this case, the question would be why would the district be allowed to invade my personal life and punish me through my employment for actions that were not performed as an employee? This was the heart of the matter. Interestingly, Judge DuBois' reasoning was in direct contradiction to the Pennsylvania tort law of negligence which states that a child's safety is of paramount importance.

In the negligence tort laws, the state has laid out the principles by which a teacher can be held negligent. If a teacher feels a child's safety is in peril, it is the obligation of that teacher to act to prevent any perceived harm. The law articulates if the teacher, in the course of this preventative action, knowingly breaks a law, the teacher is not answerable to an accusation of violation of the negligence statute.

Judge DuBois rationalized in his conclusion:

If the Court accepted plaintiff's First Amendment retaliation claim, school districts would be unable to require teachers, in their interaction with students, to comply with school policies and procedures without First Amendment scrutiny by the courts.

This was unadulterated legal compost. There were no policies or procedures stating a private citizen could not help a child outside of school. He took the easy way out protecting the school district in spite of law and rational judicial reasoning.

School districts have the right to require teachers to follow policy established to govern them as teachers during the school day. They do not have the right to reach into a teacher's private life for no viable reason other than administrative whimsy.

Again, Judge DuBois borrowed heavily from Michael Levin's defense. The judge accepted Levin's fiction that I violated **unnamed** policies and procedures. This was not up to the judge. It was up to a jury. They should decide if I breached non-existent policy. The judge suspended his obligation to accept my argument as valid and supplanted it by drawing his decision on postulations of the defendants. What these policies and procedures were he didn't say.

The judge proceeded to dismiss the Fourteenth Amendment claim that I was denied due process. As long as I was provided with the list of accusations and given an opportunity to "tell my side of the story," the school district was in the clear.

The district did not have to provide any information in reference to rules or regulations that were allegedly violated. All it had to do was accuse me. Hiding the letter from K's mother was A-Okay. Not permitting my attorney to see the WIN team letter or hear Anderson's testimony was legally honkey-dory. It does not have to be "an elaborate" process. Doesn't have to be honest either. The Rehab Act and the Americans with Disabilities Act were the next to be axed. Under these, I had to prove my activities were protected and the district took adverse action because I performed these protected activities. Here we go again. Jan DuBois decided I performed no actions that were protected by the ADA or the Rehab Act. Both of these laws stipulate there can be **no retaliation** against someone who has opposed any act or practice made unlawful by these acts. In other words, if someone provides assistance to any person protected by the ADA or Rehab Act (Kay would be included under these), there can be no retaliation against the person for doing so. This makes sense; without this protection, the disabled would go unaided if others feared punishment for their advocacy.

Once again, the judge fell back on the hollow claim that I did not make a great deal of noise about the district's negligence toward Kay. Maybe I should have mounted a major letter writing campaign. Of course, while I was producing letters of complaint and while they were being filed in the trashcan, Kay may have killed herself.

The violations of the Pennsylvania Constitution went by the wayside. The judge said no federal violation, therefore, no state violation.

The defamation claim was dismissed because Maria Salvucci was merely "expressing her opinions." As the judge opined, taking words out of Michael Levin's mouth, I had "admitted" to the facts upon which those opinions were based. But your honor: what law was violated? It's considered defamation if the subject matter is not "important." Mr. Levin said that Kay's problems were not of import to the community. This removes the public interest component of the letter which would protect it from a defamation charge.

The judge quoted the entire WIN team letter. He provided the unproved accusations in a manner that implied the letter was truthful and accurate. At no time did he point out that much of the letter had never even been addressed at the Loudermill hearing.

In addition, the letter of Allegations was also "not defamatory." Why? You may wonder? Because it was not "critical of plaintiff's talents, skills or abilities as a Special Education teacher." You don't say. Since when are charges of: **willful neglect of duty, incompetency, persistent negligence in the performance of duties, improper conduct, unprofessionalism,** and **poor judgment** considered complimentary?

The judge employed the same tactics of reciting parts of the letter as if they were true. Now remember, the judge stated the letter was not "critical of my talents or abilities as a Special Education teacher"; two paragraphs later he states, "The notice in this case is **solely related to plaintiff's employment.**" If it relates solely to my employment, then how would the accusations **not be critical of my talents or abilities as a Special Education teacher**?

The judge gutted our case. There was no recourse to anything dismissed with prejudice. In all her years as an attorney, Ms. Alberts had never lost a prima facie case on a Motion to Dismiss. I felt sorry for her because she truly believed in the legal system and the sanctity of the First Amendment. She was emotionally devastated.

A day after we read the decision Anita wrote to me:

> I am still reeling. I feel like I've just been kicked out of the John Ashcroft School of Constitutional Law. I cannot remember reading an opinion so hostile to the First Amendment in 25 years of practicing law...I apologize for believing that saving a suicidal adolescent is still a noble thing for a public school teacher to have done. September 11th must have erased the First Amendment while I wasn't looking.

She suggested that Kay and her mother could file as co-plaintiffs on an equal protection claim, although she was worried the judge "may well have the same level of contempt for the rights of the student as he has shown for the rights of her teacher."

In another letter, she wrote a fellow attorney who worked in a public law institution. Anita said the "federal gods" had "wiped out the First Amendment and the Rehab Act." She also enclosed the opinion. She questioned how my actions could not be protected speech, adding that she "could not swallow" the judge's reading of the Rehab Act, either. This is bad stuff."

She went on:

> My client went the extra mile to save a suicidal adolescent and got shafted by a smart-ass lawyer...I've opposed him before on behalf of an interracial couple

forced out of school. I won that time because there was a federal judge who understood hate. This time, [the judge] has no interest in the rights of student or teacher. The opinion tracks Levin's abomination of a brief.

She asked if the center would consider filing an amicus brief. Anita knew they were handling a case against Wissahickon at the time, and this attorney was aware of some of the things the district was doing.

In a later phone conversation, this same attorney told Anita that Michael Levin was "a scourge to Special Education." He was advising the districts to write skeletal IEPs that could be used later against the parents if they had the temerity to attempt to get mandated support for their exceptional children. She said he was "poisoning the landscape of Special Education."

The judge said we could file a Second Amended Complaint within twenty days. We did. The Second Amended Complaint presented claims under the Fourteenth Amendment concerning equal protection, discrimination, a class of one and stipulations under the Rehab Act. In this pleading Anita was attempting to show the district's violation of law in how Special Education children were handled and the targeting of teachers who were vocal in the defense of these students. She could no longer argue anything under the First Amendment because the judge had stifled that permanently.

Anita claimed there were many children "dumped" in Special Education in Wissahickon. True, especially children who did not speak English. I had three children in my class who did not speak any English. I was not a language teacher. We had a number of Korean students who were in Special Education. None of these children were tested in their native language; that would insure low-test results. Some of these students were put into Spec Ed without the paperwork or correctly signed placement forms. There was no English as second language program with a teacher who spoke Korean.

Anita claimed that WSD "maintained and enforced an unwritten policy to cut services to Special Education pupils and to punish and intimidate teachers who advocated for them." This was true, but impossible to prove.

One of the means to cut services was to write a barebones IEP. The less you promise, the less you have to provide. Michael Levin was a strong proponent of the less you write in an IEP the better for the district.

There was no mention of an emotionally unstable condition in her IEP. Why? Because if you do not mention a child is emotionally troubled, you do not have to provide Emotional Support. Mr. Levin then stated my actions were "illegal" because there were no related services in K's IEP and there was no mention of her need for psychological counseling.

And that, my friends, is how it's done. Districts avoid mention of a condition and thus are able to circumvent the intent of IDEA by not offering services to address the condition. Notice that Mr. Levin never once suggested that a troubled child, with an emotionally unstable history and a suicide attempt, did not have an appropriate IEP and was not provided the services which IDEA stipulated. In fact, look closely at what Mr. Levin was saying: if there is no mention of a child's need in the IEP and if the services are not provided by the district, then it is illegal to provide any assistance not specified in the IEP. Listen to Mr. Levin's argument repeated in every pleading: "Defendants believe [Montanye's] behavior was violative of the student's civil rights because [Montanye's] behavior was not required or implied by the student's IEP."

This is convoluted reasoning. Michael Levin said the child was emotionally troubled. He ignored the district's violations of not addressing this in the IEP. He then established that doing anything more for the child than what was in the IEP was illegal. It was a civil right's violation to provide necessary help to a student who had been denied this help by the district that was mandated by law to provide that help.

Our supervisors constantly instructed us that doing anything **less** than what the IEP called for was noncompliant; you could always do **more.** Michael Levin was postulating that a child could not be given anything more than the services listed in the IEP. Michael Levin was restructuring IDEA to be the most restrictive law applied to Spec Ed kids.

In order to support her contention that the district punished teachers who advocated for Spec Ed children, Anita offered another case of reprisal aimed at a tenured teacher at the high school. This teacher met with Anita to discuss the district's pogrom against vocal Spec Ed teachers. She had gone up against the administration a number of times. She fought the administration's illegal rule about waiting to place Spec Ed students until the end of a marking period. She refused to help the high school administration illegally suspend a Special Education senior twelve days before graduation because they "didn't want him there." Her evaluations dropped to unsatisfactory. In June, she was "reassigned" to the middle school. Transfers were used as punishment. She resigned.

The Fourteenth Amendment provides equal protection. Anita claimed the board, in failing to adopt policies for Special Education teachers and by arbitrarily applying stricter standards for conduct against them, violated the equal protection clause.

In discussing the Rehab Act, my attorney reminded the court that WSD received federal funding for Special Education children. She then wondered if the funds were used for retaining special counsel but were not identified in the public WSD budget. Good point. Where did Mr. Levin's money come from? The vote to spend it certainly never showed up in any school board minutes. We know the board didn't approve the initial outlays because it didn't know about them.

*****

We filed a Third Amended Complaint. An associate in the Levin Legal Group wrote the Defendants' Motion and Memorandum of Law to Dismiss Plaintiff's Third Amended Complaint. This was the response to our Third Amended Complaint.

Much of the content was the same as in the previous arguments. Stacy Smith (Levin Legal Group) did complain that, "these defendants must again expend taxpayer funds to respond to Montanye's unfounded allegations." Funny how the board never wanted to discuss resolving the case outside of court where it wouldn't be draining tax payer coffers.

Then Ms. Smith decided that I couldn't be a certified Emotional Support teacher because there was no such category. "...her certification is 'Mentally and Physically Handicapped.'" Wrong again. My certificate reads, under the area of certification, **Socially and Emotionally Disturbed.** The second area of certification states "Mentally and Physically Handicapped." I was hired by the district to fill an **Emotional Support** position. The supervisor of Special Education sent out notification that I was the new **Emotional Support** teacher. The school board agenda listed

195

me as an **Emotional Support** teacher. On the seniority list, I was classified under **Emotional Support.** All the students who were **Emotional Support** in my grade level were assigned to my class.

Ms. Smith re-explained how the district, through Dr. Durtan, held the Loudermill hearing as part of the investigation. Ms. Smith again stated that the school district "does not have the duty or capacity to respond to a student's needs that do not affect the student's ability to learn." Was there no one in this practice who grasped the concept that depression, anxiety, and suicidal ideation had an effect on a student's ability to learn?

Another twist Ms. Smith related was a footnote concerning my inability to understand the position of the school district.

If a parent requests a due process hearing concerning any type of issues concerning a student's IEP, the school district always has the burden to show that the actions they took concerning a student's IEP and the IEP process was [sic] appropriate. Changes to a student's IEP must be made after meetings which include the input of the students' [sic] parents. The parents must agree to changes in writing and must be given notice of their rights whether or not they agree with the IEP. If the procedures have not been scrupulously followed the school district will be held liable, at the very least, for **procedural violations** of the IDEA.

That was a mouthful. It was also irrelevant to the case.

First of all, if a parent requested a due process hearing concerning an inappropriate IEP, the hearing officer would grant the district time to change the IEP if the parent prevailed. The district usually is given opportunity to repair a problem.

Most importantly, there were **no changes** made to Kay's IEP. Therefore, there was nothing to be written. And, the only paper the parent signs on the IEP is the front page. This indicates attendance at the meeting. There is no place for the parent to indicate she has agreed to any changes made.

Procedural violations do not deny services to the student. They are usually in the form of mistakes in the writing of the IEP. They do not come with liability. *Substantive* mistakes are not having a program or not providing needed related services. I had no violations on my scorecard. WSD had a whole bunch. And, they were **substantive**.

What Ms. Smith's footnote established was Kelle Heim-McCloskey's lack of scrupulous adherence to the law: "Changes to a student's IEP must be made after meetings which include the input of the students' parents. The parents must agree to changes in writing…"

So once again where was Kay's *revised* eighth grade IEP?

The final blow to IDEA and its protection for Special Education students came two pages later. In another footnote Ms. Smith claimed:

> It is possible that, at another time in history, in the absence of IDEA and Special Education laws, Montanye's behavior in attempting to "help" (her quotes) a troubled student, would be considered **valiant** behavior, above and beyond the call of duty as a school teacher. The Defendants do not even dispute that it is possible that K's parents were thankful for Montanye's intervention. However, because of the IDEA and Special Education laws that the School District is compelled to follow, Montanye's actions were inappropriate. It is the duty of the School District to ensure that their teachers follow the law.

Wowser!!

In one paragraph, Ms. Smith establishes that IDEA forbids helping Special Education students in any manner unless it is specified in the IEP. Since the IEP does not cover life after school, Spec Ed kids are out of luck. IDEA, the law written to protect these kids, to make sure they get what other students are getting, forbids that a troubled Special Education student receive private therapy with the help from a community member outside of the school day. But wait! It's quite all right to save a regular ed student; that's valiant behavior. Helping a troubled, non-Special Education student is "above and beyond the call of duty." Helping a Spec Ed student is breaking the law, because the laws say she cannot have the same assistance. This assertion completely desecrates the intent of IDEA.

By alleging the law would intercede to prevent keeping an exceptional child alive, the defense attorney sets the value of a

Special Education child's life lower than that of a regular education child. According to Ms. Smith, the government of the United States fashioned a statute which avows that support given to a regular education child is valiant, but when given to a Special Education child, is a violation of civil rights. Ms. Smith said IDEA and PA Spec Ed regulations forbid helping a suicidal Spec Ed child. Was this because both governments felt the Spec Ed child was expendable? This idea would have found a cozy home in Nazi Germany.

The defendants also denied my claim that I could not obtain employment elsewhere. My experience contradicted this. I placed my application on a website used by all the districts in the area.

A year later, I was contacted by one district. I interviewed for this position. The first question I was asked was why I wanted to leave Wissahickon School District. I told them for intellectual differences. They wanted to know what they were. I gave them a short view of the events; the tenor of the interview changed drastically. I was shown the door without a request for references.

The summer of 2003, there was a position in a small school district where my friend lived. She gave me a personal reference. I was never even contacted.

Two friends gave me glowing references for an Emotional Support position in their district. They also spoke directly with the personnel director. The district did not contact me.

Joe was working at a private school. He had gotten a job for one of the other teachers from Wissahickon. I asked him what my chances would be. He told me there was no way they would hire someone with my "history."

A friend of mine told me about a position at the Vo-Tech school. They needed a seasoned Special Education teacher. My friend's brother, who worked there, spoke with the personnel director about me.

When I spoke with the personnel director, he was very positive about my qualifications. We would meet the next week. He also remarked that he and Stan Durtan were good friends. They played golf together on the weekends.

As instructed, I called the following Monday to set up an interview. The director would "call me back." I called Tuesday. No response. Finally, the director called me back. He "just realized" that the position was federally funded and therefore was not a good choice for me. Right. He refused to interview me.

I applied to a district in Bucks County. I had to sign a waiver stating that all of my personnel records and information were to be released to the district. I also would not hold my previous employer responsible for any statements made to this district. I would further agree to allow the hiring district to investigate my background completely. So much for that.

Ms. Smith then proceeded to present IDEA law as it applied to school district evaluations.

> The first step in determining whether a child is a child with a disability is the evaluation process. If the school district believes that a child may be disabled as defined by the IDEA, the school district shall conduct an evaluation of the student. These evaluations can only take place after written informed consent from the parents of the child is obtained.

Ms. Smith's game is subterfuge. Evaluation rules only apply to an agency.

This section specifies the local educational agency is responsible for this procedure.

I was **not** a local educational agency. **The Directives Letter said so**.

The therapist was **not** a local educational agency.

The therapist did **not** administer an initial school district evaluation.

Kay had two psychiatric evaluations **before** she saw this therapist.

Here's what Ms. Smith and the Levin Legal Group were claiming: A parent has to sign a paper saying she grants herself the right to have her child re-evaluated by a privately paid, outside therapist. Although the parent is not an educational agency and does not receive federal funding for offering federal programs, she must follow the federal guidelines. It gets weirder. Where does the parent get this nonexistent form? With whom is the form filed? If the parent doesn't sign the non-existent form, can she take herself to due process for procedural violations? You may think this is silly, but an attorney sold this tripe and a federal judge bought it.

Now let's look at defendants' other sleight of hand. She explained in detail to the court about goals and objectives found in the IEP. This was totally nonrelated to the case, but she slugged on for pages. Although she had much to say about goals and objectives, she briefly mentioned **related** services and deftly ignored the fact that Kay was not offered any. This, on the other hand, was quite relevant. The district's disregard of related services was in direct violation of IDEA.

Ms. Smith lectured that "any and all changes to a student's IEP must be pursuant to an IEP team meeting and approved by the parents in writing." 20 U.S.C. §1415 (b) (3). Not according to the actions of the administrators in the spring of 2001 as it pertained to Kay.

This law had nothing to do with me; it had everything to do with the violations on the part of the administrators.

Ms. Smith also stated I had "no authority as a teacher to engage in these activities on behalf of the school district." That's a leap. Since when does a teacher on her own time and in a non-school activity operate on behalf of the school district?

There were two new affidavits attached to this document. One from Stanley Durtan and the other from, here's a shocker, Michael Levin.

Dr. Durtan's affidavit read as if penned by Mr. Levin. It devoted a noticeably large amount of attention postulating how innocent Mr. Levin was.

> Neither Mr. Levin nor his firm had been retained to perform any Special Education work for the district.[10]
>
> We hired Mr. Levin to insure that we were acting in accordance with law.[11]
>
> Based on the legal advice that I received from Mr. Levin, my long experience as an educator and the advice from my staff, it was my conclusion that the Plaintiff violated special education laws.

Hold the phone! If Dr. Durtan, his attorney, and his staff were so adept at assessing violations of Special Education law, wouldn't that indicate they were well aware of the violations they committed in their handling of Kay?

"In fact, neither Mr. Levin nor his firm, were [sic] ever

---

[10] Not true. LLG had represented the district in a Spec Ed case previously.
[11] Who exactly is "we"?

retained to provide any services in any Special Education matters." That had such a familiar ring to it. He made the same statement on the first page of the affidavit.

The rest of the affidavit repeated his claims that the school board knew nothing. The affidavit was followed by Dr. Durtan's resume'. He had oodles of experience. He was a teacher for all of one and a half years. He went on to become a school psychologist, a principal, an assistant superintendent, and finally superintendent. Most of his career removed him from being with kids.

He also directed the Special Education program and oversaw the initial implementation of Public Law 94-142. [IDEA] With all this experience, it was amazing that Dr. Durtan needed the advice of a specially hired attorney on the ins and outs of IDEA.

It was now Mr. Levin's turn to offer his testimony. He began by reciting a litany of his accomplishments. He pointed out that he had "written magazine articles on virtually every aspect of public school law." Mr. Levin wanted the court to believe that because he wrote articles on education he would not violate its laws. Knowing the law and adhering to it are two separate beasts.

Then the counselor took great pains to point out how little of his practice was devoted to Special Education.

> Over the course of my career, I have devoted less than ten per cent (10%) of my time to Special Education. Over the past two years, I have devoted less than approximately five per cent (5%) of my time to special education. On the contrary, my time is devoted to the three main areas (1) labor and employment (11) litigation other than Special Education (111) general advice to school entities in all areas of their operations.

So, according to Mr. Levin, in his sworn affidavit, the majority of his practice was spent on matters other than Special Education. But according to Dr. Durtan, he brought Mr. Levin in on two cases against Special Education teachers, based on his vast knowledge of this particular area of law.

The district employed a Doctor in Education, whose forte was Special Education, but Dr. Durtan asked a lawyer to override his own expert. Ms. Heim-McCloskey was a supervisor in Special Education, a former teacher of Special Education, and a woman whose entire career was Special Education, yet Dr. Durtan needed the opinion of a labor lawyer to reject the IEP's Ms. Heim-McCloskey helped write and accepted as accurate. The collective knowledge of the superintendent and the assistant superintendent far exceeded Mr. Levin's percentage of expertise. Not to mention, it was up to these two administrators to hire the experts who would run the district programs.

And last, but certainly not least, there was Scott Wolpert, a lawyer with Timoney, Knox LLP. These were the hired solicitors for the Wissahickon School District. Timoney, Knox LLP was quite proud that their stable of lawyers included attorneys with varied expertise who could provide the client with the necessary skills and specific counseling. Mr. Wolpert's CV indicated that he had substantial background and working knowledge of Special Education law. In fact, he also specialized in teacher discipline and labor law. During the years of my litigation, Mr. Wolpert ran a number of CLE's (Continuing Legal Education courses) on Special Education and teacher disciplinary actions. Mr. Wolpert **was teaching lawyers about Spec Ed and teacher labor issues**. But strangely enough, Mr. Wolpert was lacking when it came time for Stan Durtan to choose an attorney to hold two Loudermill hearings allegedly based on Spec Ed issues.

Despite the rather large array of knowledge among these experts, who already worked for the district, it was Mr. Levin who was called in to provide expertise for the superintendent. Mr. Levin attests, in his affidavit to his minimal amount of experience in this field, but he was chosen over people who had him beaten on paper to oversee the pre-termination hearings of two Special Education teachers.

Ok. So here's the head scratcher. Considering Mr. Levin's background paled in significance to those already employed by the district, why would he be the chosen one? Surely, the board would have realized their own people would have the moxie to question two teachers. Oh, that's right. The board didn't hire the attorney. The superintendent did. Maybe Timoney, Knox LLP were well acquainted with the school board policy that solely endowed the board with the power of hiring an attorney and encumbering the district with any contract over $100. Maybe Timoney, Knox LLP was unwilling to keep Dr. Durtan's, Ms. Clark's, Ms. Heim-McCloskey's, and Mr. Sanni's secret from the board. We know the Levin Legal Group did not have that problem. After all, they were the ones who repeatedly said the board had no knowledge of what took place.

This next one is priceless. Mr. Levin avers he "specifically recalled Dr. Durtan and Assistant Superintendent Judy Clark stating that it was important that all laws governing the education of Special Education students be complied with by everyone in the school district including teachers." No kidding. Does that go for a superintendent, his assistant, the supervisor of Special Education, and one principal?

The next assertion was that Mr. Levin did not write the Directives Letter. He did some coaching though. "In fact, I recommended the language for the superintendent to utilize." If you recommend the language, isn't that writing it? And why didn't the letter "say what we meant it to say?"

In answering Anita's charge that: (1) Mr. Levin's fees were needless (2) Levin and the superintendent tried to justify the expense and Mr. Levin's unauthorized actions to the school board, he claimed:

> All recommendations were made by me to the School District in good faith, in accordance with my ethical obligations to the School District, and based upon my considerable experience in representing school districts across the Commonwealth. After giving the school district a description of the options that it had in this matter, the School District, through the superintendent, made the decision as to what action to take.

Hello. He made these recommendations to the **school district?** Stanley Durtan is not the school district, the board is. Durtan was not in a position to supplant the board's authority. When did Mr. Levin, in accordance with his ethical obligations, let the board know what was going on? Dr. Durtan said they knew nothing until the grievance was filed. Most importantly, why wouldn't Mr. Levin advise Dr. Durtan that the board should know a teacher supposedly "violated Special Education laws" that would put the district in jeopardy of a lawsuit? Shouldn't they know they were in jeopardy?

Did Mr. Levin rely on Dr. Durtan to inform the board about

what was taking place? Was Mr. Levin claiming that he did everything in good faith; and if someone was lying, it was the superintendent?

> After giving the school district a description of the options that it had in this matter, the School District, through the superintendent, made the decision as to what action to take.

When did Mr. Levin give the school board the description of the options? Dr. Durtan swore they did not have a description of the options before the Loudermill and Directives Letter. They didn't have a description of options until they were dragged into litigation by actions kept secret from them. Come to think of it, the whole concept of Mr. Levin submitting an affidavit was bizarre; he was not a defendant. He was not called on to provide testimony.

*****

Ms. Smith also filed a Motion to Strike. This was an attempt to keep the one page from Kay's IEP out of the court records. Although it was not very descriptive, the statement that Kay became emotionally overwhelmed indicated that school personnel knew she had problems. It also proved her IEP teacher or Special Education supervisor did not call for a re-evaluation or the revising of the IEP to provide related services.

Ms. Smith was complaining we were using the IEP without permission, because there was no "record on file at the School District...that the Plaintiff had the student's parent's prior consent to disclose this information to her attorney as required by FERPA."

The motion continued, indignantly, that these violations subjected "the Defendant School District to possible sanctions by the Department of Education, including the withholding of federal financial assistance."

It went on:

> Plaintiff's disclosure of these records to her counsel and counsel's subsequent disclosure of these records to the public at large is impertinent, immaterial, and scandalous

and is highly prejudicial to the Defendants. The Defendants are requesting that this information be stricken from the record in this case.

Let's flash back to the Loudermill hearing when my attorney asked about the confidentiality of the information being discussed. Michael Levin assured us that those present were permitted to have access to this information without a signed waiver. Now his co-hort was arguing

…when Plaintiff turned over the educational record to her counsel in this matter, she disclosed an educational record without prior written parental consent in violation of the provisions of FERPA.

Then, admittedly, when the Wissahickon School District turned over five of Joe's IEP's to Mr. Levin without parental knowledge or permission, they were violating FERPA.

But wait! Ms. Smith attached the IEP page to this document. Stapled to the IEP were the consent forms signed by Kay and her mother. So now FERPA was saying that I could not use an IEP **with** written consent from the student and her parent, but the school district, through the superintendent, could hand over other student's IEP's without permission?

The motion goes on for pages reciting verbatim parts of the FERPA law. One contention I found interesting was, "It is the School District that will suffer the consequences of the Plaintiff's ill-conceived filing. It is the School District that may be sanctioned by the Department of Education, not the Plaintiff." Let's get this straight. I could be personally liable for violations of nonexistent IDEA, but I would not be personally liable for violating FERPA?

The defendants were not just selfishly thinking of their own purposes. They were trying to protect Kay's parents.

The Defendants can see no legitimate reason to drag the parents of a disabled child and the details of their daughter's educational program into this case at this stage.

The defendants ridiculed the parents when they were begging

for help and protection for their daughter. They thrust themselves into and interfered with this family's personal decisions. They stated repeatedly that the problems of their daughter were of no importance to others. The district didn't care if their daughter slashed her throat open, but suddenly, these same people developed sensitivity to the parents' privacy?

The next pages were a replay of a defense of Michael Levin's integrity.

Rule of thumb: the more an attorney defends his integrity, the less he actually possesses. Like everything else in life, if you have it, people will know without you thumping your chest. Conversely...

Mr. Levin also included his lengthy resume´ to impress the court. Being prolific does not impute integrity; behaving honorably does.

Our response was brief. We had included the IEP page because the defendants had stated I did not follow the IEP. I had. The school district had already used Kay's records without the consent of her parents during the Loudermill hearing. Our allegations about the actions on the part of the district were true. We attached Kay's affidavit providing consent for the use of her school records and mental health information. We attached Kay's mother's affidavit providing consent for the use of the school records.

When Anita argued against striking the IEP (Plaintiff's Answer Opposing Motion to Strike), she showed the ambiguity of the defense attorney's statements.

> Defendants complain Montanye does not produce "evidence" of the wrongdoing she asserts against them-and when she does, they claim "prejudice" and seek to have it stricken off. They can't have it both ways.

We attached two documents to this-Robert Anderson's affidavit and Joe's. Mr. Anderson's affidavit recounted the meeting with Stanley Durtan and William Sanni. Included was their admonition that he should have written me up for insubordination, although I had not been insubordinate. Joe's described the events of his Loudermill including the principal's statement that these were created to "knock Joe around and put him in his place."

*****

On March 18, 2004, the judge handed down his decision concerning the Motion to Dismiss the Third Amended Complaint. He denied the motion.

He found that the claim of equal protection under the Fourteenth Amendment was valid. He also said I was justified in claiming that I was a class of one as I maintained I was intentionally treated differently from others similarly situated, and there was no rational basis for this difference. We would have to prove that the district's actions were not rationally related to a legitimate government interest.

One day short of the second anniversary of the WIN team letter, a federal judge said I had a case against the district. We were on our way.

*****

Anita Alberts and Michael Levin had a second phone conference with the judge. Afterwards, she sent me a letter with a schedule that we would have to religiously follow. If we missed a deadline, there was nothing we could do to remedy it.

Her final paragraph was encouraging.

Anyway, the judge is pretty familiar with your case now. He told us that his opinion distilled out those allegations he feels have merit—and those concern discrimination against Special Education. Judge DuBois said you are really a dedicated teacher and if we can prove discrimination against Special Education, the school district's got something to worry about.

CHAPTER FIFTEEN

Nicole

It's a grim fact of life that every year students from schools across the country will die…When a student's life is lost the resulting shock and sorrow can shake a school community to its core…Schools are about young people, and young people are about life. When a young person dies, especially when it is sudden, it completely disrupts the equilibrium of the school environment.

NEA Today: "Lessons on Loss"; Cindy Long
March/April 2010

What was I doing all the time I waited for this case to progress? According to Michael Levin and Chuck Herring (PSEA attorney), I was sitting back, popping bon-bons, and waiting to strike it rich by suing an innocent school district. Chuck Herring told the WEA president his suspicion, while Mr. Levin informed my attorney this was my goal. Strangely enough, they both used the exact wording.

Contrary to their misplaced theories, I was not living a carefree life. I could not work, I had countless emotionally distraught days, and I could not sleep. I found the best antidote to these restless hours was to research the law. I was reading everything I could get my hands on pertaining to school law, school liability, Special Education law, and civil rights. I also devoured studies on bullying and teenage suicide.

Legal cases are tedious for the beginner to slug through, but like everything else in life, ease comes with practice. Becoming familiar with the pattern that written decisions follow and acquiring a working knowledge of precedential cases helps a lot.

Anita Alberts suggested I go to law school, but I did not have the money, and I felt it would be too late to start a practice once I earned a law degree.

For now, reading the law was what I did when I was unable to sleep. That is how I met the young lady from Maryland.

Nicole Eisel, a 13-year-old student at a middle school in Montgomery County, (Maryland) allegedly became involved in Satanism. Nicole told some of her friends she intended to kill herself. The students reported Nicole's intentions to their school counselor, who relayed the information to Nicole's counselor. The counselor questioned Nicole, but the girl denied making any of the statements. The counselor failed to notify Nicole's family or the school administration about Nicole's supposed plans or the discussion concerning them. One week later at Rock Creek Park, Nicole's friend, after entering into a murder-suicide pact, killed Nicole and then shot herself with a .32 caliber semi-automatic pistol.

Nicole's father, Stephen Eisel, sued the Board of Education of Montgomery County (MD), the superintendent, the principal of the middle school, and the guidance counselor. (*Stephen Eisel v. Board of Montgomery County, Maryland et al.* No. 139, September Term 1990). He claimed it was their duty to inform him about his daughter's intentions so he could have had the opportunity to intervene. The defendants argued they **owed no duty** to the plaintiff or his daughter.

The circuit court granted summary judgment to the defendants. They decided for the school board on the grounds that the defendants owed no duty to intervene to prevent Nicole's death. Eisel, the grieving father, appealed the decision.

The Maryland Court of Appeals reversed the lower court's decision and remanded the case back to the original court for further proceedings. (Court of Appeals of Maryland, 134 Md. 377; 597 A.2d 447 1991).

This was the first time I had read a case involving the suicide of a child and the claim of negligence against the school. Eisel was not the first suicide suit against a district, but it is used as a standard in law classes.

The appellate court's decision was emphatic in its belief that a suicidal child is owed some duty of obligation. There are striking contrasts between the Eisel court's views of a suicidal child and those of the Wissahickon School District. Let's view them side-by-side.

*

Maryland Appellate Court on reasonable care:
The relation of a school: vis-à-vis a pupil is analogous to one who stands in loco parentis with the result that a school is under a special duty to exercise reasonable care to protect a pupil from harm.

Stanley J. Durtan, Superintendent, Wissahickon School District:
In short, those activities were not part of your job as a teacher and your actions to engage in those activities illustrates [sic] that you did not demonstrate a sufficient appreciation of where to draw the line between your proper duties and acts that are not appropriate.

Stanley J. Durtan, Superintendent, Wissahickon School District:
...why were you involved? You are the student's teacher. You are not the parent. You are not a social welfare agency.

Michael Levin, Attorney for Wissahickon School District:
On the contrary, Montanye was simply a teacher...
...Nothing more is alleged than that of a teacher-student relationship

*

Maryland Appellate Court on foreseeability:
Foreseeability is the most important variable in the duty calculus and without it there can be no duty to prevent suicide. Nicole's suicide was foreseeable because defendants allegedly had direct evidence of Nicole's intent to commit suicide.

Michael Levin, Attorney for the Wissahickon School District:
K had serious emotional and psychological problems and had made threats and attempts at suicide in the past. These emotional problems continued throughout the school year.

The Wissahickon High School WIN team letter:
As the high school WIN team we are most concerned about these behaviors and the continued lack of good judgment and professionalism Mrs. Montanye displays with students at risk. We ask that you take action...

*

Maryland Appellate Court: Was there a duty?
School counselors have a duty to use reasonable means to prevent

a suicide when they are put on notice of a child or adolescent student's suicidal intent.

Wissahickon High School WIN team letter:
As the high school WIN team we are most concerned about these behaviors and the continued lack of good judgment and professionalism Mrs. Montanye displays with students at risk.

Levin Legal Group:
Montanye admittedly engaged in behavior with a student, which the defendants believe was violative of the student's civil rights because her behavior was not required or implied by the student's IEP.

Levin Legal Group:
The school district does not have the duty, to respond to student's needs that do not affect the student's ability to learn.

Michael Levin, Attorney for Wissahickon School District:
In sum, Mrs. Montanye insinuated herself into the personal life of a very troubled and emotionally disturbed youth.

*

Maryland Appellate Court: How certain is the foreseen harm?
The degree of certainty that Eisel and Nicole suffered the harm foreseen is one hundred percent.

Stanley J. Durtan, Superintendent, Wissahickon School District:
Allow me to raise a rhetorical question-was it the right thing to do, because it was necessary in terms of the student's education? Or was it the "right thing" to do in terms of issues wholly apart from the student's educational needs?

*

Maryland Appellate Court: Whose problem is it?
An adolescent who is thinking of suicide is more likely to share these feelings with a friend rather than a teacher. But we all—parents, teachers, administrators, service providers and friends—can learn what the warning signs are and what to do.

Michael Levin, Attorney for Wissahickon School District:
K's emotional and psychological issues are **not matters of public concern.**

Montanye's alleged speech or expressive conduct concerned only K and her emotional issues. These issues are **not matters of public concern** as they only relate to the treatment of a single student.

Levin Legal Group:
Montanye's alleged speech or expressive conduct cannot be fairly characterized as **relating to any matter of political or public concern.**

Stanley J. Durtan, Superintendent, Wissahickon School District:
None of those activities are related to the expectations for your position, none are required by the student's IEP, and none are required by law...those activities were not part of your job as a teacher and your actions to engage in those activities illustrates [sic] that you did not demonstrate a sufficient appreciation of where to draw the line.

Wissahickon High School WIN team letter:
It has come to our attention that Mrs. Montanye has taken one of her students to three therapy sessions outside the school setting. As the high school WIN team we are most concerned about these behaviors and the continued lack of good judgment and professionalism Mrs. Montanye displays with students at risk.

Michael Levin Letter 5/15/2002:
With respect to student K, we will be inquiring whether your client made an appointment for the student with the therapist, whether your client transported the student to the therapist, whether your client participated in the therapy session with the student. If she did it, we will be very anxious to hear [the] **explanation** and **justification** for her acts.

*

Maryland Appellate Court: Why all the fuss?
The General Assembly has made it quite clear that the prevention

of youth suicide is an **important public policy**, and that local schools should be at the forefront of the prevention effort.

Stanley J. Durtan, Superintendent, Wissahickon School District:
Allegations have been made that you engaged in willful neglect of duty, insubordination, incompetency, persistent negligence is [sic] the performance of duties, willful violation or [sic] school laws, and improper conduct growing out of the following: improperly involving yourself in situations pertaining to student K...making an appointment for the student with a therapist, transporting the student to the therapist, participating in the therapy session with the student. It is alleged that these actions by you are unprofessional, and exhibit poor judgment. If any of the allegations are true, we will also want to discuss possible dismissal from employment.

Michael Levin, Attorney for Wissahickon School District:
K's emotional and psychological issues are **not matters of public concern...**

*

Maryland Appellate Court: It's not just an oversight.
The harm that may result from a school counselor's failure to intervene appropriately when a child threatens suicide is total and irreversible for the child, and severe for the child's family. The consequence of the risk is so great that even a relatively remote possibility of a suicide may be enough to establish duty.

Stanley J. Durtan, Superintendent, Wissahickon School District:
...you are directed not to engage in any act, conduct or activity with respect to any school district student that is not expressly required or reasonably implied by your job.

The school district has no duty to respond to a student's needs that do not affect the student's ability to learn.

*

Maryland Appellate Court:
To categorize youth suicides as knowing and involuntary acts which

are protected by law to be unaccountable for omissions or other acts, would be contrary to the policy established by the act itself.

Stanley J. Durtan, Superintendent, Wissahickon School District:
Your acts and omissions constituted significant wrongdoing…you are directed not to engage in such acts or omissions again either with this student or any other students.

Michael Levin, Attorney for Wissahickon School District:
(Montanye's) behavior (was) in violation of federal and state law and violate(d) the procedural safeguards guaranteed to students and their parents.

*

Maryland Appellate Court: Duty
Considering the growth of this tragic social problem…we hold school counselors have a duty to use reasonable means to attempt to prevent a suicide when they are on notice of a child or adolescent's suicidal intent.

Stanley J. Durtan, Superintendent, Wissahickon School District:
The school district has no duty to respond to a student's needs that do not affect the student's ability to learn.

Wissahickon High School WIN Team letter:
Mrs. Montanye has taken one of her students to three therapy sessions outside the school setting. As the high school WIN team we are most concerned about [the] continued lack of good judgment and professionalism Mrs. Montanye displays.

Michael Levin, Attorney for Wissahickon School District:
Montanye has also **admitted** her **misconduct** for which she was being investigated.

Levin Legal Group:
…the employee's speech or expressive conduct can not be fairly characterized as relating to **any matter of political, social or other concern to the community.**

Stanley J. Durtan, Superintendent, Wissahickon School District:
Your acts and omissions constituted significant wrongdoing...you are directed not to engage in such acts or omissions again either with this student or any other students.

*

Maryland Appellate Court: A Youth Suicide Prevention School Programs Act
Moral blame as a factor to be weighed in deciding whether to recognize a legal duty in tort is less than an intent to cause harm. The factor considers the reaction of persons in general circumstances. Is it the **sense of community** that an obligation exists under the circumstances? The youth suicide prevention programs provided for by the Act call for an awareness of, and a response to emotional warning signs, thus **evidencing a community sense** that there should be intervention based on emotional indicia of suicide.

Levin Legal Group:
...the employee's speech or expressive conduct can not be fairly characterized as relating to any **matter of political, social or other concern to the community.**

*

Maryland Appellate Court:
The act does not view these children as standing independently, to live or die on their own.

Levin Legal Group:
Montanye's alleged speech or expressive conduct concerned only K and her emotional issues. These issues are not matters of public concern as they only relate to the treatment of a single troubled student.

The court quoted from "A Youth Suicide Prevention School Programs Act" [Maryland Code]:
The uncodified preamble to the Act states that the rate of youth suicide had increased more than threefold in the last two decades...over 5,000 young Americans took their lives in 1985 including 100 young people in Maryland.

Youth suicides are knowing and involuntary acts which are protected by law and thus making them unaccountable for omissions of other acts, would be contrary to the policy established by the act itself. The act does not view these children as standing independently, **to live or die on their own.**

The Eisel court believed:
...the prevention of youth suicide is an **important public policy**, and that **local schools should be at the forefront of the prevention effort.**

Not according to the people running the Wissahickon School District and their attorney. Contrast the opinion of the court with the district's actions:

- The superintendent spent thousands of dollars to punish the employee who took Kay's suicidal ideation seriously.
- The superintendent did not find fault with the principal who would not control the bullying in his school, which led to Kay's exile.
- The superintendent did not reprimand the WIN team or the guidance counselors for ignoring a bullied, suicidal child.
- The superintendent did not reprimand the Special Education supervisor for ignoring a bullied, suicidal child who needed Emotional Support as required by federal law.
- The superintendent did not find fault with an unrevised eighth grade IEP, and an illegal outside placement, which contributed to Kay's suicide attempts.
- The superintendent wrote a Directives Letter instructing a teacher that her actions in saving a bullied, suicidal child were unprofessional and a sign of bad judgment.
- The Wissahickon School Board showed no concern about their employees' neglect of a bullied, suicidal child.
- The Wissahickon School Board paid thousands of taxpayers' dollars to establish for the record that **the problems of one troubled teenager were of no importance to the community.**
- The Wissahickon School Board, charged with the protection of its students, did not conduct any investigation into the events surrounding Kay.

- The Wissahickon School Board contended in numerous briefs, that K's emotional and psychological issues were not matters of public concern.

Although the courts are conflicted on how special relationships and duty affect the liability of school personnel toward suicidal children, I was unable to locate any case where parents of a suicidal student sued a school district because a teacher helped the child by assisting her in getting counseling from a professional therapist. Not one case was based on the premise that a teacher who helped a child live had "violated her civil rights." Parents do no sue school districts because their child did NOT commit suicide.

In my research, I never came across any school entity that promoted the malignant belief that helping a child in a positive manner was an action to be condemned. I found no mission statements from any counseling group indicating that assisting a family in getting help for their child was a breach of professionalism.

I also could not locate literature espousing the theory that the troubles of a child, which could lead to a premature death, were of no interest or concern to those around her. In all my years of extensive investigation, the only source of the contention that a child's life was of no importance or that her death had no social impact came exclusively from Michael Levin and the Wissahickon School District.

Stephen Eisel did not have the opportunity to see his daughter graduate high school and college. He was denied the joy of walking his daughter down the aisle. He was robbed of the exhilaration of welcoming his first grandchild when his daughter gave birth. Instead, he was left with the eternal emptiness that comes with the loss of a child. He spent his life existing with the personal agony of knowing his child died by her own volition and he had been powerless to prevent this. All human pleasures attendant with living and watching your child grow exploded with that bullet.

No one can say what events would or would not have taken place had Mr. Eisel been notified of his daughter's intentions. Perhaps an intervention would have put Nicole on another trajectory. Of course, the possibility exists that the outcome would have been the same, even in the presence of therapeutic steps. The answer is moot.

But I will say this: I would rather have tried to help Nicole, even if it meant failing, than to be on the other side of the argument with those defendants claiming, *It's not my fault your child is dead.*

Sallie Montanye

CHAPTER SIXTEEN

Discovery

Mrs. Montanye devoted her entire teaching career to helping and assisting youngsters who have severe emotional difficulties. To then be charged with over involvement in doing this was a major traumatic (experience)... From the standpoint of working as an Emotional Support teacher her career in that area **is over.**

This individual's vocational career, for all practical purposes has been terminated...The disciplinary charges that were brought against her and the action taken against her will be something she will not be able to overcome in the educational field. To that extent, the loss of long term earning potential over her work life will be significant.

Donald Jennings, Ed.D. Certified Vocational Expert

It was now March of 2004. I had been involved in the lawsuit for a year and a half. The pleadings and motions were stacked up in every corner. My living room floor was covered with papers. My chairs groaned under wobbling stacks of materials. Everywhere you turned there were piles and piles of pages with colored sticky notes poking out from between curled-edges. That was what a federal lawsuit looked like, at least in my house.

The next step to trial was discovery. This is the gathering of evidence supporting the claims made by the parties. Up to this point, both sides were slinging accusations left and right, without having to provide much substantiation. Discovery allows both parties to depose witnesses, collect documents, request answers to interrogatories, and agree or disagree with statements or stipulations. The judge provides a schedule for this. If a party misses a deadline, that's too bad, unless the judge ignores the rules and says it's OK. It is the judge's prerogative to ignore the rules.

Discovery has its purposes. The first is to obtain information that can later be used to bolster or impugn the testimony of a witness. It also has collateral advantages in that it is labor intensive and excessively wordy, which drives up the cost of litigation and buries your opponent under redundant verbiage. In Anita's case, this was critical because she was a sole practitioner and did not have a team of paralegals to type out repetitive pages that were variations on a theme. Discovery is necessary and vital to a case. It is also an effective weapon to crush the client who has no money.

Expert Witnesses/Expert Witness Reports

A few words about what an expert witness is, or is not. By loose definition, an expert witness is an objective professional hired to evaluate some aspect of the case. To qualify, this person should have extensive familiarity and expertise in the area for which he is testifying. Some expert witnesses testify only for defendants, others only for plaintiffs. Some testify for either side. The expert witness is supposed to bring in a trained objectivity to the case at hand. If the person is not objective, for example if the expert is someone who stands to gain or lose depending on the outcome of the trial, then what you have in essence is a hired gun.

My first witness was a vocational expert. He wrote a report as to whether I was damaged or not, and what I could expect from my career in the future. The tests cost about $1500. The expert would be about $300—$400 per hour for testifying in court. Anita was a big fan of having a vocational expert testify. I was less enthusiastic because I had to borrow the money to pay him to state the obvious.

The report opined that given the accusations against me, no district would be willing to take the risk of hiring me in a teaching capacity. No surprise there.

The expert pointed out my history at the district had been excellent until 2001.

What appears to be most interesting to this writer is that from the very beginning of her tenure with the Wissahickon District, up until her last academic year, Mrs. Montanye received excellent performance reviews…Based on the review of her performance evaluations during her tenure with the school it was obvious that Mrs. Montanye was considered a superior teacher.

The data was clear on his view of what caused my physical and emotional problems:

> The etiology of Mrs. Montanye's stressors is directly and causally related to her experience at the Wissahickon School District. Mrs. Montanye's tenure prior to the episode for which the school required the Loudermill hearing was excellent-to then be charged with the allegations concerning her over involvement with a student was extremely difficult for this patient to accept.

To have my career ended as punishment for being concerned about the life of a child turned my world upside down. Emotional devastation is the natural result of having everything you stand for used against you. Nothing this man could write would put into words what I experienced and how it left me.

Attorney Alberts found a man who provided a knowledgeable, expert opinion of the SAP and its responsibilities. James Higgins had been a family counselor, a guidance counselor, a school psychologist, a superintendent of schools, and finally an adjunct professor at a respected university. Most importantly, according to his CV he had:

> ...ten years of experience supervising the establishment and monitoring of a Student Assistance Team as well as serving as a member of said team. In addition, I also served the Pennsylvania Department of Education as a trainer for the five original Student Assistance Teams (SAP) in the Commonwealth.

Mr. Higgins believed, based on 38 years of experience in education, "there does not appear to be a foundation for the charges alleged in the May 1, 2002 letter from Dr. Stanley Durtan." He then evaluated the viability of the accusations:

- **"willful neglect of duty"** It is the duty of the Emotional Support teacher to provide emotional support as well as academic support because academic achievement is dependent on the student's emotional stability. Mrs. Montanye's actions were appropriate for an Emotional Support teacher.

- **"insubordination"** Mrs. Montanye kept her immediate supervisor informed of her actions and followed his directives.
- **"willful violation of school law"** Dr. Durtan does not state the law that was violated and in what manner it was done willfully. In my experience, I am not aware of the violation to which he refers.
- **"improperly involving yourself in situations pertaining to student K..."** The actions were requested by the student as a condition for her participation in therapy with the consent of the parent and knowledge of the principal. Concern for the student's safety was the teacher's motivation.

Mr. Higgins also found fault with the WIN team and the Special Education department.

> ...other areas that I found to be of concern were the functioning of the WIN team, the apparent lack of commitment to a quality Special Education program, the procedure to be followed in regard to out of school contact with a student or parent outside of one's status as a teacher and a pattern of intimidation and withholding of evidence in order to build a case against Ms. Montanye.

> In the functioning of a Student Assistance Program, in this case, the WIN team, it is customary to use all resources...to address student problems that are interfering with that student's ability to learn...It appears that the WIN team had a resource in Ms. Montanye that they should have used to help a suicidal student, but instead chose to be critical of her efforts while they took no action.

The conclusion of the letter pointed out that I had the support of the parents, the student, and the principal, which was a "powerful endorsement." Mr. Higgins ended by stating that I was a "flexible, caring, self-sacrificing and competent teacher…She put the education and welfare of her students first and portrays the type of teacher that I valued as a Superintendent of Schools."

I still needed someone who could refute Michael Levin's arguments concerning IDEA. PSEA (state union) employed a woman whose function was to advise the union on matters of Special Education and to testify in court on behalf of members in cases involving Special Education. Ms. Stanley-Swope was a renowned speaker and authority in the subject of Special Education. She served on Special Education boards for the governor. She was on many well-respected committees. She traveled all over the state educating professionals on IDEA, through in-services, consultations, and presentations.

The president of our local (WEA) saw her at a meeting and asked if she would testify as an expert witness for me. Ms. Stanley-Swope said she would be glad to-that was her job. I was instructed to get my information to her secretary and to procure her CV (curriculum vitae) for Ms. Alberts. Time was most definitely of the essence as there were only three days left for submission of an expert's CV. I called Anita who was pleased we had someone of knowledge and repute. Ms. Stanley-Swope was on the road that week. Following the instructions she gave to the union president, I called her secretary and arranged to have her credentials sent to Anita's office. Ms. Stanley-Swope had already contacted her secretary to give the OK for this.

A few days later I received a distraught call from KH, the union president. Apparently, when Ms. Stanley-Swope returned to Harrisburg, she was told not to get involved with the "Montanye case." In fact, she was informed she might lose her job if she were to testify on my behalf. The union president received a terse email from Chuck Herring (PSEA attorney) basically telling her to mind her own business and not to interfere. The PSEA attorney said he had informed Anita Alberts that "Liz will not testify as the expert witness." Mr. Herring instructed KH that a ship "only had one captain" and Anita Alberts was the captain on this ship.

Sometime after this, the union president ran into Ms. Stanley-Swope at a conference. Ms. Stanley-Swope told her that one of the lawyers in Harrisburg (union headquarters) went "ballistic" when he heard she was testifying for me and told her she was not to get involved with the WSD lawsuit. She was "not to testify in a federal case." She apologized to KH for the outcome. Strange actions for the people who were there to defend my rights, wouldn't you say?

This woman was employed for this specific purpose, and yet she was threatened with loss of her livelihood if she fulfilled the obligation.

The cold reality was that the union, through a letter from Charles Herring, informed my attorney that the PSEA professional, who was paid to testify on behalf of teachers concerning Special Education, would not do so for me.

Request for Production of Documents

The next part of discovery was getting our hands on written material. This is done with document requests. We requested all sorts of things. Again, the virtue of excess rules the day here.

One thing we *never* received was a copy of the Wissahickon School Board's resolution or any documentation authorizing the conducting of Loudermill hearings. They didn't exist.

No copies were supplied of the Wissahickon School Board resolutions or other documents authorizing the engagement of and payment(s) to attorney(s) hired to conduct Loudermill hearing(s) in the school district. Apparently, these didn't exist either.

We asked for "all policies, ordinances, laws, regulations, procedures, and practices from any source that were allegedly violated by Plaintiff and upon which the charges made against Plaintiff were based." The district said these would be "supplied at a later date." You would think these would be handy considering they would have been the basis for the allegations letter.

Interrogatories

Interrogatories are, as you might assume, questions. They are supposed to uncover information pertinent to the parties' positions. They are to be completed by the client and the attorney. They are serious in nature and are to be approached as such.

In my first set of interrogatories from the Levin Legal Group, the opening questions concerned an unknown person who was apparently claiming to suffer from bulimia.

Question #2:

Please produce copies of all insurance claims forms and insurance identification cards for which you or anyone on your behalf has submitted claims for services or treatment with respect to your bulimia or with respect to any injuries you claim you suffered as a result of any act or omission (name redacted).[12]

Question #23 wanted me to:
identify each employer with whom you applied for work since January 1, 1997, including each employer referred to in paragraph four of your Third Amended Complaint, stating the date of each application, the positions applied for, and the results of the application.

Now that was challenging. I was employed by the Wissahickon School District since 1994 and was still their employee. This question was also addressed to another person. Such are the perils of cut and paste. These sections were obviously in reference to some other case.

Our interrogatories were similar in style, except we only asked questions concerning our case. There were the usual mind-numbing answers such as the oft repeated, I "should have notified the WIN team." According to Dr. Durtan, he and his underlings interviewed a myriad of people, which I knew to be untrue as they included my first attorney, the PSEA uniserv rep, Kay, and her mother. My first attorney and the PSEA rep sat in on the Loudermill. That hardly counts as being interviewed. And for the record, **not one administrator or district representative** spoke with Kay or her mother.

Then it came time for the list of numerous legal violations. Mr. Levin recorded a large selection of IDEA and PA Special Education Regulations, which as you know, had no application to the behavior of a private citizen. You have to admire his pluck. Many of the parts of the list were repeated two or three times. Lists are much more impressive when they are really, *really* long.

Dr. Durtan felt I violated the Potential Suicide Policy Checklist. First of all the Wissahickon School District **did not have** any form addressing a suicide policy. This would not come into existence for years. What they had was a sequence of steps to take if you felt a child was in danger of committing suicide. When I took the note to Principal Anderson, he pulled out the checklist

---

[12] The name was not redacted in the original.

and we followed the parts that were applicable to the situation. A copy of the note was given to the nurse and Maria Salvucci, WIN team captain. I called the mother. I notified the teacher who had Kay in the room at the time. I spoke with Kay. I reported back to Robert Anderson. Despite the fact that none of the above was elucidated in her IEP, I followed the steps of the checklist. Now I am not sure where the sin occurred. I followed the checklist steps, which Dr. Durtan stated I should have followed, but according to Mr. Levin, this was a violation of Kay's civil rights because my actions were not explicitly required or implied by the IEP.

Following the list of federal and state no–no's Defendant Durtan then claimed I **violated** School Board Policy #827.

Here is Policy #827 as it appears in the WSD policy manual:

Section: Operations   First Reading: **October 28, 2002**
Title: Outside Activities   Second Reading: **November 11, 2002**
                         Adopted: **November 11, 2002**

Administrative Guidelines:
District employees shall not be entitled to engage in outside activities subject to the following guidelines:

1. District property shall not be used for personal gain.
2. District resources including...District property and time shall not be used to engage in outside activities.
3. Political activities may not be engaged in during assigned hours of employment
4. No employee shall tutor or teach for private hire any pupils taught by the employee during the school year.
5. No employee shall use school, class time, mailbox, or other building news dissemination methods to advertise an outside activity.

The purpose of this new policy was to assure that staff members maintained "ethical standards."

It was the definition that astounded me.

All District employees are bound to refrain from any private business or professional activity or from having direct or indirect financial interests that would place them in a position **where there is a conflict, or even the**

appearance of a conflict, between their private interests and the interests of the District.

Since I did not make any money by helping Kay and since there was no financial gain to my assistance, my only conclusion was I was in conflict with the district because I wanted Kay to live and they did not. I would not have been punished if my interests and the "interests of the District" had been in unison.

The next section was even more disturbing.

III. Authority
The Board reserves the right to establish standards of conduct for its employees. Employees shall be evaluated **in terms of their faithfulness to,** and effectiveness in discharging school duties and responsibilities. Disciplinary actions shall be consistent with District procedures.

I would have to believe if the district felt I "violated" this policy then it was their belief that **school duties and responsibilities** were counter to saving a child's life outside of school hours. Remember, this policy is also about what a teacher is doing **outside** of school, as a private citizen. Not only did the administration concur with ignoring a bullied, suicidal child during school hours, they took the precaution in making sure no one would or could help the child after school hours, off of school property.

The Wissahickon School district wanted to insure that its:

Employees (may) avoid situations in which their **personal interests**, activities, and association may conflict with those of the District.

I had a **personal** interest in keeping Kay breathing. This went in direct contradiction to the district's interests. The Wissahickon School District was so invested in its belief that a dead kid was of no consequence, they were willing to pass a "policy" to enforce punishing a teacher who found it difficult to live with the idea of a dead fourteen year old. Remember the words of the Levin Legal Group:

Montanye's alleged speech or expressive conduct

concerned only K. and her emotional issues. These issues are not matters of public concern as they only relate to the treatment of a single troubled student. [Motion to Dismiss Amended Complaint]

There were a few details about Policy #827 which were just a tad problematic:

- The policy was written without input from the union which is to be included for the writing of policies pertaining to personnel issues.
- The local president of the union attended every board meeting. She did not recall the required readings, she was not aware of the vote to establish this as district policy, and she had not received a copy of this policy. She had not even heard of this policy before I brought it to her attention.
- #827 was not located in the section of the policy manual where the other personnel policies were located. It was placed toward the back of the manual.
- PSEA (state union) was completely unaware of this policy. **They did nothing once they learned of its existence however.**

Now let's see exactly what section of this policy was violated by keeping Kay alive.

- I did not violate the PA code of Professional Practice and Conduct for Educators. Nowhere does it state that a teacher, on her own time may not assist a suicidal child by helping get her to therapy.
- I had no financial interest in keeping Kay alive.
- No one even claimed that I was less effective because I helped Kay.
- I was faithful and effective in discharging my school duties and responsibilities. Remember, I was a bad employee because I went **beyond** the call of duty.

Did I violate any of the administrative guidelines?
- I did not use any district property for personal gain.

- I did not use any District property and time to engage in outside activities such as the solicitation of customers: (Many administrators and teachers who sold Girl Scout Cookies did so).
- I did not engage in any political activity at any time.
- I did not tutor any of my pupils outside of school or for money.
- I did not use any school, class time, mailbox, or other building news dissemination methods to advertise and/or organize an outside business activity.

Dr. Durtan did not elaborate on how I violated this policy. He also ignored the obvious, which was this policy was passed in **November of 2002.** That would be nine months **after** my activities with Kay. It was six months **after** the Loudermill hearing. It was eight days before I filed the lawsuit.

The cornerstone of Mr. Levin's argument was that we could not prove the existence of an "official but unwritten policy and practice against Special Education children." We failed to allege who enacted this policy or when it was enacted. On the other hand, Attorney Levin and the superintendent claimed I violated a school district policy, which was *not even in existence* at the time of my hearing.

Did the school board rush to pass this policy hoping no one would be observant of the date? Was this a desperate measure on the part of the board to forestall any liability?

No and No. There was a new twist in the tale of the school board. Under *response*, on page 9, #6: (Defendants' Answers to Plaintiff's First Set of Interrogatories)

…Durtan answers as follows. The School Board never took any action with respect to the Loudermill hearing. The School Board was not even notified of the allegations against Ms. Montanye and **there was no discussion with the school board about the allegations until after this lawsuit was filed and they were individually named as defendants in this lawsuit.**

It's the old *were you lying then or are you lying now* conundrum. Up until this point, Stan Durtan had asserted the board did not know about any of these shenanigans until the **grievance**

was filed (July, 2002). In Mr. Levin's letter of October 18, 2002, he clearly stated he was representing the school district, which means the school board. Now, the superintendent was revising his assertion, declaring the school board did not find out in **July** about his actions, but only learned about them in **November,** when served with the lawsuit papers. Mr. Levin and his clients would stick by this version of the story for the rest of the litigation.

This claim raised even more issues of violations of protocol. Once the grievance was filed it should have been reviewed by the school board. There are requisite steps taken according to the collective bargaining agreement. The step before arbitration is a meeting of the board members to review the points of the grievance and decide whether to resolve it or let it go to arbitration.

Another concern would be that Stanley Durtan and his attorney brought this lawsuit on the district purely through their own, unauthorized actions. Certainly the board should have been notified about the:

- Employment of Michael Levin, Esquire
- Loudermill Hearing
- Directives Letter
- Grievance filed by the union
- Extended contract for Mr. Levin to represent the school district in the matter of the grievance. This would have required more money than was originally agreed upon for the initial services.

Mr. Levin said in his affidavit that he advised his clients of their options. He obviously wasn't advising the board if they didn't know they were involved in a matter that could turn into litigation. According to Dr. Durtan the board never had the opportunity to make any of the decisions that required their knowledge and authority. According to Dr. Durtan, he and his hired attorney made the decisions that should have rested with the school board.

There is irony in Durtan's decisions. At a 2001, fall school board meeting, the attorney for Timoney, Knox LLP, who was present at all meetings, stated aloud that the board had to make every effort possible to avoid lawsuits. The attorney maintained the costs of legal altercations were breaking the district and that every effort should be made to **prevent** litigious entanglements.

I guess Dr. Durtan did not agree with this philosophy, or maybe *his* lawyer did not present all the options available. Whatever the reasoning, these two men usurped the power and responsibility of the duly elected officials and dragged the school district into litigation that was not only financially costly, but was also morally reprehensible.

CHAPTER SEVENTEEN

Depositions

...one of the major objections I have for the process you (Michael Levin) use is that you put an employee in a position where you impose a stiff penalty...then you offer on the side to settle for less than that, even though the offense doesn't deserve a ten-day penalty...So the employee is put in a position where they can fight it if they want, but they suffer horrendous penalties to fight it, or they can agree to the lesser penalty...It's a very clever way of getting people to agree to that because most people won't fight that.... most people will opt for the lesser penalty when put in that position.

Deposition of Donald Atkiss (PSEA Regional Director/Uniserv
Representative)
June 29, 2004

In his deposition, Mr. Atkiss was testifying how Michael Levin ran his Loudermill hearings. Mr. Levin would assign an overly severe punishment for an alleged "offense." He would then speak with the union rep and agree to lower the duration of the punishment, if the employee would agree to not take the district to arbitration. He was blackmailing the employee into acquiescing the right to arbitrate an action by lowering the amount of days suspended (which means a lesser loss of money). Levin was not the only bad guy here. Why would the union ever allow this without a challenge?

In my opinion, depositions are the most interesting part of discovery. Interrogatories and admissions for the most part are restatements of arguments raised in the pleadings. I am sure attorneys might disagree with this, as they probably have greater use for the interrogatories and admissions.

Depositions are hands on. You have the witness in front of you and you ask your questions face to face. I attended all the depositions and found them fascinating.

The purpose of the deposition is to extricate information to use to impeach a witness's credibility on the stand. You want to find out as much information as possible. You are looking for witnesses to make statements that are in direct conflict with the evidence.

A good deal of the case rides on the depositions. What is said here is binding and can hinder or support a case. It is important to be accurate; any discrepancy can and will be used against future testimony and could possibly tank the case at trial.

Depositions are very effective in the hands of able litigators. The witness is under oath and expected to speak the truth. Depositions are also used to verify or disprove statements made in affidavits. Depositions trump affidavits; the statements in affidavits are not under oath. The rule of thumb in law is you never ask a question you don't already know the answer to. Depositions record those answers.

Depositions are extremely expensive propositions. The people who record and transcribe them need to be paid. The price per page is costly. With each new deposition came the need for me to get more cash advances. Then, of course, each deposition had to be copied a number of times to provide reprints for all the attorneys, two for the judge, and some for the experts.

Michael Levin dragged out depositions. He came in with a four-inch thick stack of papers with typed questions. The longer the depositions took the more money it would cost me as the plaintiff. It wasted my attorney's time, which in turn drove up her charges. Delay and Cost: the mantra of defense attorneys.

By this time I was so far into debt and so strapped for money, it seemed more prudent to resign myself to the fact that I would never again have a decent credit rating, and that it was wiser not to answer the phone unless it was a friend calling.

Anita Alberts and Michael Levin had distinctly divergent styles. Michael Levin used his questioning to intimidate the witnesses. I felt he sometimes did this at the expense of gathering information. He seemed more intent on embarrassing the witnesses or making them feel stupid than finding out what they knew.

Anita did not write her questions down: she let the deposition unfold.

She preferred to question the witness and let him take her down paths with the answers. Attorney Alberts gave me a paper explaining depositions and the expected behavior of those involved. The instructions said that the witness could not confer with his attorney; he had to answer the questions put to him without assistance. It also said that witnesses were forbidden to discuss any matters related to the case during breaks or meals. I found our depositions to be less formal.

The first deposition was Robert Anderson's, the former Wissahickon High School Principal. Michael Levin deposed him. It took well over five hours. Mr. Levin covered a number of subjects, some of which were way off topic. Because there is no judge to determine what should or should not be included, the deposing attorney can ask any question he chooses; the witness is bound to answer the question. The information may not be admitted at trial, but you are still required to respond to the attorney's query.

Weeks before the deposition, Anita requested information from the school district on Robert Anderson. She received it the afternoon before the deposition. This was done in order to limit her preparation time. In addition, there were papers which were not included that should have been. That's the way this game is played.

Michael Levin had a huge packet with exhibits he used for Mr. Anderson's deposition. It had every transcript of Anderson's educational background including high school. Robert Anderson's grades in high school did not have much bearing on the matter at hand, but there they were. There were many emails and letters that had nothing to do with the case; yet, Mr. Levin tried to use them to impeach Mr. Anderson's competency, which in turn would show that he only supported me because he was a poor administrator.

Mr. Anderson testified that there were children who could not speak English who were placed in Spec Ed classes. He had asked Kelle Heim-McCloskey about two children in particular. He wanted to know if their paper work was in order. She said, "we're working on it." By law, the paperwork needed to be completed before the placement. This supported our argument of discrimination against Special Education.

When questioned about the letter from Kay's mother supporting me, Mr. Anderson stated he brought it to the Loudermill hearing but was told by Judy Clark and Bill Sanni to put it away. In other words, he was *instructed* to suppress evidence.

When the suicide note was discussed, the principal reiterated what he had already said. He copied the note, took it to the guidance suite, and instructed the secretary to give it to Maria Salvucci who was unavailable. He took the second copy to the nurse's office to give to Imelda Kormos. She said she was busy. He placed it on the counter in front of her, told her it was important and that she should read it as soon as she could. He also confirmed that he had instructed me to find Kay and speak with her.

Toward the end of his deposition, Robert Anderson dropped the bombshell that he had asked Kelle Heim-McCloskey (Supervisor of Special Education) if I had broken any rule or law by helping Kay. According to Principal Anderson, the supervisor's answer was **I had violated no law or regulation.**

Do you think Dr. Durtan secretly fired Robert Anderson because that would keep the superintendent's actions toward me and his negligence toward Kay under the school board's radar? That made sense. Dr. Durtan could not risk a board hearing for Robert Anderson. He also could not legitimately "fire" Anderson without the board's involvement. Dr. Durtan allowed the board to believe the resignation was spontaneous and motivated by other employment. Stan Durtan admitted this when he claimed the board knew nothing about the events concerning me until the lawsuit was filed. Had Dr. Durtan been honest with the board, they would have known why Anderson left. Mr. Levin confirmed this when he stated our accusations would be "shown to be totally frivolous…such as the assertions the School Board Defendants had anything to do with the events in this case."

The packet of deposition exhibits contained few new documents, and most of it was extraneous. Intimidation through copious replication. Michael Levin was trying to make Bob Anderson out to be a liar, thus limiting the damage his testimony would do on my behalf.

One of the exhibits I found interesting was the manual from Robert Anderson's training for the SAP program. He had received training before all this took place.

In the Risk Assessment Guidelines (for at risk children), the suggestions were:

- Listen for feelings and help student to clarify them.
- If you determine that the student is at risk (no matter what level) begin linking her up with the next level of resources.
- Encourage the person to seek help from a school counselor, a school psychologist, mental health specialist, minister or someone who can help solve the problems.
- **Offer to set up the first appointment with them.**
- **If need be accompany the student to the next line of assistance.**
- While teachers cannot solve a child's problems...they, nevertheless, can truly make a difference in the child's life.
- Members of the SAP team should not participate in group or individual treatment sessions without the consent of the student.
- Pursuant to federal and state confidentiality regulations, confidential information such as that related to the student's treatment may not be released to a SAP team without the student's written consent. Written or verbal consent from the student's parent(s) will not satisfy the regulations.
- Student Assistance Program personnel receiving client information must be made aware **they are prohibited from re-disclosing the information.**

According to the manual, the WIN team (SAP) was the impediment to helping this suicidal child.

*****

The second deposition was at Anita Albert's office. We were deposing Donald Atkiss, the Uniserv representative (Region Field Director) from PSEA (state union). Mr. Atkiss had spoken a few times with Anita prior to the deposition. In one conversation he told her that Michael Levin had approached him and asked what he intended to say about him. During this phone conversation Atkiss once again repeated the statement Michael Levin made at the Loudermill hearing: **"I can't get her on anything because the principal knew about it."** Anita and Don Atkiss had at least two phone conversations before the deposition. On two separate occasions, the union rep recited this statement. Don Atkiss and I had three conversations in which he recited to me Mr. Levin's Loudermill lament. Keep this in mind.

Anita began her questioning by asking about the Loudermill hearings. She asked Mr. Atkiss how the Loudermill hearings were used. All quotes are directly from the deposition.

> **Atkiss:** It was the whole process itself that I consider to be improper...it followed similar problems...we were not given evidence prior to the hearing, which are procedural violations. And then the end result we think was violative of Sallie's rights.

On Michael Levin's consistent refusal to provide information to the accused teacher:

> **Atkiss:** That's another dispute I have with Mr. Levin...when we are first notified of a Loudermill hearing we would ask for copies of any statements, any evidence, any documentation on which the investigation is based and he routinely refuses to give that to us.

Mr. Atkiss also had issue with the use of "evidence." He cited a case from another district where a woman and a janitor were accused of putting a hat over the lens of a surveillance camera. She was found "guilty" of this charge based on a tape that showed her smiling into the camera. The janitor testified that the woman had nothing to do with placing the hat on the camera. Despite this, Mr. Levin, the district's attorney, found her "guilty." She received a suspension.

Here's a recounting of a Loudermill hearing in a neighboring district. It makes you wonder about the professionalism in these matters:

> **Atkiss**: I tried to take down his (Levin's) opening statement...he would not permit me to do that...I asked him to slow down...and he stood up and we had a screaming match...he accused me of trying to obstruct the process...He turned to the employee and said 'you're suspended without pay until further notice'...it was a

fairly minor incident for a Loudermill hearing...then he walked out...I then attempted to contact him to resume the hearing...he wouldn't open the door to the personnel director's office...I had to slip a note under the door saying we were willing to continue the hearing under protest...we ended up reconvening the hearing after what I considered to be a very childish exchange of letters.

I could not believe this was being said in public. I felt embarrassed for Michael Levin. Care to guess what would happen to a teacher who behaved in this manner?

Mr. Atkiss also testified that he felt the way Mr. Levin conducted the Loudermill hearings was unjust:

> **Atkiss:**...in my opinion, the way the Loudermill hearings are conducted are [sic] not appropriate. In fact, we ended up filing a class action grievance in that district over the Loudermill hearings process itself after they had become, in our opinion, abusive.

Donald Atkiss also stated that in the eight years he had been a Uniserv rep, he did not recall any Loudermill hearings in Wissahickon until mine. He said he was told there had been two others before he came to this region, "which took place around 1995 or prior to that."

The nature of Mr. Levin's Loudermill hearings:

> **Atkiss:** In many cases, the district, through Mr. Levin, is looking to entrap people...entrap people into making inconsistent statements, then discipline them based on those statements.

Donald Atkiss returned to his concern as to how the Loudermill hearings had undergone a remarkable change from the original Supreme Court decision. A major issue was the fact that the district lawyer, Mr. Levin, refused to provide any information prior to the hearing. Mr. Atkiss found this particularly problematic because there was no way of knowing if the exhibits introduced by the district had been doctored or altered.

He further found fault with the method of committing the

hearing to paper. Although he was not a court stenographer, and hardly objective, Mr. Atkiss pointed out that Mr. Levin recorded all the information himself.

Atkiss: Well, I don't like the fact that you take notes of your version of what happens and then ask employees to sign an affidavit of your version.

The deposition became more animated when the Directives Letter was addressed.

Atkiss: It was our opinion that the letter...put restrictions on her that were in violation of her constitutional rights and others under the law. Particularly, she wasn't allowed to speak to parents outside of the school setting...That in our opinion is way out of bounds.

Anita: In your mind was this a disciplinary measure against my client?

Atkiss: Yes...because it put restrictions on her...we considered it to be disciplinary...that's why we filed a grievance. Again, part of the basis of the grievance was they were putting conditions on Sallie, including conditions about her conduct outside of the school that were unreasonable.

Mr. Atkiss elaborated on the Directives Letter.

Atkiss: This is a classic of the difficulty I have with some of the things that Mr. Levin does. This is a setup...to say...you're directed not to engage in any conduct, act, activity with respect to any school district student that is not expressly required or reasonably implied by your job etcetera...you could trip up any teacher in the Commonwealth of Pennsylvania on that statement.

In response to the complaint from the defense that the Directives Letter was being misconstrued:

Atkiss: We understand what it means…if I run into somebody at the supermarket, I'm supposed, before I talk to them have them, sign a statement that I'm acting in my personal capacity…that's absurd in our opinion.

Anita asked Mr. Atkiss if he had any explanation of the reason why the June 3, 2002 "improvement plan" was written after this Loudermill hearing.

Atkiss: …I have an opinion…In our opinion the district could not impose discipline because nothing was done wrong, yet they wanted to-they wanted to impose discipline but they couldn't support it through evidence, so they wrote the letter that was very restrictive, very accusatory, and then called it a non-disciplinary letter. It was a way of disciplining Sallie without, in their opinion, I guess, subjecting it to challenge.

Ms. Alberts asked Mr. Atkiss if he felt any teacher would be able to follow the guidelines of the Directives Letter. She received an emphatic, "no."

My attorney asked about IDEA and other specific rules pertaining to the hearing.

Anita: During the hearing, when Mr. Levin asked Sallie Montanye questions, did he ever allege or state that she had violated any particular rule, regulation, policy or law?

Atkiss: I don't recall any specific statement.

Anita: At any time during the Loudermill hearing, did Mr. Levin discuss or ask questions concerning IDEA and the writing procedures of an IEP?

Atkiss did not recall any mention of IDEA or Special Education Law.

Sidebar: It is *of significance* that Mr. Levin did not ask any questions about Kay's IEP, which was provided, or anything that pertained to Special Education law or procedure during the Loudermill hearing.

IDEA and its fellow statutes did not show up until the lawsuit. Remember they couldn't "get me on anything"; had IDEA been applicable and had I truly violated Kay's civil rights they could have "gotten me" on that. The Directives Letter said, depending on the facts, I *could have* violated Kay's rights. Suddenly, when the district had to justify its actions, I *did* violate her rights. IDEA was dragged out and given a mangled interpretation to cover up the lack of law and reason for what they did. In the world of magic, this is known as a misdirect. IDEA was Michael Levin's legal misdirect.

Attorney Alberts then asked if we were permitted to hear Robert Anderson's testimony.

Anita: Who made you aware of Mr. Anderson's testimony?

Atkiss: I believe Mr. Levin.

Anita: Was Mrs. Montanye allowed to present any witnesses to support her side of the story?

Atkiss: No.

Anita: Did Mr. Levin say anything to the effect that what you [Mrs. Montanye] did was wrong because you put the district in jeopardy of a lawsuit?

Atkiss: Yes…

Anita went to the suppressed letter from Kay's mother:

Anita: Were you aware that Robert Anderson had provided a letter from K's mother to Mr. Sanni and Judy Clark before the hearing started?

Atkiss: No. I was not aware of that.

Anita then asked Mr. Atkiss to recount the discussion that took place in the parking lot at the conclusion of the Loudermill hearing.

Atkiss: That was when he met with us, and he appeared to be frustrated to be honest, and he told us they weren't going to take any disciplinary actions against Sallie…I believe Mr. Levin said to me-because of that [the principal's knowledge of my actions] they couldn't take any action against her.

It was Michael Levin's turn to question Mr. Atkiss. He spent a great deal of time asking about the procedures in the Loudermill hearing. Mr. Levin also posed many questions about the hearings in the neighboring district.

Eventually, Michael Levin turned his attention to the Directives Letter.

Levin: Now you referred to a couple of hypotheticals that you thought were unreasonable in this letter.

Atkiss: I said that the directives were such that she couldn't do that. Any teacher would have violated this. It's a set up. The restrictions placed on her would have required her to report personal conversations in a grocery store.

Levin: And you think that this letter should be interpreted that if there is a chance meeting…

Atkiss [interrupting him] I didn't even get past first base on this letter, Mike, it was just so unreasonable…it's not even worth trying to go through and saying one little piece would be acceptable. It's so outrageous that it is objectionable in its entirety.

Donald Atkiss then addressed the authorship of the Directives Letter.

Atkiss: We were trying to figure out who wrote it because it's not his [Durtan's] writing style; it is yours.

Michael Levin went through a litany of questions to establish that nothing Mr. Atkiss said had any validity because he did not have enough "degrees" or "licenses." Levin to Atkiss:

- Have you attended law school?
- Are you certified as a teacher by any state agency?
- Do you have any teaching degrees?
- Do you have any governmental licenses for any profession?
- Have you ever had any governmental licenses for any profession?
- Have you ever represented any school district or other public school entity in any capacity?
- How many times have you represented a school district in a Special Education case?
- Have you written any books or articles about employee investigation?
- Have you written any books or articles about supervising employees?

The questions went on for pages in that vein. Questions such as these do not elicit information. The constant negative responses are designed to make the one being questioned look and feel inferior.

Of course, when these questions are being shot at you one after another, the most genuine response is defensiveness or just caving in.

But while the questioner was busy disparaging Mr. Atkiss because he lacked Mr. Levin's background, he asked what I considered to be questions laced with unwitting irony.

For example:

- Has any public school district or any other public school entity ever hired you to **advise them with respect to reducing or eliminating legal liability?**
- Are you a **risk analyst?**
- Do you have any training in **assessing risk?**
- Do you consider yourself to be an **expert in assessing risk?**
- Have you ever worked in a **risk management position?**

Too bad Mr. Atkiss couldn't ask Attorney Levin how, despite his *substantial knowledge of risk assessment,* he didn't see my lawsuit coming. Not only didn't he see it coming, he and Dr. Durtan were the ones who created it and brought it on the district. Obviously, Levin's views on the risks he and the superintendent (not the board) were taking were not sound. At no point along the path did Mr. Levin seem to consider that his actions were not legitimate and would possibly beget the very legal action he "feared." All they had to do was drop the Allegations and the Directives Letter. Mr. Levin and Stanley Durtan dragged this district into a five-year federal lawsuit based on lies and administrative arrogance.

Speaking of risk assessment. Aside from all the illegal activities preceding my assistance to Kay and ignoring all the laws violated by Imelda Kormos and the WIN Team, how did Mr. Levin assess the *risk* of a successful suicide attempt by Kay?

Did his clients care about the *risk* they were placing Kay in when they would not allow me or anyone to help her? Why was putting a child's life in jeopardy not considered a *risk*? **Because it's only risky if you have something to lose.** Mr. Levin and the Wissahickon School Board did not view the life that hung in the balance as a *risk* because the outcome would not affect them. After all, "**K's emotional and psychological issues are not matters of public concern...**"

Mr. Levin wanted to establish that he was operating in "good faith." That's the standard cry when a person acts without it.

Levin: As far as you know, our differences of opinion [concerning the Loudermill hearings] are in good faith, right?

Atkiss: Oh, I wouldn't characterize them as that, no.

Levin: Why not?

Atkiss: Because I disagree strongly with the way you run those hearings.

Levin: And you have a good faith disagreement with me, right?

Atkiss: I wouldn't characterize it as good faith, Mike.

Levin: You would not characterize your viewpoints and your opinion about the Loudermill hearing process as being made with good faith?

Atkiss: Mine are, yes.

Levin: But you don't think mine are?

Atkiss: No.

Levin: And what basis do you have for coming to that opinion?

Atkiss: Because I believe that you use that process to violate rights.

An example that Atkiss offered to this was Mr. Levin's blackmailing technique:

Atkiss: In several of the cases, he (Levin) would meet with me and say we're going to suspend somebody for a long period of time unless you reach an agreement (not to grieve the punishment). We'll agree to do two days or one day. In my opinion it's an abusive leverage, if you will, to try and threaten a heavy penalty and then agree to a lighter penalty. It puts the member in a very difficult spot.

Another reason Mr. Atkiss believed that Mr. Levin's operational faith was not "good" was his use of the Loudermill to push teachers out of the district.

Atkiss: You used this process in Joe's case to try to find some way to get him, and in several cases people just resign over that—previously a very good teacher.

Sidebar: Mr. Levin was not a stranger to the idea of people resigning due to Loudermill hearings or the aftermath.

Administrations could and should avoid the embarrassment of first learning exculpatory information during the school board hearing. A confrontation [Loudermill] with the employee has provided benefit analogous to pretrial discovery in judicial proceedings…The school district can also thereby prepare to meet the employee's contentions where the employee, during the pre-hearing investigation denies the truth of the allegations against him.

Translation: The employee has to answer all the questions and provide all information demanded; the school district uses this to build a case against the employee. Conversely, the district does not have to provide any requested information, and, in my case, has the opportunity to manipulate materials to negate any evidence in favor of the employee.

Mr. Levin continues:

Finally, the recommended process has eliminated the necessity for dismissal proceedings in some instances by stimulating the employee to resign rather than face the ignominy of having formal charges filed against him and a public record made of a dismissal cause. (*2002-2003 Pennsylvania School Personnel Actions*, Michael I. Levin, ed.§ 5.2/Chapter 5 Practice Note p 188).

*****

Michael Levin wasted an inordinate amount of time pouring over the contract between the district and the union. Anita sniped that we did not have enough hours left in the day to go through the entire contract. Oh, those billable hours!

Attorney Levin asked a few questions concerning the grievance. He wanted to know who filed it, was it filed on time, and what was the situation pertaining to the grievance as of that date. When told it had been put in abeyance, Levin asked if there were any papers or documents which indicated this was so. I did not understand the implications at this juncture, but I would learn what he meant in time.

Finally, Mr. Levin switched to the "affidavit" he had written for me, allegedly containing accurate quotes from the Loudermill hearing. He wanted Don Atkiss to validate its contents.

Atkiss: I have a problem with the whole concept of it because they are your notes and your version. So you are operating from your version…

Anita stated pointedly that Mr. Levin was testifying, and he was not a party to the case. It was ridiculous to ask Don Atkiss to substantiate a document he did not write, had never seen, and which referred to a meeting that took place two years earlier. I also refused to substantiate the contents of the affidavit. Michael Levin wanted someone to do this.

Lastly, we had the privilege of listening to Michael Levin touting his book: These were his questions/statements:

Levin: One of the resources that you use when you research the law is my textbook on personnel actions, is that correct?

Levin: And PSEA buys copies of that book for the staff, is that correct?

Levin: It is considered to be authoritative and accurate?

Levin: And the lawyers at the PSEA use the book regularly, correct?

One final note to this deposition. Attorney Alberts posed a few questions after Mr. Levin had wrapped up. She asked Don Atkiss if he recalled what Michael Levin had said when he spoke in the huddle in the parking lot after the Loudermill. Mr. Atkiss said he did not recall the **exact** words. Interesting. In five phone conversations, three with me and two with Anita, Donald Atkiss recited the "I can't get her on anything" statement attributed to Michael Levin. You will remember from earlier, the last time he quoted this was only a week before the deposition. Now, under oath, he could not remember this.

I cannot prove that Don Atkiss truly couldn't recall the exact words. The information I had at the time is presented here. I will state for the record there would come a time when he would contradict a previous assertion he had made and I could prove it. I strongly suspected that he was either told to omit this part of his account or decided on his own not to repeat it verbatim. He did a great job of supporting me during the deposition. But his memory lapse, for whatever the reason, caused me worry. The Liz Stanley-Swope incident made me painfully aware the union was not on my side.

CHAPTER EIGHTEEN

Sarah

Dear Judge Dubois:

I am Sallie Montanye and I have a Civil Suit pending before you. Unfortunately, there have been unforeseen problems which have impeded progress in this case.

Ms. Anita Alberts is my attorney of record. In July, we had an appointment to discuss my concerns about the progress of the case. She handed me a letter with a one week ultimatum. After I read the letter, she informed me that she did not intend to wait for a response, that in fact she quit.

I took her at her at her word, and proceeded to look for a new attorney. To this date, I have been unable to obtain counsel.

Ms. Alberts sent me a draft of her petition to withdraw. I do agree this is no longer a productive, professional relationship.

As I have yet to find another attorney, I am at an impasse as to what action to take.

I write to your Honor to clarify the events. I will continue to make every effort possible to procure an attorney. I would appreciate any guidance you wish to offer.

Sallie Montanye
Letter to Judge DuBois
August 28, 2004

We still needed an IDEA expert. Although Michael Levin's first pleading argued that federal law, such as the Rehab Act, **could not apply** to a private individual, Anita believed if I did not produce an expert the court would side with the district's illogical argument that IDEA (federal law) applied to *me* as a private citizen. Apparently contradictions within your own argument do not counter how "things appear". Although it was difficult to accept that anyone would buy into this argument, I still had to spend thousands of dollars for an expert.

I was in a difficult position; no one in the area would testify; they did not relish taking an opposing stance against a school district with whom they worked or may work. There was no doubt that many of the experts feared testifying against a school district. Up to this point I had not realized what a closed community local academia was.

I went looking elsewhere. I contacted Peter Wright, a renowned attorney in Special Education. Peter Wright was a learning disabled child who went on to become one of the top education lawyers, arguing cases for exceptional children.

In 1993, he successfully represented Shannon Carter before the United States Supreme Court. Thirty-four days later, the Court issued a unanimous decision in *Florence County School District v. Shannon Carter*. This was a decision of far reaching impact; it held if a public school defaulted in providing an appropriate education for a disabled child and a private school could provide it, the school district would have to pay for the private education.

I wrote to Peter Wright explaining my situation. He did not respond. I called and spoke with his secretary. She assured me he had received my letter and knew who I was.

I wasn't expecting Mr. Wright to be an expert witness, but I was hoping he could write me a supporting letter and direct me to someone who could testify on my behalf. Surely he would not want to see IDEA reduced to a law that forbids Special Education students from getting help. I could not believe he would not refute the proposition that saving the life of a regular ed child was valiant, but saving the life of a Special Ed child was a civil rights violation.

Reminding Mr. Wright about the incidences which led up to the lawsuit and pointing out that a judge had shaped the complaint into a discrimination case, I sent off letter number two by certified mail:

> If you defend children, then help us, because we are the only voices raised in this area and the district has all the money and power. The only thing we have is the truth and a bunch of kids we care about...
>
> The law is useless if the teachers are frightened into silence and cannot stand up for the children. Without us watching, the law isn't worth the paper it's printed on.

Whether it lacked significance for someone of such repute, or whatever, Mr. Wright did not feel it necessary to reply. Mr. Wright made a good living training parents with his lectures, his boot camp, and his consultation services. As he was crossing the country delivering the message of how to obtain rights for exceptional children, Michael Levin was whittling them down to nothing.

I was back to searching.

While I was conducting my legal expedition, Michael Levin's office was sending out letters to all my experts requesting everything they had ever published, everything they had ever read, every organization or professional group to which they had belonged or did belong, every course they took in all their years of education…and on and on.

What I did not know was that the Levin Legal Group did not have the right to send out such letters at this stage of the proceedings. This request was not to be submitted until the part of discovery that dealt with expert witnesses. There was a designated period reserved exclusively for this. Anita said this was an intimidation tactic. Well, it worked. My SAP program expert was very upset. He did not have publications. He lived quite a distance from our area, and Mr. Levin was demanding that he come to his office for questioning. Also, remember, this would all cost me a great deal of money, as I would have to pay the experts and my attorney for their time. Either way Michael Levin would be successful at causing me harm.

$$*****$$

Lawyers love letters. They love sending them to each other. They must. They produce them by the truckload.

Lawyer letters have a pattern. The first line or lines start out by thanking the other attorney for whatever letter he is responding to. He lets the attorney know when he received it. He is gracious.

If he is writing an angry or rebuttal letter, in the next paragraph he launches into his argument that refutes, disparages and belittles whatever the initial letter contained and with which he takes great, indignant exception. If he is merely irritated, he ends on a light, snippy note. If he is considerably agitated, he threatens to do harm to the other's reputation. All of this is laced with protestations of the profusion of his integrity and the other's appalling lack of it. He ends with a "thank you" and signs off with "sincerely."

There were many letters that flew back and forth between Anita Alberts and Michael Levin. One of these was the Stipulation letter. Michael Levin was demanding that a letter be written to establish guidelines for using student information. His suggestion was a three-page, jargon-laden explanation of how and why the information would be used. Anita did not agree to this because the wording was intimidating and slanted in favor of the district. We did not need this stipulation because we had permission from the parents and the students to use whatever records we needed. It was the *district* that did not have permission.

Anita bristled at Levin and he seethed back at her. The judge had left it up to the attorneys to arrive at a solution. It was a motion before the court. Mr. Levin suggested that until it was resolved the records would be redacted. The records were redacted. That's how they were handled for the entire case. The motion just faded into obscurity. I point this out because much of the arguing on matters was later jettisoned, which indicates that it was not deemed important, just fodder for delay.

There was another set of letters dealing with my Family Medical Leave time. Levin misinterpreted Anita's response; he was so furious that he accused her of being illogical and irrational, and threatened to "report her to the Ethics Board." (Letter 5/20/03) This shook her. As seasoned as she was, she was unaccustomed to being subjected to such threats. As I said, the letters were numerous and nasty.

*****

I performed a number of legal jobs with Anita's blessings. When we received piles of papers from Michael Levin, she instructed me to go through them and filter out the relevant ones. I helped write the affidavits for some of our witnesses. I wrote up the witness list with the annotations as to what these witnesses would contribute to the case. I wrote suggestions for two sets of interrogatories.

In July (2004) Anita interviewed Joe for approximately two hours. She spent most of the time asking Joe about a disagreement he had had with an instructor during a two day Wilson training session. Joe's argument with the presenter did not have any connection with Special Education. Anita was annoyed with my interruptions;

however, I did not feel she was pursuing a line of questioning which would be useful. Joe's major contribution to my case was the illegal use of the Loudermill and the obvious Special Education violations on the part of Michael Levin and the school district. These were never broached during the discussion.

Joe and I went to lunch. He spoke honestly; he had strong concerns about my attorney and where the case was headed. I was terrified to say anything because time was running out and I did not have another lawyer. I did not know what to do or how to do it. I didn't want to do anything to hurt the case and was not sure enough of myself to rely on my own instincts.

I called Anita the next day to talk. I was worried, no petrified, because we had only one deposition to our name. Anita told me that she was only going to depose Stanley Durtan in addition to Donald Atkiss. The Atkiss deposition was a bone of contention. Anita said it was vital to our case. I was not so sure. Atkiss's deposition went to Michael Levin's illegal and questionable tactics; however, it did not establish that the district used it against me for reasons of discrimination because he was unable to address any Spec Ed issues.

According to Anita, we would not need to question anyone else. I did not see this as being sufficient. Anita informed me we would not need the records of any students. That struck me as seriously dangerous. Kay's records proved she was the victim of negligence. I had other students as witnesses who had a history of neglect or abuse at the hands of Wissahickon. Our contention was that WSD was using the argument of Spec Ed law as a pretext to cover their illegal actions. In order to prove their willingness to ignore law in other cases, I would *need* other cases. The district could have countered by saying Kay's situation was a fluke. This would be less disputable if I provided more than a few examples of legal violations being the usual practice. Furthermore, Anita had made some sweeping statements about minorities and non-English speaking students. How could we prove these if we did not have the records?

We made an appointment for the following Monday.

After ten minutes or so, I was escorted into her office. She handed me a letter, told me to read it, and then leave her office. The letter stated her feelings about the case and me. It also gave me an ultimatum: I had until the next Friday to decide if I wanted to keep Anita as my attorney. We had a discussion that did not turn out well, and Anita said she wanted out of the case.

I left the office crushed. I thought we had a good relationship. When I was working on the case, it was at her instruction. I thought we were fighting this together. I never pretended to know the law or to argue it. I provided information about Spec Ed and the practices in WSD. I researched Spec Ed law for her. I did not challenge her decisions; although, I was very worried about some of them.

I felt I had a right to be concerned. We had one deposition. Anita had never spoken to Kay or her mother. She was only going to depose Stanley Durtan. She was not going to use any student records. The records that would have supported our claims.

In a letter she sent me the next week, Anita gave me her interpretation of what had happened. She told me that she would need the name of my new counsel in order to request permission to withdraw from the case.

Anita was a bright and successful attorney; however, I had lost confidence because she was veering off in a direction that was difficult to prove, and one that was not centered on the real questions of the case.

When the judge dismissed the First Amendment case, Anita told me she was not sure she could take the case further because of the educational arguments, as she was not well versed in this area. Part of my involvement was that I was knowledgeable in this. I also stressed that discrimination existed specifically toward Emotional Support children and there was plenty of proof to substantiate this. There was a definitive link between discrimination against these children and their teachers who are put in direct opposition to the district's lack of services and programs.

Anita kept calling me. I would not answer the phone. I avoided her because I did not know what to say. I had no one who could advise me. I cringed every time the phone rang. I was sick to my stomach with every trip to the mailbox because she was sending me letters with great regularity. This case had been extremely emotionally demanding, and I did not need to add physical and mental stress caused by dissension between my lawyer and me.

I was distressed at the lack of documents we received for discovery. We only had a few items, and they were not particularly germane. I was well aware that I was not an attorney;

however, I knew that we did not have enough information to combat Michael Levin and his mountains of papers. We could not go to court and claim the district violated children's rights without some form of proof. We made these claims in the pleadings; we needed something to back them up.

Anita had also told me that she had decided we would not need any experts other than the vocational and economic expert. She did have a report from Dr. Higgins (SAP expert), but his testimony only addressed the WIN team. He was not an expert on IDEA. I thought that this was very chancy given that Mr. Levin was intending on having a cast of thousands for experts. We would need someone to counter their arguments. We had no one.

Anita sent me a letter:

Enclosed is a partial draft of a Petition to Withdraw, which must be filed with the Court. It must also be served to Michael Levin which would give him great pleasure...It will be difficult finding an attorney who understands this case and would be willing to undertake it on a contingent fee halfway through litigation. I do not want to prejudice your interests and I also have invested a considerable amount of time and energy in this matter. We appear to have Levin where we want him, i.e. worried, with hands shaking.

I am not sure what gave rise to this observation. True, Levin seemed unnerved at the deposition of Donald Atkiss, but he had sufficiently recovered and was back to his old form.

The letter ended by saying: "She could not give me professional representation when there was so much dissension between us."

I suspected that some of the aspects of the case upset Anita. She had never lost a prima facie case on a Motion to Dismiss. This was a first. It was a major emotional set back. In addition, Anita was a "believer." In other words, she truly had faith in the sanctity of the Constitution. She also was burdened by a strong belief in the legal system. She had a commitment to the law and its meaning in society.

Anita was a sole practitioner. That meant that every case she handled had to have some remunerative value or else the rent did not get paid. When you charge $300 per hour and spend 100 hours on pro bono work, that is a loss of $30,000. If you are the only one shouldering the expenses, this has quite an impact. Anita was also not making money from my case: nevertheless, she was spending a great deal of time on it.

The most important point to remember is Anita gave this case credence. She breathed life into it. For that I was extremely grateful. Sometimes the attorney who starts the case is not the one who finishes it. It was what it was.

I started another search. I had no doubt in my mind that I would find someone to take the case now that a judge had accepted it. This was a hot case, and I was going to bequeath it upon some well-deserving attorney who was committed to truth, justice, and the American way. This delusional thinking died a quick and painful death while I was out pounding the streets looking for representation. It was worse the second time around because I had to convince someone to take the case when it had already been defined by another attorney's work.

Many lawyers don't look favorably on clients who are shopping for new representation. They suspect the person is lying about what went wrong or that the case was a loser to begin with. Some lawyers do not want to be saddled with another lawyer's parameters.

In addition, I had to let the judge know that the case had to be suspended until I engaged another attorney. I hadn't the foggiest idea how to accomplish this. No one could give me advice because no one I knew had any experience with the legal industry. I wrote the judge a letter explaining my situation and that I needed more time to find a new lawyer. He extended the hearing for thirty days. When I did go to court, I would have to state why Anita and I were no longer working together. It would be up to the judge to grant her leave of the case. Great. Not only could I not find a lawyer, I would have to show up in court without one.

I spent my days calling attorneys. I spent my nights quaking in fear.

My first interview was with a partner in a law firm of two, which specialized in litigation. This meant they did not settle most cases; they went to trial. My kind of legal eagles. I met with Sam in July. Like those before him, he echoed the familiar refrain: why would anyone possibly want to do this to a teacher who helped a student?

Sam said he would have to speak with his partner who was on vacation for another week. He also said that my case was legally frightening: because if I won, the floodgates would open. Once people found out what was taking place and once community members started inspecting their districts, he felt there would be a reckoning. Kind of a Spec Ed Pandora's box. Of course, none of this had any bearing if I couldn't get the case into a courtroom.

Two weeks later, Sam told me he and his partner felt my case was too time consuming and they would not be able to handle it. I am not sure if my need for a contingency agreement had any influence in this decision. I suspect it did.

Anita sent me another communication. She advised me of the hours she had spent on the case and that she wanted me to pay her the enclosed Statement of Costs (about $90,000) if I no longer wanted her services.

I traveled to Lancaster to meet with another attorney. She looked at the Third Amended Complaint, announced that it was disorganized and that the judge obviously had to connect the dots. She told me to call her with certain information. I called her; she was not in. I left the information with her secretary. I called everyday for the following week. I received a letter from this attorney telling me she was not interested in the case because she never took contingency cases. She then proceeded to chastise me because I did not "call her" with the information she requested.

Then there were the ones who just blew me off on the phone.

- My case was "stupid."
- I didn't have a case.
- Just because a judge accepted it, didn't make it a case. Judges are idiots.
- I could get help if I had $60,000 as a down payment.
- I should go back to work and keep quiet.
- I didn't stand a chance against a school district.
- No one cares what happens to teachers.
- No one likes teachers.
- Juries don't care about dead kids; they care about their taxes being raised.

- Special Education students are of no interest to the general public.
- Bullying was just the cause of the week.
- Not a school's problem if a kid kills herself.
- I was wasting my time and money.
- We only take cases that are important.

Eventually, I called a practice one of the other lawyers had recommended. I was put on hold. A minute later, a man answered the phone. It was not the name of the person I was to talk to, but I assumed this was the person designated to deal with me. Jeff listened to the story. He would read over the complaints and the judge's decision. He would get back to me.

Surprise! He did call. He was unable to take the case because the partners voted against it. He had spent the entire Labor Day reading every paper from the case. He made statements I would hear many times:

The judge's decision to dismiss the First Amendment case made no sense. It was illogical and disjointed. His honor did not take into account any of our points, relied entirely on Levin's interpretation and used outdated and inapplicable case law to justify his decision.

Jeff then explained step by step how I had to sell the case to get a lawyer. He took over an hour "training" me. The irony of our meeting was that Jeff had answered the wrong phone. He was not supposed to have picked up the line I was on. No such thing as coincidence.

Armed with my new approach, I called an attorney in nearby Glenside. Her write up included a Special Education background.

I sat impatiently waiting for Sarah Dragotta to meet with me. She was on a conference call. When she was done, I was ushered into her very small office. I told her my story á la Jeff's instructions. She did the devil's advocate thing. Sarah kept trying to offer me viable reasons for the actions the district had taken. I was tired of hearing they had their reasons. They didn't. Their outrageous statements proved this.

I had people coming for dinner that night, and I was tired of wasting my time with the same old recitation. I told her about the hearing before the judge, which hung over me. Attorney Dragotta offered some suggestions: say as little as possible and stick to the basic facts. She wished me luck. I needed more than luck.

The two weeks flew by, and I was no further along in my search. Let's put this on the terror spectrum. I was going into a federal court, before a federal judge with Michael Levin on one side and Anita Alberts on the other. *Seriously awkward and considerably frightening, to say the least.*

The night before the hearing, I had a voice message on my cell from Sarah Dragotta. She was interested in the case and wanted to know if I would mind if she came to the hearing. IF she came to the hearing!!

"Sure," I said. "You're more than welcome." (I was in stroke territory by this point.) I did not shriek until I pushed the end call button. Sarah didn't say she would take the case, but at least I wasn't walking into that courtroom alone.

The federal courthouse is imposing because it is the federal courthouse. When you enter large, somber buildings, with no idea of where to go, you become small and intimidated. I ran into Anita in the lobby. This was of little comfort. She was angry with me. She had been holding Mr. Levin off as long as she could before telling him she was no longer representing me. When Mr. Levin learned what was taking place, he blasted her with one of his trademark nasty lawyer letters.

Before the judge entered, Sarah Dragotta came in. She took a seat behind us. The judge walked in with all the pomp accorded the position. If people knew the truth about many of these professionals, they would question their entitlement to this obligatory show of esteem.

The judge is merely a human being, given not only to mistakes, but corruption. Nevertheless, federal judges have their jobs for life. They cannot be challenged for the most part; they have to commit some disgusting act before they are relieved of their positions. If they make horrendous decisions that don't follow law, they remain unscathed. No matter how outrageous a decision, no matter how far it strays from legal practice, even if it makes no sense whatsoever, federal judges, who are appointed as a political pay back, stay safely ensconced in their imposing, black leather chairs. It has nothing to do with talent or skill. It has to do with a politician owing a favor to someone and with a system that protects its own.

The judge asked Anita to explain her request for withdrawal. Anita informed the court:

I have filed a petition for leave to withdraw as plaintiff's counsel. I believe that Mrs. Montanye and I mutually respect each other but we disagree on the expectations for the outcome of this case and strategy as to how to get there. And we've tried to repair our disagreements and it hasn't worked.

I listened as she spoke. Her voice was wavering. I could feel her shaking while she was speaking. I wondered if she was worried about what I was going to say. We had never discussed this.

The judge made his speech about the "test for withdrawal." An attorney can be granted leave if the client no longer accepts the recommendations of the attorney, and the attorney has decided that he or she cannot proceed. He asked Anita if that was where she found herself. She told him she believed so.

His honor then took a moment to comment on his surprise at this turn of events. He told Anita:

...this is a difficult case...and some lawyers like to back out of cases when they find them difficult. You are not such a lawyer. You have not had a case in my court which I would characterize as easy...they've all been difficult. And you've been steadfast and stuck through them to the end; in some cases I know it must have been difficult. So this is an unusual motion, at least from my perspective, for you.

Anita agreed, saying, "It's the first time I've filed one, your honor." We were just breaking all sorts of records.

He said he would not dismiss the case. He would give me a "reasonable amount of time to obtain an attorney." He continued:

I'm concerned with case management, although I think we've finished with everything in the case. Well maybe not...I know I've written a lot in this case but I'm not so sure my opinions have all dealt with the myriad of complaints that you filed. Are we at the summary judgment stage yet?

Summary judgment comes after discovery is completed. There are a number of steps taken after discovery that precede summary judgment. Summary judgment is the last decision as to whether the case will go to trial or not. I guess the judge didn't do a once over of the case before coming into the courtroom.

Michael Levin volunteered we had not reached summary judgment. He told the judge that we were in discovery, "and once this problem surfaced, we kind of put discovery on hold."

The judge and Levin then had to hash over the confidentiality issue. Michael Levin pointed out this had been put temporarily aside because of "this matter." Considering Anita said we were not going to use student records and Mr. Levin claimed they were not intending to do so, these people were pretty preoccupied with this non-matter.

Finally, the judge asked me what my opinion was of my relationship with Anita. I could "tell him anything" I wanted that related to the motion. I told him I agreed with everything Ms. Albert's said.

The judge said he would give me some time to find another attorney. He looked beyond us to Sarah and asked, "I gather Ms. Dragotta, is that?"

Sarah perked up, "Yes, your honor."

Sarah said she was considering taking over the case. The judge said he would give her a reasonable amount of time to get acquainted with it.

Then these words boomed out: "Ms. Dragotta, are you a member of this Court?"

Sarah's answer resounded off the walls of Courtroom 12-B, coming to my ears in an aural slow-motion echo: "No your honor. I'm actually a new member of the bar, I was admitted in 2002, and I have not come to this court yet."

I wanted to sink into the floor. Levin was on the other side of the room, jumping and clicking his heels for joy. Easy pickins! Anita was tittering; she told me I wouldn't find someone else to take this case.

Sarah was just taking the bar exam while Wissahickon was putting me through a Loudermill hearing.

What the hell else could go wrong?

The judge and Sarah conversed a while longer about Sarah being admitted to federal court and what she had reviewed pertinent to the case. He suggested she read the entire file. He was instructing her to read all the pages? She was an attorney, not a first grader.

He then asked Anita what her plans were for turning over the file. Anita provided the answer: "I'd be glad to turn over the file to anyone who wants this case, your honor."

Anita and the judge discussed her fee. She said she had a great deal of time in the case and wanted to be reimbursed for her efforts. She planned to apply an attorney's lien to the case, meaning she would get paid from any amount we would win. Her fee would come before Sarah's.

The judge said that Anita had done extensive work after the first Motion to Dismiss had been granted. The judge then said he couldn't remember some of the pleadings but he had "read all the opinions, re-read the opinions that I've issued." He then said he thought, "The claim was still alive." He *thought* the claim was still alive? What were we doing in this courtroom if the claim was not alive? I wouldn't need an attorney, nor would we need more time if the claim were dead.

Here was part of the exchange:

Judge: I think that claim is still alive. Am I correct Ms. Alberts?

Anita: I'm not sure which one you're talking about

Judge: I'm talking about the second, the third amended...

Anita: On the third amended complaint, yes

Judge: So whatever, well, I guess there was a second amended complaint.

He seemed confused. He went on about the time line and how he would give us additional time if we needed it.

Then he turned his attention to Michael Levin, who had violated the court's regulations and now the judge was calling him on it.

Judge: One word to you, Mr. Levin. You got the impression I was not pleased with...

Levin: Yes, sir.

Judge: What happened with the experts? I'm not sure it was intentional, I think maybe that's the way you operate, but I don't operate that way and I never did as a lawyer. And I'm very concerned about contacts with expert witnesses.

Levin: Well, we really didn't have any contact.

Judge: Yes, you did, you served a subpoena. That's contact. See, if you had no contact the expert witnesses would not know who Levin, Michael I. is, but they know because you served them with a subpoena which has the effect, just in case you didn't know, of *chilling a witness' ardor to participate in a case* and particularly if they're told they have to produce something, particularly since under the rules you were entitled to that information on the schedule that I set forth in my scheduling order. You were going to get it. The subpoena was out of order and I want you to know that.

Michael Levin had sent subpoenas to my experts before the time of discovery for expert witnesses. He jumped the gun. The judge was not sure if this was "intentional?" Just what did the judge think it was? As Mr. Levin pointed out at my Loudermill hearing, he had been doing this for more than twenty-nine years. But, Mr. Levin did not know not to contact expert witnesses until the discovery time allotted for expert witnesses? This was not Mr. Levin's first federal rodeo. Surely, something as elemental as this should not be so confusing.

The judge knew why attorneys do this. They do it to scare the expert witnesses so they back out. Michael Levin, who deliberately sent out premature subpoenas for the unethical purpose of scaring away my witnesses, was being told he was out of order? Michal Levin violated rules of the court, with deliberation. His unethical behavior resulted in some of my experts leaving, and the best this judge could say was Levin was out of order. Why bother to have rules if they are not applied? This was foreshadowing. This judge was extremely liberal with Levin's behavior. Slapping the hands of people like Michael Levin demeans the rules, skews the case, and reveals the arbitrary application of regulations. What's the point of having these guidelines if they can be ignored with no consequence?

His honor announced that he wouldn't tolerate the acrimony that had built up in this case. Then after lecturing about sanctions and how he **wasn't** going to impose them, the judge said he "was not going to tolerate that." His reference was cryptic because he had been discussing sanctions. He then cleared up his lack of toleration with, "There will be no interfering with expert witnesses." I have news for this judge; not only had he tolerated this interference, he *allowed* Levin to interfere and refused to do anything more than comment on this. No sanctions. No reprisal.

Michael Levin "apologized" to the court. The judge then made him "apologize" to Anita.

There was discussion about mediation. Judges are big on this because it saves money, and better than that, it decreases their workload. Approximately fifty percent of all cases are settled or resolved through mediation. When the judge was discussing settlement, Anita chimed in that I had not agreed to this. Did she not recall Michael Levin's responses to her settlement offers? They were loud and clear no's. First, Levin said they would not remove the allegations or the Directives Letter. The next overture Anita made was during the phone conference when Michael Levin said his carrier (insurance company) had not given him permission to discuss any settlement. Whether I liked the idea of settlement or not, Michael Levin and the Wissahickon School District were not interested.

Levin and Anita had sent a mutually agreed upon letter to the judge addressing the question of settlement. It was on Anita's stationery, signed by both of them. It read:

> In light of the pending petition for leave to withdraw I am unable to represent to the Court that my client agrees to a settlement conference before a Magistrate Judge or mediation.

This was news to me. Anita had spoken about mediation; however, she had never suggested we do it, nor had I nixed the idea. She told me that somewhere down the line we would have to do this. She maintained throughout that Levin would not discuss settlement. I could go back to work and live with the Directives

Letter. That was the extent of Michael Levin's interest in resolution. Anita's interpretation of my preventing these talks was off base. She did not refuse to take part in settlement agreements because I had nixed the idea. I was beginning to wonder if there was something in the air that affected the reasoning ability of some of those with a law degree.

The judge asked Michael Levin if his clients would be willing to "approach this undertaking (mediation) in good faith." Of course, Mr. Levin assured the judge they would only operate in good faith. I felt uneasy. I was concerned that the spiritual force in the universe would be so offended by Levin's string of aspersions, it just might send a thunderbolt down through the ceiling in good old smiting fashion. I didn't want to be standing too close when this happened.

Sarah, Anita, and I rode the elevator twelve floors down. It was an exceptionally uncomfortable ride. Sarah was enthusiastically asking Anita questions about private practice. Anita was giving curt answers. They were the kind intended to shut down the questioner, but Sarah, not one to be easily put off, continued her spirited conversation with Anita. After an eternity and a half, we arrived at floor level.

Anita Alberts told Sarah to call her and arrange to get all the materials from the case. She gave me a quick kiss good-by and told me to be well. I needed some air desperately.

Sarah and I sat outside at 601 Market Street and spoke about our plans. She said she was sure she wanted the case. Her exact words were, she would be "honored" to represent me. (HONORED!!!) I was dumbfounded. When I finally figured out how to form words, I told her another attorney had expressed an interest. I just wanted a few days to relish the idea that two people said I had a viable case and they wanted to take it. It was a pretty heady feeling, one I wasn't used to it.

What I said was true. A week after I met Sarah, and two weeks before the hearing, I met with Chris, an attorney who had been referred to me. Chris was enthusiastic. After the hearing, he called. I told him how it had gone. I also told him I was going to use Sarah to represent me. Chris told me if it didn't work out with Sarah I should give him a call. He then said, if he had enough money, he would get rid of all his cases just so he could take this one. This time I was the one who felt honored.

I called Sarah and said it was a go. She thanked me for having faith in her. She also told me the attorney who rented her space in his building was a Harvard graduate and would be helping with the case. I remembered meeting the Harvard graduate the first time I met Sarah. He was wearing work clothes spotted with tar. He had been fixing the roof. He had a stentorian voice and towered over us. He was exceptionally intelligent and could still fix his own roof. Apparently, Harvard hadn't ruined him.

Now it was the three of us; petite, untried Sarah, tall commanding Attorney David Brooks, and I. We were off to make the world a safer place for troubled kids.

*****

On October 7, 2004, I watched as Sarah was sworn in as a member of the Federal Court. I knew in my heart that she was sincere about her promise to uphold the law and the honor of the court. Given my experience, the court was getting the better part of the deal. From my perspective, the law had little to do with what went on in the court, and I certainly had seen little evidence of anything analogous to honor.

I told Sarah that day, and many times after, that I was sure Michael Levin was chuckling in his contemptuous manner that she (a newbie) was the best I could do. Damn straight. I could not have done any better.

CHAPTER NINETEEN

Boundaries

And make no mistake, as these EducRAT$ model bullying to our children, our children learn that bullying… is the way for them too! Each time you hear about a bullied student hanging himself, know that this was a student crying out for help from this toxic system…Read one of many stories about educators being ordered to cover up bullying because those running our schools need the public to think they care about children…"The EducRAT$' Way to Deal with Suicidal Students: Pretend You Don't Know!",…Sallie Montanye's PA story about how she was harassed for helping her suicidal student because "helping a student not commit suicide was not in this student's IEP." It doesn't get much more ruthless than that…This is so much more than workplace abuse against teachers; this is the destruction of the American dream in progress.

Karen Horwitz, President, NAPTA

Once Sarah Dragotta took over the case we were back on the discovery track.

We had quite a number of depositions that proved most enlightening. I will let these people *speak for themselves, in their own, recorded, sworn testimony.*

MARIA SALVUCCI DEPOSITION
February 23, 2005
School Guidance Counselor/Leader of the WIN team

Maria Salvucci began her deposition by assuring Sarah she would "tell the truth."

Ms. Salvucci offered that the "WIN team got its information through observable behavior from members of the team… and emails received by one of the team members." Apparently, I had been under observation by the members of the team. Although nothing was recorded, the principal was "told" about my activities. Imelda Kormos (school nurse) and Judy (guidance counselor) reported me to the administrators. What did they report? "Seeing Ms. Montanye outside the school building with K on the front lawn…"

When Attorney Dragotta asked how the information of my observable behaviors came to Ms. Salvucci, she snapped, "*It* came to the **WIN** team …we had a team meeting and we discussed it." She couldn't remember the date of this meeting, but she knew they had one. My *non-observable* behavior was information Imelda Kormos got from K's mother and relayed to the team.

Imelda Kormos "reported to the team." In other words, in violation of state mental health laws, Mel Kormos discussed confidential information, without consent, to the WIN team for the purpose of stopping me from helping my student. Ms. Salvucci and the WIN members did not detect a problem with this.

Maria Salvucci wanted to make something perfectly clear; she "did not write the letter, the team did."

It was not me …it was the WIN team…And the WIN team are the people that got together when behaviors were increasing, when things were taken to administration and nothing changed and then the therapy sessions started.

Let's clear this up right now. The WIN team letter was dated **March 19th**. The last time I had gone with Kay to the therapist was the end of February. Thus, the WIN team was responding to Imelda Kormos's gossip and the fact that I had been seen "talking with Kay."

Maria Salvucci told Sarah about the "incident" where I was seen sitting on the grass listening to Kay. That was the only "incident" she was aware of. Ms. Salvucci did not know if this was the same "incident" reported to Principal Anderson by Imelda Kormos or reported by Angie, K's guidance counselor.

According to Ms. Salvucci, this information about the "incident" was presented at a WIN team meeting. She "couldn't recall" who told the team. Naturally, there were no notes taken to support what allegedly had taken place.

Here's Maria Salvucci's rendition of how the WIN team letter came to be:

Salvucci: ...people presented what they knew and that's what resulted in the letter.

Attorney Dragotta: Was the letter written at that meeting?

Salvucci: No, ideas were formulated.

Attorney Dragotta: Were those ideas written down?

Salvucci: I believe so.

Attorney Dragotta: Would there be a log of that WIN team meeting?

Salvucci: No.

Attorney Dragotta: ...how soon after that meeting was this WIN team letter written?

Salvucci:...maybe a week later.

Attorney Dragotta: And do you know who typed this letter?

Salvucci: I typed it.

Attorney Dragotta: And to what did you refer when you typed that letter?

Salvucci: Notes that I had gathered from the meeting.

Strange, she *believed* there were notes taken but she *knows* she used them. Maria Salvucci typed it then took the letter back and read it to the WIN team. She couldn't "recall exactly" what had to be changed, but she did know there was a correction that had to be made so she re-typed the letter. Remember the team members, other than Imelda Kormos, told Robert Anderson they had no knowledge of a letter being written.

When asked if anyone ever bothered to speak with me, Ms. Salvucci said she didn't know. When asked who decided that a letter should be written to Robert Anderson, Ms. Salvucci stated that it was the idea of Thomas Speakman, the assistant principal. Mr. Speakman was one of the people who told Robert Anderson he was not aware a letter had been written.

Maria Salvucci then went on to explain that I **had to be stopped** because someone had "to set some boundaries between a teacher and a student."

Attorney Dragotta: What kind of boundaries?

Salvucci: Where a teacher is not in a therapeutic relationship with a student.

When asked how Ms. Salvucci *knew* it was a therapeutic relationship, she offered "when a teacher is seen a number of times talking with a student or when she takes them to therapy." One would think taking Kay to a therapist was an indicator that I felt I was not qualified to give her therapy.

Maria Salvucci then listed the steps taken after a child is referred to the WIN team. She also explained that the IEP team was a different entity and therefore not privy to WIN team information. She stated that confidentiality prevented the team from telling anyone that Kay was suicidal. This is ridiculous, as you know.

Then there was a discussion of the "log" which was to be filled out on each student. There were six entries on the log. Here they are:

9/5   Police report student held knife to her throat. Intervention planned.

9/11   Meeting w/parents who down played knife situation. Blamed trouble on middle school...under psys[sic] care. **K doesn't want forms released.** Debating on Spec placement.

Most of this was unintelligible. When questioned, Ms. Salvucci could not say whether Kay was seeing a psychologist or psychiatrist. She did not know what forms were being addressed and the "Spec" placement could not be explained.

2/12   Was picked up by the police and arrested—Mom looking into having committed to Norristown St.

She was *not* arrested. Mrs. Kormos and the WIN team got this wrong.

2/14   Supposed to be released on Fri. from Norrist.St

3/12   As per Bob Anderson K to see Kathleen M; (Drop-in Center counselor) refused to come. Instead sitting outside w/ Sally [sic] M.

Here was proof that Kay would not speak with the counselors, and yet Dr. Durtan kept saying I should have had her speak with them.

3/14   Admitted to Abington ER

Heaven only knows for what. This was the extensive log kept on Kay. This was all the information they had on her. The one other form that should have been a record of behaviors, grades, and teacher observations was blank, except for her name in the upper corner.

Maria Salvucci admitted:

- She had never attended any special meeting concerning Kay.
- She had never met Kay.
- She had never spoken to Kay.
- She had never met Kay's mother.
- She had never spoken to Kay's mother.
- She had never spoken to me about Kay.
- She had never spoken to Kay's IEP case manager.

- She had no idea of Kay's history prior to coming to the high school.

Ms. Salvucci alleged she had not seen the suicide note after Robert Anderson left it at guidance. The first time she saw it was when Stacy Smith [Levin Legal Group] came to prep her for the deposition. Strange how both she and Nurse Kormos never saw this note.

Then Ms. Salvucci took the tried and true method of accepting accountability. She blamed Angie, Kay's guidance counselor, for the lapse in care. The WIN team leader knew nothing about Kay or her history, nor did she feel compelled to find any of this out.

Salvucci: K's guidance case (manager) Angie, who was not sitting on the team, was her counselor. The person that is aware of the IEP for each of the students is their current counselor. So Angie...even though she was not sitting on the team, would have been aware of this as a need in her IEP (referring to the line in the IEP about K becoming overwhelmed.)

Ms. Salvucci continued to throw Kay's guidance counselor and her colleague under the bus:

Attorney Dragotta: Was there a specific procedure in disseminating information from the WIN team to the IEP team?

Salvucci: There was no specific procedure. And as I stated before, often the school counselor would be the person to talk to the people that needed to know if there was something that was needed to know.

Attorney Dragotta: And if the information was discussed about a particular student who was a Special Education student and that student's counselor wasn't there, how would that information get to the IEP team or the student's counselor?

Salvucci: The school counselor would ask one of the team members or come to another team meeting...or one of the team members would tell the counselor what was happening.

Talk about falling through the cracks.

Although Ms. Salvucci said that she considered the note from Kay a "suicide note," she was shakier on Kay's mental health.

Salvucci: I cannot speak to her mental health...

Attorney Dragotta: How about at the start of the school year, entry 9/5/01 student had held a knife to her throat, would that be a suicidal attempt?

Salvucci: Possibly, yes

Attorney Dragotta: What else would it be if it wasn't a suicidal attempt? What would you consider a student holding a knife to her throat---

Salvucci: It's a suicidal attempt.

Attorney Dragotta: ...if the WIN team felt that a Special Education student needed counseling, would that counseling be provided for the student within the school day or would the WIN team recommend that the student go outside of the school day?

Salvucci: Outside of the school day.

Remember IDEA says children with therapeutic needs should (but didn't) receive therapy as a **related service?** And why must WSD children receive outside therapy?

Salvucci: Because none of us, as far as the counselors within the school system are trained as therapists.

So I was wrong because I didn't make Kay see someone who **was not** a therapist, but I was also wrong because I got her to someone who **was** a therapist?

Ms. Salvucci stated that "files" were kept on each student for monitoring purposes. She had no reason to offer as to why Kay was an exception to this.

The last questions held some zingers. One of my witnesses was a boy named J. Although the WIN team discussed him at length (again Imelda Kormos), he was not a WIN team student. Therefore, discussing him was gossip, not assistance.

Attorney Dragotta: was J referred to the WIN team?

Salvucci: No.

About me "giving therapy":

Attorney Dragotta: Any other serious repercussions?

Salvucci: A student's mental health. If you have an unqualified person counseling and giving therapy to a student, then an untrained person ---I am not qualified to do psychotherapy with a student...

Attorney Dragotta: To whom were you referring when you said an unqualified person?

Salvucci: Ms. Montanye

When asked if I "counseled" Kay, all Salvucci could offer was that I "crossed the boundaries with this student as far as the WIN team observed."

Finally, when Michael Levin asked Maria Salvucci if the WIN team had any contact with Kay after her stay at MCES, she stated that there was no longer any cause or need for intervention by the WIN team. Why? Because **"she was in the mental health system by this point."** So there you have it—under oath—Ms. Salvucci explains why the WIN team really had no active involvement with Kay. **She was in the mental health system.** Once that happens the WIN team is not a component in the child's treatment.

Someone needed to explain this to Stanley Durtan. **Kay WAS IN THE MENTAL HEALTH SYSTEM BEFORE COMING TO THE HIGH SCHOOL.** Maybe that's why the WIN team ignored her, but this slipped Ms. Salvucci's mind in her zeal to prevent me from helping this girl.

Imelda (Mel) Kormos Deposition
February 18, 2005
School Nurse/WIN team member

Ms. Kormos informed Sarah that she knew I was suing the school district because

I was "not happy with the discipline I was given."

Ms. Kormos was then asked about her background.
She took student assistance training in about 1990 and remained on the WIN team until she retired in 2002. "That became a **major** part of my job." In addition she took courses on "suicide" and on "children at risk." She was also coordinator of nursing services for the district. Ms. Kormos stated that she was able to assess children at risk. She would know the signs and symptoms of a student who had a drug or alcohol problem. She did not diagnose the problem, but she would be aware there was one. It got more interesting when the subject of suicide came up.

> **Attorney Dragotta:** ...what would be some signs and symptoms of a high school student who had suicidal tendencies?

> **Kormos:** Well we had ---would have---on occasion we had other students that would tell us, somebody talked about suicide. We would have a student that had written a note, given a note to someone. We could–basically those were the, you know, or the child himself and they talked about it to a friend or to a teacher.

She denied getting K's suicide note from Robert Anderson. "I know I didn't." She identified the WIN team log page but said she had never seen the one filled out about Kay. The nurse also incorrectly stated that Maria Salvucci made all the entries on Kay's log. (She did not.)

She was foggy on the log entries.

Kormos: And honestly I did not remember the first part until I saw it now.

Attorney Dragotta: What do you mean by the first part?

Kormos: The first part that says, police report, student had held a knife to her throat, intervention planned...I did not remember that part.

Her understanding of Kay was even shakier.

Attorney Dragotta: When did you first hear about her?

Kormos: I guess K would come into my office and not want to stay in school, would want to go home. This was a constant battle, when I didn't think she was ill where she could go home. That was most of my exposure with K, this not wanting to be in school.

Attorney Dragotta: When she first started coming to your office, would you have been aware that she had held a knife to her throat?

Kormos: I knew she was a troubled student.

Imelda Kormos declared that she knew Kay was under psychiatric care and that she had had problems in the middle school. However, Nurse Kormos did not see any signs of suicidal tendencies or drug and alcohol use. According to Ms. Kormos, Kay did not like some of the kids at the high school. Kay felt the "kids picked on her."

The nurse's memories were somewhat muddled; she did not know when Kay was on homebound or when she tried to commit suicide. She was, however, certain that a counselor from the middle school met with the high school WIN team, and that was when she became acquainted with Kay.

Attorney Dragotta: Do you remember K's name being discussed at this time?

Kormos: Yes. I do know that—I do know that's when we knew she was a troubled young lady.

Unfortunately, this was not the case. Kay was not on the SAP roster at the middle school, so her name would not have come up. In fact, Kay was on homebound placement, so no one knew if she would even be coming to the high school. Furthermore, the police notified the high school about the suicide attempt. The middle school would not have known about this.

All Ms. Kormos knew was that there were no records that had come from the middle school; there were no logs. The students' information was "word of mouth only." She couldn't remember if the high school team wrote the names of the students down during this meeting. "We *probably* did."

Ms. Kormos was having problems remembering because these events happened three years prior. However, she was able to recall an incident in March 2002 because it was "very vivid in my mind." The incident involved Kay coming to the nurse's office asking to go home. According to Nurse Kormos, Kay "was very mouthy and carried on" in the office. The next day the nurse received an apology email from Kay's mother. Ms. Kormos asked Kay's mother if the child was in counseling. The mother replied she was and told Kormos that Kay and I had gone to the therapist together. Imelda Kormos wanted the name of the therapist so they could "communicate and they could give us advice." She also informed Kay's mother "teachers are trained educators, not therapists..." The next email Nurse Kormos sent to Kay's mom said:

This is TOTALLY inappropriate—teachers are NEVER to cross lines like this—Sally [sic] has a MAJOR problem with knowing BOUNDARIES—I am struggling with the ethics of my knowing this information and not being free to say something to Mr. Anderson...this is a dangerous situation. (email 3/06/2002 Imelda Kormos)

Attorney Dragotta (reading from the email)...even though they are special ed teachers they should not be therapists or counselors.

Attorney Dragotta: To whom were you referring?

Kormos: Mrs. Montanye

Attorney Dragotta: What were you saying...in that?

Kormos: ...that K would not go to class and instead would go to Mrs. Montanye and this was not good, that she was escaping from this class and going...I would see Mrs. Montanye sitting on the curbstone with a student, sometimes it was K, talking, I guess counseling. I don't know what else she would be doing at that point...

Attorney Dragotta: ...let me ask you this, you said she would be counseling...

Kormos: Well she would be sitting out there talking to her, okay.

Attorney Dragotta: So is that counseling?

Kormos: Well I guess---I don't know the conversation that was going on but it could have been.

Attorney Dragotta: Did you ever ask Mrs. Montanye what was the conversation that was going on?

Kormos: No.

Nurse Kormos admitted that Kay would also come to her office complaining of illness to "escape" from class. But the nurse said she would either send the child back to class or send her home. Attorney Dragotta asked Ms. Kormos if she spoke with Kay on these occasions, asking her what the problem was. Ms. Kormos agreed that she did ask Kay questions. Sarah then asked the nurse if this might have been what was taking place between Kay and me. The answer: the nurse had "no idea."

Attorney Dragotta: So you don't know what she was saying?

Kormos: No.

Imelda Kormos justified her horror at my speaking with Kay by claiming the Drop-in Center counselor was a "trained therapist." According to Ms. Salvucci and others, this was not so. The Drop-in Center counselor was not a therapist and could not administer therapy.

Ms. Kormos addressed the "lines" that I crossed:

Kormos: Going into therapy with a student, sitting in with the therapist. I don't consider that professional at all. That's not a teacher's responsibility nor should she do that.

Now the medical professional, who studied suicide and at risk children testified:

Attorney Dragotta: These were serious issues...

Kormos: Yes.

Attorney Dragotta: Of a student who had suicidal tendencies?

Kormos: This at the point was not about a suicidal student.

Attorney Dragotta reading from the log: Student had held a knife to her throat. Would you consider that a suicidal tendency?

Kormos: That was 9/5/01.

Attorney Dragotta: And what was the main issue as you saw it for the incident in March?

Kormos: A student who didn't want to stay in class. And had emotional problems as such. Suicide was never discussed at that point.

Attorney Dragotta: ...what was so serious about K...beyond not wanting to be in class?

Kormos: ...at that time I think she was having quite a few absences and she was very emotional, not suicidal.

Ms. Kormos had a confused version of the MCES incident. First of all, she claimed that Kay's mother was hysterical and unable to pick her daughter up, which is why the police did. Not true. Nurse Kormos **instructed** the police to do this. Kormos knew that they brought K to school, but she skipped her part in this decision. She admitted, "It was a traumatic incident, I don't remember specifically."

She stated that I was an impediment to the SAP process because they were not informed that Kay was in therapy. Thus, I was "keeping it to myself" and interfering with a relationship between the therapist and the school. The fact that Kay would never have granted permission for this had no bearing. According to the nurse, the WIN team would establish a relationship with the therapist. She was skipping the permission part.

Again, when the nurse was asked if I ever gave Kay therapy, the answer was, "That I don't know."

Attorney Dragotta: reading from the WIN team letter...jeopardizing the health and welfare of these children...to what were you referring?

Kormos: That if they are in emotional crisis they should be seeing a trained therapist.

Here is one of the saddest responses of the whole case:

Attorney Dragotta: But until they get to a trained therapist, sometimes the children reach out and go to the nurse's office, right?

Kormos: But they wouldn't be there for a long period of time and (they) wouldn't continue to come.

Ms. Kormos was saying, under oath, that she would give a suicidal child a negative reception that would encourage the child to leave without seeking help and not to return if she needed assistance. Using this technique, the nurse would make sure the child "did not escape" from class. Unless, of course, she killed herself.

There is another matter to consider. Where I kept Kay in school by talking with her, Ms. Kormos would send her back to class. Kay would then return to the nurse's office and the medical expert would call her mother, and Kay would go home. This was the procedure as the nurse testified. So, although I allowed Kay to talk to me, I kept her in the building and somewhat involved. The woman who didn't want her to escape kept sending her home.

I also want to make another thing perfectly clear. Kay was in my room for:

(1) English (2) Social Studies (3) Study Skills.

This was her original schedule. When she withdrew from French, she was also put in my class for study help/support. Ms. Kormos and Ms. Salvucci, unaware of her schedule, assumed she was cutting class and coming to my room. They were incorrect. They didn't bother to find out what my schedule was or what Kay's was. They just assumed that I was "counseling" while I supposed to "be teaching." Their accusatory method was obviously easier than obtaining the facts. The reality that they could have cost a child her life makes that more menacing.

Ms. Kormos exhibited a unique approach to this suicidal child. When Sarah questioned the nurse about the log and the entry concerning the knife to the throat, she wanted to know if Ms. Kormos considered that an instance of suicidal ideation and therefore should be taken seriously.

Kormos: That you have to realize, that did not happen -- if that happened in the school building, this [taking all suicide threats seriously] would have applied.

Attorney Dragotta: So then it would be factored that she had suicidal ideation on at least one occasion?

Kormos...Did not happen on our watch.

Attorney Dragotta: If a student has a previous suicidal incident, whether it was in school or out of school, did you take that into consideration?

Kormos: If another incident occurred and she held a knife to her throat again, sure. If she did something in school that was suicidal, absolutely.

Attorney Dragotta: Did you have in mind that here is a student who had a previous suicidal incident?

Kormos: No.

Attorney Dragotta: Do you discount the fact that K has suicidal ideation?

Kormos: If she had therapy and felt that this was no longer an issue. **Because once you have suicidal ideations, doesn't mean that it lasts for ever and ever...Even a suicide attempt every student that has had a suicide attempt we don't look at them forever as whenever if they don't want to go to class that they're suicidal...**

Attorney Dragotta: Did you ever consider that K might be suicidal thereafter because at one point she did hold a knife to her throat?

Kormos: If she gave me an indication that she was, I would have acted immediately. I had no indication of that.

Ms. Kormos stuck with part of the story of how the WIN team letter came about. There were a few discrepancies with Ms. Salvucci's rendition. Ms. Kormos now claimed she read the letter before it was sent out. She did not claim that the entire team read the letter together. She also said there were no changes and the letter was sent out as the first draft. If you remember, Ms. Salvucci testified in her deposition, that the entire team read the letter together, and there was a mistake which had to be corrected and involved retyping the document. Quite a difference in recall.

Ms. Kormos got around her illegal behavior with this logic:
Kormos: It involved a kid at risk and an incident that put the kid farther at risk, so therefore it would certainly be my responsibility to the SAP team.

In Kormos's confused thoughts, I had put Kay farther at risk because I had gotten her to see a therapist that the WIN team did not have contact with.

The final questions dealt with my witness J. Two things stood out. One was a conversation Ms. Kormos had had with him. He told her he felt comfortable talking to his therapist and to me, his teacher. This sent Ms. Kormos into a writing fit; she sent an email to Judy Clark noting her deep concern about this situation.

The second interesting factor concerning J was that Ms. Kormos said he had been discussed at the WIN team meetings. When asked if this child had been referred to the WIN team, she said he must have been or why else would they have been talking about him.

J had an outside therapist. He had never been referred to the WIN team. He was not on the at risk list of the WIN team. Ms. Salvucci established that in her deposition. The WIN team was discussing him because they did not like my relationship with him.

It was in J's IEP that I was to be in constant contact with his therapist. These people had no concern for children. They were only concerned with a hyperbolic sense of their own importance.

Stanley J. Durtan
January 31, 2005
Superintendent of Schools

> **Attorney Dragotta:** During the 2001-2002 school year did Wissahickon School District have a policy regarding transportation?

> **Durtan:** I do not believe that we have a school board policy but I believe each school has a procedure suggesting that teachers get parental permission before doing so.

> **Attorney Dragotta:** And where would that procedure be?

> **Durtan:** I believe it would be in the faculty handbook in each school

Wouldn't the superintendent have knowledge of a school board policy pertaining to transportation? In light of the fact that this was a violation he was saddling me with, one would think he would be certain. Not only was he unsure about the lack of a policy, he was ambivalent about where anything pertaining to transportation would be located. In fact, there was no school district policy. In addition, there would be no binding procedure if suggestions appeared in each school's manual. Yet again, another policy I violated that did not exist.

> **Attorney Dragotta:** Did Sallie Montanye violate any Special Education laws? What laws did she violate?

> **Durtan:** She violated the Pennsylvania State Board of Education Regulations which address Special Education. And the Federal IDEA law.

> **Attorney Dragotta:** And so how did she violate—what specific portions?

> **Durtan:** Well there are requirements in both those laws, in that law and regulation that before services are delivered to an exceptional student that there has to be

notification prepared that certain documents have to be provided to the parents of that student.

Attorney Dragotta: And to what services are you referring?

Durtan: Counseling services that were given to the student...by the psychotherapist that Ms. Montanye drove the student to and sat in on sessions with.

When asked if I received an unsatisfactory rating for this breach of state and federal laws, the answer was no. That defies any kind of logic. And since when do outside services not provided by the school require notification prepared by the school? That would be a bureaucratic nightmare.

About informing the board:

Attorney Dragotta: Any time during that 2001, 2002 school year, regarding Sallie Montanye, was there ever an occasion where you informed the board of school directors about Ms. Montanye?

Durtan: No.

Attorney Dragotta: Was it your decision to contact Attorney Levin?

Durtan: Yes.

Attorney Dragotta: Was the board informed of your decision?

Durtan: No.

Attorney Dragotta: ...was it your obligation to inform the board?

Durtan: No.

Attorney Dragotta: Why did you make that decision?

Durtan: Mr. Levin has served the Wissahickon School District for many years as a special counsel in personnel cases.

This is what passes for an answer in the WSD. Dr. Durtan was a master of the nonresponsive response.

Durtan repeated the party line about the Loudermill hearings: "It's an opportunity for employees to present their side of the story when allegations are made against them." He would repeat this phrase seven times throughout the deposition. It was an automatic reply.

According to the superintendent, the WIN team letter was now a "report."

Attorney Dragotta: What inform... do you remember on what information they were [Bill Sanni and Judy Clark] relying?

Durtan: They were relying on a report from the WIN team.

Attorney Dragotta: A report from the WIN team?

Durtan: Yeah. Verbal report that was subsequently reduced to writing and the interaction that they had had with the building principal.

This would be version #3 of the WIN team letter creation story. According to Dr. Durtan, the "report" was verbal and then whoever wrote the letter (WIN team/Salvucci?) put the gossip into writing. This story was exceptionally different from the first two.

When presented with the suicide note, the superintendent stated he had only seen this note for the first time a couple of weeks ago. Possibly, my first attorney had been correct when he said that Stanley Durtan had slept through the Loudermill. I talked about the suicide note at that hearing. He was there.

The potential suicide checklist, which was so important to Dr. Durtan in his affidavits, presented more of a challenge. This was the form that Robert Anderson and I followed when the note was discovered. Durtan stated that I did not adhere to this document. Of course, he had never seen the document before the Loudermill and was not certain when he first saw it or where it was located.

Attorney Dragotta: Did you ever see this before, Dr. Durtan? (showing him the potential suicide checklist)

Durtan: Yes I think. (He thinks?)

Attorney Dragotta: Did you see this document before the Loudermill hearing?

Durtan: No.

Attorney Dragotta: When was the first time you saw this document?

Durtan: I'm not sure.

Dr. Durtan "believed" it was an excerpt from the crises response manual that "exists" at the high school.

He "believed" it was in use at the high school in 2002. There were no crisis response manuals at any other schools? He "thinks" he may have seen it: he "believes" it may have been in use at the high school: he had never seen it before the Loudermill: he was not sure when he first saw it, but he **knew** I had violated it.

The letter from Kay's therapist equally confused the superintendent. He wasn't sure when he had seen the letter. When asked if he had seen it before the Loudermill hearing: "I don't know. I don't know."

Sarah then asked Dr. Durtan if he copied anyone on the Directives Letter. Although there was no notification of any copy, Dr. Durtan was "sure" he had sent a copy to the personnel office. When asked if he had sent a blind copy, he gave his standard response: "I don't know."

Sarah asked why he wrote the Directives Letter.

Durtan: Well it was written to Sallie because the information that I had gathered about this case suggested that she exercised poor judgment in performing her responsibility. That she *probably* has an ethical violation in regard to her interaction with a student. That she placed the district at very severe risk of liability. That she exhibited no awareness of or sensitivity to the appropriate bond of the student-teacher relationship because she violated state Special Education regulations and because she violated federal Special Education laws.

This from the man who allowed Kay to be brutalized and then sent her home to die.

The superintendent also stated, "whenever district personnel do not follow regulations, policies, procedures, and the law with regard to students, the district is potentially liable for that action." This was obviously not of great import when Dr. Durtan and his administrators were denying Kay FAPE, pushing her out of school without benefit of an IEP meeting, putting her in an illegal placement and denying her related services for the emotional turmoil she suffered at the hands of the bullies the superintendent did not bother to control.

If there were any doubts that Kay even existed in this man's mind, his next words banished that misconception.

Attorney Dragotta: Dr. Durtan, did you ever have conversations with student one's (K) parents?

Durtan: Yes.

Attorney Dragotta: Mother and father or just one or the other.

Durtan: I believe it was both.

Attorney Dragotta: What was the nature of those conversations?

Durtan: My recollection is that the parents scheduled an appointment with me to discuss the educational program that was being provided to their daughter at the school.

It's one thing that Durtan did not recall who Kay was before the Loudermill hearing. Obviously, the violations he committed did not give him much pause for concern. But one would think, that any person in his position would have made the minimal effort to find out the facts before coming to the deposition. Kay's parents weren't discussing her program. They were taking her out of school because not one administrator at that table gave a rat's tail that she was being physically and emotionally hounded and her parents feared for her safety.

When asked if Durtan could say what WIN stood for, the answer was "not really."

Sarah requested that Dr. Durtan read over the cryptic WIN team log entries. Most of his answers were that he couldn't make out what it said or he didn't know what the writing meant. Despite admitting that the log was virtually useless, the superintendent said he considered it to be adequate.

The superintendent was "not sure" if he ever saw the fax from Kay's mother.

Even after seeing the note from Bill Sanni on the bottom, Dr. Durtan could still "not recall" if he had ever seen the note.

Likewise, Durtan could not remember if he had seen Robert Anderson's affidavit.

Demonstrating that he knew exactly what was going on:

Attorney Dragotta: Did she [Sallie Montanye] transfer the student from the school to the therapist?

Durtan: That's my understanding.

Now here's a stumper: Dr. Durtan testified that he had problems with Robert Anderson telling the truth. He was referring to the conversation that he and Bill Sanni had with Mr. Anderson the day after the Loudermill hearing.

Durtan: What I meant, what I attempted to convey to him is that both the board and me personally had a number of concerns about his lack of ability to tell the truth. There were a number of events which led us to that conclusion and this (my Loudermill) was the culminating event.

Stanley Durtan had this conversation one day after the Loudermill (May).

According to his testimony, the board had no idea about these events until the following November, because Dr. Durtan had kept it a secret. Therefore, the board was not aware of the "culminating event."

Attorney Dragotta: Were you aware that Sallie was having difficulty in preparing her side of the story because she couldn't get any documents from the district, were you aware of that?

Durtan: No, I had no awareness of any problem of that nature.

Then how would he explain these?

#1
From:Warren S
To:Stan Durtan
Sent:Friday, May 17 2002 11:04 PM
Subject:Sally [sic] Montayne [sic] DISCLOSURE AND LOUDERMILL HEARING

Hi Stan,
It has come to my attention that Mr. Anderson has not given Sally [sic] Montayne [sic] copies of his file on her. She needs this to prepare for the hearing. I have been told that Mr. Anderson has been told not to give this information by Mr. Levin.
I don't believe this is legal. Delays can often be done to get around the spirit of the law.

#2
From:Stan Durtan
To:Warren S
Sent:Friday, May 17 3:04 PM
Subject:RE: Sally [sic] Montayne [sic] DISCLOSURE AND LOUDERMILL HEARING

Warren: This is a serious situation. Mrs. Montayne [sic]should have legal counsel. Her legal counsel should contact Mr. Levin to acquire any information she wishes to have. District personnel will neither be discussing this situation nor providing any written information prior to the Loudermill Hearing. Stan

#3
From:Warren S
To:Stan Durtan
Sent:Friday, May 17 2002 3:17 PM
Cc:Montanye, Sallie; Donald Atkiss (email)
Subject:Sally[sic]   Montayne   [sic]   DISCLOSURE   AND
LOUDERMILL HEARING

Hi Stan,

This is dead wrong. Sally [sic] should be entitled to copies of certain materials that represent communications to her over the last year. Some recent materials that may be related to a criminal investigation, she may not be entitled to receive. I don't believe there are such materials.

I have asked our attorneys to request the material. I am told the denial of disclosure could cause the District difficulties in the future should disciplinary action be determined as warranted.

Honest people have nothing to hide. The adversarial aspect of legal proceedings should be tempered with justice and certain legal ethical values.

I have no recourse but to leave this dispute with the lawyers.

Warren

I included a good deal of these depositions so you could see what was really taking place; the case against me was built on lies, misinformation, incompetence, unethical behavior, legal fraudulence, suppression of information, manufactured policies, imaginary regulations, falsified documents, and perjured testimony. Had there been any legitimacy to these charges, Dr. Durtan would have followed the course of his responsibility and included the school board, our employer. He could not, however, let them in on the secret, as they may have been unwilling to finance a case fraught with deceptions and malevolent intent. They may not have felt secure backing the man in charge, who answered, "I don't know" or "I can't recall," more than twenty three times in a short period of questioning.

After Dr. Durtan's deposition the woman typing the record took me aside. She was shaking her head. She told me she had a nephew who had special needs. She said, "Promise me you won't give up on this. Please promise me."

A few months later, Sarah called me. She had just finished re-reading the depositions of Stan Durtan and Judy Clark. She was amazed at how many questions these people answered with "I don't know" or I can't recall." Sarah wanted to know if the two most prominent leaders were so mystified about the goings on in their schools, then "who was running this district?"

CHAPTER TWENTY

Final Depositions

This was part of the affidavit Kay wrote with Sarah Dragotta.

11. My IEP said that I should speak with an adult of my choice...I chose to speak with Mrs. Montanye, because I felt comfortable with her.

13. Mrs. Montanye helped me go to therapy.

14. I was never asked by the WSD to sign a student release for the use of my student records, including records and documents noted above.

15. No guidance counselor, Special Education Administrator, High School Administrator, or any staff person from WSD asked me to sign a consent form to use my records against Mrs. Montanye.

16. No guidance counselor, Special Education Administrator, High School Administrator, or any staff person from WSD asked me to sign a release form to discuss my therapy.

17. I did not know Mrs. Montanye was punished for helping me.

18. I did not know my confidential records would be used by the district to punish my teacher.

21. I did not give oral or written permission for an outside agency, such as the Levin Legal Group, to use any personal information, including records and documents noted above, to prosecute my teacher.

25. At no time was I informed of the fact that my personal information ...would be seen and/or discussed by the Superintendent of WSD, the Assistant Superintendent of WSD, the Personnel Director of the WSD or any staff at WSD, and an outside agency, Michael I. Levin, *Esq.,* of the Levin Legal Group.

27a. I state here that I grant Sarah Dragotta... and Sallie Montanye permission to use all of my present and past IEP's, and oral information from discussions, any information from my therapy sessions or any other information, including records or documents noted above, pertaining to me that she needs in her complaint against the WSD.

Judith Clark
February 23, 2005
Assistant Superintendent

Judith Clark's deposition was the last of the district's upper administrators. One remarkable aspect of Clark's testimony was how often she "did not recall, wasn't aware, didn't know, wasn't sure" of any information. There were numerous questions to which she responded, "not specifically." Another one of her favorite answers was, "not to my recollection." Of course, there were also a number of times she "was not aware" of something.

She informed Attorney Dragotta that she believed the reason for my lawsuit revolved around the "incident."

Attorney Dragotta: You refer to "the incident," to what are you referring?

Clark: The situation with K...

Attorney Dragotta: And what is that situation?

Clark: The situation is when Ms. Montanye transported the child to the therapist, sat in on a therapy session.

Sarah pursued the transportation issue. She asked the assistant superintendent who would be the personnel that could transport students. Again, there was no transportation policy referred to because none existed. There was also no law quoted to sustain the argument that transporting a private citizen was a violation of statute. K **had returned home**; she was no longer the district's responsibility.

Ms. Clark stated that only **bus drivers** would transport students.

Attorney Dragotta: Would it have been permissible for staff to transport students?

Clark: No.

Attorney Dragotta: Are students ever transported by staff for athletic purposes other than bus drivers?

Clark: I don't know the answer to that.

As assistant superintendent, she should have known the answer to that. That's why school districts have policies. As one of the people responsible for hiring an attorney and accusing me of transportation violations, Ms. Clark should have been aware of children who were transported from school by personnel other than licensed bus drivers.

There were a number of instances where faculty members transported children.

(1) The assistant principal of the high school transported his wrestling students daily from home to school for practice. Additionally, he would transport students to the matches. There were no signed permission forms. This was common knowledge in the district. He also testified to this in his deposition. This had been taking place for years and continued after I was charged with transportation transgressions.

(2) The students from *Camerata,* (a choir), were transported by a teacher to singing engagements. Again, this was common knowledge. This continued after I was charged with transportation violations.

(3) During the strike of 2003, Superintendent Durtan, **in a letter sent to all district parents**, assured them that, "District staff will transport students to away athletic events; however, no after school activity buses will be provided." You can be sure the "district staff" were not bus drivers. They were coaches and teachers. (Durtan

293

Letter/August 2002/In the event of a strike) The man who said I had violated the transportation policy, and who hired an attorney to press those charges, wrote this letter.

(4) Then there was the incident where another assistant principal transported students to a math competition. While driving the students home, the assistant principal was ticketed for failure to observe a traffic sign. Breaking the law while transporting students is an offense punishable by termination according to PA law. Although he stated in his deposition that he reported this incident to the administration, the assistant principal did not undergo a Loudermill hearing. According to his testimony, there were no consequences. This incident occurred well after my Loudermill hearing. The difference being Dr. Durtan was this man's mentor; he did not hire an attorney to see if this incident required investigation or discipline. (Deposition)

The next subject was Kay's homebound placement. Ms. Clark was in charge of the billing for all homebound placements.

There were forms to be completed in order to monitor the progress of homebound students. Although we requested these, they were never provided. The forms required parental signature. Kay's mother stated she was never asked to sign any papers.

On Kay's homebound placement:

Attorney Dragotta: Are you aware of any incident at the Wissahickon Middle School where students were placed on homebound because of bullying issues, they were afraid to come to school?

Clark: Not specifically.

What should happen when a homebound student returned to school?

Attorney Dragotta: ...would there be any specific services necessary for a student [this one in particular] who was out on homebound placement for posttraumatic stress disorder?

Clark: ...there would be discussion with the child's counselor to monitor the child because of the length of time they had been out and see if there is any transitional issues that occur as a result of that absence from school.

Attorney Dragotta: Did you know if there were any transitional services in place for this student when she returned to the school in September of 2001?

Clark: I do not.

Attorney Dragotta: Do you know of any of the circumstances surrounding this diagnosis of posttraumatic stress disorder?

Clark: Not specifically...Dr. Durtan and I did meet with the parents...they had asked to come in and just meet with us regarding some of the difficulties they were having with their daughter...Dr. Durtan and I primarily listened to their concerns.

Attorney Dragotta: You were just saying that the parents came in and spoke to Dr. Durtan and yourself, what time period are you talking here?

Clark: I can't recall the exact time period.

Attorney Dragotta: ...would it have been before homebound placement or after?

Clark: I'm thinking it may have been after, where there was an incident with K in the summertime but I'm not...that's what I can recall at this point.

Attorney Dragotta: Are you aware of the reasons why she was out on homebound instruction, aside from reading the words posttraumatic stress disorder?

Clark: Not specifically. I do not have awareness of all that went into that placement.

Attorney Dragotta: Do you have any awareness of what went into that placement?

Clark: In my capacity I needed to rely on the team…we have 4400 students in the district.

Sound familiar? It's the same argument employed by Hugh Jones. He could not protect Kay because he had 1200 other students to care for. Dr. Durtan, recipient of all the letters concerning Kay, was not aware of Kay's predicament. Clark relied on some "team" to keep her informed. Although she would have access to the mother's letters and was included in the meeting, she had no idea what was transpiring in the district in relation to this child. After all, there were 4400 other students. The WIN team was busy with many children on their list. They did not have time for Kay. But *all these people* had time to go after me for helping her?

Allow me to point out that Ms. Clark initially may have been ignorant about the specifics of Kay's situation; however, after her "investigation" there was no excuse for not knowing the story behind this child. According to her deposition and Dr. Durtan's deposition, those who failed Kay were viewed as "professional."

Clark went on to point the finger at the supervisor of guidance who would "speak with her." This person was responsible for informing the assistant superintendent about Kay and the events surrounding her. Unfortunately, Ms. Clark could not "recall exactly that conversation."

Attorney Dragotta: Were you aware of any bullying issues that affected this student?

Clark: Not specifically.

Attorney Dragotta: Do you know if she was a Special Education child before she was placed on homebound?

Clark: I don't believe I knew that at the time, again with the number of students.[13]

---

[13] AGAIN with the number of students!

Attorney Dragotta: If a student is a Special Education student and there comes a need for that student to be placed on homebound, is there a need for a re-evaluation or an IEP change or something to designate that homebound placement?

Clark: Normally it would be documented through the IEP process.

That would be a yes. And by the way, Ms. Clark *would have to have known* that Kay was a Special Education student. There would be no other reason for having Kelle Heim-McCloskey at the meeting. The supervisor of Special Education did not attend random meetings for regular education children. In addition, someone should have had Kay's records at the meeting, or did all these professionals show up empty-handed? Didn't Dr. Durtan say the parents wanted to discuss their daughter's educational program?

Durtan: My recollection is that the parents scheduled an appointment with me to discuss the educational program that was being provided to their daughter at the school.

But the parents never mentioned their child was classified as Special Education? Exactly what part of the education program was being discussed?

Recap time:

- Ms. Clark and the district were unable to provide us with the documents, required by the state, pertaining to Kay's homebound progress. They didn't exist.
- Ms. Clark was not aware that Kay was placed on homebound as a result of relentless bullying.
- Ms. Clark was not aware that transitional services for a returning homebound student, who was also Special Education, were not offered.
- Ms. Clark met with the parents to listen to their "concerns." At no point in time did Clark realize that bullying was an issue, although it was the reason for the removal of this child from school.

- The parents just wanted to vent to Dr. Durtan and Ms. Clark. They were not looking for assistance or resolution.
- Ms. Clark was not aware of "all that went into the placement." In other words, the parents were taking their daughter out of school for her own protection; Clark was unaware of this one condition that required Kay be removed from school.
- Ms. Clark did not question anything about Kay's placement, despite a diagnosis of posttraumatic stress disorder, and the radical move to place a student outside the school setting.
- Ms. Clark cannot be held accountable for any of the infractions surrounding Kay because there are 4400 students in the district.
- Ms. Clark relied on a "team" to keep her informed. If she didn't know what took place, it was the fault of the team.
- The supervisor of guidance should have reported to Ms. Clark about Kay; unfortunately, Ms. Clark could not recall anything about that conversation.
- The IEP process should have been used to document Kay's placement and program, but it wasn't because no one, including the supervisor of Special Education, knew this child was in Special Education.
- Despite all Ms. Clark's conversations and investigation, she still had no clue about this child, her history, or her needs.
- The only sure thing that Ms. Clark **knew** was that I should not be allowed to help this child as a private citizen.

It is interesting how the WIN team and Ms. Clark applied similar arguments to excuse their deliberate indifference. The WIN team log said the parents "played down the knife incident." Clark met with the parents who never mentioned the bullying and the trauma to their child. What parents play down a suicide attempt? What concerned guardians meet with the superintendent and assistant superintendent to discuss their fears for their child's physical and emotional safety and neglect to refer to the threatening incidents during the course of the meeting?

Sarah asked what I did "wrong," Clark responded, "She crossed the line between her professional responsibility as a teacher with a student." **I should have referred her "to someone**

that was trained to deal with her problems." Of course, that is what I did, but **that** was wrong also.

As far as counseling went, Ms. Clark admitted that I never tried to pass myself off as a psychologist nor did I represent myself as such to anyone else. Again, my sin was not referring K to a **trained professional** and making sure she saw one.

> **Attorney Dragotta**: Was K identified by the school district's at risk team?

> **Clark**: My understanding is that...information regarding K had come to the WIN team, I am not clear exactly on where that was in the process when this incident occurred and what their next step would have been.

In other words, the assistant superintendent had no idea whether Kay was on the WIN team roster, what the WIN team did or did not do, and how dire the circumstances were surrounding this child. You would think the WIN team letter would have made her curious. Apparently not. The Loudermill hearing should have piqued her interest. It did not. The neglect and animus that pushed Kay out of the district were pushing me out too.

According to Ms. Cark, Dr. Durtan, Dr. Sanni (personnel), and she held a discussion that resulted in the decision to hold the Loudermill hearing. What Ms. Clark did not mention was how the decision to hire Michael Levin came about, and who made the decision to keep this a secret from the board.

> **Attorney Dragotta**: So this was a serious matter? [my interaction with K]

> **Clark**: Absolutely.

> **Attorney Dragotta**: Did you ask to have Mrs. Montanye removed from working with the student?

> **Clark:** I would not have done that until she had had an opportunity to be able to respond to the allegations.

Once she was sure I was not going to therapy, Ms. Clark did not feel the need to remove Kay from my presence.

BUT WAIT! This was in contradiction to the testimony from Durtan, Salvucci, and Kormos. They all stated the danger of my relationship with Kay was that I was "counseling" her. Ms. Clark did not think I was counseling Kay. I was just getting her to someone who could and that had to be stopped.

Sarah next addressed the letter from Kay's mom that was kept from me, and the "record" of the Loudermill hearing. Sarah showed Judith Clark the letter; the assistant superintendent could "not recall" when she had first seen it.

Attorney Dragotta: ...the home speed fax from the parent was it your decision...not to have this letter present at Sallie Montanye's Loudermill hearing?

Clark: It was not my decision.

Attorney Dragotta: Whose decision was it?

Clark: I don't know that. I do not know that.

Attorney Dragotta: Were you a part of any decisions with regard to whether this letter, this home speed fax...should be withheld or not?

Clark: Not to my recollection.

Attorney Dragotta: Did Dr. Sanni share this letter with you before the Loudermill hearing?

Clark: I believe that he did.

Attorney Dragotta: Did Dr. Durtan ever discuss this letter with you?

Clark: We may have had a discussion after the fact but I can't recall.

Attorney Dragotta: Did you have discussions with Attorney Levin with regard to this letter?

Clark: Most probably.

Ms. Clark was not taking the fall for suppression of evidence; she exonerated Dr. Sanni because he turned it over to Michael Levin and showed it to her. Dr. Durtan denied seeing it at all. That left one person who could decide to keep the letter secret—the attorney, Mr. Levin.

For the grand finale, Ms. Clark established that the permission form to see an outside therapist was a figment of Michael Levin's imagination.

> **Attorney Dragotta:** Do parents need the permission of the school district to take their children to outside therapists?

> **Clark: No they do not.**

> **Attorney Dragotta:** Do students need to go through an evaluation process to go to **an outside therapist?**

> **Clark:** That's not a requirement that we evaluate and then the parents can take them to a counselor or outside therapist. Parents can do that at any time they want.

What the assistant superintendent was saying with this statement was:

- Parents do not need to have their child evaluated by the school to see a private therapist.
- Parents can take their child at any time to a private therapist without notifying the school.
- There is no form required by the school for taking your child to a private therapist.
- There is no evaluation performed by the school to decide if a child should go to private therapy.
- Therefore, there is **no form** because there is no evaluation performed before parents take their child to a private therapist.

Our evidence requests only served to back up Ms. Clark's

testimony that there was no permission slip which the parents had to sign to take their child to a private therapist. In every document request, we asked for a copy of this alleged form. Of course, we never received one because one didn't exist. The only paper we ever obtained from the defendants was the form used to grant permission for the **school district to evaluate the student for Special Education placement.** Despite Mr. Levin's constant assertions to the contrary, there was no such form because **parents do not have to grant themselves permission to take their children to private professionals.**

What I found interesting was that Judy Clark attended most of the depositions and took voluminous notes. Yet, this woman did not have one sentence recording anything having to do with Kay, nor did she have anything to which to refer in relation to my activities and the district's responses. No meetings, no discussions, no emails, no personal observations. **Not one single note.** And yet this was a very "serious matter."

Judy Clark's deposition was remarkable due to its omissions. Ms. Clark who was in charge of the Special Education program when she was Director of Pupil Services did not breathe a word about IDEA. When asked what I did wrong, she did not offer the Special Education referral routine, nor did she recite the supplying of services not in the IEP as a basis for concern. It does not make sense that Durtan and his attorney based their arguments on the alleged violation of IDEA and PA Regs, while the assistant superintendent, a woman who sported a legacy of familiarity with Special Education, did not see this as worthy of note when asked what I did wrong. According to Judith Clark, suggesting the therapist and going with Kay to the therapist's were my only sins. Not only did she not refer to IDEA at any time, she studiously avoided it. This was a strange break within the ranks, especially from the woman who told Robert Anderson his duty "was to protect the superintendent."

*****

The final depositions are with Kay, her mom, and the two assistant principals from the high school. Kay's deposition did not come without problems. She wanted her mother to be with her during the deposition; but in order for that to take place, Kay's mother had to be deposed first and Kay would have to wait a few hours. This upset her greatly. With angry tears, she threatened to leave and not return. Michael and Sarah were arguing back and forth about whom, what and where. Finally, they took it in the back room, where Michael Levin wanted to know why this was such a big deal. As he said to Sarah Dragota, Kay should be told what to do; she was "just a goddamned kid."

I had learned something very quickly, which Michael Levin had not yet grasped. You better be careful what you say to Sarah. She doesn't forget, and she will memorialize something in writing if she thinks it's important. She did as much in a letter to Levin, following up Kay's deposition. Referring to a bullied, troubled, suicidal, emotionally tormented child, as a "goddamned kid," did not rest well with Sarah Dragotta. You do not want to poke this mamma bear.

Finally, after much ado about everything, Kay agreed to be deposed without her mother present.

Kay
February 18, 2005
Student

Michael Levin started by asking Kay if she attended WSD. She informed him that she did not; she was finishing high school at Montgomery County Community College. Kay could not get away from Wissahickon fast enough. She started a year earlier at the college. She would be allowed to walk at graduation with her high school class but she refused.

Then the questions turned to me:

Levin: One of the reasons that you liked her (Mrs. Montanye) was because she let you talk to her and she spoke to you about things, right?

Kay: Yes.

Levin: Can you tell us some of the kinds of things you talked to her about...?

Kay: Well, I would come to Ms. Montanye for just about everything. If I needed help with a fight I got in with my mom, I would just ask her if she thought I was wrong in a way or if I could have done something different. We talked about things from important things to dumb stuff like our nails and some things like that.

Remember the accusation that I did not inform the WIN team that Kay was using drugs? There was a reason:

Levin: I understand you may have had some drug problems?

Kay: Yes

Levin: And did you discuss drug problems with Mrs. Montanye?

Kay: I don't think so. *(She never mentioned this to me until years later.)*

Mr. Levin wanted to know if her problems had any impact on her education.

Levin: And did you think that these emotional problems that you were having adversely affected how you were doing in school, you couldn't concentrate in school because you were having those kinds of problems?

Kay: Definitely.

Mr. Levin wanted to know if she left classes to discuss her problems with me. She admitted that she had done that once in a while when she got upset: "I would usually start breaking out in tears in the middle of class, and I would get embarrassed...Mrs. Montanye was the only one I felt comfortable discussing my problems with." Kay pointed out that this **"didn't happen a lot."** Mr. Levin then put his spin on what she said:

Levin: So is it fair and accurate to say that on **numerous** occasions you would leave your academic classes and go to Mrs. Montanye's class?

Kay: I wouldn't say numerous.

Then Michael Levin asked about seeing me outside of the school. I'm not sure what his goal was: was he asking about socially or the times we sat outside the school building? It was difficult to discern.
The next discussion pertained to the therapist.

Kay: ...I needed to see a therapist, I knew that myself, I didn't want to admit that at the time but I knew I did...I told her that the only way I was going to go see another doctor is if she came with me.

Levin: What were your problems?

Kay: I think the reason she [Mrs. Montanye] told me that (Kay needed to see a therapist) was because I was more suicidal at that point because everything was going wrong between school and friends, I couldn't deal with everything.

Levin: Okay. So some time before mid December you were-you thought you were suicidal?

Kay: I was suicidal since eighth grade, since Wissahickon took me out of school because they couldn't provide protection for me. And that's when I became depressed and was put on medication for the first time and that's when I started abusing the use of drugs.

Levin: ...when you put the knife to your throat were you trying to commit suicide or were you trying to get the attention of your mother for some reason?

Kay: Honestly, at that time I would say I was trying to commit suicide.

Levin: Did you ever try to commit suicide at any other time?

Kay: Yes.

Levin: When?

Kay: I think it was actually a few weeks before that …

About my attendance at the therapist's:

Levin: How many times do you remember her driving you to or from Dr. Ex's?

Kay: She only came a few times with me because I just wanted her to stay until I got comfortable…

Michael Levin then turned his attention to the class switch. He asked her why I changed the schedule for her:

Kay: …because they had put me in a class where pretty much I was being, I guess you would say picked on. It was all of the people I had problems with the former year, that was the reason Wissahickon took me out of the school; they put me right in the class with everyone I was having problems with.

Kay remembered that she was put back in the class. "I don't know why…" Kay then admitted that she missed "a lot of that math class (when she was returned to it) because of that situation. I would leave because I didn't want to go there."

Mr. Levin attempted to get Kay to admit she also cut the math class I had put her in. Kay said she didn't. She was right; she was in my room for math and she never cut the class for the few weeks she was there. It was not until the assistant principal placed her back in the math class with her tormentors that she began to cut again.

Kay retold the story of the day the police picked her up. She was quite emphatic that while at the police station she "was calm."

Kay: I was calm when I was in the police station. After I left and found out that I was going to the school I became very mad because I did not want to be seen by anyone in the school and I did not know why they were even bringing me there in the first place. When the car stopped…my mom was there, Mrs. Montanye was there then-I know the school nurse was there and they were trying to get-the school nurse wanted me to come into her office to talk to her, well she in my eyes knew nothing about my problems.

Levin: Was that Mrs. Kormos?

Kay: Yes it was.

Kay went on to describe how upset she was and how the time in the police car seemed to last forever. From school she was taken to MCES. This entire incident was unnecessary and was the disastrous result of the nurse's ignorant interference. It was the nurse's demand that Kay come into the school, so she could not "escape," which caused the hysteria that resulted in Kay's second time in a mental facility. Imelda Kormos certainly didn't handle Kay like a "troubled young lady," but rather wanted her cornered and forced into doing what the nurse felt she should be doing.

Kay also mentioned that she often spoke with Ms. P, who was her IEP case manager. She refused to speak with the Drop-in Center counselor because she was "not going to talk to a complete stranger." She also noted that the counselor wasn't there much of the time; so if she needed her, chances were she wouldn't be available.

At the end of her deposition, Kay was describing an incident to Sarah that took place the year after I did not return to school (2002-2003).

Kay was in tenth grade. She was attending a class that was in the room I had occupied the year before. Kelle Heim-McCloskey (Supervisor Special Education) had come into the room and was speaking with the substitute teacher.

Kay: This was our English class and we watched movies...Mrs. McCloskey was going through the books that were in Mrs. Montanye's old room, saying oh, this looks like they weren't used. That upset me because they were trying to imply, in my eyes, that Mrs. Montanye didn't teach us anything.

Attorney Dragotta: Who is they?

Kay: Mrs. McCloskey [Kelle Heim-McCloskey] and the substitute teacher...They both stood there and tried saying that Mrs. Montanye never taught us anything, never used any of the books...And I stood up and got very mad...and I said you don't know what Mrs. Montanye was doing, you weren't here and I told Mrs. McCloskey about how our new teacher was just letting us watch movies...

Attorney Dragotta: Okay. Is there anything else...

Kay: Yeah, Mrs. McCloskey told me to sit down, that I already started enough problems---caused enough problems.

Attorney Dragotta: Can you try to think exactly what she said to you...

Kay: She told me---I remember her exactly saying sit down, Kay, you started—it was either you started or caused enough problems. And she said my name, which surprised me because at that time I didn't know who she was...

*****

Kay's Mother
February 18th/March 11th 2005

Kay's mom spent a good deal of her deposition describing how she could not obtain help for her child. She referred to Kay's gym class in the high school: "Basically, quite a few of the girls that were harassing her in eighth grade were in that class and Kay was frightened." She also explained why Kay had a cell phone: "Kay would call me crying hysterically, extremely upset...I would say where are you, she would say I'm in the bathroom...hiding in fear that she would again be beat up by certain girls in her class."

She explained why Kay would come to me: " Quite often I would say who are you comfortable with and she would say Ms. Montanye, I would say if need be go to Ms. Montanye. Ms. Montanye was the only person Kay felt comfortable with."

Kay's mom was asked about emails exchanged between her and Imelda Kormos and why she was angry with the nurse.

Mother: Because Mrs. Kormos did something I told her not to do.

Levin: Which was?

Mother: She broke my confidence in her. I specifically said to her, confidential, for you only. And she did not listen to that directive.

Levin: In what way?

Mother: She went to someone else with this information.

Kay's mother was also vocal about Robert Anderson and me.

And I still to this date feel as if Mr. Anderson was extremely helpful or tried to be extremely helpful with the situation at hand...First of all he talked to me on numerous occasions...I believe I said to him...that I would like Ms. Montanye involved in all of the conversations. I made her aware of everything that was being discussed because she played an integral part in Kay's life, in keeping her in school, keeping her on track, and keeping her alive.

She pointed out that she had given permission for me to talk to the therapist, "And to take her because I knew that Sallie was the only one that Kay trusted at that point and that was the only way that I was going to get her to have the therapy she needed."

In contrast to the WIN team accusation that I had the parents excluded:

...Kay had indicated to her [the therapist] that she would like to have Sallie. Sallie was invited in and I believe the therapist had said something to me that because Sallie is familiar with the circumstances did I feel comfortable with her being in there initially and I said fine.

Kay's mother read over notes she had taken from middle school on:

- Kay told me on numerous occasions that she was afraid to walk through the halls
- Wanted to die; she discussed this numerous times
- I [mother] was crying almost every single time I was in contact with somebody at school. I was in constant fear that Kay would hurt herself.

Then things turned hostile:

Mom: At this point I was aware of the fact that that Ms. Montanye had been reprimanded, which infuriated me no end.

Levin: Why did this infuriate you

Mom: Because Mrs. Montanye was the only one who salvaged or even cared about my daughter in 9th grade...I would like to know why it is that the WIN team, who met with my husband and I on September 11, who were supposedly there representing the school district and supposed to be helping my child, did not inform any of her teachers of her background and emotional distress.

Mr. Levin then had Kay's mom read over the WIN team log entry. She had some choice words about that.

Mom: I'm having a hard time reading this. "Meeting with parents who downplayed knife situation." I don't think you can really downplay a knife situation when a child is standing there with a knife about this long...Blamed trouble on the middle school. Oh definitely. The middle school was not there to support her when she needed it, nor was the district. Mr. Durtan did nothing to help her.

The next exchange erupted into an emotional outburst.

Mom: (looking at WIN team log) There's such a wonderful gap between September 11, 2001 and 2/12/2002. What were we doing in the meantime?

Levin: Why are you being very sarcastic?

Mom: Because I am very angry.

Levin: Why are you angry?

Mom: Because my daughter's life was at stake. Do you have a child?

Attorney Dragotta: Let the record reflect that mom is angry and she is crying.

Mom: I would like to know does Mr. Levin have a child? Has his child, if he has a child, ever tried to commit suicide in front of you? Did your child ever try to jump out a window...Mr. Levin doesn't understand the situation, neither did the school. The school didn't try to get themselves involved...

At this point, Sarah and I took Kay's mom out of the room to help her regain her composure. I understood exactly how the mother felt. I had watched child after child being deserted or screwed over by the very people who were supposed to protect them. You listen to their double speak, you know what exists in reality, and you want to explode in anger and frustration.

Kay's mom had a different recollection of the meeting in the Spring of 2001, when Kay was put on homebound.

Mom: ...my husband and I did go to the district office. We sat down with Dr. Durtan and a group of people.

Levin: What was discussed at this meeting as you recall?

Mom: The neglect of the school district of handling my daughter's situation in 8th grade...In summary the school district wasn't going to do very much, even though they said they would cooperate with me.

The rest of the deposition was spent going over all the communications Kay's mom had sent to the district, including Dr. Durtan. Some of the letters asked for more assistance for Kay, which was understandable. Kay's mom feared if she became totally dependent on me and I was not there, then Kay would not be able to cope with whatever the problem was. This makes sense. What this child needed was a support system.

Kay's mom was not pleased with the email sent from Imelda Kormos, nor was she happy with the nurse's desire to make sure I had no contact with Kay.

> ...I already knew at that point that the only person who Kay was ever going to go to would be Sallie, and the only way that we would get her through the year would have her be involved with Sallie. If I recall there were numerous times, during quite a few meetings where I said, I want Sallie in the loop. I want her in the circle. I never asked for her to be excluded.

As I see it, the major problem boils down to this: Kay's mother and I wanted to protect and help her; the others could have cared less.

A proud note: One of my students was going to be deposed by Michael Levin. Stacy Smith (of LLG) called this boy, and attempted to talk him out of coming. She told J that the district had a strong case; in fact, both Kay and her mother were going to be testifying against me. J didn't bite. This eighteen year old, shy child, who was terrorized by many things, walked bravely in with Sarah and me to take on Michael Levin. The attorney would never understand any of this. It had to do with loyalty and honor.

CHAPTER TWENTY-ONE

Experts

It does not appear as if any other responsible party, such as the WIN team, was assuming this role and, so, it would be natural for a caring professional special educator, such as Ms. Montanye, to do so...The fact is that Dr. Ex, as stated in her letter, supported the actions of Ms. Montanye and further remarks that "sometimes a special bond with just one teacher can save a child's life."

...in stark contrast to the district's portrayal of an insubordinate, improper or neglectful individual, in my professional opinion, I see a caring teacher who, on her own time, cared for the emotional needs of this student. Who, in discussion with a parent, provided the name of a qualified therapist, transported the child to therapy and participated in the beginning of what was hoped to be effective treatment for this child.

I see a teacher who exhibits characteristics I strive for when looking for quality educators. She put her duties for this child first. Imagine what could have happened if Ms. Montanye had not intervened.

Susan Roberts Bolash, M.Ed

It was now time for the expert witnesses reports. Remember when I said an expert is *supposed* to be impartial or objective? Well, that is not always the case. The district's list of "experts" could not have been considered unbiased:

Dr. Stanley Durtan	Defendant/Employee WSD
Ms. Judith Clark	Employee WSD
Imelda Kormos	Employee WSD
Thomas Speakman	Employee WSD
Barbara A. Rizzo, Esquire	Defendant's Acquaintance
Barry O. Smith	Defendant's Acquaintance

Their reports echoed each other in thought and mode of expression. It was as if they had all been penned by one person, or the authors were following a script.

Stanley Durtan

There was nothing very new in Durtan's "report." He answered a number of repetitive questions. He was still hiding behind the false premise of IDEA:

> Of particular concern are the facts that she failed to secure written permission of Student #1's parents before subjecting her to an evaluation and related therapy, she did not provide parents with the required procedural safeguard notice, and she failed to make the appropriate Special Education referral.

Do you recall Ms. Clark's testimony pertaining to this elusive form?

Attorney Dragotta: Do parents need the permission of the school district to take their children to outside therapists?

Clark: No they do not.

Again, Durtan inexplicably complained that I did not refer Kay to the WIN team. He skipped the part about the WIN team's knowledge of Kay and her problems. He also overlooked the fact that she was in the mental health system already.

What is unfathomable is Dr. Durtan's claim that I should have referred her to Special Education. How could I refer to a program she was already in?

The report restated these ideas several times:

- My behavior was damaging because I denied Kay contact with professionals who were trained to help her.
- Kay needed in-depth therapy and I should not have interacted with her.

- I should have contacted the appropriate personnel to get Kay help.

- I should have initiated a review of services. (*This would not have helped much because we had no services to provide Kay and re-evaluation can take months. Additionally, only the case manager of the IEP is the one who can make this recommendation and have it taken seriously. Don't forget the assistant principal's admonition that I should not be involved with any student who was not on my IEP caseload.*)

Judith Clark

Ms. Clark's report was almost a carbon copy of Durtan's. She had a few absurdities that didn't make much sense.

"She did nothing to assist K properly and also violated the IEP as she was not providing appropriate academic or emotional services." That was a new one. Clark was now saying that I was not teaching Kay and that I didn't provide her with the Emotional Support services which were not written in the IEP.

Another questionable declaration: "In my opinion, Ms. Montanye violated professional and ethical behavior when she unilaterally made the decision to discuss the suicide threat with her, assessing her mental condition, and subsequently sending her back to class."

Suddenly, Ms. Clark is concerned with FAPE (free appropriate public education): "She failed to react appropriately thus denying Kay's opportunity to FAPE." Was it not Judy Clark and the rest of the district administration that ejected Kay from school when she became a problem for them?

"Much could have been done to assist Kay. Examples of this would include referral to a psychiatrist for clinical assessment. However, due to the inappropriateness of Ms. Montanye's course of action, all of the possibilities available for Kay were negated." It's a wonder these people could sleep at night.

Interestingly enough, Ms. Clark who did not mention any IDEA violations in her deposition had a great deal to say about it in her report. This came right after the section that said I denied the WIN team the right to act.

Imelda Kormos

Ms. Kormos spelled my first and last name incorrectly throughout her "report." Either she lied or was confused about Kay's drug use and my knowledge. Kay distinctly said I was not aware of her drug use. Ms. Kormos believed that an "intervention by the team, which would have included the parents, would have been very beneficial to this student."

I "fostered a dependency" between Kay and me, which was why she wouldn't talk to anyone else in the school. *(Kay spoke with her IEP teacher many times. This was in her deposition.)*

Ms. Kormos was upset because I would sit on the curb and talk with Kay. She was concerned that parents would see this and what would they think?

I should not have let Kay return to class after I spoke with her about the suicide note. Ms. Kormos said that although Kay appeared calm, "calmness in a suicidal student can be a red flag as that could mean they are now at peace and can complete the act." Despite her extra course work in identifying at risk kids and her ability to detect at risk behavior, do you recall the red flags Imelda Kormos missed?

> **Attorney Dragotta:** And what was the main issue as you saw it for the incident in March?
>
> **Kormos:** A student who didn't want to stay in class. And had emotional problems as such. Suicide was never discussed at that point.
>
> **Attorney Dragotta**: …what was so serious about K…beyond not wanting to be in class?
>
> **Kormos:** ---at that time I think she was having quite a few absences and she was very emotional, not suicidal.

Not to be ignored was this item included in Ms. Kormos's resumé:

Psychologically Battered Child [course at Intermediate Unit]

But surprisingly, all Ms. Kormos saw was a child trying to "escape" from class.

Thomas J. Speakman

Let's refresh our familiarity with Mr. Speakman. He was the assistant principal at the high school. He was the administrative member of the WIN team who never uttered a word about Kay to the principal or the Spec Ed department. He alleged he did not know the WIN team letter was written, while Maria Salvucci said it was his idea to do so. Now, he was an expert.

He did seem somewhat misguided when speaking of the counselors and the medical professional: "These certificated professionals know the policies and procedures for working with students at risk. They also possess the human qualities of warmth, caring and understanding which are essential when dealing with students" *(and noticeably absent in the depositions of the nurse and guidance counselor).*

Then there was the ultimate sin: "As a member of the WIN/SAP team as well as an administrator, I believe that Mrs. Montanye's actions with Kay (but he used her real, full name), such as sitting on the grass in front of the school building, to be totally unprofessional." Considering the amount of classes held outside on the lawn, I found this a gross generalization. I had taken my students out to read on the lawn for all the years I had taught in this district and no one said word one. There were a number of classes held outside on nice days. If he had been so upset by this, why didn't he say something to me; he was an administrator for heaven's sake.

Mr. Speakman describes the WIN team process:

Upon receiving a referral, the trained members of the WIN/SAP Team will gather data on a student who may be considered at risk. Once the team receives the completed data from all the student's teachers, the team would analyze the data then decide to invite the student and parents to attend an Intervention Meeting. During the Intervention, the data received from the teachers would be presented to both the parent [sic] and student. Following a discussion about the data, strategies to address the concern are presented to the student and parents. In many cases, an assessment is recommended.

There are a few problems with this:

(1) The WIN team knew about Kay in **September.**
(2) I didn't even start talking to her until **October.**
(3) The WIN team did not send out data retrieval forms for Kay.
(4) The WIN team had no feedback from teachers for Kay, before, during or after my relationship with her.
(5) The team **had** an intervention meeting.
(6) Kay was **ALREADY** in the mental health system.

It was Mr. Speakman's understanding that "none of the Special Education teachers at Wissahickon High School were designated as Emotional Support teachers." Had Mr. Speakman looked on the teacher's roster and the teacher's seniority list he would have been shocked to find that there were **FOUR** Emotional Support teachers in his school that year. We had children classified as needing Emotional Support; that requires at least the pretense of Emotional Support teachers.

Then there was the specter of me destroying Kay. "By assuming the role of counselor, Mrs. Montanye discussed with Kay some very sensitive issues that potentially, if handled improperly, could have damaged or possibly proved fatal for the student." (If-could-possibly- these words sound familiar?) This is the land in which Mr. Levin resides; the land of accusing people with "possibilities."

What about the people who hurt this child in reality, not possibility? **I** didn't send her home into complete isolation that triggered a suicide attempt.

Then the assistant principal confusingly said: "It is my opinion that Mrs. Montanye's rapport with Kay was not genuine; she did cross the line by driving the student to therapy and participating in therapy sessions." (I have no idea what he meant by this.)

It was my fault others weren't working with me. "It is my opinion that for Mrs. Montanye to really help this student she should have work [sic] collaboratively with the nurse, the guidance counselor, her teaching colleagues and the WIN/SAP team." I would have gladly worked with any and all of these people. The guidance counselor was not interested, the nurse thought Kay should to be forced to go to class, and the WIN team never contacted me, but instead studied my interaction with Kay. This was my first year in the high school, and I found many of these people to be aloof and uninterested. My Special Education colleagues were the only support I received that year. But there was little we could do for Kay.

It still begs the question why this administrator did nothing, said nothing, wrote nothing, advised no one about all this danger I was putting Kay in. He knew about her from the first week of school and yet said **nothing**. Why didn't he at least say something to the principal during their weekly update meetings? And why, pray tell, did this administrator find it totally acceptable that the WIN team had no data forms ever filled out for this child? And why didn't he know there was an intervention meeting with the parents? Didn't he see the log? Didn't his WIN team compatriots tell him about Kay, her history, and the intervention?

Barbara A. Rizzo, *Esquire*

Ms. Rizzo worked in a practice in central Pennsylvania. I wondered if she knew Michael Levin from law school.

I'm not sure where Ms. Rizzo was gathering her information, but it all sounded very unfamiliar. For example, despite a lack of transportation policy, Ms. Rizzo knew that "prior written permission from a parent is necessary to transport a student and any such transportation is not done by a staff member other than a bus driver or van driver." There was nowhere in our district where this was committed to writing. It wasn't in Pennsylvania law either.

Here's a new twist that was not mentioned by any of the administrators in their testimony. According to Ms. Rizzo, prior to 2001-2002 the WSD adopted a procedure by which referrals for outside therapeutic services were provided through **one of the student assistance programs** and provided by guidance counselors or school psychologists. This was not a policy. In fact, this '"procedure" was not listed anywhere nor was it common knowledge among the staff. School psychologists just do testing. They do not give or recommend therapy or therapists. Again, there was only **one** student assistant program. Same mistake or deliberate false information—Michael Levin kept supplying.

Ms. Rizzo claimed there was a "protocol" that had been established (teachers not allowed in therapy with students) "and was to be followed by the teachers of the WSD regardless of whether a parent approved any action by the teacher inconsistent with the procedures or policies." I have not found any of these protocols or policies. In addition, Michael Levin never provided any quote from this fictitious protocol. Neither did Ms. Rizzo.

To add support to her thoughts, Ms. Rizzo invented a number of policies that I allegedly violated:

(1) District policy relating to student schedules. *(There was no policy for this; the schools had their own way of doing this.)*

(2) Failure to comply with school district policies relating to transportation. *(We already know that didn't exist.)*

(3) Failing to follow a policy concerning a process to refer a student for an outside intervention. *(There was no such policy.)*

(4) Exceeding the appropriate boundaries of the student/teacher relationship by going to therapy without prior written permission and consent of the parents and prior written approval of supervisor.

(This is a crock. Apparently our legal counselor had not heard of the PA Mental Health Laws that would preclude written approval from parents and supervisors. Kay was the only one who could do this.)

(5) Failure to comply with federal and state law by failing to refer K for re-evaluation to address her emotional difficulties. (*Gee, shouldn't Kelle Heim-McCloskey have seen to that, considering she was putting her out of the district on a posttraumatic stress disorder diagnosis?*)

Despite the extensive investigation Dr. Durtan and his assistants conducted, Barbara Rizzo emphatically states that he had no idea of the suicide note before the Loudermill, (according to his deposition he had no idea of it **after** the Loudermill.)

In a footnote, Ms. Rizzo pointed out there "was no reference made to the suicidal [sic] note nor a copy of it provided, at the Loudermill hearing." Well, counselor, there was a reason for that.

Number one: who was taking notes at the Loudermill hearing? Mr. Levin. Mention of the note would not benefit the district as it proved my point about Kay's situation and the need to respond to her precarious predicament. In keeping with the suppression of evidence, Mr. Levin did not ask for the note or a copy of it. Of course I had it with me; the attorney brushed over my reference to it. Do you want to know why? Because they really weren't interested in **my side of the story.**

Ms. Rizzo proffered that Dr. Durtan was correct in holding a Loudermill hearing because the high school principal " had not acted appropriately to preclude Ms. Montanye taking such actions and/or to rein her in …"

Ms. Rizzo discussed the schedule change in depth, but then dismissed it as moot. Of course she did not get it quite right: "As noted, the building principal, Mr. Anderson, had previously issued a memorandum to Ms. Montanye to address the schedule change issue." The assistant principal wrote the memorandum to me. He was the one who put Kay back in the class with her persecutors. (footnote #3/p.13)

Now here is the crux of the matter:

> Thus, it was appropriate for Dr. Durtan to address these concerns in writing to Ms. Montanye, particularly in light of her representations at the Loudermill hearing that she believed what she did was right, and the suggestion implicit in those comments that she would take the same action again if she had to do it all over again.

I was not contrite. I did not apologize for helping Kay. I maintained that keeping a child alive was an appropriate act, not one deserving of punishment. I did not agree that a dead kid had no impact on the community. I did not sign on to the idea that her problems were **her** problems. I could not support the philosophy that turning your back on a desperate child was professional. I could not join Dr. Durtan and his colleagues in their deliberate indifference and the pernicious eradication of moral and ethical responsibility.

Sidebar: One day Attorney Dragotta and I were walking through Grand Central Station. She was discussing the district's "fear" that I might repeat these actions. Suddenly, Sarah put her bags down, raised her hands, and called out at the top of her voice: "Will someone *please* stop this woman before she saves another child's life!"

Ms. Rizzo, who as an attorney would know that supposition must have evidence to back it up, gives a list of "district policies" that I violated. In her long list of resources used, she did not list the policy manual of WSD or the faculty manuals. Instead, she used Durtan and Clark's "testimony" which asserted the same claim but lacked any evidentiary proof.

> Moreover, as Dr. Durtan and Ms. Clark...testified, it is not appropriate or the role of a teacher to actually participate in a therapy session with a student not her own child. Notably this protocol had been established, and was to be followed by the teachers of the WSD regardless of whether the parent approved any action by the teacher inconsistent with the procedures or policies.

Unfortunately, Ms. Rizzo cannot cite where these policies and procedures are located. They don't exist! The one policy I violated was created months after the alleged violation. I do not believe this was included in the list of items.

Again, the "expert" parroted Mr. Levin's arguments. I kept Kay from the WIN team; I kept her away from the crisis counselor. (That would be the Drop-in Center counselor who was **not** a crisis counselor and was only there part time, and who sat on the WIN team and thus was already aware of Kay.)

What was amusing was Ms. Rizzo's staunch advocacy of Dr. Durtan: he protected the district from potential costly liability exposure (the parents' lawsuit because their child was not dead?) and his Directives Letter removed or reduced the potential for legal action against the district. Ms. Rizzo didn't see the defects in her argument: (1) Durtan did not protect the district from a lawsuit; he brought one to it. (2) Durtan (and his attorney) didn't even notify the district it had a potential lawsuit until the papers were delivered. (3) The Directives Letter was the main catalyst for the lawsuit. All these violations and machinations: the superintendent, the assistant superintendent, the supervisor of Special Education, the director of human resources, the hired attorney never felt the need to let the school board in on the secret?

Dr. Barry O. Smith

I believe Dr. Smith worked for the Office of Dispute Resolution in Harrisburg. Dr. Smith started off his letter with "Dear Mr. **Levine**." Not to feel bad, he also spelled my last name incorrectly all the through the report.

Dr. Smith first threw his support behind the WIN team. He focused on the accusation that I should have been in class when I was seen outside. Keep in mind both Salvucci and Kormos could only identify one "incident" of me sitting outside with Kay which was reported a number of times. Neither woman knew my schedule, and neither one checked on this schedule when they noticed me out front. As you may recall, Kormos's best estimation of when she saw me was whenever she looked up from her desk. Not likely.

He also quoted the wrong classification for my certificate.

Then he started with the party line:

- I admitted to determining which counselor Kay would see.
- I provided transportation to the sessions.
- I participated in the sessions.
- I did not refer Kay for a re-eval for her IEP. (I was not the case manager—she was the only one allowed to make a formal recommendation).
- It was my fault she had an inadequate IEP (even though I did not write it).
- AND! I did not notify Kay and her mother of their procedural rights, despite the fact that this is done at the end of an IEP meeting or WHEN THE DISTRICT IS PROVIDING A SERVICE. I was not the district. The therapist was private. The procedural rights said **nothing** about private therapy or services parents received **outside** of school. One would think a hearing officer would know this bit of information.

Dr. Smith put a new twist on an old saw. Because I exceeded my responsibility as a teacher and used poor judgment, I "placed the District in the position of denying Kay her civil rights." Now, I had forced the district into colluding with me to deny this child her civil rights by not letting her die. But I couldn't be in collusion with the district: because when they had the opportunity to help Kay, they booted her to the curb. They had plenty of practice in violating her civil rights. In fact, they had the entire district administration and the middle school principal denying her an education.

Not to be outdone, Dr. Smith brought in those infamous "lines."

...This area of certification...allows a teacher to teach. It does not extend to the type of discussions that K testified about in her deposition. Teachers need to interact with students and be empathetic to their needs. However, teachers must also know there is a line, which they should not cross. Montayne [sic] does not know either where that line is or refuses to recognize that the line exists.

In fact, "in forty years of public education I have **never** encountered a teacher who lacked the understanding of the responsibilities of a teacher demonstrated by Montayne. [sic] "

Not to be left out, Smith went after Joe's IEP's. He found two of them too vague and one barely passible. He tried to suggest that Joe had written some of the speech goals. No way. But for some reason he had no problem with the fact that they were accepted and filed as adequate. Does Dr. Smith think that no one checks these? Say a supervisor of Special Education?

These reports were all renditions of the same thoughts, the same inaccurate information based on the same make believe policies and procedures. Not to mention the fact that three of Joe's IEP's went to Dr. Barry Smith **without parental permission**. In one case, the child's full name was used. Plus, Kay had never signed a release to WSD to send her IEP to Ms. Rizzo or Dr. Smith. So much for the letter of the law.

*****

My experts were not related to me, (Imelda Kormos was mother of board member Donna Leadbeater), did not work for me, had not entered into deceptive behavior with me, nor did their well being depend on my largesse by agreeing with me. I never met my experts except for the vocational therapist who interviewed me. The others were faceless strangers.

Allan M. Tepper, J.D. Psy.D

Dr. Tepper was a psychologist and an attorney. Unlike the district's experts, Dr. Tepper was succinct. His discussion contained two paragraphs. He believed that Kay was in a serious psychological situation and that it was reasonable to institute a plan of action to diffuse the threat of self-destructive behavior. Sarah believed this was good because it was both legal and psychological. Seemed a little skimpy to me.

Susan R. Bolash

Ms. Bolash had great credentials:

- 33 years in a public school setting
- Special Education teacher
- Special Education coordinator
- Supervisor/Director Special Education in Easton Area School District
- Facilitator for crisis intervention teams
- Supervisor of daily duties for certified school psychologists

She went through most of the testimony and evidence from the whole case.

She started off with:

I am experienced with working with administrators, teachers, parents, and support personnel in addressing student needs and am, quite frankly, shocked at what has occurred to this high school Special Education teacher, Ms. Montanye, as a result of attending to the very real and serious needs of her student, Kay.

Ms. Bolash obviously understood the concept of a family in crisis:

> Ms. Montanye went the extra mile…she notified the appropriate school supervisor…and facilitated appropriate interventions…Ms. Montanye demonstrated compassion not only in helping Kay, but also in assisting the parent through what appears to have been most trying times.

Ms. Bolash questioned the district's reaction:

> In light of Ms. Montanye's knowledge and training as a Special Education teacher, taking action to ensure Kay's safety in the manner in which she did was the responsible action to take. The actions of the Wissahickon School Board, Superintendent, Stanley J. Durtan, and the Wissahickon School District in formally reprimanding Ms. Montanye and subjecting her to a Loudermill Hearing are actions I find unfathomable when the steps taken by Ms. Montanye were not only appropriate but, also, necessary by both moral and educational standards.

My expert saw the charge of the schedule change for what it was: "The issue of changing a class and notifying a principal seems to be one that should have been reasonably corrected. In my opinion, the heightened scrutiny this particular event was given was unwarranted.[14]

Ms. Bolash stated my actions in reporting the note to my supervisor, following my supervisor's instructions, and reporting back to my supervisor were appropriate and done in a timely fashion, considering the immediacy of the situation.

Unlike the district, Ms. Bolash was not impressed with the WIN team.

> The quality of the WIN team's response is what should be questioned in that there appeared to have been no level of intervention from anyone on the team. In the Anderson Affidavit, he states that when he gave the note

---

[14] In "real" life something like this wouldn't warrant more than a verbal reminder.

to the school nurse, a member of the WIN team, she said she was "too busy to read it at the moment."

Furthermore, it appears that one of the only actions taken by a member of the WIN team was to discredit and discourage any assistance from Ms. Montanye...The letter from the WIN team to Mr. Anderson was particularly disturbing and, at the same time suspect in terms of motivation. Why, indeed, would a "team" write a letter of concern and then not sign it? Seeing the level of support this teacher was capable and willing to provide this child, why did the team not embrace Ms. Montanye's involvement as part of the WIN team in serving this child? I can't help thinking there may have been personal/professional animosity as a motivating factor rather than professional responsibility.

Ms. Bolash was appalled that a member of the WIN team, "didn't have time to read" a potentially serious suicide note, especially about a student who (according to Ms. Kormos) was a troubled girl. Quoting Mr. Anderson, she questioned why the team did not provide "some sort of support." She then added, "that thankfully, 'that support' ...was provided by Ms. Montanye, a caring, diligent teacher."

Kay's IEP was found by this expert to be sadly lacking.

The resulting IEP does not mention or take into account Kay's known hospitalization for emotional and suicidal ideation. Furthermore, this IEP dismisses any behaviors that impede learning by answering NO to section 1(C) of the IEP. I believe emotional issues were evident and that a behavioral support plan and/or interventions were indicated but not developed. (*I was not present at the writing of this IEP.*)

While one can make the argument that perhaps the particular IEP team members did not know of any prior emotional problems[15], it remains the responsibility of the

---

[15] That would be an omission on the part of the previous IEP team and the Supervisor, Kelle Heim-McCloskey.

WSD and Superintendent to ensure that information comes to the table when IEP's are developed.

As Ms. Bolash pointed out, the fact that it was noted that Kay became overwhelmed and needed to speak with an appropriate adult demonstrated that there was some awareness of this child's emotional distress. This sentence indicated that Kay's emotional issues could impede her learning. By developing a purely academic IEP without related services, such as counseling, made the document inadequate.

Ms. Bolash also took umbrage with Dr. Durtan's philosophy from the Directives Letter:

> that the "fundamental mission of the school district is to educate students...the school district has no duty nor even the capacity to respond to a student's needs that do not affect the student's ability to learn."

My expert pointed out that a school district "does in fact, have an expressed obligation to ensure that a child with a disability, as in the case of K, has all the related services necessary to access that education. It's the law.

As far as IDEA and PA law were concerned, Ms. Bolash found the district in violation of these:

- 34 CFR 300.347 (a) (3) required related services
- 34 CFR 300.30 public agencies must provide counseling services
- 34CFR 300.24 (b) (9) related services—psychological services

Furthermore, Ms. Montanye in no way violated IDEA or PA Chapter 14 by providing the name of a therapist.

Ms. Bolash followed this up with:

> As with any medical intervention...a parent always has the right to provide private counseling/therapy for her child...Kay's mother recognized a need for therapy and in discussion with Ms. Montanye, a trusted individual, was advised of the name of a counselor. Kay's mother

exercised her parental right to provide therapy for Kay at her own expense. To suggest that this is in any way a violation of IDEA or Chapter 14 is ludicrous.

Also of note, Ms. Bolash pointed out the difference between seeking therapy and seeking an independent evaluation. Kay's mother was not seeking an evaluation or a re-evaluation at the district's expense; hence, no form was required.

To suggest that the district be given the opportunity to address Kay's mental health needs through a re-evaluation that could take up to 60 school days would have been an irresponsible action. Sixty days to do what?

It was clear that the IEP team did not address Kay's needs in providing specially designed instruction to succeed emotionally in the classroom. It is clear that the WIN team failed Kay in providing intervention. Now it is suggested that the parent wait 60 days to allow this same school district the opportunity to evaluate?

Ms. Bolash did not feel that I had "crossed the lines" that the district felt were ever present.

Clearly, this teacher recognized that individual counseling was the responsibility of a licensed professional as demonstrated by her referral for outside counseling. Most appropriately, she provided a name of an individual who was listed on the district's recommended list of counselors...Ms. Montanye's assistance after school on her own time should be admired not admonished.

******

Although not an expert opinion, there was a surprise affidavit written in May 2005. It was included with a pleading. It was written by Charles Herring, attorney for PSEA. It was written for the defendants.

- The affidavit stated he had attended two Loudermill hearings in the 1990's. Neither was held for a Special Education teacher.

  This was designed to discredit our assertion that I was the first to undergo a Loudermill Hearing. I am not sure these hearings were labeled Loudermills.

  The fact that two Loudermill Hearings were held ten years before mine and they were not held for Special Education teachers was supposed to nullify the charge that WSD was targeting Spec Ed teachers.

- Mr. Herring represented the WEA (local union) with respect to an unfair labor practice charge for Ms. Montanye.

  He did not point out the unfair labor practice had been dropped by the union.

- Mr. Herring filed a grievance pertaining to Ms. Montanye.

- He also stated that the grievance was processed in accordance with the grievance provisions of the collective bargaining agreement. *(Keep this in mind for later on.)*

- Additionally, "by agreement of the parties, the grievance is now being held in abeyance pending this lawsuit."

The Levin Legal Group received the affidavit on May 10th.

Sarah Dragotta was incensed. By this point, nothing surprised me as far as PSEA was concerned. Mr. Herring justified his actions because it would preclude being called to court, and he "didn't want to be dragged down to Philadelphia in mid-August." Maybe Mr. Levin and Mr. Herring "joked around" about this. To me this was not a joking matter. According to my attorneys this was collusion: *def.* to appear as adversaries though in agreement.

CHAPTER TWENTY-TWO

Falsus Uno, Falsus Omnibus

And the question is whether you want to use this opportunity not just to do justice in this case, which sorely needs some justice, but whether you want to use this opportunity to give some power, some breathing room to those who want to make things better, to those who want to be advocates for kids, or whether you want to strengthen the dead hand of this bureaucracy whose face you've seen.

Attorney Kafoury: Closing Argument from
Settlegoode v. Portland Public Schools

Summary judgment is rendered when the court decides the pleadings, depositions, answers to interrogatories, admissions, and affidavits show there are no genuine issues of material fact and that the party applying for summary judgment is entitled to it as a matter of law. In other words, when all the evidence is considered, if there is no decision for a jury to make, the case is dismissed. At this point, the judge is to consider the evidence in favor of the non-moving party. Also included in this definition is the caveat: …The Third Circuit (eastern district courts) urges special caution in granting summary judgment to an **employer** when its intent is at issue particularly in discrimination and retaliation cases. In my case, intent was definitely at the heart of the matter, and it was a discrimination charge.

Joshua Axlerod, a new addition to the Levin Legal Group, wrote the memorandum of Law In Support of Defendants' Motion For Summary Judgment. Josh graduated law school with Sarah Dragotta. Six degrees of separation.

The motion stated that Superintendent Durtan, "believed that the School District had an obligation to investigate the allegations and to take action reasonably calculated to end any improper conduct" (Durtan Affidavit). If this were the case, one would ask why Dr. Durtan did not notify the school district that he "believed he had an obligation to investigate the allegations…" Dr. Durtan was **NOT** the school district, the school board is.

Next, Mr. Axelrod assured the court that, "The draft affidavit accurately summarizes the information provided at the *Loudermill*/investigative meeting (Ftnt #4 pg 4). This was done to legitimize the affidavit that was not signed or endorsed by me. It was not an "accurate" summarization of the Loudermill hearing; it was Michael Levin's filtered rendition of what was said.

Mr. Axelrod compounded his misrepresentations by misquoting Kay's therapist. In a footnote, he claimed that Dr. Ex "represented Montanye as an attorney later in 2002." This was an out-and-out falsehood; this was not in Dr. Ex's deposition because it had never happened. She never provided me with legal representation.

Mr. Axelrod held to the LLG theory that accusing someone of an act that is not associated with any particular law is the same thing as finding someone guilty of violating a law. In response to our statement, "Defendant presented no evidence to support the charges made in the May 1, 2002 letter," Mr. Axelrod said:

> This allegation is peculiar and troubling. The factual allegations in the Loudermill notice letter were: "improperly involving yourself in situations pertaining to student 1, making an appointment for the student with a therapist, transporting the student to a therapist, participating in the therapy session with the student…How Montanye can possibly allege in her Third Amended Complaint that the Defendants presented no evidence when she admitted those factual allegations is mystifying.

What Mr. Axelrod neglected to understand was that there were no laws against any of the above-mentioned activities. Evidence is material that shows a statute has been violated. An action is not equivalent to a violation of law if there is no law to address that action.

The old arguments were trotted out again. In essence, this was what they were claiming:

- An IEP addresses a child's needs after school hours, for services not provided by the district.
- An IEP addresses a child's needs once the child has gone home.
- A school district is technically delivering a service when a child receives private therapy outside of school hours.
- Private therapy is equivalent to services provided by the school during school hours.
- Private therapy paid for by the parents, provided by the parents is covered under IDEA, although the parents do not receive federal funding for it.
- A parent must sign an apocryphal permission slip granting herself permission to take her child to private therapy.
- If the child is fourteen years or older, she must sign an imaginary permission slip granting her parents permission to take her to private therapy.
- A school's evaluation for Special Education placement is the equivalent procedure as a private therapeutic session with a student after school hours.
- The Procedural Safeguards Notice that provides parents with information to redress the district if they feel their child is not receiving programs from the school that are guaranteed by law is applicable to a private therapist who is not operating under the umbrella of IDEA.
- A fourteen year old child cannot choose who comes into her private therapy session unless the school district grants permission.
- A non-existent school district transportation policy applies to a student once she has returned home from school.

The irony of the district's argument always was that they were not responsible for all the harm Kay underwent in school and for the denial of an education. However, the district claimed it had a say in what the child did **after she left their care and during her private life when she was not in school?** This argument was rooted in two documents: (1) The Procedural Safeguards Notice which only applied to the school district and the programs provided to the students (2) a permission form that did not exist (Clark Deposition). The district was arguing that Dr.

Durtan's actions were rational based on the fact that I did not get a **non-existent** form signed, and I did not give the mother a paper that was not applicable to private therapy.

Mr. Axelrod stated that Dr. Durtan had "numerous reasons for holding the Loudermill hearing and issuing the Directives Letter...and they were certainly all rational." He then listed those rational reasons which included an interest in ensuring that:

(1) The school district avoided legal exposure.
   (That would be the parents suing the district because they were upset that their child was still alive.)
(2) The school district's students were safe.
   *(Maybe other students were, but Kay wasn't safe from the time she was the target of the bullies and was pushed out of school and beyond; she was **never** safe during her ninth grade year.)*
(3) There was compliance by the Plaintiff with the law and school district policy.
   (As a private citizen, after school hours, IDEA did not apply to me, and I did not violate any district policies—written or unwritten.)
(4) School district programs were used.
   (Spec Ed was used, the Child Study Team was not because Kelle Heim-McCloskey did not recommend Kay to them; the WIN team ignored the suicide note and their knowledge of Kay's first suicide attempt).
(5) A proper teacher/student relationship was maintained.
   *(Their **only** definition of **improper relationship** was paying attention to the needs of this child).*

And of course, there was the notion that the WIN team (my peers and co-workers) believed I had acted inappropriately. Let's see what my "co-workers" were actually saying under oath:

- **Maria Salvucci** said that once a child was in the mental health system the WIN team had no responsibility.
- **Maria Salvucci** denied she was given a suicide note.
- **Maria Salvucci** discussed a child not on the WIN team during WIN team meetings.

- **Maria Salvucci** assumed I was giving "therapy" despite not having any idea of the content of those conversations.
- **Maria Salvucci** provided a disjointed and conflicting scenario of how the WIN team letter came to be.
- **Imelda Kormos** violated the confidentiality of the student's mental health record.
- **Imelda Kormos** whose interference landed Kay in a mental health facility.
- **Imelda Kormos** "forgot" about Kay's suicide attempt.
- **Imelda Kormos** denied receiving Kay's suicide note.
- **Imelda Kormos** didn't "feel" Kay was suicidal.
- **Imelda Kormos** knew Kay was troubled but wanted to keep her from "escaping" class.
- **Imelda Kormos** admitted another violation of confidentiality by discussing a student at the WIN team meetings, although he was not part of the WIN team.
- **Thomas Speakman** an assistant principal **never** discussed a suicidal child with his principal.
- **Thomas Speakman never** spoke with the principal about the team's "concerns."
- **Thomas Speakman never** spoke to me about his concerns, which as my supervisor he would have been well within his right to do.
- **Thomas Speakman** should have referred Kay to the child study team.
- **Thomas Speakman** who should have contacted the supervisor of Special Education about his concerns but chose not to.
- **Thomas Speakman,** who according to Maria Salvucci, came up with the idea of writing an anonymous letter condemning me for helping a desperate child.
- **Thomas Speakman** denied knowing about the existence of the letter he allegedly proposed should be written.

In order to decide whether my co-workers had any legitimate intentions, you have to choose which story of the WIN team letter you want to believe:

(1) Salvucci wrote the letter, Kormos read the letter, and no one else knew about it? In this case, it was not my co-workers. It was an angry nurse and resentful guidance counselor who fashioned this epistle.

(2) The entire team wrote the letter, and not *one* person thought to discuss any of this with me? Not *one* person went to the union rep to check on protocol? The rest of the team was too ashamed or afraid to sign individual names to this letter?

The lawyer for the district then declared that "the entire WIN team" believed my actions were inappropriate. This was based on the inconsistent stories coming only from Maria Salvucci and Imelda Kormos.

The attorney then transitioned to the IEP. "The IEP team is to revise the IEP to address lack of progress, necessary changes arising from re-evaluation of the child..." Would this be the IEP team meeting that was never held when Dr. Durtan forced Kay out of school in March 2001? "The law is clear that when information justifies the reconvening of an IEP team, such a team needs to be reconvened." The law does not exempt the superintendent, assistant superintendent, Special Education supervisor, or middle school principal.

Next came the Directives Letter. Here is an assumption that made no sense. "By issuing the Directives Letter...Durtan sought to insure that the Special Education laws were followed in the future if Montanye **elected to have a relationship with a student like she had with student 1**[Kay]." But I thought I was never to repeat this behavior. Wasn't their fear based on the assumption I might save another child?

Durtan was also defended with the argument of *professional judgment*, which states if a professional makes a professional judgment that judgment is automatically considered valid. Funny, I was a professional, and thought I was making a professional judgment.

The school board was off the hook because they didn't "know about" it. A school board member, Marjorie Brown, wrote yet another affidavit declaring that no one on the school board knew about any of this. How she knew what everyone on the board knew or didn't know was never established.

*****

Sarah Dragotta came back with the Plaintiff's Response to Defendants' Motion for Summary Judgment. Her theme was *falsus uno, falsus omnibus.*[16] Retaliation was one of her first talking points. Sarah pointed to a new case, *Jackson v. Birmingham Board of Education* No. 02-1672. It established that a coach who complained that his girls' team had been discriminated against, in violation of Title IX, was fired in retaliation. The Supreme Court upheld the charge of retaliation. Thus, Attorney Dragotta claimed that because Kay fell within the bounds of IDEA and ADA, I had a claim of retaliation, as the district had no legitimate reason for what they had done.

Another point she made was new, and cogent:

> Moreover, Defendants' actions toward Plaintiff and others interfere with the constitutional rights of parents and guardians to direct and control the upbringing and development of their minor children, whose liberty rights are protected in the Fifth and Fourteenth Amendments of the U.S. Constitution.

Then she added, Kay's mother decided to send her child to this therapist and paid for the service. Wissahickon School District, under the guise of being concerned for an ignored, suicidal child, argued through the superintendent that I was not allowed to accompany the child as she had requested and her mother had permitted. Once again, the district interfered to Kay's detriment. She also pointed out that no one with a rational mind could accept the reasons the district was desperately manufacturing.

Sarah introduced another new case: *Settlegoode v. Portland Public Schools* 371 F. 3d 503 at 514 (2004). The decision of *Settlegoode* stated: "Teachers may therefore be the only guardians of these children's rights and interests during the school day." Additionally, the court added, "Teachers are uniquely situated to know whether students are receiving the type of attention and education that they deserve and, in this case are federally entitled to."

---

[16] false in one, false in all – lie to one person, lie to everyone

Background: *Settlegoode v. Portland Public Schools*

Dr. Settlegoode was an adaptive physical education teacher. She was concerned how her disabled students were treated. She was also upset about irregularities in IEP's (back dating) and in students **not** getting what was stated in the IEP. [17] She wrote letters pointing these things out. She was told by her supervisor to stop writing letters. Settlegoode received good evaluations until she started her letter writing. Suddenly her evaluations were negative. Her supervisor advised that she not be rehired for the next year. The teacher wrote to the superintendent of Portland schools, claiming discrimination against her for advocating for her students. Her letter was ignored and she was not rehired. Dr. Settlegoode sued. The defendants presented many arguments about the teacher's "deficiencies." One of their complaints was her writing of the IEP's. They presented thirty IEP's to the jury to show the "flaws" in the documents. When asked by Settlegoode's attorney if the district revised the lacking IEP's, the answer was no. (Sound familiar?) Settlegoode eventually won her First Amendment claim.

Attorney Dragotta pointed out that my work environment was "hostile" and I was punished and intimidated for advocating for Special Education students. She ended with, "An adult in a position of authority who acts to save the life of a child is to be commended." She then requested summary judgment in our favor.

She followed this with Plaintiff's Memorandum of Law Opposing Defendants' Motion for Summary Judgment. In this pleading, Sarah went through Kay's entire history, the story of the district's neglect, and my assistance to her in ninth grade.

Attorney Dragotta pointed out that Dr. Durtan's:

...allegations of potential liability are pretextual because during the 1999—2000 school year through 2004-2005 school year other administrators and WSD teachers transported students in their own vehicles, sometimes without parent permissions and sometimes in violation of motor vehicle laws.

---

[17] There are no cases where a district was sued for providing more than the IEP promised. Wissahickon was the only district that lived in fear of this charge.

Importantly, during the 2001-2002 school year, Defendants did not have (1) a written policy for transporting students, or (2) a procedure that suggested that teachers get parental permission before transporting students.

What was more damning was her paragraph that dealt with Kay and the probable outcome if she had killed herself. Attorney Dragotta stated unequivocally:

> Most importantly, if K had killed herself and it was determined that Montanye and Defendants WSD, School Board and Superintendent Durtan knew of her suicidal tendencies and attempts and did nothing, their liability would have been incalculable.

Funny that Michael Levin with his risk management background and Dr. Durtan with his expertise in education did not consider this. Of course, there may be another explanation. Perhaps these people did consider the ramifications of Kay successfully committing suicide and a resulting wrongful death lawsuit from the parents. I was the teacher who could prove that Kay was ignored in the high school and continued to be harassed. I was the teacher who could link them to a charge of negligence. Maybe they thought if they got rid of me then they would not have to worry down the line if Kay were able to carry out her dark wish.[18]

Part of Kay's therapist's deposition was quoted on my behalf:

> **Levin:**... Did you write that letter on or about May 22, 2002?
>
> **Therapist:** Yes, I did.
>
> **Levin:** Did you write that letter because you wanted to help Ms. Montanye?
>
> **Therapist:**...I wrote that letter because I had strong feelings about some of the actions that Ms. Montanye had taken, and I felt that I wanted to go on record about that.

---

[18] Getting rid of Robert Anderson made it a clean sweep.

339

Levin: Why did you want to support Ms. Montanye?

Therapist: Well, because I feel so often teachers do not go the extra mile, and that when I observe someone that cares enough to take their time to help a student, I wanted to make sure that I underscored my thoughts on it.

Sarah addressed the inferior WIN team log entries and the lack of information to be found in them:

> Put simply, the Defendants, including the WHS WIN team, were deficient in their own policies and did nothing to secure the protection and education of K.
> After March 14, 2002, the WHS WIN Team focused all of its efforts on silencing Montanye, who helped K complete the school year.
> Rather than follow up with K's parents or link K to appropriate supportive services in the school and community, which is its responsibility, the WHS WIN Team wrote a letter against Montanye…In fact the WIN Team accuses Montanye of being an impediment to a process that it did not even implement. It was Montanye who provided necessary help and support to a student and her family in their time of crises.

Attorney Dragotta wanted to make sure the judge understood that my "affidavit" from the Loudermill was a fraudulent representation of the hearing. (This will prove an important point later on.)

> There was no record made of the Loudermill Hearing. Nevertheless, the defendants stated in their Motion for Summary Judgment that the information provided at the Loudermill Hearing is accurately "summarized in a "draft affidavit" prepared by Defendants' Counsel, which was never signed by Montanye. However, the Defendants' recollection is not to be trusted.

The absurd contention of Thomas Speakman's affidavit stated that there were no Emotional Support teachers in the high school was her next target:

Moreover, the Defendants have attempted to portray Montanye as not being an emotional support teacher. In stark contrast, Montanye was appointed by the Wissahickon School District Board of Directors as a Special Education Emotional Support Teacher in her area of certification at the Wissahickon Middle School.

As Attorney Dragotta illustrated, by law the district was required to offer an Emotional Support program. We had children who were classified as Emotional Support students. Their IEP's stated they were in the Emotional Support category. Now the district's assistant principal was swearing there were no teachers present to work with this group in the high school. In an effort to please his employers and cast doubt on me, Thomas Speakman was stating the district was out of compliance with IDEA. Consequently, Emotional Support children were not being given the services and support guaranteed by IDEA and PA state regulations. Being out of compliance suggests illegal placements and gross negligence on the part of the administration, the board, and the district that purports to follow the IDEA. Speakman did not think his lie through. *Falsus uno, falsus omnibus.*

Sarah brought to light one of our witnesses who proved the lack of programming for children with emotional issues. Student J was placed on homebound for a year. Although enrolled in WSD, the psychological report implied that J was on homebound all year from another school. Not so. He came to WSD and was put on homebound by the district, *for an entire school year.* The psychologist opened his IEP meeting by saying J could not stay home because it was illegal. He had to come back to school. The district had no program, no plan, not one idea about what to do for this kid. He suffered from social phobia, but he was put in all regular classes (although his testing showed him to be gifted). He started out sitting in the guidance office. That was Maria Salvucci's idea. He came in, sat, and read by himself. Ms. Salvucci was frantic to get him out, but I had to wait for the return of the IEP before taking him into my room. The "plan" was: if J felt he could not go to class, I was to decide if he was truly too anxious or if he merely didn't want to go to class. For someone who allegedly was only capable of providing instruction, this was a great burden to put on me. The guidance department refused to do it and so did the administration. I alone was to discern the depth of his need and the veracity of his feelings.

In addition, he had been assigned to a huge study hall in the auditorium. He was totally overcome by this placement.

There were days when he would ask to go home. I was supposed to call his therapist and discuss this. The therapist was rarely available, so I let him call his mom from my room, get her permission and then walk down to the nurse's office to sign him out. Imelda Kormos was livid at this arrangement because he was supposed to ask **her** first if could go home. That's not how it was written in the IEP, but she didn't care. Despite their contentions, there were no programs for these children other than imaginary ones written on paper. I was also required to keep in contact with J's therapist and share information.

When I didn't return the next year, J had some rough going. His guidance counselor did nothing for him. He had spent many hours hiding under the staircase, not attending class. Finally, he, like Kay, got out of Wissahickon to finish high school at the community college.

The next area of discussion was the Directives Letter, which required me to

(a) Attend an appropriate seminar or training session in "where to draw the line" which is vague, overly broad and nonsensical in that it essentially directs her to learn to walk away from a suicidal child.

Attorney Dragotta also questioned the defendants' assertions that I was not disciplined, suspended, or discharged, and yet the Directives Letter was in direct contradiction to this. If nothing else, the Directives Letter was specifically designed to make it appear "to parents and others that Montanye cannot be trusted with children she is charged with educating."

Finally, Sarah asked the court to grant summary judgment to (me) the Plaintiff, citing case law that provides "if there is a conflict between the plaintiff's and the defendant's allegations or in the evidence, the plaintiff's evidence is to be believed and all reasonable inferences must be drawn in [her] favor." The judge is supposed to question if a fair-minded jury could return a verdict for the plaintiff on the evidence presented. In other words, if we had produced even the smallest amount of a genuine issue of material fact, then the judge would be compelled to either grant summary judgment to us (not probable) or deny summary judgment to the defendants and proceed toward trial.

Because I had helped my student, I underwent a list of "firsts":[19]

Montanye endured a series of firsts because she refused to resign with each increasingly differential step of disciplinary treatment toward her by Defendants.

- First teacher written up by the WIN team
- First teacher subjected to Loudermill hearing for helping a child
- First teacher given a Directives Letter which subjected her to constant scrutiny, being watched by her peers, and being put in a position to be regarded as suspect by parents/ guardians
- First teacher to have her personal freedom restricted under threat of termination of employment

Sarah ably provided arguments against qualified immunity for Durtan. He operated outside of his authority and with retaliation. His "professional" actions were not professional and did not warrant the protection of the Professional Judgment Rule. The school district lacked any policy that designated for its administrators to conduct investigations of employees or that indicated the administrator could enter into a legally binding contract with an outside agent, i.e. Levin.

As to the "affidavit" of Board member Marjorie Brown, Sarah pointed out the citing of huge amounts of money allegedly spent on Special Education did not in any way prove that the programs are offered or were of any value. Remember Mr. Speakman's affidavit: there were no Emotional Support teachers in the high school to work with the Emotional Support children.

Marjorie Brown also claimed that she was well acquainted with Special Education law. Sarah countered by saying the board member should then have had knowledge of the irregularities taking place in her district toward Special Education students.

---

[19] This was just the beginning of a long list of "firsts" and heightened scrutiny.

Sarah wanted to address some other aspects of the case, so she filed a (ready?)

PLAINTIFF'S SUPPLEMENTAL MEMORANDUM OF LAW IN SUPPORT OF HER INITIAL RESPONSE TO DEFENDANTS' MOTION FOR SUMMARY JUDGMENT.

Technically, this was a lengthier discussion centering on facets that Sarah believed had not been fully explored in the first pleading. If you are sensing a perfectionist in Sarah, you are correct. She wanted to emphasize:

- I was one of four Special Education employees targeted in the WSD.
- She introduced part of a local newsletter that contained a letter from board member Barbara Moyer complaining about the high cost of Special Education. (Moyer was specifically referring to the costly Shorehaven case, which we will see later on.)
- Sarah spent quite a few pages exposing the Loudermill irregularities and baseless charges against Joe.[20]
- The persecution and hostile work environment created around LA, a Learning Support Teacher.
- A fourth targeted teacher, VR, resigned after a flurry of personal and professional attacks by the administration, particularly when she refused to illegally keep a child out of school.
- Finally, Robert Anderson was targeted for his support of me during the 2001-2002 year.
- She also drew heavily from the Atkiss Deposition about the Loudermill hearings used to "get" teachers and the Directives Letter which was a "set up."

Her work was thorough and truthful. These are often dispensable qualities in the legal industry.

---

[20] Included was his reason for resigning: "I resigned primarily because I was told – there were unidentified administrators …going to put pressure on me and were going to continue to go after me until they made my life so miserable that I wasn't going to be able to stand it, and I would have to quit."

Of course, Mr. Axelrod came back swinging with routine arguments: Durtan didn't know about the suicide note (even after the Loudermill), the board didn't know that I had advocated for my students, etc. Mr. Axelrod was rather testy:

> However, to the extent that Montanye is trying to paint herself as the only person in the School District who cares about children, she engaged in extremely reckless behavior by making a suicide assessment and sending the student back to class.

Don't be silly; I never considered myself the only person in the school district who cared about children. But, given the actions and words of the district administrators, the school board and their attorney, it was more than evident I was the **only** person in the school district who cared about Kay.

As far as I had done it on my own time, he contended I should have worked within the system and not waited until after school hours. I was just operating as a "free agent."

It gets better. He said I did not do this on my own time because I "admitted" in my deposition that I had discussed the idea of going to therapy with Kay when we would talk during the school day. "Montanye was reacting to what occurred in school…and she *hatched the scheme* of the evaluation and treatment while in school…"

Let's get this straight: when you plan how to defraud an insurance company, you are "hatching a scheme." When you take action in response to a suicidal child, you are trying to save a life.

The rest of the argument was the usual rhetoric: I should have known better and those in charge knew nothing.

And on and on it went. When we weren't submitting briefs, we were sending in mounds of paper evidence. When an attorney sends a document to the court, she must always send a copy to opposing counsel. Sarah was obedient in this requirement. Michael Levin's office, which was operated with a number of lawyers, for some reason, could never send us their papers. There was always something wrong with their fax machine or ours. They always received our deliveries, we always received faxes from everyone else, but LLG could never seem to get those papers to fly between Huntingdon Valley and Glenside. This is an old stall tactic. It goes hand and hand with lawyers who don't number their pages. Lack of pagination can be extremely time consuming for the people reading and working with the multitude of pages. (I know you think I'm kidding, but it's the truth.)

FINALLY. Sarah decided to call it a day. After months of launching repetitive papers at each other, Attorney Dragotta filed a request to preclude further filings. She listed the myriad of filings already made and pointed out that further filings would become redundant. (would?) She also made clear that unlike the district that had deep, taxpayer pockets, I had limited resources. Michael Levin was banking on those limited resources. He did his best to deplete them.

She ended with a quote from the Federal Civil Rules Handbook:

...so long as more than one reasonable inference can be drawn, and that inference creates a genuine issue of material fact, the trier of fact is entitled to decide which inference to believe and summary judgment is not appropriate.

CHAPTER TWENTY-THREE

Summary Judgment

NEA Kate Frank/DuShane Fund. Another benefit of NEA membership is the availability of legal assistance from the Kate Frank/DuShane Fund (the "Fund"), which was established by the Representative Assembly to protect the **human, civil and professional rights** of educators…The 1993 RA voted to pay up to 46% of state costs of legal representation to guarantee adherence to local contracts and collective bargaining agreements; to uphold state fair dismissal laws; to protect constitutionally guaranteed free expression rights…For 1993-94 almost **$17 million** was budgeted for the DuShane Unified Legal Services Program.

> The NEA and AFT: Teacher Unions in Power and Politics
> Myron Lieberman, Charlene K. Haar, Leo Troy
> Pro >Active Publications

Our practice is DYNAMIC. We often find ourselves making new law through successful advocacy on behalf of our clients, generating news and even spurring new legislation as we go.

> Levin Legal Group.com

The waiting was excruciating. We sent in a pleading. We waited. The response would come. Back and forth. Always anticipating what would be said or what was going to happen. When everything was said and done, we waited for the judge to make his decision. The pace of my life was constantly shifted from off, to on, to off. When we were on, there was never enough time to get done what needed to be done. We were moving at breakneck speed. When we were waiting, time moved as slowly as ten dead men.

I would keep busy by reading law or exploring the Internet. One day I happened upon the Oklahoma Education Association page where I read about the Kate Frank/DuShane fund.

The fund was established in honor of Kate Frank, a teacher from Oklahoma who was fired without warning or an opportunity for a hearing. She was dismissed for being an Association activist. NEA President DuShane convinced the Executive Committee to put aside $10,000 for her legal defense. She won her case, and in 1945 was reinstated. After all bills were paid, $948.39 was left. It became the basis for the Kate Frank/ DuShane Fund. **"Today the fund insures that no member's rights can be exploited for lack of a legal defense."**

The NEA claims this fund is used to protect teacher's civil rights and freedom of expression. In order to start the requisition process, you have to talk to your Uniserv rep. I did just that. I asked Don Atkiss about it. I got a blank stare back. He knew nothing about it.

Not to be discouraged, I asked Chuck Herring if he knew anything about it. Nope.

Plan B: I would write (again) to Michael Simpson the assistant General Counsel in the NEA office of the General Counsel. I told him:

- I had written to the lawyers of PSEA in Harrisburg asking about the Kate Frank/DuShane fund.[21]
- I included a quote Mr. Simpson had sent me in a previous letter: "From my vantage point, it appears that teachers of special needs students are more likely than regular ed teachers to experience employment difficulties as a result of their advocacy on behalf of students"
- I asked for assistance from the Kate Frank/ DuShane fund because if I lost this case, teachers would not have any First Amendment rights.

Mr. Simpson responded. I had misunderstood the nature of the fund. I could apply for assistance through the state affiliate (PSEA).

---

[21] I had done so. Their letter in response was that I had no constitutional cause and I was *selfish* because I insisted on a lawsuit rather than trust arbitration. I wasn't "thinking of my fellow union members."

The state affiliate then would decide whether to provide legal assistance and what form that would take. I was already provided legal representation in the form of the grievance challenging the Directives Letter. Expenditures incurred "by hiring your own private attorney are not supplemented with the fund."

True, I had hired my own attorney. Why?

- I asked for assistance from the Kate Frank/ DuShane fund because if I lost this case, teachers would not have any First Amendment rights.
- Chuck Herring initially said there was nothing I could do.
- Chuck Herring was reluctant to help the grievance chair file the grievance.
- Chuck Herring believed what I did was "foolish."
- Chuck Herring informed me the union would not go to court for a civil rights action (although state unions have done so).

I had a meeting with Mr. Herring in March (2003) to go through my records at PSEA. That's how I got the Loudermill affidavit, which had never been sent to me. Mr. Herring seemed very pleased with me at the time, stating that I had the "perfect case" because I had done "nothing wrong, violated no law, or committed no illegality." He was quite positive at that moment.

I noted that Michael Simpson had written articles on teachers who had gone after districts for violations of First Amendment rights (e.g. Settlegoode, McGreevy, Mayer). Although Mr. Simpson extolled the virtues of these "brave" teachers, he never once pointed out that they had to finance their own legal actions without assistance from the union. Additionally, they were forced to seek outside legal representation because the union was either not interested or unwilling to take the case. Remember, the union lawyer gets to cherry pick the cases. Why get embroiled in the mess that is a civil rights battle when you don't have to? Arbitrations are easier, shorter, require less attorney effort, and allow for a 3:30 tee time.

*****

Attorney Dragotta was in contact with Attorney Alberts (Anita) while she was writing the pleadings for summary

349

judgment. Despite the fantastic job Sarah did with these, she was still new at the game. Anita helped her out on numerous occasions. They were getting along well.

One afternoon Sarah called with a question. As the client, the answer was completely up to me. Anita wanted back in. She would be second chair; she wanted to take the case to the end, and she liked working with Sarah. I knew Sarah wanted her to be part of the team. Who wouldn't? Anita knew her way around a courtroom. She was a seasoned civil attorney and would know instinctively things that Sarah was still learning.

Anita had given birth to this case, so I said yes. The next week I had to deliver pleadings from Sarah to Anita. I was thrilled for us all to be together. Sadly, not everyone was happy. Sarah delivered the notice of appearance when she went to a meeting with Mr. Levin. She said he was aggravated when he read Anita's name on the paper. He was not excited to have Attorney Alberts back.

*****

Just because we were waiting for a decision doesn't mean Attorney Dragotta was not busy with the case. First, she had to submit a lengthy Pretrial Memorandum, (forty-one single spaced pages) which was a review of the case, a list of all the witnesses, and a compilation of all the evidence. The electronic filing showed the memorandum was submitted at 11:08 PM. That was not unusual. Many nights Sarah would leave the office at one or two in the morning and was always back in the office by six the next morning.

The defendants also filed their memorandum. They listed **46** witnesses. They were calling:

- the last two superintendents before Durtan (one was terminated, the other was found guilty of crimes and had served time)
- Charles Herring (PSEA Attorney)
- the attorney who represented me at the Loudermill hearing (the man Michael Levin called unprofessional)
- a teacher and guidance counselor from the WIN team who were no longer working at WSD
- each board member

- the nurse's assistant
- the middle school principal who retired years before any of this took place
- the director of Special Education who had been gone from the district for years (and was never involved when he was there)
- Denise Fagan-former Director of Special Education. She was the Director of Special Education the year Kay was placed on homebound.

Strangely missing from this group were:

- the assistant principal who dealt with Kay in the middle school (all three years)
- Hugh Jones, the principal when Kay was in the middle school
- the teacher who delivered Kay's homebound instruction (still in the district)
- Kay's middle school guidance counselor (all three years)
- the nurse from the middle school
- the IEP case manager from the middle school

In the Defendants' Trial Memorandum, they were vehement in arguing that I should have done something because I believed Kay's IEP was inadequate. Let me put this to rest. Many of the IEP's that were written were inadequate, especially for children with emotional issues.

- There was no Emotional Support program other than the classification of children in this category.
- There was no counseling within the school; remember, Maria Salvucci said NONE of the counselors were qualified to give therapy.
- The Drop-in Center counselor was NOT qualified to give therapy, plus she would only see a child six times before recommending the child to (you guessed it) the WIN team.
- If there was no one who could provide counseling and no program for Emotional Support kids, how would I change the inadequate IEP?

- Again, only the IEP case manager could change the IEP. You could recommend it but the changes weren't going to take place, especially when there was nothing to offer the child.
- If there had been a program, why hadn't Kelle Heim-McCloskey recommended the IEP be changed? Was she indifferent to this child's life or was there nothing to offer her?

Inadequate IEP's were nothing new; they were a way of life.

*****

The next document to be submitted was the Motion in Limine: this is an argument explaining why your opponent should not be able to have certain witnesses. Anita told Sarah she would write these if Sarah promised she could cross-examine Stanley Durtan. The deal was struck and Attorney Alberts was back in rare form. She started with:

- Durtan was listed as a fact witness, not an expert, thus misleading the court.
- Clark, Speakman, Kormos were listed in Pretrial Memorandum as fact witnesses and were now being used as experts, again, misleading the court.
- Durtan's expert report was self-serving.
- The expert reports of Durtan, Clark, Speakman, and Kormos did not state objective or independent findings. They merely repeated their boss's views:

These four proffered "experts" are not qualified to render expert opinions in any case because they lack required credentials. They are not recognized as authorities, have never produced learned treatises and have no specialized knowledge or ability beyond their school district jobs...They are holding themselves out as "experts" to protect their jobs.

Anita claimed that Durtan, Kormos, Clark, and Speakman should not be "permitted to render expert opinion because they are unqualified, and because their opinions are biased, self serving, unreliable, and unduly prejudicial."

According to Attorney Alberts:

None of these so-called "expert reports" contains an independent thought, opinion, or analysis. The questions asked in each report were written by defense counsel Michael Levin. Levin also ran Montanye's infamous Loudermill meeting for Durtan. Levin also drafted Montanye's pre-termination charges and the punitive "Directives" letter following the discharge of Principal Anderson, who supported Montanye's actions. Levin probably wrote the "experts'" opinions too.

Anita was correct in her assumption that the testimony of these people would be unduly influencing if elevated to expert level. Durtan's testimony would carry more weight as an "expert," and he would be able to talk his way around the laws he broke which made him a defendant, not an expert. As Anita pointed out, these people did not have an area of "expertise"; all they had was a "job title and a job resumé."

There is also repeated discussion of a mysterious LINE.

What is this LINE? Where is this LINE? They claimed Sallie Montanye, a Special Education teacher finding a student's suicide note, crossed "A LINE." A line between two things? Right and Wrong? She says she did the RIGHT thing, and she saw no LINE barring her way. The four "experts" want to see her punished, but they're not sure for what. They'd like this case to be about transporting a child to a doctor's office. Suicide note? What suicide note? The four WSD "experts" said she was WRONG but they cannot say what LINE was crossed nor can they point to any prohibition, anywhere for Plaintiff's perfectly proper conduct...So Durtan & Co. want to draw a LINE somewhere, and they need to be on the other side of it, they think, to remain employed.

Anita Alberts then turned her attention to another witness, Barbara Rizzo, *Esquire.* Anita's contention was that Ms. Rizzo was usurping the judge's role because it was up to him to provide the law to the jury. An expert may not instruct the jury on law.

The trial court has the authority to appoint an expert witness concerning the law, "especially where the parties' experts appear to lack independent judgment."

She then presented her learned opinion of Ms. Rizzo's real purpose:

> In the present case, defense counsel Michael Levin, *Esquire*, who considers himself an expert on school law and the IDEA, has apparently realized he cannot testify to his own legal opinions, and has therefore retained another attorney who agrees with him to do so. This is not proper. Should the Court desire expert legal advice on IDEA or any other law, the Court has the power to appoint such an expert, and should not rely on an adversarial party appearing before it to supply legal advice to the jury.

The defendants had a good deal to say about our witnesses also. Ms. Bolash did not review enough materials to make an expert opinion. They also claimed her opinion was based "totally on incorrect facts" and thus will be "deemed irrelevant." The defendants asserted that Ms. Bolash's testimony was "based merely on subjective belief and/or speculation." In addition, the defendants argued that Ms. Bolash knew nothing about the law because she was not a lawyer. This seemed to be a favorite refrain. Durtan needed a lawyer to tell him what was right/wrong in Special Education law. Ms. Rizzo was an expert in Special Education because she had a law degree? If this is the case, then all school districts should have had lawyers heading their Spec Ed departments, the assumption being educators are not bright enough to grasp the nuances of the law.

Ms. Bolash was also not a superintendent, which defendants argued made her unable to evaluate the behavior of a superintendent. Unfortunately, they could not use this argument against James Higgins because he had been a superintendent. The case against Higgins was that he had not reviewed all of defendants' materials. His report had been written at the beginning of the case. Plus, the bulk of Mr. Higgins' report dealt with the purpose of the SAP team and Special Education, both of which were his areas of expertise.

Dr. Tepper and Dr. Jennings were also no good because they did not read the materials the defendants wanted them to. Dr. Jennings's report had little to do with who was at fault. His statements were more aligned with the results of what had taken place.

Finally, defendants wanted to exclude any information pertaining to Kay, with the exception of her IEP and Notice of Recommended Assignment. They also wanted to jettison the WIN team records and the suicide note "allegedly drafted by Student 1." Allegedly?

Next came the proposed Jury Voir Dire questions from each side. These are questions written by the lawyers that try and root out bias or prejudice on the part of prospective jurors.

After that came the jury instructions that were prepared to tell the jury what they could or could not consider and how to apply applicable law to the case. The defendants had approximately seventy pages. We had three.

There were many more pleadings that were restatements of what had already been said. We kept the economy going with all this rehashing. Everything had to be copied at least a few times for evidence and records. Meanwhile we waited.

Our answer came on November 3, 2005. Sarah called me at home. Out of respect, she had called Anita first. Anita, hearing Sarah's voice, said, "We are being called to trial, right?" Sarah broke the news.

The Motion for Summary Judgment was granted to Defendants. In other words, the district won the case without benefit of a trial. Judge DuBois' decision was riddled with mistakes. Let's look at the errors his honor made in merely reciting the facts:

Judge DuBois: "Plaintiff found an outside psychologist for K to see."

The judge was quoting from my "affidavit," the one written by Michael Levin. I did not "find" an outside psychologist.

Judge DuBois: "K requested that plaintiff join her."

Not so. She *refused* to go to therapy if I did not go with her. This ignored both Kay and her mother's depositions. It also minimized the urgency of my attending the sessions. Kay refused to go without me.

Judge DuBois: "Principal Anderson was aware that plaintiff made the therapy appointments and drove K to psychologist's office."

355

Untrue, again the judge was paraphrasing Michael Levin. Principal Anderson **did not know** Kay had made the first appointment after school. I just told him we had an appointment. Kay made the second appointment after the first session. He would not have known about that. Mr. Anderson was not aware that I **drove** Kay to the psychologist's office, because I did not take her from school. The ONE time I drove her there she had already gone home. Principal Anderson knew I went to the therapist with Kay. I told him before we went and after our first visit. He was not aware of driving arrangements or when the appointment had been made. It did not occur to me to report my private activities such as driving.

Judge DuBois: "In the original complaint, plaintiff named the District, the School Board, the individual members of the School Board and Superintendent Durtan as defendants."

Again, incorrect. Maria Salvucci was also named in the original complaint. Remember, this is the law, a profession that turns on every little detail.

The next section of the decision included inaccuracies that overlooked the **district's** wanton disregard for the law. This information was vital to the case. It was their disregard and ridiculous application of IDEA that proved our contentions: there was no legitimate government interest for their behavior and the district's actions were pretextual. The judge gave his opinions; he dispensed with the irritations of following the evidence.

Judge DuBois: (stating the law)

Where an equal protection claim is based on selective enforcement of valid laws, a plaintiff can show that the defendants' rational basis for selectively enforcing the law is a pretext for an impermissible move.

Translation: If I could prove that the district enforced "valid" laws with me, but did not apply them to others, then I would have met the burden of proving their actions were impermissible. The district (the administrators) broke the following laws, which were VALID and APPLICABLE in Kay's situation:

(1) state harassment laws violated
(2) denial of FAPE
(3) illegal homebound placement
(4) homebound papers not completed as required by state law
(5) no IEP team meeting
(6) IEP revisions
(7) no recommendation to the Child Study Team
(8) IEP illegal because it did not reflect change in program
(9) IEP illegal because it did not reflect change in placement
(10) put in most restrictive environment
(11) no provision of counseling (no related services)
(12) no reference in 9th grade IEP of special needs
(13) violation of mental health laws by revealing fourteen-year old child's mental health history without permission
(14) placement back in math class—denial of FAPE
(15) placement back in math class—endangering the health, safety and welfare of a student

Those were the **real** laws the district violated.
Now let's look at the "pretend" policies that really didn't exist:

(1) policy #827
(2) made up transportation policy
(3) regulation to have a non-existent form signed
(4) non-existent policies concerning recommendations of psychologists
(5) Special Education laws which were not applicable to students outside of school

Recap: The administrators of WSD violated IDEA and PA Special Education laws, but that was acceptable. I did not violate IDEA and PA Spec Ed law, but I was charged with created offenses.

Despite many employees in the district transporting students, I was charged with violating a transportation policy which did not exist and which the superintendent could not locate or articulate.

And yet, the learned judge ignored the testimony, which established the selective enforcement of the law (and non-law), and found that defendants' actions were supported by a rational basis. One of his contentions was Dr. Durtan had a duty to protect the children. Had the judge skipped over the parts of Kay's torture in school? Who was protecting her then?

The judge then addressed our claim of being treated differently than those similarly situated. We claimed that I was the first person to undergo a Loudermill hearing. We argued: "Plaintiff was intentionally treated differently from others similarly situated."

His honor did not agree because another teacher had received a Loudermill notice the same day I did (Joe). Of course, his Loudermill hearing was cancelled and not held until three months later. There had been no Loudermills for at least ten years. (At that time, the hearings were not called Loudermills.) DuBois blew off the proof that Joe's Loudermill was a sham and mine had nothing to do with IDEA or the arguments the defense was employing now.

The coup de grace was the refutation of our claim based on Charles Herring's affidavit for the defense:

> In addition, defendants have submitted an affidavit from an attorney who attended two Loudermill hearings on behalf of teachers in the District in the mid-1990s.

Herring: Affidavit
Our union dues at work.

The judge also decided I was not the first to have a Loudermill hearing because the district produced **two other letters of allegations**. However, there was no proof the hearings ever took place. I know for a fact one of them did not. We were remiss because we could not "prove" that these letters did not result in Loudermill hearings. The district did not have to prove these "hearings" took place; they merely had to produce letters that suggested they had taken place.

The judge also said that others were accused of "similar charges." Considering the district and Mr. Levin used a form letter that lists all the reasons a teacher can be fired, it is not extraordinary that everyone is "similarly charged."

But wait, you may wonder what about the people who drove

children in their private cars to events? Wouldn't they be in a **similar situation**? No, no, no, says the judge. Why not? They drove children without written parental permission to and from school. Yes, says the judge, but the issue is not the transportation of a student. The issue is driving her to be examined by a psychologist; the issue was "plaintiff's conduct in connection with the examination of K."

Regarding the Directives Letter. The judge admitted the district could not produce evidence of "directive letters" sent in multiple cases. But that was okay by his honor, because it was up to me to present evidence that other teachers who "**violated the same or similar District policies and federal law did not receive Directives Letters,"** and I had not done so. This would be proven how?

Notice the judge had decided that I violated district policies and federal law. **What about a jury?**

Now the judge turned his attention to whether there was a rational basis for what the district did. There was. The WIN team letter. The judge recited Durtan's argument **directly from his affidavit.** The judge then quoted from my "affidavit" (Loudermill) where again he reiterated Michael Levin's words: I made the appointment with the psychologist. **A federal judge quoted from an unverified, unsigned, non-endorsed affidavit written by the defense counsel**, Michael Levin.

Well, you may wonder, did she really violate federal law? Michael Levin advised Stanley Durtan that I did. Although IDEA applies to school districts and not private citizens, this judge felt I violated federal law by making sure Kay got services that were not offered by the district and were not in her IEP. Again, you may question, why wouldn't **a jury** be charged with the decision of whether I violated law and policy? Why, indeed.

Then, showing no command over the concepts of IDEA, the judge stated I did "not follow the **parental consent procedural safeguards** required by the IDEA." I have no idea what the **parental consent procedural safeguards** are. The judge bastardized two separate entities: (1) the parental consent form, which allows the district to test children (2) the procedural safeguard notice which is given out at IEP meetings.[22]

---

[22] By the by – Procedural Safeguards Notices were to be given to parents in their native language. This was never done when I was there.

Completely ignoring federal law and the deposition of Judith Clark, the judge decided on his own, that I had to have the fictional parental permission form signed. Clark stated there was no form to be signed to take a child to private therapy. Apparently, that held no interest for the judge. Also, following the judge's reasoning, any **outside** service comes under the IDEA requisites. Therefore, any parent supplying outside services to his child should use this argument to have the district pay for the services. A federal judge decided this was the law.

Another question comes to mind. If the examination had required a consent form, why wasn't the district going after the therapist? In the district, no psychologist would conduct testing without the signed form in hand. Wouldn't the district, afraid of "legal reprisal," have contacted the therapist to advise her of their precarious position if she did not have a consent form?

Actually, no one ever spoke to the therapist until her deposition which took place at the end of discovery. In her deposition, Michael Levin did not ask her why she conducted the "examination" without the school district's signed parental consent. Of course, he would not ask this because he would have looked stupid: (1) Kay would have had to sign it and (2) the form doesn't exist.

The judge went on to assert that I had violated school district policy. He did not list any policy by number. He maintained that the policy followed the requirements of federal law. Again, he said that seeing a private therapist outside of school hours, paid for by the parents, was the **same** as receiving services from the school district during school hours under IDEA.

Making up the law as he went along, Judge DuBois stated, "meeting with an outside psychologist qualifies as additional assessment since this service was not in K's IEP." Interesting. As I pointed out before, the therapist was also a lawyer; a lawyer who was not aware that every time she initially saw a Special Education child outside of school, she was violating the law if she didn't file a non-existent form with the school district?

So the judge, following Michael Levin's reasoning verbatim, based on no real concept of the law, citing the absence of **parental consent procedural safeguards,**[23] and quoting almost

---

[23] Whatever that is.

exclusively from Stanley Durtan's affidavit,[24] ruled that all was fair because the defendants decided to make IDEA applicable to private citizens and any interaction they might have with children classified as Special Education.

What I was never able to fathom was how the judge could ignore:

- what the district did **not** do for Kay (especially in light of Jan DuBois' later decision)
- what the district **did** to Kay
- the contradictions in Levin's legal arguments
- the extensive violation of federal law by WSD administrators
- the lies exposed by the depositions
- the policy created months after I "violated" it
- the fact that I was operating as a private citizen
- the fact Dr. Durtan (the man who had to protect children) allowed a male employee with a pornography binder, an illegal lock, and a dildo in his desk to remain employed with only a three-day suspension and no Loudermill hearing (but was not afraid of any legal ramifications?)
- the fact that there was no mention of IDEA or IEP writing at my Loudermill
- the lack of specific school policies violated (except the newly made one)

In addition to all this, we had an extensive amount of evidence which showed violations against Special Education children to prove our discrimination charge. None of this was even referenced by the judge. His entire argument rested on Michael Levin's newly created IDEA, Durtan's affidavits, my "affidavit," and unnamed policies and procedures. Oh, and of course there was the **parental consent procedural safeguards,** which I had not followed because, like many of the other contentions, there is no such thing.

*****

---

[24] Affidavits are notoriously inaccurate.

Two years later, I was speaking with an attorney who was presenting a CLE (continued law education) at Lehigh University. All the presenters were knowledgeable in the area of Special Education. In our conversation, he asked me my name. It seemed to register. He then asked if I was **the** Special Education teacher named Montanye. Yes. He shook his head. He recalled reading the decision. He said he had no idea what the judge was thinking or saying. The decision made absolutely no sense. Neither does letting a kid die.

CHAPTER TWENTY-FOUR

The Appeal

A teacher who saved the life of a suicidal child was disciplined as a direct result of her advocacy of this student who is protected by the Individuals with Disabilities in Education Act and Section 504 of the Rehabilitation Act. As a result of Ms. Dragotta's representation of the teacher and the case, the United States Court of Appeals for the Third Circuit heard oral arguments in January 2007. Although the outcome of that case resulted in the Third Circuit affirming the District Court's ruling, Ms. Dragotta still believes strongly in the rights of teachers when those rights impact what a teacher does on her own time. She believes that these are the cases for the courts to hear.

Sarah Dragotta—Philadelphia Area
Constitutional Rights Lawyer

We were at an impasse. To be more exact, we were seriously screwed. Writing and defending an appeal requires very specific knowledge and abilities, bolstered by a great deal of experience. It's literally another world from the lower court. And of course there is the added benefit of extreme cost; the average appeal can run anywhere from $200,000 to $500,000.

Sarah and I spent much of our days on the phone, trying to figure out what to do and what we "wanted" to do. We were both exhausted emotionally and physically. I was in such debt that I would never be able to climb out of that hole, and Sarah's practice was circling the drain. Even Attorney Brooks was in financial uncertainty due to all his time and resources donated to my case.

I wasn't sure I would have enough strength to go on even if we could find someone to take it. My life was in tatters; my marriage was seriously damaged from all the stress, my kids were growing up while I was at the office organizing evidence, and my friends had to be sick of hearing about this day in and day out. (God bless them. They were beyond patient.)

A therapist I was seeing after the initial litigation told me he had watched many of his clients become totally consumed with their lawsuits. I certainly was. First, I am the type of person who fully commits to a project; secondly, I so strongly believed in the heart of the matter, the importance of the life of a child. Every time I decided the fight was over, I would think of what I assumed to be the horror of burying a child. That would spur me on.

Sarah Dragotta was another person who threw herself into a project wholeheartedly. Finally, we agreed if she could find someone to take the case, we would pursue it. And that is exactly what she did.

It took a couple of weeks; but once again, Attorney Dragotta pulled the rabbit out of the hat. She may be the size of a Chihuahua, but she has the tenacity of a pit bull. Sarah set her sights on the number one First Amendment attorney in the country. He was not in town. Not to worry, she tracked him down in Boston and got him to agree to consider the case when he returned to Philadelphia.

His name was Gregory Harvey and he was the most respected authority on First Amendment issues. He worked for an elite firm in Philadelphia. He thought it was a great case. He even got the firm to let him take the appeal for only $20,000 (only).

Mr. Harvey told Sarah that he was intending on retiring soon and he wanted to go out on a case he truly believed in. When Attorney Dragotta mentioned her concerns about the outcome of the lower court, Mr. Harvey assured her he had no intention of exiting the profession on a loss. We were ecstatic.

The next step required the presence of Anita Alberts, Sarah Dragotta, and me in the imposing marbled conference room at MMW&R. Attorneys Alberts and Dragotta had to sign away their right to any money that was recovered by Harvey's firm. If there was any left over, it would go to them. Both women were aware this was not very probable. They were very willing to do it. Anita Alberts was quite impressed at Sarah's coup. She knew how amazing this feat was.

Attorney Harvey assured both women they would be involved with the writing of the briefs and the decision making during the case. He assured Sarah she would be right by his side at the table for the entire life of the suit. She was in seventh heaven. Me? I was amazed that I had to give permission for these two women to sign over their financial claims. I was surrounded by a pretty heavy-duty brain trust, and the deciding factor was my signature? Heady Stuff.

*****

Before the writings of briefs and the preparation of oral arguments, both parties were required to submit a confidential mediation statement to see if there existed any possibility that a resolution could be reached, thus keeping the case out of court. Gregory Harvey was my attorney, but he was not the one who wrote it. A woman named Catherine Merino Reisman did. I was a little disconcerted. We had hired the best, and now he was farming us out to someone else?

When I read the mediation draft, my concerns were put to rest. Catherine had a laser style of writing: pointed, sharp, and able to cut through the legal garbage. She was an artist with her verbal scalpel, and she knew what she was talking about.

Recap: Initially, Anita Alberts presented a First Amendment argument, based on *retaliation.* The lower court dismissed this and fashioned a Fourteenth Amendment case based on *discrimination.* Now my appellate attorneys were re-presenting the First Amendment argument, which was always the most valid claim for this case.

In essence, the argument was: (1) The district retaliated against me for my advocacy of a Special Education student which would be protected speech (2) the Directives Letter impermissibly "chills" the exercise of my First Amendment rights in the future. The appeal was based on the concept that the lower court incorrectly dismissed the case because I failed to identify any protected speech. In other words, DuBois did not apply the correct analysis.

Catherine began the brief with instructions for FAPE and the IEP that is the "centerpiece" of IDEA. She pointed out that IEP's are required to address the educational, emotional, and social needs of students. In addition, in Pennsylvania, pursuant to the *Cordero* case, "there are particular administrative requirements for Special Education students placed on homebound instruction."

In this case, there is ample evidence that the District, *prior* to Mrs. Montanye's involvement, deprived K of her right to a FAPE. Because K's emotional needs were not met, she was placed on homebound instruction. The District failed to report K to the

Pennsylvania Department of Education, as required by the *Cordero* Order.

Attorney Merino Reisman provided these examples for the court:

- When a school district knows or should have known that an IDEA eligible child is not receiving an appropriate education, the district may be liable for compensatory education.

WSD knew that Kay was denied FAPE.

- When a local education agency's (LEA—the school district) abrogation of its duties under the IDEA results in actual physical harm to the child, the LEA can be responsible for extensive monetary damages.

WSD sent Kay home illegally, did not provide her with supplemental services as per the *Cordero* order, and as a result of this accumulated abuse she tried to kill herself.

At this point, Catherine Merino Reisman produced a case new to us: Cynthia Susavage.

Background: *Susavage v. Bucks County Intermediate Unit No 22,* 2002, was a case where the court held the Bucks County I.U. responsible for the death of a child. Cynthia Susavage was transported in a harness (car seat) that was known to be dangerous for her. The court observed that BCIU "had time to make unhurried judgments to insure Cynthia's safety," because the BCIU had received "various written reports and other communications" related to the inadequate transportation services.

Attorney Merino Reisman noted the consistencies between our case and *Susavage:*

In this case [mine], the District admits to knowing that it had not met K's social and emotional needs in the past, which necessitated her placement on homebound instruction for the previous school year. The District failed to report her as a *Cordero* case, which reporting could have resulted in increased social/emotional supports through the intensive inter-agency process. As in

Susavage, the Board was deliberately indifferent to K's needs and the Board's failure to train responsible teachers and administrators resulted in actual harm to the child.

But there were more than similar behaviors linking these two cases together. The WSD Board, the superintendent, the assistant superintendent, the nurse, and the guidance counselor all claimed innocence through ignorance. And of course, these folks who did not know what was going on under their noses would hardly be up to date with contemporary court cases. **But their lawyer would.**
Ms. Merino Reisman stated:

Insofar as the Levin Legal Group represented the Bucks County Intermediate Unit in *Susavage,* it would be presumed, especially in the context of a motion to dismiss, the defendants were aware of the potential liability for failure to provide appropriate related services to K. (footnote 2:Confidential Mediation Statement)

The Levin Legal Group had defended the Bucks County Intermediate Unit. It was LLG's job to push the child's death off on to someone else. It was their task to convince a court that a child was mortally hurt, not because the adults around her refused to take protective action, but rather as the result of cruel providence.
Remember Mr. Levin's letter of October 18, 2002?

I suggest that if the Education Association were more interested in improving teacher performance, and ensuring that its members do not engage in the kind of inappropriate conduct that this teacher engaged in, that there would be fewer attacks on public education and on the teaching profession…

Mr. Levin wanted to improve the educational landscape by ridding it of teachers like me…but the question is, what would remain in education if you did get rid of "teachers such as this one"?
A world populated by the administrators I worked under and a world "cleansed" and defended by Michael Levin would be strewn with the bodies of dead children. In both Kay's case and Cynthia's case, Mr. Levin was defending the values of people

who would let children be hurt or killed.

The reality is the public should be aware that there are people in this business who are indifferent to the children they "are here for"; there are those who feel exonerated if a death does not "happen on our watch." In my case, these malevolent people persecuted me for my efforts to keep a child alive and then spent huge amounts of other people's money to put forth the scurrilous argument that saving a child's life was a violation of her civil rights.

It was the Levin Legal Group that Stanley Durtan chose to employ to attack me for saving a child's life. Think about it. The *Susavage* case was decided in January 22, 2002. That was four months before my Loudermill hearing. One would think, given Mr. Levin's knowledge of the outcome of *Susavage*, he would have run the other way when he heard K's background. Now, assuming that Durtan, Sanni, and Clark were not forthcoming about the truth surrounding this child, Mr. Levin would have had no clue until the Loudermill hearing when he heard "my side of the story." But he wasn't paid to find out the truth; he was hired to get rid of me. Plus, he didn't check out any facts before buying into the myths floated by the administrators. No matter what the strained reasoning, Attorney Levin knew that a district could be found guilty of a child's death if put on notice of the possibility. But rather than advise his clients to get over whatever petty reason they had to pursue this case, this lawyer seemed to egg them on. When he couldn't "get" me with the Loudermill, Mr. Levin endorsed and most likely wrote the punitive Directives Letter.

Dr. Durtan seemed to have no fear of liability. His lawyer, on the other hand, should have had a heart to heart with his client; or maybe Cynthia was just another dead child who was of "no importance" to the community.

Whatever the thought process, Michael Levin, knowing the parameters of *Susavage,* should have steered his clients clear of this quagmire. Instead, he played fast and loose with questionable advice. If nothing else, this cost the district and those who support it thousands upon thousands of dollars. I wonder how pleased the "community" would be, knowing it was paying to advance the idea that the death of a child was of "no importance" to them.

*****

I spoke with Catherine a few times. In our first call she said she could not believe an attorney would have written a rant like the Directives Letter. She also found the arguments of the district to be absurd.

The next conversation was with Gregory Harvey who told me the mediator said we were too far apart to attempt mediation. The mediator suggested we ask LLG for $10,000 to settle. Ten thousand dollars for a child's life. It wasn't about the money.

*****

The appellate court guidelines for submitting briefs differ from the lower court. The appellate court sets limitations to avoid the extensive overuse of words so evident in some attorney's pleadings. The plaintiff presents her case, the defendants submit their rebuttal, and the final argument comes from the plaintiff's response to the defendant's refutation.

There is even a rubric of how many words can be used for the briefs. The plaintiff's first brief may contain no more than 14, 000 words. To some attorneys this is a virtual gag order. When you write appellate briefs, you have to cut to the chase, get your point across, and supply all the necessary citations without leaning on the crutch of verbosity. The best analogy I can think of is lower court pleadings are prose with endless verbiage, while appellate briefs have to reflect the concise precision of poetry. Even the typeface size is dictated. I am not sure whether that has to do with saving the judge's eyesight or keeping attorneys from using the old high school ploy of writing in smaller type to squeeze in more than the allowed words. I tend toward the second thought, as I heard appellate judges do not read most of the briefs. This task is left to their clerks who do the grunt work.

My brief was very well done in only 9,223 words. Catherine Merino Reisman was the author, combining information from Gregory Harvey, Sarah, others in her firm, and me. It is no easy task to merge information and ideas from various sources and produce a coherent one-voiced argument. Her style was direct and succinct; the appellate poet.

The brief begins by citing the lower courts decision. It contains a footnote stating we were including all the information pertaining to the dismissal of the **First Amendment** claim which supported our argument; however, at the insistence of the defendants [i.e. Michael Levin] the information gathered under the claim we were not arguing was also included, despite the fact that the court was not supposed to consider any of this information.

To clarify: We were arguing only the Amended Complaint which dealt exclusively with the First Amendment and the Rehab Act. Almost all of the information gathered for discovery was done under the Third Amended Complaint; therefore, it should not have been considered, as it had, according to rules of jurisprudence, no relevance to the matter at hand. The defendants could request the inclusion of irrelevant material (you can ask for anything); however, if the court followed its own protocol, it would not consider any of this material. In reality, courts do not have to follow their own guidelines if they are not in the mood.

Mr. Levin wanted the material included for two reasons: (1) it added a great deal of confusion to the argument (2) judges are not inclined to slog through mountains of paper and their clerks lack the time to do so. Despite the strident regulations of the appellate court, Levin was able to bury the issue in a mountain of paperwork, a tactic he held most dear.

Our first claim was the school district violated my rights by retaliating against me because I advocated for a Special Education student who was protected by IDEA and the Rehab Act. The second claim was that the district retaliated against me because I provided services the district failed to give the student. It also included the fact that the district interfered with Kay's rights under the Rehab Act.

The recitation of Kay's history pointed out:

- The district did not respond, as mandated by law, to Kay's problems despite the fact these interfered with her education.
- The WIN team did not follow the state required procedures of referring Kay to multi-disciplinary evaluations to determine eligibility for psychological services.
- The district failed to comply with state mandated procedures when it did not report Kay's homebound placement and did not supply her with intensive interagency supplemental services.

The brief then pointed out that the district used the argument of liability for the actions taken against me; however, despite the failures on the part of the WIN team, the school nurse, and all the other employees who completely disregarded the law and their job responsibilities, I was the only employee to be disciplined.

To claim the fear of liability because a teacher makes an effort to keep a child from killing herself, while extolling the virtues of all the other professionals who, with full knowledge, ignored the law and the requirements of their positions is ridiculous. It would be laughable if this argument did not cloak the darker agenda of punishing teachers who helped special education students either because it overtly pointed to the district's lack of compliance or, worse, it exposed the deep seated dislike for children who were not cut out of the correct academic cloth or were not accruing glory for the district.

The *Pickering* case was the lead off once again, making the point of public concern and the district's inability to point out how I had damaged the education system by keeping one child breathing. In accordance with this, the credibility of the feeble explanation offered to justify the district's adverse employment actions was something for a jury to decide **not a judge.**

Much of the brief mirrored the argument found in the lower pleadings; however, there were a few interesting additions.

Shore Regional High School Brd. of Educ. v. P.S. was a new case decided in 2004. In this case, the Third Circuit (our circuit) stated a child had been denied FAPE because he was harassed.

Background: *Shore Regional high School Board of Education v. P.S. on behalf of P.S.*

A child was victim of relentless physical and verbal harassment as well as social isolation by classmates. After his grades slipped badly he was tested and placed in Spec Ed; his low academic work was due to the bullying rather than cognitive deficiencies. His parents wanted him moved to another public high school and for the district to pay for it because he was being denied FAPE. He was allowed to change classes at different times to avoid hallways. In eighth grade P.S. attempted suicide. He was placed on homebound. He was re-evaluated and changed from a learning disabled student to Emotional Support.

Here's a novel idea: "The Child Study Team believed if P.S. attended Shore Regional HS he would experience the same harassment because (and this is really deep) **"the bullies who were responsible would also be there."** An **administrative law judge (ALJ)** said P.S. was denied FAPE due to the harassment. The **Third Circuit upheld this ruling.** The Third Circuit said P.S. was denied FAPE because he went through everything Kay had gone through. The decision was unanimous.

What made this decision so interesting was the list of the presiding judges who fashioned it. One of the judges was sitting in as a substitute. The judge was from the Eastern District Court. Care to guess the name? Yes indeedy, **the Honorable Judge DuBois.** The man who ignored all the evidence of the WSD's myriad of violations toward Kay turned around and attached liability to a district, which committed the same violations against P.S.

The argument will be made that this appellate court was only deciding the merit of a denial of FAPE claim, and that my case had to do with First Amendment violations. Nice try; however, it was this judge's refusal to attach any liability to the district, which weakened our argument that I was acting against an illegal practice. Instead, the Honorable Jan E. DuBois ignored all the relevant evidence, pretended Kay's rights were not violated, and therefore my actions were not protected.

Catherine added a few new views to the Directives. She pointed out that it not only regulated my conduct by prohibiting me from engaging in a particular action, it also mandated what I was to say to my students and their parents. The requirements of the Directives were designed specifically to "chill" my inclinations to exert my First Amendment freedoms due to the requirements of "reporting" interactions with student or parents to the district personnel.

Now comes an even more astounding aspect. Every law student or paralegal is taught when looking up a case the **most important** step to be taken before quoting it *is to make sure the case is current.* Cases undergo differences in interpretations, extensions, or limitations of applications, or complete reversals over the course of time. In order to assure the decision is applicable and supportive to the case in which it is being cited, you must *always* check for changes to the case or more importantly, if the case has been superseded by a newer one. This is a hard and fast rule. According to my professors, it is written in stone.

A judge can dismiss an action, which relies on a case that is outdated, because the changes can no longer be applied to the matter at hand. Aside from being inaccurate, it is also evidence of sloppy legal work, which taints the rest of the cases that are offered in support of the argument. If the inclusion of a case that has been reversed is not due to inferior legal abilities, it would stand to reason its use would be an attempt to mislead the court in the hope the judge does not catch this.

Part of the argument of First Amendment protection rested on the question of whether my actions would be protected because they were *expressive*. The lower court applied two cases that were outdated:

(1) The court dismissed my First Amendment claim because my conduct did not "possess sufficient communicative elements to fall within the protection of the First Amendment." This was decided using *Steirer v. Bethlehem Area School District*, (1993) a case whose standards were no longer viable after *Hurley v. Irish-American Gay, Lesbian, and Bisexual Group of Boston, Inc.* (1995). In *Hurley* the court modified the test for what determines speech. These standards were broader based and would have supported my argument.

(2) The court applied the *Spence-Johnson* test (*Spence v. Washington*)(1974) that required a "particularized" message for protected speech. Therefore, DuBois said my speech wasn't protected. But the *Spence–Johnson* was found to be too restrictive and "could no longer be viewed as criteria"; in *Tenafly Eruv Ass'n, Inc v. Borough of Tenafly* (2002) the court rejected the *Spence–Johnson* test, replacing it with this reasoning:

Conduct is expressive if, considering the nature of the activity, combined with the factual context and environment in which it was undertaken [the court is] led to the conclusion that the activity was sufficiently imbued with elements of communication to fall within the scope of the First and Fourteenth Amendment...

The newer cases stressed that context was crucial to examining an expressive conduct claim. Judge DuBois, following the older, outdated cases supplied by defendants, performed no contextual analysis, "instead dismissively stating that Montanye was 'just doing her job' and comparing her actions to 'walking down the street.'" Had the judge not religiously followed the line of reasoning provided by defendants, he may have used apropos cases, rather than outdated ones.

By refusing to take into consideration that the district had violated Kay's rights and had placed her in peril, the court removed the prime motivation requiring my involvement. The district's illegal behavior added credence to my actions and certainly eradicated the bogus assertion that any of their actions were borne of the need to protect the children. Furthermore, given the list of district IDEA violations, it would strain credulity that the administrators who were perpetrators of these violations were going after someone who had not violated any laws because they wanted "strict adherence to the law."

The brief also pointed out that not once had the district been able to offer any example of how my actions caused the school to run with less efficiency or impeded its daily operations. This is a very salient factor: if a government agency restricts the rights of an employee, it has to offer reasons as to why it is forced to do so. In other words, the impingement of rights has to be justified on proof that the employee's actions in some manner caused the agency problems in how it operates. The defense was never able to conjure up an iota of evidence that keeping Kay alive was interfering with business as usual.

The *McGreevy* case was another Third Circuit decision.

Background: *McGreevy v. Stroup*, 413 F.3d 359 (Third Cir. 2002)
This case involved a nurse who was given an unsatisfactory rating because she advocated on behalf of two Special Education children. The principal did not appreciate her advocacy and used her annual rating to demonstrate his displeasure. McGreevy, a professional who had received nothing but outstanding ratings, was suddenly "unsatisfactory." She sued, and like me, she lost in the

lower court. When she reached the appellate level, which, like mine, was in the Third Circuit, the decision was reversed, because the district was unable to prove that her advocacy caused such disruption it would warrant the denial of her civil rights. The Third circuit quoted the Supreme Court's decision in *Jackson* stating that the importance of protecting teachers and professionals who advocated on behalf of individuals who were themselves protected by broad statutes, was of "paramount" importance. The Supreme Court acknowledged in *Jackson* that laws protecting students would be worthless if districts **were allowed to strong arm anyone who had the audacity to point out how administrators ignored what the law specified for the students.**

To me the most damning part of the brief was the reality that my actions exposed the district's failure to follow IDEA and the Rehab Act. Even a superficial reading of this case made it obvious that Kay did not have the support IDEA required, that Durtan and his cronies repeatedly ignored every responsibility imposed by federal and state regulations, and most tellingly, everyone from the superintendent on down had been made aware of this.

Thus, Catherine posited the lower court erred as the judge ignored existing, applicable law.

*****

I had a long conversation with Linda McGreevy one summer day. She was passionate and committed to the kids and the laws that protect them. Her stories of how these disabled children were humiliated and brutalized by the district would have been shocking had I not witnessed Wissahickon's behavior. It is sickening that two professionals can play "I Can Top That " relating horrifying stories of neglect and raw animus toward any student, let alone those who may need more attention.

By the way, Linda McGreevy was president for her local union (part of PSEA) for twelve years. She said she was the poster girl for union membership. What do you think her local or PSEA or NEA did for her? If your answer is nothing, give yourself a gold star.

CHAPTER TWENTY-FIVE

Fraud Upon The Court

In this case, Montanye clearly believed that the right course of conduct was to commit acts of advocacy for the rights of K., and the message she sent was clearly understood by others, including Defendants who retaliated against her.

Catherine Merino Reisman, Esquire

Now it was the defendants' turn. I want to point out that Stacy Smith (of LLG) began her argument with a deceit. On page three, she stated: "... and a Special Education student, K. was assigned to one of Montanye's classes." K was assigned to two of my classes per day. When she withdrew from French class, she was assigned to my room for Study Skills. She also had permission to come to my room from her other Study Skills class. This means she was in my room at least three periods per day. This was interpreted by the defendants as K "leaving classes" to come to my room. Not true. She was assigned there for a better part of the day. This may seem like a small distortion; however, it is yet another example of how these people misrepresented information and twisted it to serve their purpose.

As you might expect, the arguments concerning IDEA and the IEP were presented. On page 5, Ms. Smith had a three quarter page footnote making a good attempt to get around the standard of review concerning an appeal of a ruling on a Motion to Dismiss.

Translation: My lawyers and I knew that the rules of the court forbid using any information gathered under the other complaints. Only information obtained under the First Amended Complaint was admissible. We knew it and Levin knew it. The LLG desperately wanted to get in the data collected under the Fourteenth Amendment complaint. We were not appealing that. What to do? Ms. Smith thought of a way to squeeze in non-applicable information. She didn't want to violate the court's rules but she HAD to because the Pennsylvania Rules of Ethics "required candor to the court," and her integrity, *forced* Ms. Smith to forgo the evidence ruling because of her "duty to candor." This was how Ms. Smith introduced a great deal of information that should have been excluded from the case. She didn't want to bring in forbidden information but the "honesty" requirement of her ethics coerced her into doing so. Of course, the information was the LLG interpretation of the facts, which coincidentally was not disputed by us. Why? **We were following the rules of evidence.** Ms. Smith recited part of the Summary Judgment decision which also should have had no bearing on this case.

Ms. Smith discussed the disadvantages if the defendants were forced to follow the law and why they should not have to:

> In this case, by the nature of the issues that she is appealing, Montanye has placed Defendants in an awkward situation. Although the law required that the Court view facts, as pled in the Amended Complaint, as true, the Defendants know through years of discovery, including Montanye's sworn deposition, that some of the facts alleged in the Amended Complaint and the inferences requested [sic] in her brief based on the facts alleged are simply untrue. Under Rule 11 of the Pennsylvania Rules of Ethics, the Defendants believe they have an obligation to be candid to the Court concerning these inaccuracies despite the fact that the law requires analysis and argument based on the Amended Complaint alone.

Pretty gutsy for someone who opened her brief with an inaccuracy. Even gutsier for a practice that had already violated countless ethics laws.

Ms. Smith did hold onto a familiar refrain: "Further, her [Montanye's] behavior and speech only concerned matters of private concern, i.e. the counseling and therapy of K, which is undeserving of protection under the First Amendment." She then went on to refer to *Texas v. Johnson,* which was the outdated case and "test" superseded by *Hurly* and *Tenafly.*

Then the implications started. "From the allegations, the defendants assumed she had spoken with student K and at least her mother if not other members of her family. She provided counseling to an emotionally troubled student and her family." (Now I was counseling the entire family.) Ms. Smith then denied that I ever said I advocated for disabled students. She was ignoring the evidence she felt had to be brought in, due to "candor."

Ms. Smith contended that even if my conduct could qualify as "speech," it would not be protected because it was NOT A MATTER OF PUBLIC CONCERN. A dead kid is not a matter of public concern. I will never get used to this argument.

Attorney Smith went on to the argument that I should have had the IEP changed, providing Kay with the needed therapy. Was Ms. Smith reading any of the candor-compelled evidence? WISSAHICKON SCHOOL DISTRICT DID NOT HAVE AN EMOTIONAL SUPPORT PROGRAM, nor was I the IEP case manager.

- Ask Ms. Salvucci; no one in the school was qualified to give K therapy. (Deposition)
- Ask Mr. Speakman; there were no Emotional Support teachers at the high school. (Expert report)
- Ask the assistant principal who said (in writing) I should not "interfere" with students who were not on my IEP caseload.
- Ask Stanley Durtan who could only offer that I should have recommended Kay to Special Education or the WIN team, both of whom were well aware of her existence.

Let's examine the WIN team's existence in light of an Emotional Support program. In the middle school, students in the Special Education (Emotional Support) program were generally not referred to the WIN team; it was felt they had their issues addressed by the department, the IEP, and the Special Education program. None of my students in the middle school were part of the SAP process.

In the high school, that was not the case. Obviously, the WIN team felt that they were the only ones who should be addressing "students at risk." This could be viewed as an admission that no Emotional Support program existed; and as Ms. Salvucci stated, the only therapeutic support was the private therapy parents could pay for outside the school day. If the district were meeting the needs of Emotional Support children, many would not need to be linked up with outside agencies. The SAP program would be for regular education students who would not have access to the "Emotional Support" program. SAP was supposed to catch the kids who "fell through the cracks." Special Education by its legal definition should have prevented children from falling through the cracks. It did not.

And while we're on the subject, if Kay had been willing to talk to the Drop-In Center counselor, wouldn't that have to be added to the IEP? According to the Levin Legal Group: if it is not written in the IEP, it is **illegal**. That would mean that any guidance counselor, principal, or teacher who ever spoke with a Special Education child about anything other than academic subjects, would be in violation of law, unless these conversations were included as part of the child's program as per her IEP. This is what they were putting out there.

Catherine went after the "candor" issue in our rebuttal brief.

Neither the Pennsylvania Rules of Professional Conduct nor any federal rule requires this Court to ignore the applicable standard of review on a motion to dismiss. Under the guise of complying with the duty of candor to the tribunal, Defendants rely extensively upon the District Court's subsequent grant of summary judgment in their favor in its final judgment of November 4, 2005 (A3-A4) **on an unrelated claim.** Defendants cite to the alleged factual findings on summary judgment to challenge the truth of the Amended Complaint's allegations.[25]

Next Catherine discussed the Directives Letter. She explained how the Directives Letter "chilled" my exercise of free speech: (1) prohibiting certain speech (2) imposing arduous and

---

[25] Their argument compared apples to oranges.

overbroad reporting requirements (3) mandating what I had to say to students and their parents.

In an effort to "limit the scope" of the Directives Notice (make it more palatable) by claiming the letter only "requires Montanye to inform parents, students, and the School District when she engages in conduct outside of school..." As Attorney Merino Reisman observed:

> Under this reading the letter simply directs her to follow the same laws and school policies applicable to any special education teacher at the WSD. However, such a narrow characterization of the Directives Notice is inconsistent with both the expansive language of the document itself as well as the allegations of the Amended Complaint, which must be accepted as true.

She reminded the appellate court that the District Court applied the no longer valid "*Spence-Johnson* test." This was no longer used in the courts.

Catherine then proceeded to use the words of the defendants to show how the lower court had not taken the correct legal steps:

> In Defendants' own words, "[c]ontext is crucial to evaluating an expressive conduct claim because 'the context may give meaning to the symbol' or act in question." However, Defendants do not recognize that the District Court itself failed to undertake this contextual analysis. By failing to apply the correct legal standard, the District Court committed clear legal error.

Remember when I said the judge's refusal to acknowledge the violations on the part of the district was damaging to my case? This is why: my actions were responses to defendants' failure to comply with the law, the advocacy on my part "represents a quintessential example of speech protected from retaliation by the First Amendment." Catherine was referring to *Leary v. Daeschner*, a case that averred that speech relating to legal violations "is undoubtedly of the highest public concern, since they hint at possible wrongdoing by public officials." This makes sense. If WSD had addressed any of Kay's issues, I would not have had to act as a private citizen. It was their lack of legal cooperation that prompted my actions; therefore, my actions were impelled by their violations of law.

One of my greatest difficulties with LLG was their insistence on arguing two sides of an issue. (Remember the contradiction of ADA not applying to board members because they did not receive federal funding, but IDEA applying to me as a private citizen even though I did not receive federal funding.)

Catherine pointed to this trend when she addressed the fractured nature of defendants' argument:

> In their zeal to establish that Montanye did not speak out on a matter of public concern, Defendants go so far as to assert that the psychological counseling was a purely private matter. Yet, this assertion appears clearly inconsistent with their other recurring claim that Montanye violated IDEA by arranging for and attending therapy sessions. If the counseling was a purely private affair concerning K., her mother, and Montanye as an ordinary citizen, **Montanye could not have violated special education law.** She should have the same rights as non-teachers to help someone outside the school setting. By punishing Montanye for doing so, Defendants violated the First Amendment.
>
> **In the end, Defendants cannot have it both ways.** They cannot claim that everything Montanye said and did here concerned a merely private matter while at same time arguing that Montanye violated IDEA.

And yet, despite the glaring contradiction in their argument, the lower court judge bought it lock, stock, and barrel.

According to Attorney Merino Reisman, the assertion that we had failed to allege any crime against individual WSD board members was without merit:

> Montanye does allege that the School Board must have authorized these acts against her pursuant to their 'policy' against special education. It was further alleged that the members played a pivotal role in the actions against

Montanye. This included approving the expenditure of money to hire a special counsel to terminate selected professional staff.

Catherine also pointed out Defendants could not defeat this claim by simply referring to discovery materials that have been shown to be irrelevant to any determination under Rule 12(b)(6). But they sure gave it a try.

Catherine's conclusion said it all:

> The Amended Complaint sufficiently alleged that allowing the WSD to discipline and threaten Montanye because of her attempts to get necessary services for a disabled student sends a clear message to other teachers, as well as parents and students, **that they better keep quiet.**

We were granted the appeal and given a date for oral arguments. Sarah was calling me every ten minutes. She kept asking, "Can you believe it? We're going to the Third Circuit?" I did not realize what a unique opportunity this was; but from the excitement in Sarah's voice, I knew it was an event of a lifetime. Very few cases make it to the appellate level. Most attorneys will never be in that courtroom. It's a walk off grand slam in the show. And it all came about because of Sarah's determination and faith.

*****

January 19, 2007 was a cold and ice-ridden day. My husband and I caught the train, picking up Joe on the way. Joe had supported me through all of this; he also loaned me the money for the appeal. He was one of the reasons it was happening.

Sarah Dragotta and Attorney Brooks were waiting in front of the courtroom.

My friend Jim was there as well as KH (president WEA). Anita Alberts was stuck in Doylestown in the ice storm.

Attorney Brooks took me aside, and in his deep basso, Atticus Finch voice, instructed me not to make a sound and to keep a straight face at all times. He said I was to be unreadable and unresponsive no matter what. We went into the hearing room, taking up a whole row of seats.

Gregory Harvey and Catherine Merino Reisman came in and took their places. Attorney Dragotta and Attorney Brooks sat in the front row behind the two presenting lawyers.

Michael sat alone.

Arguments were slated for 9:00. About ten minutes after nine the clerks came out and placed the papers of the judges at their respective seats. The air was thick with awe and respect.

The clerk called out *oyez* and the shadowy forms of the judges filed in.

Gregory Harvey said this was the best group of judges we could hope for; they had a reputation for being liberal.

The judges –

Midge Rendell:

- She was appointed her judgeship as a thank you from Clinton to her husband for delivering Pennsylvania in the presidential election.
- Judge Rendell's husband, at the time, was the governor of Pennsylvania. As such, he was the head of the school systems.

Dolores Sloviter:

- First female federal judge who was appointed by Jimmy Carter.
- She was reputed to be very liberal, having forged the way for women in the judiciary.

Richard D. Cudahy:

- The third judge was sitting in to help out the third circuit due to their vacancies. He was from the Eighth Circuit Court of Appeals.

The judges took their seats.

Gregory Harvey walked up to the lectern. He spoke in measured tones. His voice betrayed no nervousness. He addressed the judges and then requested two minutes for rebuttal at the end of defense attorney's argument. This was readily granted.

I settled in to hear the argument of a lifetime. Sarah had been in overdrive since December in anticipation of hearing the revered speech of the number one attorney on First Amendment issues. This was history in the making.

Attorney Harvey began his argument by stating this was a case that clearly suffered from "over-lawyering." He then cited a barrage of legal cases, none of which I was familiar with from the briefs. He seemed to be reciting a list; he never said anything that sounded familiar, nor did he present any argument that bore a resemblance to anything having preceded this case in any discussion. I kept waiting for him to hit upon a topic that sounded remotely connected to the case. This did not happen.

After a few minutes, he paused, waiting for the judges to question him. Judge Rendell posed the first question: "What did Mrs. Montanye do to protest the actions of the school district?"

Harvey stopped dead. There was no response. The silence went on indefinitely. It was a most uncomfortable moment. I was watching the expiration of my case. It had just gone on life support.

The most respected man in the United States reputed to know more about the First Amendment than anyone in the nation was losing his battle for one simple reason—he did not know the case.

After what seemed to be enough time to read *War and Peace* cover to cover, Mr. Harvey said something that didn't even register. I was madly writing down the answers:

- She saved the kid's life by acting as a private citizen and providing assistance that the district was compelled by law to provide.
- In the evidence was a letter which clearly established my advocacy for the students.

All that work, all the emotional cost—shot to hell.

I was frantically passing notes to Sarah. She was reading them, but she didn't feel comfortable passing them on to Catherine. I believe that a few of them went up to the table, but Catherine did not have time to read any of them. She was moving at warp speed, paging through huge books looking for whatever Harvey was whispering in her ear.

Michael Levin was next. He was nervous; however, he must have sensed that Mr. Harvey was not well acquainted with enough information to refute anything. Michael had cited a ruling that he alleged we violated in our first brief. He and Judge Sloviter went round and round about this for many minutes, which is a good deal of time when your limit is twenty. Finally, the judge, tired of Levin's insistence, told him that whatever he was talking about was not in the body of Federal law and she was not going to accept it. Michael reluctantly let it go.

Mr. Levin argued as I expected him to. The surprise was the court's acceptance of his violations of the rules.

- Michael pointed out that we had lost in summary judgment. **Not admissible.**
- Michael referred to depositions. **Not admissible.**
- Michael stated that I "admitted in my testimony that I hadn't had the IEP rewritten." **Again, not admissible.**

Understand, that every time I suggested the use of information of evidence that was accrued **after** the dismissal of the First Amended Complaint, I was told by Catherine that we could not use any of these materials because they came under the aegis of the Third Amended Complaint which we were **not** appealing. Yet, here was Michael Levin anchoring his argument to the very documents and materials the law explicitly stated were not allowable under this appeal.

When Levin made the statement about my "admission," Judge Sloviter said that she saw no reason as to why they should exclude my deposition. Her words were:

"It seems ridiculous to me that we ignore evidence that we have already..." So much for following the dictates of the court. She then went on to ask why this wasn't a case of a "disgruntled employee who wasn't happy because she was disciplined." Apparently, Gregory Harvey wasn't the only one who didn't bother to read the case. Given Mr. Harvey's lackluster performance and the judge's willingness to ignore protocol, Michael was probably doing internal handsprings.

Not one to let an opportunity slip by, Michael Levin decided to end his argument with a monumental lie. And why shouldn't he? It was apparent that none of the judges were acquainted with the case, nor did they wish to be burdened with considering the information before them. Attorney Levin finalized his argument by stating that this case was comparable to the *Garcetti* case, because:

- My actions took place during the school day.
- They were done on school time, and
- I had performed them as an employee of the district.

I adhered strictly to the admonishments of Attorney Brooks and sat there stone faced and mute. Those on either side of me were not as self-composed. My husband said in a loud, growling voice, "No!" Attorney Brooks shot him the disapproving Harvard scowl; however, it was too late. On the other side, KH, the local union president whispered, "That's not true." She didn't bother looking over to get the legal eyeball. Sarah maintained her poise; however, she stiffened noticeably, and her eyes widened in horror.

- Levin stated in his briefs that the district did not pay for the therapy nor did they contract for it, yet tried to link it to *Garcetti*.
- Levin stated, in pleadings and the Directives Letter, this action was **not** part of my job—yet tried to link it to *Garcetti*

Background: *Garcetti v. Ceballos,* 547 US 410 (2006).

Ceballos a supervising deputy district attorney criticized the legitimacy of a warrant. He was then passed over for promotion. He sued claiming that he had First Amendment rights, which protected his speech for criticizing the warrant. The Supremes did not agree with this. The judges stated because his statements were made pursuant to his job, his speech was not protected

Therefore, Mr. Levin was trying to claim my actions took place pursuant to my job. I would not be protected under the First Amendment. Of course this proves confusing as Mr. Levin said my actions had no relation to my job responsibilities and that's why I was a bad teacher.

Gregory Harvey showed no reaction. In my opinion, this was not due to years of training at being impervious to startling information; rather, he was not taken aback because he didn't realize Michael I. Levin was lying.

Mr. Harvey had already dealt with the Garcetti decision. In a letter sent to the court before oral arguments, he pointed out the vast differences between my case and *Garcetti.*

First, application of *Garcetti* must consider whether actions are pursuant to official duties. Mine were not. The district SAID they were not. I was in trouble because my **actions were not part of my duties**. The district, through the superintendent and their attorney, stated time and again that what I did was "wrong" because it was not part of my duties.

Also, *Garcetti* did not apply to me because the Supreme Court refused to make a decision dealing with this ruling in relationship to education.

Additionally, the Court specifically declined to extend *Garcetti* to teachers employed by educational institutions, stating:

> There is some argument that expression related to academic scholarship or classroom instruction implicates additional constitutional interests that are not fully accounted for by this Court's customary employee-speech jurisprudence. We need not, and for that reason do not, decide whether the analysis we conduct today would apply in the same manner to a case involving speech related to scholarship or teaching. (Letter: Harvey 5/31/2006)

Translation: *Garcetti* did **NOT** apply to me because:

(1) I was not performing or acting in my job capacity (as fully established by all of the district's arguments).
(2) The Supreme Court reserved analysis of the application of *Garcetti* on "academic scholarship or classroom instruction" cases. Once again, *Garcetti* was **not** applicable to my case.

Falsus uno, falsus omnibus.

Mr. Harvey took the floor for his final statements, and the absurdities of the proceeding were unveiled in full. Judge Rendell queried if we were appealing only the First Amendment complaint or were we appealing something else? This could be an indicator that not only had she not read the brief; but, apparently her clerk had not given her a memo about the case. Mr. Harvey said we were appealing only the First Amendment claim.

She then asked if we were expecting the court to ignore the evidence gathered under the Third Amended complaint. Mr.

Harvey said that while we were not in agreement with any of the "findings" from the Third Complaint, we were only addressing the first one. He respectfully asked the court to follow its own rules by not considering evidence that should not be admissible as it applied to another complaint.

Judge Rendell then reiterated her question about what I did to oppose the district's illegal policy against Special Education children.

Harvey was again silent.

She said specifically to him that she was hoping he could provide one example for her. I guess the letter I wrote, which was included with the brief, was written in invisible ink. Finally, Attorney Harvey, in a desperate attempt to cover this legal catastrophe, said that I opposed the Directives Letter.

It was the death knell to five years of Herculean efforts we all had made.

He added that the principal had also been fired, which Judge Sloviter immediately dismissed with the observation that the principal was not a plaintiff. In forty minutes he gave away years of sacrifice and work.

When we left the courtroom, Attorney Brooks took me into the anteroom to explain to me how brilliant Mr. Harvey had been and how the judges were able to apply the facts and the law once they consulted the briefs. He tried his best, but I had been around long enough to know that this case was over. I had never agreed that Judge Rendell was to our benefit. After all, her husband was the governor of the state and the head of the schools. He certainly wouldn't want to see a school district have to shell out any money no matter how offensive its actions. Furthermore, given the long list of Special Education travesties, a decision in my favor would invite closer inspection that could open the floodgates for more lawsuits. Better to leave this alone and keep the lies covered. It struck me that she should have recused herself from this case. But then again, all the talk of propriety went the way of rules and procedural processes.

Gregory Harvey came into the room and started laying the groundwork of excuses in the event that we lost. He went on about the slim chances and the difficulty facing any First Amendment claim in the repressive climate of 2007. I had heard all of this before.

Catherine came in to say goodbye. She stood in the doorway looking at me; then she said in her quiet voice: she had children who were special needs kids. She said it gave her hope to know there were teachers like me out there. She concluded by saying it had been an honor to represent me.

I finally allowed myself some tears. The day had been a fiasco, yet this woman, whom I only knew through phone calls, ended it with such kindness.

*****

It came as no surprise. The Third Circuit upheld the lower court's decision. The judges applied the *Spence-Johnson* test using the outdated parameters of cases from 1989 and 1974. My actions were not protected because I did not convey a message. The Rehab Act basically went the same way. I was not protected from retaliation because I *merely* assisted the student. My actions weren't affirmative. In other words, acting as a private citizen I did not have protection because I did not openly criticize the district for failing Kay. Had I criticized the district for failing Kay by writing an article in the paper, then I would have been protected as a private citizen. The irony was the district could punish me because I did not criticize it openly. For some reason I lost the protection a private citizen assumes she has. But then you may wonder if I didn't say anything negative about the district what prompted their actions?

Now that you are well acquainted with lawyer letters, we can deal with specific categories. When a case is over, the client receives a letter ending the relationship at least for the particular part of the case that has concluded. If the case is won, the letter is self-congratulatory. If the case is lost, the lawyer supplies the reasons, none of which have anything to do with him. The letter ends with some form of "you were a great client."

Mr. Harvey's letter began with a recitation of what had occurred and how useless any follow up action would be:

- The Third Circuit based its ruling on the merits of the district court; they dismissed the case using the same argument as the lower court.
- The judges were a favorable group but that did not help.

- He noted that the oral argument had gone **well**.
- He assured me there was no chance of obtaining a rehearing from the three-judge panel and no chance of an en banc hearing (where the case is re-heard by a panel of eight judges.)
- There was no chance for a Writ of Certiorari from the Supreme Court. We could not appeal it any further.
- Based on this, nothing could be done by way of appellate proceedings on my behalf.

Now we get to the part where he explains how the outcome was destined to be, because of a cruel twist of fate—the *Garcetti case.*

One matter we did not discuss on Friday was the adverse decision of the Supreme Court of the United States on May 30, 2006 in the *Garcetti* case. We spent considerable effort preparing a letter to the Court that distinguished the result in that case from your situation and the panel did not cite the case in their opinion. However, the *Garcetti* decision was a major adverse development that occurred after we had filed our briefs on your behalf. As I said in opening my oral arguments, "Because the Supreme Court's *Garcetti* decision does limit the First Amendment claims—significantly but not fatally—I start with the Rehabilitation Act claims...

Once again, in *Garcetti,* the public employee was executing his job responsibilities. Thus, the First Amendment did not protect him.

Why then you wonder would this have any impact on my case? It wouldn't. I was acting as a private citizen which was established in my pleadings and in the defendants' pleadings and the Directive Letter, "None of these were in your job description..." Plus the district was using the argument that I "broke the law" because I was acting outside my duty as a teacher. So much for *Garcetti.*

You may also recall, at the end of the *Garcetti* decision, the court states it reserves its opinion of applying this decision to education. That would be for another time and another case. Gee, I was in education.

Other than the above, there is a third reason to believe that *Garcetti* was not considered in the decision. It was never mentioned. The reasoning for a court decision is backed up with court case citations. In fact, the only mention of *Garcetti* was when Michael Levin lied to the court and said I was performing my actions as a teacher, during school hours.

The kiss off lawyer letter ended with regret "that we were unable to obtain a reversal, but it was a pleasure to become acquainted with you..." He wished me the best in my future endeavors.

He Cc'd a copy to Sarah and spelled her name wrong.

*****

We were disheartened. It had been a colossal undertaking replete with more resolve and passion than finances or advantages. We had our day in court and it was a bust. I had my lawyer's kiss off letter saying it was over.

A district that fabricated a law and connived to invent a "policy" for that law had won. A district that ignored a distressed child had triumphed over someone who helped her. The people who argued that dead kids are insignificant were victorious. Dead kids don't learn and evidently they don't matter.

I was crushed. I had jeopardized my entire future to fight for a cause I thought was worthy, only to lose to Michael Levin's distortions and legal subterfuges.

I went looking to see if this in fact was the bitter end. What should I discover on my legal search, but the concept of *fraud upon the court.* So I figured I'd give it a go. After all, I would never have to write another brief.

I set out on my mission. The brief could only be fourteen pages. It had to be addressed to the court and was a request for a full panel review of the decision. Did I stand a chance of winning a review? Hell no. Would there be all kinds of sniggering while the esteemed judges looked over my work? Hell no. They wouldn't bother reading it. My motion would be thrown at some rookie law clerk who would be instructed to make it go away.

Never one to let a lost cause slip through her fingers, I wrote the brief. I was petitioning the court to reconsider because Michael Levin had lied to the judges when he said what I did was as a teacher, during school time. In order to meet the qualifiers of fraud upon the court I had to prove:

(1) The fraud was intentional.
(2) The fraud was made by an officer of the court.
(3) The lie was directed to the court itself.
(4) The lie was made to deceive the court.

I jumped right in:

> At oral argument, January 2007, Michael Levin, defense counsel for the Wissahickon School District et alia, deceived this panel, by stating that Plaintiff Montanye, was functioning "in the capacity of a teacher and an employee of the school district, during school hours" when she helped parents to obtain independent, private therapy for their suicidal daughter.

I then pointed out that Mr. Levin's intention was to link my case to *Garcetti,* as Garcetti's actions were considered part of his job and therefore he had no First Amendment protection. Mr. Levin wanted this panel to view Montanye's activity as having occurred during the work hours to subvert its decision.

It was not difficult to prove #2; Levin was obviously a member of the court. The next three prongs could be proven by Levin's words:(1) spoke to the court; he was directing his comments to the panel (2) intended to deceive because what he was saying was in direct opposition to his words in his brief (3) his lie was intentional-because it was **a lie.**

Let's take a look at Mr. Levin's contentions:

> In the (Directives) Letter Durtan informed Montanye that in his opinion, "**None of those activities are expectations for your position, none are required by the student's IEP, and none are required by law. In short those activities were not part of your job as a teacher...**"

and

K's private therapy sessions ...**were not a part of any related services set forth in K's IEP...**

and

The recommendation of a therapist, evaluation by the therapist, transportation to the therapist and attendance at the therapy sessions **were not condoned, approved or paid for the by the School District as part of K's Special Education services.**

and

Explaining the Directives Letter:

...directed Montanye to act in accordance with the law and school policies and instructed her on a plan of action **if she chose to engage in contact with students and their families outside her scope of employment**

This was to ensure that parents and students are aware that counseling services that she was providing were **not done pursuant to her role as a teacher with the School District.**

and

It should be noted that the services that Montanye suggested, scheduled, transported and attended were **private counseling session**, not condoned, authorized or paid for by the School District as any related service of K's IEP...Montanye's actions were **unrelated to K or her parents' attempts to procure additional services from the district.** (Defendants Appellate Brief)

While I was on a roll, I threw in the Loudermill "affidavit" for good measure. After all, Levin had been passing this puppy off as legitimate since the beginning of litigation, and Judge DuBois *quoted it* quite a few times in his decision.

Mr. Levin created deceptive documentation in which he inserted his words while attributing them to another [me] for the purpose of misrepresenting the truth. The "affidavit" is a fictitious document because: (1) it is the summary of the Loudermill hearing which Mr. Levin records on his laptop (2) there is no validation of what transpired as no other recording method is used (3) Mr. Levin uses his terminology to convey meaning conducive to his argument.

Mr. Levin included this document as evidence; Montanye refuted it in its entirety during deposition. This document was presented as valid although it **was never signed.** The document states it contains 'sworn' testimony although an oath was never administered.

I spent the last paragraphs apologizing for any mistakes of form or substance. By this point, I was exhausted and defeated. Things like this only happen in Franz Kafka novels.

CHAPTER TWENTY-SIX

Writ of Certiorari

When a public employer takes action against an employee for reasons related to the employee's out of work activities, the employer should consider whether the employee's activities would be protected by the Constitution and whether, despite such protection the employee's actions are reasonably justified to achieve or serve a legitimate government interest.

Michael I. Levin,
Pennsylvania School Personnel Actions

The Supreme Court has commented that any inhibition of freedom of thought and of action upon the thought in the case of teachers brings the safeguards of ...[the First and Fourteenth Amendments] vividly into operation. Yet, the Third Circuit, through lack of analysis, did not justify or find fault with the Directives Letter.

Montanye v. Wissahickon, et al Writ of Certiorari

We had arrived at the end of the judicial road; to be more precise, we had come to a cliff and the ground crumbled under our feet.

The Third Circuit, not unexpectedly, denied the request for an en banc hearing. There was nothing more to be done. I had addressed the court about Michael Levin's deception. They were not interested. In all fairness, the Third Circuit's decision did not cite *Garcetti*, so Mr. Levin's lie fell on the same deaf ears as my accusation of fraud upon the court brief.

The only step left was to write a brief petitioning the Supreme Court for a Writ of Certiorari. This is a request for the court to hear a case to decide whether it should be reheard or to allow the court to make clear the intent of the law. This is how cases come to the Supreme Court and how we in turn get the landmark decisions that define and refine the law.

Looking around I realized there was no one to write this. Sarah was too busy, she had no experience doing so, and besides she had lost so much money with the unpaid time invested in my case. She had to take other clients if she wanted to pay the rent. Sarah had given every ounce of devotion and energy to this endeavor. It was time for her to let it go.

This left me in the wretched position of begging some unknown lawyer to consider helping me. It was a detestable place to be.

I compiled a list of organizations and some private practices that claimed to deal primarily with civil rights.

My first stop was the ACLU. I did this out of morbid curiosity because by now I was definitely convinced the ACLU was not all it purported to be. I had read too many articles, listened to quite a few former ACLU employees, and studied enough of their recent cases. These people were too busy defending twelve year olds who claimed their parents had no right to listen to their phone conversations.

I sent a fact sheet; by now, I was proficient at summing up the case. I included a cover letter explaining the importance of the case, which held the bold assertion that bullied, suicidal children have a right to look to teachers for help, and those teachers have the right to help them.

The reply arrived. The April 23rd letter began with "Dear Sally Montaynye." They started out with the explanation that they existed to preserve certain constitutional principles, most of which are found in the Bill of Rights. They followed with the "we don't have enough people" to take many cases, ending with the proclamation that they only deal with cases in which there is a *significant civil liberties issues*. I wrote them a letter helping them out: I let them know that the Bill of Rights contains the First Amendment, and I pointed out that there are some people who might consider the loss of any personal freedom outside the workplace a significant civil liberties issues.

It may not have compared to **Bong Hits 4 Jesus** but it did have some significance. The Bong Hits 4 Jesus case was *Morse v. Frederick*, 551 U.S. 393 (2007). During oral arguments, Chief Justice John Roberts asked the court why this case was even being heard. The ACLU represented Morse, a teen who claimed his First Amendment rights had been violated because he was suspended for making a pro-drug banner held up at a school event. Now that's a *significant civil liberties issue.*

Although an attorney at the Law Center had defined Michael Levin as a "scourge on the educational landscape, that needed to be stopped," he was unable to help out. Strike two.

The other rejections trickled in with each mail delivery. The American Center for Law & Justice, which is "committed to ensuring the ongoing viability of constitutional freedoms" and is "dedicated to the concept that freedom and democracy must be protected," was unable to handle the case because it "was outside of the scope of issues being handled by the ACLJ."

In the summer of 2006, the Supreme Court handed down a decision in *Burlington v. White,* which redefined retaliation in the workplace. The court found for the employee, Shirley White. It was a unanimous decision with Judge Alito (from the Third Circuit) weighing in by saying there was retaliation outside the workplace if the employer in some manner caused harm or engaged in harassing behavior when the employee was not at work. I looked up the name of the attorney who handled the case at the Supreme Court level. I called and spoke with his assistant, who instructed me to send the information. Of course I did not hear back, so I called. His boss was not interested in the case.

And then there were the others:

✓ Center for Individual Freedom—VA
✓ Lawyer's Committee for Civil Rights—DC
✓ The American Civil Rights Union
✓ Atlantic Legal Foundation
✓ Case Investigations at Institute for Justice—VA
✓ Center for Constitutional Rights—NY
✓ Public Justice P.C., "America's Public interest law firm," couldn't accept my case because they had limited funds. They encouraged me to continue pursuing my claims through other channels. The letter went on to advise me that I should do this a quickly as possible "as there are legal time limits...and because these legal time limits vary from state to state..." Obviously, these folks had

thoroughly read my material because they completely missed that this was a *federal* case. Strangely enough, the time limit for filing a writ of cert to the U.S. Supreme Court is the same in every state.

A number of private firms sent letters of rejection or left messages saying they could not take the case. One firm sent a long letter stating I did not provide a phone number or else the attorney would have called me. My phone number was on the last page where I listed all contact information for me and for Sarah. How *did* these people get through law school?

One of the nicest letters I received was from Bonnie Robin-Verger. She took the time to explain to me the ins and outs of the Third Circuit's decision. She listed the qualifiers the Supreme Court looked for in granting a Writ of Cert. She suggested I file it myself if no one would help me. She even went so far as to include the information on how to do this. It was an extremely thoughtful gesture in a rather thoughtless profession.

At this point, April 2007, I was working for Sarah and Attorney Brooks as a paralegal. I did not have my certificate yet, but I was taking classes at night. I was spending all of my spare time researching law for the Writ of Certiorari. I had a deadline, ninety days after entry of judgment; it had to be met. No one could help me in the office because I was filing pro se (writing my own brief), and the rule was it could not be ghost written by an attorney. Sarah and I never spoke about it. She did not see the completed project until long after it was sent.

On the morning of April 14th, 2007, the police were at my front door informing me that my twenty-year old son had been in a horrific car accident. He had been flown to the Hospital of the University of Pennsylvania. I knew this meant he was either dead or dying. When I called the ER, I was told there was no one there answering his description. That had to mean he was in the morgue.

On the long ride down to Philadelphia, all I wanted was to die before I got there, to not have to hear he was gone. I cannot describe the feelings I experienced.

My son did not die; his doctors considered this a miracle. I tell this part of my story for one reason. I sat in my son's room, day after day, watching his coaches, friends, aunts and uncles, and his father sit by his comatose body, crying with deep heartbreaking sobs. Attorney Dragotta said to me, "I guess this puts everything in perspective." I know she meant dealing with our disappointments of the last few years.

It did put everything in perspective. I *was* right. There is nothing worse than burying a child. Parents should not have to bury their children. I was no longer imagining the horror; I had a taste of it. My child lived, but I will never be completely over that day.

The Wissahickon School District said filling out a non-existent paper was more important than saving a child's life. Can you imagine any lawyer arguing that a piece of paper held more weight than a young life? Think about what they did to me because I didn't want Kay's parents to have this experience. School administrators, the school board, and Michael Levin (the father of a daughter) collectively argued that standing by while a child self-destructs instead of responding to open cries of help is "professional." Shame on all of them!

There I was, dragging my rolling backpack filled with computer and books, sitting in the chair in the hospital room corner, writing my Writ of Cert. It was a race getting the writ in on time. Concentration was a major effort.

Finally, the forty-page brief was completed and ready to go, all ten copies. I sent it express from a stationery store. They promised me the package would be there by the next day. It was not. The papers arrived the day after which made them "untimely filed."

A week or so later all hell broke loose. Because the case hadn't been filed, Michael Levin's office could not find the docket number. They wanted to know what was going on, so they contacted Sarah demanding information she did not have.

We had a big powwow in Attorney Brooks' office. Sarah was upset because she thought the case had been tossed. I assured her I had taken action.

What do you do when you screw up in the legal world? You ask some hapless clerk to forgive your idiocy and then beg him to accept this late entry. I explained that the papers were to be delivered the day before, but they were not delivered on the date promised. I also explained that I should have mailed them earlier; however, my time was taken up by a very sick child. I sent the four-inch medical file along with the motion. Even without a medical degree, one look at these records you could tell this boy was in trouble.

Michael Levin sent a motion telling the court why they should not accept my late entry. Number one, Mr. Levin said, she claims her lateness was due to "her son's **alleged** injuries." Alleged?

Mr. Levin also received the packet of medical records, as he was provided everything sent to the court. I guess if dead kids are of no importance, then ones lying in a coma, only half dead, are completely insignificant.

Despite Mr. Levin's protestations, the court did schedule my case for review. Sarah was beaming when the notification was faxed over. To be honest, I believe at one point we were jumping up and down on the pavement outside the law offices.

I realized the chances of being heard were slim to none, but I was proud that I had gone the distance. The brief was a decent effort.

My argument was that I was operating as a private citizen; the behaviors they "criticized" were done after school hours and off of school property. I had violated no law or moral code while I was helping Kay as a private citizen. I did not openly criticize the district, so *Pickering* was not relevant. If I didn't do anything against the district and I was operating as a private citizen, then the district had no authority over what I had done, nor did the federal government.

*****

It was time to go back to school. I received a letter from Dr. Durtan addressing my long awaited return. It was a three page reminder of how I did all these terrible things, how I violated this child's rights, how I put the district in extreme jeopardy, and how I would be expected to follow the laws which applied to everyone and to make sure to comply with all district policies.[26] It was a nasty, demeaning letter. The writing had a familiar ring to it.

I thought of all the things I could write back in response to this letter. I sent back one-sentence: " I will be returning to school in August."

---

[26] I wondered if that meant written AND yet to be written.

Now that I was returning to WSD, it was time to decide what to do with the grievance. As you recall it was supposedly put in "abeyance" with the intention of taking it out of mothballs on my return. We had an exceptionally strained meeting that August. Chuck Herring was not in attendance. Instead, PSEA sent a lovely young lawyer who did as she was told.

The beginning part of the meeting dealt with those in charge trying to explain to me why they couldn't really follow through on the grievance. Yes, they had promised they would. But, now they couldn't. Sometimes it is not so satisfying to be right; but I *told you so.*

Of course, I always had my suspicions. These were exacerbated by the questions Michael Levin asked at Don Atkiss's deposition. He spent a good deal of time asking about the status of the grievance and if Atkiss believed this status to be accurate. Also, Michael Levin's letters about the grievance indicated that it had not been filed in time and correct steps had not been followed, which would render it invalid.

The grievance revolved around the Directives Letter. Mr. Atkiss repeated the comment Dr. Durtan had previously made to him: "the worst decision of my professional life was signing that Directive."

Nobody seemed to know what to do, but they were definitely scrambling for reasons why the grievance was dead.

Atkiss gave it a try. The *Hanover* decision would not apply here. (If there is no specific language in the contract about discipline, then the just cause clause is implied and applied.) Suddenly *Hanover* underwent a revision à la PSEA. According to Atkiss, if the contract does not have specific language about discipline, but the union tried to have that language put in, then the *Hanover* decision would not be applicable. And, he pointed out he would be called to testify to this and he couldn't lie under oath. Does this make any sense? No. Does it matter? No.

It was lady lawyer's turn. "Well, Sallie, you see, if we did take this to arbitration, we would lose because of *Garcetti.*" GARCETTI? Was she kidding? Then it hit me; she was getting her advice from Michael Levin or someone was getting it from Levin and passing it on to her. My money said she had never even read *Garcetti.* When I asked her exactly how this case would apply, she was mute. Then I got some legal mumbo-jumbo about how high the standard was to prove our case and we would not be able to meet that standard. When all else fails, drag out the trusty standards argument.

I asked about taking it to the court level. No, no, no you can't do that. Well, you see, the grievance may have been filed late. I asked if that was my fault. Yes, I was told. Although I did not file the grievance, it was my responsibility that it be filed on time. Fine. Then I would go to court. No, no, no you can't do that because the union owns the rights to the grievance; so even though it was mine, it really belonged to them, and they would not allow it to go to court.[27] I owned it at the moment of filing but not after that. I had learned by now that fighting this type of illogic was impossible.

But, lady lawyer had an idea. I should rewrite the Directives Letter to say what I would be comfortable with. Wait a minute. That was taken from Michael Levin too. He had asked me what discipline I felt I deserved and now my union was saying the same thing. I should admit that I was a bad girl and write my own "you were a bad girl" disciplinary letter, and then everyone would be happy. I looked over at the WEA president. Her face was a reflection of the turmoil taking place inside. I looked at Don Atkiss rocking back and forth on his chair. Lady lawyer was sitting there expressionless. I was done. I was burned out completely from this long battle and my still very damaged son. I didn't even have the strength to summon up any contempt. I stated that it was obvious they never intended to do anything with this grievance, and my return to school was both unexpected and inconvenient. I left.

Before leaving this scene, I do want to turn your attention to a comment Don Atkiss made at a WEA (local) meeting. It was the union board, Don Atkiss, and I. The local union was going to endorse me and give me $1000.00 toward the case. Believe me in this district that takes a lot of courage. It was at this meeting that Atkiss said he had never heard of the Kate Frank/DuShane fund. He also stated that the "union did not know what was really going on with my case." This was true for PSEA and the local union. PSEA only knew what Attorney Herring was telling them. My local union members knew nothing about what was going on. My

---

[27] Joseph Heller would be proud; it was a perfect Catch-22.

lawyers wanted me silent about everything. I read sometime after this that unions and lawyers do a disservice giving this advice to their members and clients. It serves the purpose of the district to have everything cloaked in secrecy; that way their lies will not be refuted. It also protects the union because it keeps their lack of support a guarded secret. Most teachers will never need union legal protection; most educators will never learn it is nonexistent.

On the first Monday in October, the Supreme Court dismissed my case.

Now it was over.

CHAPTER TWENTY-SEVEN

Target

"I just pass them through and let life sort them out."
WSD administrator referring to disabled students at the end of an IEP meeting, after the parents left.

September 14, 2007
I had a meeting with Judy Clark (Assistant Superintendent) and KH (President of WEA local union). Ms. Clark said they wanted me to "be successful." She wanted me to meet with Jim Malley (Supervisor of Special Education) for three separate sessions to go over the modifications made to IDEA in the last five years.

When I left, Ms. Clark told KH she wanted Jim Malley to work with me because she had been named in the lawsuit and Jim Malley had a neutral background. Judith Clark had not been named in the lawsuit.

Jim Malley never complied with these instructions.

*****

Before we experience the next few years, let me explain how a district can "target" a teacher. There are some remarkably effective methods:

- Set the targeted teacher up to ensure she fails or looks bad to superiors.
- Make things difficult for the targeted teacher's students.

- Set the targeted teacher up by giving her instructions; when she follows them, deny your instructions, then write her up for her actions. If she doesn't follow the instructions, write her up for insubordination.
- If you're a supervisor, you can manufacture mistakes in evaluations to justify unsatisfactory ratings.
- Let it be known that other teachers can gain "bonus" points with the administration if they report anything on this targeted teacher (the accusations **do not** have to be true).

Targeting a teacher also includes targeting the students. Lest we forget: this was a district that punished me for saving a child's life; they would have no reservations of merely hurting a student to satisfy their retaliatory agenda.

September 2007
My schedule for the 2007-2008 school year was as follows:

Itinerant Support:
This was similar to a study hall where I would help Special Ed pupils with projects/assignments.

Study Skills:
This was a supportive study hall for Special Education; it also included the twenty-minute "mini" lesson.

Biology co—teaching: three classes

This was an exceptionally difficult schedule. The students in the Itinerant Support room were from all four grade levels. In addition, they were from all different classes and teachers; they had assorted assignments and different homework. My job was to assist these children in any phase of their work. This meant I was reading at least five novels at once, four history books, and many other texts. I had to know the material to assist the students. If I just let them work on their own, it would have been a cake assignment. However, if I were to work with them one on one, my time for each was extremely limited.

For the biology classes, I rewrote the notes to adapt them for the students. I rewrote the chapters from the book to make them easier to understand. I also made study guides for tests. I had to rewrite the tests so they were adjusted for the students' abilities. This was very time consuming. Special Education teachers were assigned to regular classes every other day; however, one of my biology classes conflicted with the aide's lunch schedule, so I attended that class every day.

My study skills class was similar to Itinerant Support, except the pupils were scheduled every day at a specific time. Again, they were different grades, had different abilities, and used various levels of material. These children usually needed a great deal of assistance. On top of this, I was expected to teach a twenty-minute "mini" lesson covering material from the PSSA tests to help raise the students' scores.

I had students scheduled during my lunchtime. I had students scheduled during my planning periods.

September 2007

I was given a new teacher's packet to help re-acclimate. There was a section with all the board policies pertaining to teachers. There was no policy #827. Now where did it go?

September 2007

I was the case manager for a student who had just returned from an alternative placement. His IEP called for therapy and a therapeutic environment. I asked Jim Malley what to do. We did not have either one of these for this child. Malley assigned the IEP to another teacher. It was written in May of 2008 (eight months late). In the new IEP, the student had been illegally re-classified as learning disabled. And that's the way to get rid of emotional problems.

September 2007

An IEP meeting was held for a student who became upset frequently in the classroom. The IEP stated the child could go to the guidance office when she needed to do so. Maria Salvucci said this was not acceptable. The student could go to the Resolve Room when she needed to. The Resolve Room was where Special Ed children, who were experiencing difficulty in a regular class, would go until they have calmed down or "resolved" their issues. This room, which would be populated with problem children, was going to be manned by aides. No teacher would be in the room. A certified teacher was not needed to supervise the children.

The only problem—there was no Resolve Room. There never had been a Resolve Room. I found quite a few IEP's that stated the child should go to the Resolve Room. The children were guaranteed assistance with emotional turmoil in a fictitious room.

October 5, 2007
I emailed Jim Malley about problems in scheduling students. I pointed out that I had students during lunch and planning periods. Mr. Malley responded by asking for another copy of my schedule because he had lost his copy. There was no further response. The teacher schedule made all the Itinerant Support Room IEP's out of compliance.

October 2007
The department had a meeting with a behavior management consultant. He was supposed to teach us how to write Emotional Support goals. He pointed out that we did not have an Emotional Support program. His suggestion was not to classify children as having emotional problems; thus, the lack of the program would not be so noticeable.

November 2007
Jim Malley said Judy Clark wanted the Resolve Room up and running by 2008. It was never established.

December 2007
A troubled twelfth grade student who stopped in my room to talk was no longer in school. He was not Special Ed. He should have been. One day at lunch he had sucked the liquid out of a glow stick to see if his tongue would glow. He went to the nurse because it was stinging. There was an ad hoc emergency meeting with Thomas Speakman (expert witness), the nurse, and Maria Salvucci, his guidance counselor. It was decided his action was a "suicide attempt." The student was sent home. He drove himself there and was at home, alone, the rest of the day. Potential Suicide Checklist anyone?

December 2007
Ninth grader Ebony Dorsey was brutally murdered. At a faculty meeting the next morning, Maria Salvucci said she was up all night trying to think of what to say to the distraught kids. Bill Hayes, principal, said on TV that this event was even more tragic because Ebony had been popular and an honor student. At the memorial service, a guidance counselor in the first row was sobbing. She had not known Ebony. She had been Kay's guidance counselor. **But I thought these things did not affect the community?**

January 10, 2008
I had a meeting with a parent and Jim Cairnes (assistant principal). One of the Spec Ed teachers was not following the IEP for a child on my caseload. Mr. Cairnes told me I should speak to the teacher about this. I told him I was not in the position to tell a veteran Spec Ed teacher what to do. Mr. Cairnes said I should report if she was not following the program and he would speak with her. I did not feel comfortable doing this. You *made your bones* in the high school ratting out other teachers. Anyway, he knew there was a problem; this was the second meeting about this matter. Mr. Cairnes's response: I was not doing my job as advocate for the student.

January 27, 2008: IEP Meeting
Parents at this meeting asked for a provision to be put in the IEP. The guidance counselor, who was not at the meeting, asked to have it removed when she learned about it. She was upset with this request because it required her to check on the child once a day when he returned to school. Jim Cairnes agreed with this provision at the meeting. The guidance counselor sent an angry email demanding it be removed. Jim Malley, who was not in attendance, emailed her, and said, "Sallie should not have put that in the IEP." I asked Malley what I should have done; Jim C. had agreed and I could not refuse to write it in the IEP. Malley did not respond.

January 28, 2008
I had another IEP meeting, which would become a part of the accusations used against me. I include parts of it to demonstrate Jim Malley's accusatory responses and his dishonesty.

IEP meeting:

- The mother, another teacher, and I waited fifty-five minutes for Jim Malley. During that time, he had gone down the hall past my room; he had completely forgotten about the meeting.
- Jim Cairnes did not show up at the meeting at all.
- When Malley, who finally arrived, told the mother there was no Special Ed math program, she abruptly ended the meeting. Nothing was discussed or signed.
- The mother wrote to district administrators about this problem; she wanted it resolved before she would consent to the new IEP. Until this resolution, the child's IEP was out of compliance.

January 29, 2008

Jim Cairnes literally yelled at me in the hallway about the provision for the guidance counselor in the IEP of January 27th. He **never** agreed to the provision about the guidance counselor. He has **never** agreed to anything like that.

The parent of this child sent me *two* emails **confirming** that Mr. Cairnes had agreed to the provision at the meeting.

He went on to address the IEP meeting he had not attended the day before. He told me **never** to have IEP meetings anywhere else but the main office.

I did not have the option of holding the meeting anywhere else but my room because I knew it would run over into first period. There were children coming to the Itinerant Support Room first period for testing, and no teacher would be there. I had to stay in the classroom to be available for the students. No one could cover for me; it was a testing day and all teachers were assigned to test rooms.

January 30, 2008

The mother who had shut down the IEP meeting two days before wrote a letter to Judith Clark and others in the administration, addressing the district's lack of programs for Special Ed children.

Her first statement concerned the lack of decent programming for the children. She also pointed out that there was no LEA (local education agency) at the meeting for the first hour.

She finished her letter declaring that she had been given promises that were never kept. (Broken promises were our specialty.)

January 30, 2008

Jim Malley responded quickly to the mother's letter. His answer to these complaints: it was my fault.

He wanted to clarify the "facts" to the mother.

There was indeed an LEA at the meeting. He was the LEA. The reason he showed up at the meeting: he just *happened* to be walking by at the time and saw there was a meeting. He neglected to mention he forgot about the meeting.

Malley said Mr. Cairnes was not present because he did not know where the meeting was being held. When he didn't see us in the office, he assumed it had been cancelled. He too had been sent a reminder of when and where.

Malley said I had students taking tests in the hallway. He saw **seven** students there. Why would he include this unnecessary information in the letter to a parent? The letter was going to Judy Clark.

Mr. Malley claimed he saw seven students taking a test in the hall. *He saw three.* These were the kids taking their quarterly exams. I had to stay in the room for them because there was no other teacher until 8:00 and testing started at 7:35. Their IEP's said these children should take the test in the Itinerant Support Room. When the other teacher arrived, she sat outside in the hallway with them. The high school administration **would not** provide coverage for these testing periods. I had asked numerous times for coverage.

Malley shifted tone in his letter by telling the parent I would be instructed to do things differently. He said I would no longer hold IEP meetings in my room; in doing so, I was "denying these students an education because they were in the hallway." Why would this have any bearing on this parent's concerns?

Malley then stated that he had drafted specific language to be placed in her child's IEP. He drafted nothing. He also claimed that math goals were to be placed in the IEP. No math goals had been discussed.

He said I would be sending the completed IEP, and he would review it in a couple of days. This was a total fabrication. He knew there was no IEP coming; the mother had ended the meeting. Nothing more had been done.

The IEP was not written until April (five months out of compliance); the mother would not do so until she had some assurances about her child's program. When I was charged with late IEP's, this was one of them. I had nothing to do with the delay, and Jim Malley was completely aware of this. Interestingly, the mother ended the April IEP meeting by stating that the district was just pushing these kids through school, and no learning was taking place. She said I was one of the few teachers who did not do this.

January 30, 2008
I sent an email to Jim Malley telling him I had eight classes in one day in order to keep the district in compliance with the IEP's. I also noted that students in the Itinerant Support Room needed more assistance than we could provide.

No response from Malley.

January 2008: Letter to Jim Malley
This time I wrote a letter. I thought that might be harder to ignore. I told Malley the IEPs were not in compliance; the room wasn't open enough periods of the day. This meant that itinerant help was not available as per the IEP.

I had more IEP's than anyone else except my co- Itinerant Support colleague.

I could not help students and get IEP's done. I had to make a choice. Could he please help me?

No response from Malley.

January—June
Frequently I told Jim Malley in person that I did not have time to write IEP's, address the needs of the Itinerant Support Room, and make the adaptations for bio. Malley said he understood. He did nothing. He also never made any comments about IEP's being late.

January 31, 2008
I broke a tooth at 5:30 A.M. I went to the dentist's at 6:30. I thought I would make it to school on time. No one is in school to take a call until 7 A.M. By that time I was numb and being drilled

and couldn't call. The dentist is only five minutes away from school. I went directly to school after my tooth was fixed. Jim Cairnes reported me to Bill Hayes. I had no students during first period that day, so there would be no one in the room for me.

Mr. Hayes sent an email asking me why I was late. He told me "You need to call the **office** if you can't arrive by 7:30." I apologized and said I would do this in the future.

January 2008—June 2008: The Aide

In January, WSD hired an aide who was also a certified teacher. He was assigned to me for fourth period study skills class. This man worked only four periods a day. He worked half a day, had lunch, and then spent the second part of the day doing homework for his own college classes, reading the paper, or sleeping. The other aides who had only a twenty-minute break for lunch resented this. This oversight was reported to their union officials and the higher administrators at Central Office.

The many times I told Jim Malley I needed help, he did nothing. The aide continued to work only half a day. When I asked the aide for additional help, he said Malley had told him not to change his schedule for me.

When I told Malley that I made myself available during my planning period, my professional period, and other times when I was not scheduled for the Itinerant Room (in order to comply with the IEP's), Malley replied, "That's your choice."

Did this affect me? It most certainly did. Rather than give me assistance, this aide sat doing nothing while I tried to cover more children than was humanly possible. Had I had more time, I could have spent more time on my IEP's. An aide in the room would have greatly ameliorated this situation. Withholding assistance that was readily available did not seem like they wanted me "to succeed." Then there's the other side: the district was paying someone to play or sleep. That's not very frugal.

Non-Special Education student in Itinerant Support Room

We were told to keep a regular education student in the Itinerant Support Room; this student was **not** classified as Special Education. As you well know, this is against IDEA and PA state regulations. It's illegal. Remember all the carryings on by

Michael Levin and Co.? Special Education laws had to be **strictly** followed.

Jim Malley was contacted through emails. The guidance counselor was contacted via email. We were told the child stayed in the room.

February 2008

Sometime in February, I learned that my students were being called down to the office and questioned by the principal and assistant principal. This happened a number of times throughout the year.

According to my students, Bill Hayes and Jim Cairnes asked repeatedly if I ever talked about a lawsuit.

February 17, 2008

I spoke with KH. A parent had called her and told her about the questioning of students. KH said she would speak with Mr. Hayes about this. Meanwhile, the parents must have wondered what kind of danger I was to their child to warrant all these inquisitions?

Some of the questions asked of my students:

- Did I say negative things about the school district?
- What did I say in class?
- Did I talk about my lawsuit? (None of the kids knew about the lawsuit until the administration brought it to their attention. *Then* I had to explain it.)

I spoke with my student T. She was extremely upset that they had called her in to ask questions about me. She was crying when she told me about this. She said I had done so much for her and this bothered her terribly. This was a student with major anxiety issues. Asking her questions to incriminate her teacher would not have been recommended to ease her apprehensions. Using children is despicable behavior for anyone, especially "educators."

My co-teacher in the Itinerant Support Room was also called in and questioned by Mr. Hayes and Mr. Cairnes:

- Did I talk about legal things?
- Did she recognize people coming into the room to speak with me?
- Were people (unspecified) coming in and out of the room?

She was told to monitor my moves and anything I said. She was directed to report back to the administration.

This co-worker was called down a number of times. She was even called over the loudspeaker to report to the office **while we were administering the PSSA test.** The all call was not to be used during testing. When I heard it, I thought it **had** to be an emergency. When I asked, her answer was, "What do you think they wanted?" During the middle of state testing? Seriously?

February 19, 2008

I gave papers and emails to the union rep about the harassment I was experiencing since my return. He said no one wanted to handle it because there were "so many layers." Translation: forget about it.

February 26, 2008: First Period

I spoke on the phone with Ms. S, a parent. She, an attorney, was furious about the mistakes in her child's IEP. I did not write the IEP. The teacher who wrote the IEP used two different names in place of her child's. One of the names was not even the child's gender.

I hung up when the bell rang. I gathered my books and went tearing across the building. I was about five minutes late getting to bio. Now understand, the regular teacher was in the room, so the children were not alone or unsupervised.

Jim Cairnes was there for an observation. Teachers are usually told when they are going to be observed. I had not been notified.

Jim Cairnes sent an email asking why I was late to bio. I explained.

March 12, 2008

Once again, I sent an email to Jim Malley. It was basically the same old song.

- My scheduling problems were impacting on FAPE for the students.
- It was impossible to keep many students passing because they required more time then they were getting.
- We were making promises in IEP's which we were not keeping or for which there was **no program.**

I received no response.
Meanwhile the aide was still unoccupied for half a day.

March 24, 2008: Spring Break

I spoke with KH. She had asked Bill Hayes why they were questioning my kids. Mr. Hayes responded, "A staff member came to him stating I was doing something they should investigate." He did not say what the investigation would entail.

There was no "investigation" because they found nothing to investigate; the kids denied the information given to the administration.

KH asked him how I was doing. Mr. Hayes had said I was fine. I stayed pretty much to myself and did my job.

March 25, 2008

I sent another email to Jim Malley about problems with QPA's (Quarterly Progress Assessments) scheduling. Students came to the Itinerant Support Room to take the test. The problem: there was no teacher there because I was in the library with my bio students and the co-teacher did not come in until 8:00. That left a twenty-five minute gap. If I covered the Itinerant Support Room, then I was not there for my bio students. If I covered the bio kids...No matter how many times I told the high school administration, they did nothing about it. Neither did the supervisor of Special Education.

March 26, 2008

Jim Malley came to fourth period study skills class to observe me. He said my schedule looked "good on paper but obviously didn't work in real life."

When the class was completed, Malley was apoplectic because the aide was reading the newspaper during the observation. Malley said the aide "lacked initiative." You think?

During this observation, I did not realize what the aide was doing. I was working with some of my study skills kids and dealing with a problem concerning other students from the Itinerant class. At the beginning of the class, I told the aide to work with some pupils doing maps, which he did. I was unaware that he had returned to his seat and was reading the paper. He knew what he was to do during this period. He was a certified teacher for heaven's sake.

March 31, 2008: Jim Malley's Observation Report
Under the suggestion section, he said I should talk to (teacher's name) to find out how to use the aide in the room. I told Malley there was no way I would sign this as the aide did the same thing in (teacher's name) classes. Malley was angry because he felt the aide had been disrespectful to him. He knew this aide only worked half a day. Suddenly he was concerned with theft of service?

April 2, 2008
Jim Malley changed the observation; he switched the name of the person who would help me to "learn what to do with an aide." Because this was on my observation, it meant I was held accountable for the actions of the aide. The implication was that I had let the aide sit and read the paper, or I didn't know what to do with an aide. The aide knew that Malley was aware of his empty schedule; maybe he figured Malley wouldn't mind if he sat and read the newspaper.

April 2008
I spoke with Jim Malley about Student D. I told him D failed two classes for the third marking period due to his disability. His IEP was woefully inadequate. He was categorized incorrectly and in the wrong classes. Malley had helped write this IEP. Mr. Malley needed to speak with the teachers to allow D extra time to remediate his work. He would look into this. He never did.

This was a great student who struggled horribly to meet the expectations of the regular classes. He deserved better.

April 2, 2008
I wrote a memo to Jim Malley, Bill Hayes, and Jim Cairnes about the aide and the problems with not having enough time or personnel to address the students. I received no response from anyone.

April 2, 2008
I sent an email to the woman in the high school who scheduled the school testing. I told her the aide did not show up for first period testing: he told me he forgot. I explained I had to leave one

set of students with another aide in another room because I had a different group coming into the Itinerant Support Room to take the tests. I didn't want to get the aide in trouble, but I wanted her to know what was taking place if I were reported not present at one of the rooms. The woman wrote back that it was my fault; the schedule had been out for two weeks. I could not have known the aide was going to forget to come to the class.

April 3, 2008
I had a meeting with Bill Hayes and Mr. Cairnes.

I was informed by both men it was my fault the aide was reading the paper during my observation. I had not "given him specific enough instructions." It was my fault that he might "lose his job." He would not lose his job; he was a coach.

I addressed the need for help and the aide's free time. Both men ignored this.

Jim Cairnes then said he had spoken with a student who told him I refused to help her with her work. When I spoke with this girl, she said she most definitely did not say this.[28] She said Mr. C. was lying.

April 4, 2008: Email to Jim Malley and Kathleen Hauk
The aide told me that Mr. Hayes and Mr. Cairnes were questioning him about me on a regular basis. I told Malley and KH I was being harassed and I would take legal action if it continued.

KH could do nothing because the union attorney would not take any action.

No response from Malley.

April 8, 2008
During study skills, I spoke with the aide. He remarked that our class was one of the best he had seen. He had been in study skills classes where kids slept or played cards. He didn't understand why they were going after me.

April 14, 2008: Annual Evaluation meeting
Present:
William Hayes-Principal WHS

---

[28] Believe me, this girl would tell you exactly what she thought or said.

Jim Cairnes-Assistant Principal WHS
Jim Malley-Supervisor Special Education
KH-President, WEA
Jim Cairnes ticked off the points of my observation of 2/26/08:

- 5 minutes late
- good job going around the class
- good job making sure the IEP kids on task
- good job making sure they were processing the info
- good job making sure that they were taking notes
- try to work more closely w/ Dr. R

At the bottom of the observation the following comments were made:

1. Have draft IEP's available and hold IEP conferences in common, designated areas.

The first meeting I had had that year (October) I did not have a draft IEP. We were going over some provisions in an already existing IEP. We were not rewriting the IEP. There would not have been a draft. Mr. Cairnes sent an email that day saying there should be draft copies. I always had draft IEP's after that. He knew this as he was at most of the IEP meetings.

He stated I should hold IEP meetings in common areas. He did not say what I should do with the children who showed up for testing and found no teacher in the room.

2. Secure prior approval from a building administrator for late arrival, early departure or other exceptions.

This was addressed in the January email from Hayes. It had not happened again. It was the first time this had happened in fourteen years. It is hard to get prior approval for medical emergencies. Mr. Hayes had told me to contact the **office.**

3. Be on time and in attendance for each of your scheduled classes and remain in a supportive manner the entire time, unless otherwise directed by building administration. (?)

4. *In addition,*
   a. *do not communicate with parents about issues not in your job description*
   b. *do not communicate with colleagues about student issues not in your job description.*

KH asked what number four meant. The principal could not provide an answer. She asked if I had done any of these things; the principal said no, but he wanted to make sure I never did.

I was then presented with a memo from Bill Hayes and Jim Cairnes.

Subject: Notice of Unsatisfactory Performance

On the following dates you engaged in the following conduct:

Jan 15, 2008—Wrote a letter of recommendation for a WSD applicant and included the name of a WHS faculty member without that faculty member's knowledge or approval.

January 31, 2008 reported 42 minutes late to school without notifying administration for approval.

February 26, 2008-reported 5 minutes late to second period Biology class

March 25, 2008—failed to attend your 4th period Study Skills class

April 3, 2008—failed to attend your 4th period Study Skills class

Your conduct has negatively impacted the instructional program of the students by failing to be on time or in attendance, when required, for your scheduled classes.

Jim Malley said nothing. Judging from the look on his face, he was as surprised as KH and I were. Malley was my direct supervisor; he should have been informed I was receiving an unsatisfactory rating. Two unsatisfactory evaluations were cause for dismissal. With the exception of the five-minute lateness, none of the other criticisms were part of an observation. I also was never informed or written up for the letter of recommendation or leaving the aide with the study skills class.

And while we are at the intersection of hypocrisy and this only applies to you, let's clear some things up. I was getting an unsatisfactory because I had written a complimentary letter about someone and typed the co-writer's name on it. This was reason for an unsatisfactory? This from the district that let Michael Levin and Stanley Durtan drag them into a legal imbroglio based on the unprincipled WIN team letter, which lacked **any** signatures?

Explanation:

January 15, 2008 I wrote a letter of recommendation for a WSD applicant and included the name of a WHS faculty member without that faculty member's knowledge or approval.

I wrote a letter recommending a one-on-one aide for a permanent position. My co-teacher wrote it with me, looked it over, put in corrections. When I typed it, I included her name. She supposedly denied this to Kelle Heim-McCloskey when asked if she had written it with me. Why the district would even care about this is mystifying. By the way, the aide I recommended was hired later and remains employed in WSD today. She was also present when the co-teacher and I wrote the letter.

January 31, 2008—reported 42 minutes late to school without notifying administration for approval.

Already addressed in the email to Mr. Hayes.

February 26, 2008—reported 5 minutes late to 2nd period Biology class

I was on the phone with a parent on school business. I know of no teacher being written up for being late, including ones who were chronically 10—15 minutes late or didn't show up at all. Notice the problematic IEP was of no consequence.

March 25, 2008—failed to attend your 4th period Study Skills class

I was at a meeting with a parent. The guidance counselor had arranged the meeting. Aides are left in the room to supervise when the teacher is not there. This was STANDARD OPREATING PROCEDURE. No one told me I was the only teacher in the district who had to have substitute coverage when I could not be in the class. As it was common practice, I would not have known this was an offense.

Here is an example of the policy that was and is practiced in WSD:

Dear Staff,

Please note that there have been a great deal in the way of requests for coverage...With regard to IEP's or brief conference attendance at meetings on students, please note **if you have an assistant (an aide) in your class...additional coverage is not needed to attend these meetings for a period or two.**

Email from WSD principal (2010)

April 3, 2008 —Failed to attend your 4th period Study Skills class

This was a lie. I went to the class and got the students settled. I then went two doors down to scribe for a child whose IEP **required this.** She wanted to finish her PSSA writing test, and she was too self-conscious to do it in front of other kids. Jim Malley would put it into her new IEP that this was to be done in private. Mr. Hayes and Mr. Cairnes told KH I should have had the aide scribe for her. Jim Malley told me it would not have been appropriate for the aide to do this. But Malley let this stand.

There was a discussion following this presentation:

- I stated we were not meeting the needs of the Itinerant Support students.
- ✓ Malley said we were. He later admitted to me we were not

- I said we were being told to violate Spec Ed law by having a student in the room who did not qualify for Spec Ed, did not have an IEP, and did not have a NOREP.
- ✓ Mr. Cairnes got visibly angry; he said **it was not my place to question this**. The order to have this child in the room came directly from the **assistant superintendent** (Judy Clark). If she said the student should be there, then I was to do what I was told. Wasn't this the very woman who told Michael Levin that everyone had to follow Special Education law, even the teachers? That was Mr. Levin's claim in his affidavit. He recalled her saying these words.

But here is the email from the guidance counselor:

Friday, 05 September 2008

Name,
You have student name on the IEP list under Sallie Montayne [sic]. [Student name] does not have an IEP. He was given study skills even though he did not qualify for an IEP. The parents went to the superintendent and threatened. I was told he is to be put in study support. Just wanted to let you know.

Maria Salvucci

She was no longer worried about serious repercussions when the district broke the law? And while we're on the subject of hypocrisy, remember this from Judith Clark's expert report?

Special Education teachers have a duty to follow the Special Education processes which are specified in IDEA and PA Chapter 14. These regulations are put in place to protect handicapped students. No teacher or administrator is in a position to ignore or compromise those regulations.

- I stated that I left study skills to scribe for S.
- ✓ Malley said nothing.
- I said I was at a meeting on 3/25/08.
- ✓ Malley said nothing. Jim C. said I could not leave the aide alone in the room. "It was against policy." There was no

policy about this. It was an accepted practice and done all the time. When I asked for the policy and where it was located, no one could provide me with an answer.

✓ Remember the Resolve Room was to be operated by the aides? They would be in charge of angry students who were removed from classes due to behavioral issues.

• I pointed out that I had more classes than others because I allowed students to come for help most of the periods of the day. The IEP's said students could come to take tests or do work, but the room was not open much of the day.

✓ Jim Cairnes said it didn't matter. I was given the periods required by the contract; it wasn't on them if I gave them up to help kids. (But wasn't it **about the kids?**)

Mr. Cairnes asked what duty I had. I had not been assigned a duty. He asked why I did not inquire about a duty. From what I gathered it was incumbent upon me to go and ask for a duty, although I didn't gather anyone else was expected to go hunting down a duty. We didn't have assigned duties in the middle school. I would not have known to do this. He said, "I have **never** seen a teacher as irresponsible about her obligations as you are." This comment came on the heels of my pointing out that I was with children every period of the day.

Keep in mind all three of these men knew the aide had half of a day free.

KH asked Hayes why he had told her everything was fine three weeks before I was given an unsatisfactory. Mr. Hayes said, "We didn't know about these at the time." Three of the listed charges were dated before the conversation in March. Secondly, KH had told Mr. Hayes she wanted to be notified if any problems arose. She was never contacted.

*****

WEA filed a grievance for the unsatisfactory. One concern was that the observation was dated February 29th but the evaluation was not given until April 14th. They violated timelines and falsified the dates; the annual evaluation was dated February 29th, not April 14th.

April 28, 2008
I wrote a letter to Bill Hayes disputing the annual evaluation. Once again, I explained the medical emergency. I addressed the lateness to bio class. In my explanation concerning the phone call I included a statement the union rep advised me to put in: "**The district has lost millions of dollars in lawsuits regarding Special Education. I made a judgment call based on what I thought was for the best interest of the district.**" The rep felt I should justify my actions.

May 5, 2008
KH and the union grievance chair met with Mr. Cairnes and Mr. Hayes. Jim Malley was supposed to be at the meeting. He did not show.

- The administration wanted a note from the dentist.
- The administration wanted to know how I knew about the lawsuits against the district. This referred to the line in the letter about monetary losses.
- The administration wanted to know the name of the parent I was speaking with on the phone.

May 9, 2008: IEP Meeting (S)
This IEP meeting was two weeks late because for one month, Malley would not commit to a date. I had sent constant email requests for a confirmation. When a date was finally decided on, Malley showed up twenty-five minutes late. He stated that just one goal (in her former IEP) was not satisfactory; he approved that IEP.

Malley wanted this modification added to the new IEP: *teacher will scribe for student in small room or private area.* Remember, doing this for the student was used as a basis for my unsatisfactory.

Jim Malley said he would talk to the school psychologist and get advice for best wording of the goals. He would then write them for me to complete the IEP. This was **never** done.

May 22, 2008
Malley sent an email to Spec Ed staff advising them of a ten-minute meeting on 5/27/08. I did not receive this. Malley then sent another email saying I was not on his distribution list. This could explain why I was not aware of many matters during the year.

June 2, 2008
The study skills aide told me he got an excellent evaluation. He thanked me for the good things I said about him. I never responded to the email asking for input for his evaluation, yet the aide stated I made complimentary comments. Jim Malley was responsible for writing the evaluation. The aide was hired for the coming year as a teacher.

June 2008
Kelle Heim-McCloskey called during a class. I was expected to stop the class and talk with her. She had a list of IEP's that were allegedly outstanding:

The first one she named had been turned in. The parent confirmed that she had received the IEP a week after it was written. It was not entered into the system at Central Office.

The second IEP was not one that I had written or processed. Jim Malley had taken care of this IEP. It was for a new student. It took Malley from August to the end of December to get this done. Apparently, he had not handed it in.

The third IEP was outstanding because Malley had not written the goals. This was the one he told me not to complete until he could supply the goals.

*****

Finally, I made it to the end of the school year. I was so tired from looking over my shoulder, worrying about everything I did or said, and having my heart stop every time I was called to the office or visited by a supervisor. My nerves were strained; my hands shook. I was afraid to ask questions, but I was afraid of doing something wrong if I didn't. I felt like I spent my days walking in a minefield. I couldn't trust anyone. Now that it was

June, I could take a few weeks, relax, and keep my meals down. Maybe I could start feeling human again.

July 5, 2008: Certified Letter from Jim Malley
Although I received this letter on July 5, the date on the letter was May 13th.

> There are three concerns I have regarding your performance in your position as teacher of special education at Wissahickon High School.

#1: He listed overdue IEP's. The majority of late IEP's were beyond my control. It should also be noted that no other teachers had been penalized for late IEP's. The letter also claimed a re-evaluation was missing. It was not. It was done on time and sent over to Malley. He never turned it in. Malley stated that three IEP's were still outstanding:

- He did not supply the goals for one.
- One was for a child who was no longer attending school. (I had emailed and asked Malley how to write an IEP for a child who was not in school.) He never replied.
- The last one was the mother wanted to put off writing the IEP until a later date. I had tried to contact her during the summer but could not get her.

#2: I was guilty of "altering" a form. I had printed questions (we had to ask them during the IEP meeting) on a landscape set up rather than portrait. The wording was exact. Jim Malley told me I could not alter it because it was "from the state" and said I should not use it again. I did not. I had used the form one time.

#3: Malley claimed I forgot the paper containing these questions at an IEP meeting. I did not have them with me so I obtained them. I was not the first teacher who forgot some papers.

Malley ended with:

> In conclusion: A critical aspect of your job description is to maintain Federal and State compliance with every

aspect of the Individual Education Program. Overdue IEP's place WSD and these students of Special Education in legal and academic jeopardy. The following actions need to take place:

1. Hold all IEP meetings and write IEP for any student overdue. (only one was overdue)
2. Turn in re-evaluations for three students (all three had been sent to Malley at Central Office). This was never addressed again because they must have found them.
3. Review email about the four questions.
4. Destroy any copies of altered question forms. (I had already done this; Malley knew it.)

The letter was sent to Judith Clark, Assistant Superintendent. Many of the concerns were moot. Malley knew the lateness of some of the IEP's was his fault or the problems encountered with parents. He knew much of this letter was false. Although he was **concerned,** he did not send the letter until July. Why?

Guess what came via registered mail about two weeks later?

July 21, 2008 Letter of Notice of Allegations and of Conference:
Allegations have been made that you engaged in the following conduct:

1. You failed or refused to complete IEP's on a timely basis.
2. You made inappropriate statements. (?)
3. When told that IEP's were overdue, you were directed to hold IEP meetings and write IEP's for any student overdue on your caseload, but you have persisted in not accomplishing that.
4. You made false statements about special education settlements and losses.[29]

---

[29] The *Shorehaven* case had a projected cost of at least three and a half million dollars, and that was just one child. According to Barbara Moyer, board member, in 2003 the district had six cases similar to this one.

This conduct, if true as alleged, may constitute incompetency, willful neglect of duty, persistent negligence is [sic] the performance of duties, persistent and willful violation of or failure to comply with school laws of this Commonwealth (including official directives and established policy of the board of directors) and may be a basis for disciplinary action against you, including dismissal.

The hearing was set for August 6, 2008. Loudermill hearing number two.

The letter was written by Mr. Levin. Notice that charges one and three are the same, as are charges two and four. Why? Because four charges are twice as impressive as a mere two.

The hearing was postponed at the district's request.

I had always been under the impression if I had gone back in 2002 and just been quiet about the Directives Letter they would have left me alone. I was so wrong. I was going to pay for my belief in the value of a child's life with my career.

CHAPTER TWENTY- EIGHT

Homecoming

[Don't] send emails to administrators about problems you find...just document it for yourself and move on.

WEA President email to me 12/16/2008

2008

August 28, 2008: In-service

At this meeting, Jim Malley emphatically stated **NO** students could be placed in Spec Ed without being tested and having a Notice of Recommended Educational Placement (NOREP). It was illegal. I had a student who was not Spec Ed (2007-2008.) Judy Clark had put him there.

Later, Jim Malley told me he was only worried about one of my IEP's from the previous year. Then explain to me why I had an allegations letter threatening me with termination in connection with a long list of IEP's.

September 3, 2008

Remember how I "put the district at risk" when I left my study skills class with the aide? This was the basis for two reasons in my unsatisfactory. The second day of school, the students in the Itinerant Support Room had no teacher for all of second period and half of third. No teacher. No aide. No adult. The administrators forgot to provide a sub.

September 5, 2008: Email to Student's Mother
This was the child I had spoken with Malley about the previous year. He had an inadequate IEP, was incorrectly identified, and had no modifications for his disability. His IEP said nothing. Nothing is what he got.

At my suggestion, the mother wrote a letter to Judy Clark. This was sent on to Malley, who responded by feigning he had no idea what had taken place the year before.

He responded by an email, which was copied, to Judy Clark and Bill Hayes. He related:

(1) the two goals concerning written expression were addressed in D's IEP.

This was true. They had been addressed in the IEP I had written in April. For most of the year, the IEP in place was one that said his **strength** was written expression. His **need** was written expression.

(2) Malley then said, " a comprehension goal should be added."

This would be useless. There was no class that worked on reading comprehension because there was **no** reading program.

(3) Malley had "additional concerns" which were the fluctuating grades during the child's sophomore year.

Those would be the grades I kept asking him to address during the year.

He added, "I will track and assist Mrs. Montanye supporting D's progress."

He was going to meet with the teachers and speak to them about D. He wouldn't do that when I had asked him to the year before.

September 9, 2008: Email from Jim Malley
Jim Malley was upset about my 4th period study skills class of 9/08/08; the students were "not getting an education" because I left the room for four minutes at the end of the period to get a file

for a student's graduation project. He noticed me "sitting at my desk" in the room two doors down from the assigned room. He wanted to know:

1. What time did I leave the students?
2. Why did I leave the assigned classroom and leave the students **unattended by a certified teacher?**
3. Why were the students permitted to end class/stop working at least four minutes before the ending bell?

September 10, 2008: Response to Jim Malley's Email:
1. He did not notice me sitting at the desk. I was standing with my student from the study skills class, handing him a folder. Malley saw me as he went by, because I saw him.
2. I was not in the study skills class for four minutes. (Keep in mind this is a **study skills class.** The students worked independently on their assignments. They were not missing instructional time.)
3. He was concerned because there was not a certified teacher in the room with the students.

I pointed out:
a. Kelle Heim-McCloskey had stated repeatedly that assistants could stay in the room with students as long as no direct instruction was taking place.
b. According to the teachers and educational assistants, aides were permitted to stay with a class when teachers had to leave the room.

Therefore, I had to ask Malley:

- Why would another supervisor state information contrary to your assertion?
- Why have you allowed this practice to continue if indeed it is not acceptable?
- Is this practice only unacceptable when it concerns me?

I pointed out that in all of the classes the students packed up about three to five minutes before the bell if the lesson was completed. Plus, as we were at the very beginning of the school year, the study skills students had little if no homework. We had had a twenty-minute review of English vocabulary at the beginning of the period; then they were allowed to work on whatever they had for another class.

No response from Malley.

September 10, 2008: Board Hearing

This took place in the evening. I was to present my arguments for the first grievance (the unsatisfactory evaluation) before a few board members. It was a waste of time because the board rubber-stamped what the administration told them, or should I say what Michael Levin told them.

September 11, 2008

At this point if anyone from the administration or the union showed up at my classroom door, my stomach would lurch, my breathing would become labored, my palms would sweat, and my heart would race. No one was coming to my room with good news.

The day after the board hearing, the president of WEA came to my room at 11:00. I was wanted in the office.

Jim Malley, Jim Cairnes, and Bill Hayes were waiting for me.

Bill Hayes said he was not going to "discuss or explain anything to me." I was being suspended (with pay) because I had put the health, safety, and welfare of the students in jeopardy. I would be out until the "investigation" was completed. I turned in my MAC book, my keys, and left.

September 19, 2008: Amended Allegations Letter

This letter recited the four allegations from the summer allegations letter.

1. You failed or refused to complete IEP's on a timely basis.
2. You made inappropriate statements.
3. When told that IEP's were overdue, you were directed to hold IEP meetings and write IEP's for any student overdue on your caseload, but you have persisted in not accomplishing that.
4. You made false statements about special education settlements and losses.

In addition, after the original notice was sent advising you of the allegations against you, you returned to work and it is alleged that you engaged in additional acts of wrongdoing including the following:

On September 3, 2008, you were not in your assigned room during assigned period with 4 students for 35 minutes.

On September 4, 2008, you were not in your assigned room during your assigned period with 4 students for 24 minutes (both of these would be changed because they were incorrect; he meant 4th period, not 4 students).

On September 5, 2008, you sent an email to a parent, a copy of which is attached hereto, making inappropriate statements to the parent about your relationship with a supervisor and falsely stating that you could not get Mr. Malley to help with a student last year.

They had enough time on their hands to read through my email? No wonder everyone was too busy to get things done for the students.

Enclosed was a memo from Bill Hayes about classroom supervision dated **September 15, 2008:**

On April 14, 2008, you were directed to be on time and in attendance for each of your scheduled classes and remain in a supportive manner the entire time unless directed to do otherwise by an administrator.

On September 3, 2008, you were not in your assigned room during assigned period with 4 students for 35 minutes.

On September 4, 2008, you were not in your assigned room during your assigned period with 4 students for 24 minutes

On September 8, 2008, you were not in your assigned room with your assigned period with 4 students for 4 minutes.

I had left the study skills class the first two days to get the schedules changed for my students. Some of them had been scheduled for seven periods of study hall **per day.**

Your conduct negatively impacted the instructional program and jeopardized the safety of the students in so much as they were denied appropriate instruction as per IEP and proper supervision. You also exposed the district to possible liability in the event a student would have been injured due to lack of supervision. In addition, your failure to follow the directive constitutes insubordination.

Effective September 10, you were placed on administrative leave with pay. A copy of this letter will be placed in your personnel file.

September 24, 2008: Loudermill Hearing #2

In attendance: President of the local union, PSEA Uniserv rep, Jim Malley, Bill Hayes, Jim Cairnes, Stanley Durtan, Michael Levin and one of his trainees.

I had hired an attorney on a recommendation from another lawyer. Unfortunately, he turned out to be worthless. He had gone to law school with Michael Levin. He spent most of his time during the Loudermill shmoozing with Levin and talking about the past. When there was a break, he was on the phone with his secretary going over other cases. My attorney had not bothered to meet with me to discuss the case before the hearing. When I asked him when we should do this, he said not to worry; we would talk before the Loudermill. We didn't.

Initially this man said he would represent me and also thought we should sue for retaliation. He said what they were doing certainly sounded like retaliation.

Michael Levin presented me with a spreadsheet that purported to list all my IEP's, their due dates, when they were initially received at Central Office, if they were returned for corrections, when they were returned corrected. This form had been designed specifically for me. No one else had this type of record kept.

I asked where the "W" IEP was; it was the only one missing from the list. Levin said there was nothing wrong with it. I said that was not true: it was four months late and it was an intake IEP which meant the student was being denied services while the IEP was being written. It was way out of compliance, but that was Malley's fault and no one wanted to talk about that.

I handed over my evidence packet, which addressed **every** IEP with emails and letters. This was a thorough compilation of materials that proved most of the IEP's were late for reasons beyond my control. Levin copied it, then put it aside.

We went over each IEP. I noticed while I was testifying, that Mr. Hayes and Dr. Durtan were leaning together talking and laughing.

I was held to standards which did not exist or which were violated with regularity. One teacher remarked to me if everyone who had late IEP's were disciplined, they wouldn't have any Spec Ed teachers left.

I was reprimanded for the email to the parent because it was wrong of me to send it. I was "lying" to the parent according to Mr. Levin.

My attorney whispered that I should apologize for writing the email. I said I was sorry for making the wrong decision on how I handled the situation.

My attorney asked no questions. We did not review my extensive evidentiary packet. What happened to my side of the story? My attorney wanted me to tell the collective audience how much I cared for the kids and how I wanted to keep my job. He said I should show them I was sorry.

I looked at the faces opposite me:

- Stanley Durtan, who allowed a child to be bullied out of her education, but protected an employee in possession of a sex binder, a dildo, and an illegal lock on his office door.
- Jim Malley, who felt he was one of the good guys. Malley, who said to me, "These are very vindictive people," (referring to Durtan, Clark, and Heim-McCloskey). Malley who took every opportunity he could to curry favor with these people by setting me up or reporting me for giving a child a folder?
- Bill Hayes, who threatened me weekly with termination.

I had a paperclip in my hand. I just stared at it. I couldn't think of any words. All I could think was these people said it was okay to let a child die; and if I agreed with them by apologizing for doing nothing wrong, then I became part of their depraved indifference toward a child's life.

Six years of frustration, humiliation, degradation, and emotional strain came bursting through my façade. I cried tears of anger, tears of resentment, and tears of powerlessness. I could not control the outburst. Finally, I had to leave the room, having said nothing.

When I returned, my attorney made nice with my antagonists. He said I was "rough around the edges," but I should be given another chance because I "really, really cared about the kids." Really. Didn't he realize **that** was the problem?

While I was having my breakdown, my attorney met with Michael Levin and the administrators. He had much to say about the information he gained from them.

1. Malley said I was a good teacher, but I wasn't "friendly." Malley felt that I was hostile, although he had no idea why.
2. When I told my attorney that I kept to myself and didn't bother anyone, he suggested I should spend more time being "friendly" and establishing relationships with my peers so people would "like me better." I should go to parties or gatherings to network with others.
3. My attorney said I did not understand "how an institution worked." I had to learn to blend in more. He assured me, if I socialized with people more, I would be all right.

Basically, he said if they liked me, they wouldn't go after me. I had to start doing things to make them "like" me.

My attorney also said he had asked Malley if everything in the May 13th letter (the one accusing me of incomplete IEP's) was accurate. Malley admitted there was information in the letter that was not true. There were two union people present when he said this. No one seemed to think this should be challenged. What did it matter if the letter, upon which the allegations were based, was false? If I went to more parties, they would like me better and this wouldn't happen.

The administration would "get in touch" with my attorney by Friday, Sept 24th.

October 9, 2008: Letter from My Attorney

The decision:

- Thirty-day suspension without pay (Remember, I had not been working since Sept 15th)
- I would be given a last chance warning.
- I would have "training" available on the "rules."
- I would get a 2nd unsatisfactory rating.

The attorney said although this was not great it allowed me to continue to teach.

They were willing to settle:

- I could come back to work immediately.
- I would be paid but the 30-day suspension pay would be subtracted from my wages and I would get a smaller check over the remaining year.
- I would still get an unsatisfactory evaluation and a last chance letter.

BUT

- In order to come back immediately, I had to withdraw the first grievance.

My attorney thought this was a "good resolution." Good resolution? For whom? They wanted me to withdraw the grievance, which meant I would have two unsatisfactory evaluations. Two in a row = termination. All I had to do was come back and sneeze, and I was toast.

The attorney who had urged me to sue for retaliation, my overpaid, non-defending lawyer wanted me to sign the "affidavit" which, as usual, was the hearing summed up in Michael Levin's words. If I thought the first "affidavit" was bad, this one was beyond comprehension.

Some examples of Mr. Levin's misquotes:

- On April 23, I sent an email to a **teacher**. (Affidavit)
  *No. I sent an email to **Malley**.* (What I said.)

- With respect to Student 18 I held a phone conference. (Affidavit)
  Not so. I did not say this. There was no phone conference.
- There was no one else at the IEP phone conference. (Affidavit)
  There was no phone conference!
- No one seemed to know what to do. (Affidavit)
  Malley did not respond to my email. (What I said.)
- *I believe that everyone was delayed and handed in late IEP's for similar reasons.*
  I have **no** clue what this means.
- At the end of the year the Central Office was piled high with IEP's.
  The high school office had stacks of IEP's to be sent over to Central Office. (What I said.)
- I called the mother to see if she had a copy from the mother. (?)
- I emailed Mr. Malley to tell him the child did not belong in the **gifted** class.
  *No, it was an **honors** class.*
- Concerning student #10 I said at the end of the IEP meeting "We're done here."
  No. The mother said that when she closed down her child's IEP meeting.
- It has been acceptable practice for me to leave when I have to cover. (?)
  No idea what this meant.

Most of what was written was not applicable; some was incomprehensible. It was obviously time to sever ties with my attorney.

I had no choice. I met with Chuck Herring. No outside lawyer could handle the grievances. When we had our first face-to-face conversation, Mr. Herring wanted to know if he "could trust" me. Now that was funny. This from the man who bragged many times that he could "sleep walk through these arbitrations." And who did.

I told him I would not drop the first grievance. They were blackmailing me. As far as the affidavit, I was not dignifying one word of Levin's confabulations with my signature.

October 28, 2008: Letter from Superintendent Durtan
This listed all the allegations from the previous letter, with the exception of these two charges, which were omitted:

On September 3, 2008 you were not in your assigned room during assigned period with 4 students for 35 minutes;
On September 4, 2008 you were not in your assigned room during your assigned period with 4 students for 24 minutes.

These were the charges that earned me the paid suspension, and yet they were never broached during the Loudermill hearing and now they had mysteriously disappeared from Durtan's letter of accusations.

After investigating these allegations and hearing your side of the story at the Loudermill hearing it is our conclusion that the allegations are true.

This conduct constitutes unsatisfactory work performance, willful neglect of duty, **intemperance** [new one], persistent and willful violation of the school laws, and persistent negligence in the performance of duties.

These acts and omissions come after a directives letter where you were told that you had violated special education law and in which the following was told to you:

There are procedures and processes in place that must be complied with. Based upon your statements at the Loudermill hearing, we are not sure you appreciate that fact.

Does this have a reminiscent ring to it? It was from the June 2002, Directives Letter. The 10/28/08 letter continued:

The acts and omissions enumerated above come after an unsatisfactory rating. Therefore, taking into account the egregious nature of the wrongdoing in which you engaged, we are imposing the following:

1. 30 day suspension without pay
2. unsatisfactory rating
3. training; you are expected to obtain training with respect to special education requirements. The School District will pay for the training. You are to work with the Principal to select the necessary training.
4. Directives: You are hereby additionally directed as follows:
    a. Comply with all requirements of your job and all applicable special education laws;
    b. You are not to leave your classroom unless an emergency arises;
    c. You are to comply with all directives given to you by supervisors, including the directives in this letter;
    d. You are not to send inappropriate letters, email or other correspondence to parents or others as you did with the September 5, 2008 email.
5. You are not allowed on school property during your suspension.
6. Because of your repeated and longstanding failure to do your job as required, you are being given the **LAST CHANCE WARNING.** [author's emphasis] Failure or refusal to comply with the directives contained herein may lead to additional discipline and possible discharge.

2008-2009: Second Unsatisfactory Evaluation
This one was interesting because it dropped some of the charges which would not be noted anywhere so they still existed even though they weren't written up.

I was found unsatisfactory for:

- Failing or refusing to complete IEP's. The IEP's were completed.
- Making inappropriate statements. (?)
- Refusing to hold IEP meetings for overdue IEP's. Again, this had been completed.
- Leaving the study skills class (with an aide), four minutes to procure a file folder for one of my students.

- Sending an email to a parent falsely stating that you could not get Mr. Malley to help you with a student.

Notice there was no mention of the two times I left the study skills class to work on the students' schedules that were done incorrectly. Those were the incidences which won me the paid suspension in September (2008.) Why were they not mentioned? Because they could not use the argument that I had left the room with an aide. There was a teacher in the room both times I went out. The administrators had been watching the tapes of me walking into the room, but they didn't know the other teacher was in there; she had entered the room the prior period when they were not watching. With all the problems of running a high school and meeting Special Ed needs, these people had so much time on their hands they could watch me on monitors to note my comings and goings? Too bad they couldn't transfer their dedication of "getting" me to helping our students.

November 5, 2008: Dates of Suspension
I received another letter from Superintendent Durtan. He was annoyed that I did not drop the grievance.

The dates of your suspension were not specified in the original letter 10/28/08 because the District was trying to accommodate you in the event that you truly wanted to return to work. The District would have been willing to designate days that you have already been out of work and consider those days as part of your suspension. Because it appears to be an impossible course of action, your suspension begins...

November was a three-pay month; I lost all three checks. I was docked future pay to cover the benefits for that month.

December 19, 2008: Return to WHS
We had a meeting with the usual suspects: Bill Hayes, Jim Malley, Jim Cairnes, and the local union president.
Bill Hayes said, "We are moving on from this point."
He then handed me a list of new directives:

1. You are to obtain training with respect to special education requirements. The training and location will be arranged by the district.
2. You are to remain with your students at all times, unless you have received prior approval from an administrator.
3. Emails to parents and teachers pertinent to school business must be copied to the appropriate grade level administrator.

Later Mr. Hayes said the email should be copied to Jim Malley. I asked who else should get these? He said copy to anyone I thought should get them.

As far as the training, that would be fulfilled when I met with Linda, the attorney who was going to train me on how to write IEP's. Keep in mind I **had not been accused of writing poor IEP's**. There was never one word uttered that my IEP's were not up to par. The one and only accusation hurled at me about IEP's had been their timeliness. Now a lawyer was compensated with taxpayer dollars for three hours to go over how to write an IEP.

My training was excellent. Linda taught me how to write impeccable IEP's. Unfortunately, the Wissahickon School District did not follow these rules with their IEP's. In fact, according to her teachings, most of the IEP's in the district were not in compliance, and in many instances denied FAPE, and violated requirements of IDEA and state regulations. Based on what I learned, there was not one IEP in my caseload that had been written correctly. Previous teachers had written these IEP's, and they had been accepted by Jim Malley as correct.

We did not do the testing required for levels. In addition, we had no reading program. IEP's address reading and math. It's hard to state a child will improve in an area of reading when there is no reading program. Jim Malley always said we could not be cited for not offering reading to Spec Ed children because we didn't offer it to regular ed children.

Second grievance filed.
This addressed the second unsatisfactory.

2009

January 6, 2009: Email from Central Office
A student was tested in the SUMMER. The secretary from Central Office wanted to know if I had completed her IEP. This IEP was six months overdue. Malley said the IEP had "slipped by him."

January 8, 2009
The department chair of Special Education had a meeting during second period. She left her study skills students with the aide for the entire period. Just saying.

January 12, 2009
My car would not start so I immediately called school. I told the secretary I would be in as soon as I could and why I was going to be late. I asked her to get me class coverage if I didn't make it by second period. I got to school at 9:00. I had no students first period. I didn't need coverage. I checked in with the secretary when I came in. I shook for the entire day.

January 21, 2009
L wanted help with her English midterm. She could not do it alone. The only time she could do it was 10th period. I was assigned to an English class 10th period. I could not leave the class even though most of the time I just sat there because the teacher lectured a good deal.

I had to hover in the corner reading the test to L who had to concentrate on the test with the noise of the class. Part of the purpose of giving the student the test in the Itinerant Support Room is that there is little distraction. Not so in an active classroom. She had a great deal of difficulty.

Was this a violation of her IEP? Absolutely. It specifically stated in her IEP that to assist her with concentration, she would be given tests in the Itinerant Support Room.

January 22, 2009: Special Education Meeting
We were told to conduct mini lessons during study skills class, which consisted of instruction for half the period; then kids could focus on their own work. The department chair told me everyone was "doing the lessons differently."

Jim Malley handed out curriculum for "mini lessons" which was nothing but a rough outline of the content of PSSA tests. Our department chair said it was less than worthless.

February 2009: Email to Union President
I explained to him: we have to do progress reports for the IEP goals every marking period. This was the goal for one of my students:

> Given randomly selected passages at her instructional level, X will utilize the word attack strategies taught to her and score 80% or better on curriculum based assessment.

Here are my concerns:

1. I have never **seen** this child.
2. I have no idea what her instructional reading level is; she was not tested for this and it is not in her IEP.
3. No one is teaching her word attack strategies. She is not in a reading program nor does she see a reading teacher.
4. She was not tested on her ability to utilize the word attack strategies, which would stand to reason, as she is not being taught any word attack strategies.

What do I put on the progress report? If I question anyone about this then I am causing myself more problems; if I don't put anything on it, they can use it against me. If I do write something, it can also be used against me because whatever I put would have to be a lie.

P.S. According to my training of 12/19/08 this IEP was illegal for many reasons.

February 2009
Our department chair said she had no time to do anything. She had three overdue IEP's.

February 10, 2009
It was 4th period study skills, and I had presented a mini lesson on fractions. (Always a crowd pleaser.) About 10:30 my students were getting out their work. Two assistant principals, Jim Cairnes

and Tom Speakman, knocked on the door. They wanted to see C. They remained outside the room with the door closed until C left with them.

February 10, 2009: Email from Jim Cairnes (assistant principal)

Sallie,
When I came to your 4th period class today to speak with C, I noticed C was playing an electronic gaming device [PSPplayer]. I asked him why he was playing it and he responded he had no work to do and you gave him permission. Please respond to why you were not following the newly designed curriculum for Study Skills that was distributed to all Special Education teachers at the last Special Education Department meeting.
Jim

February 10, 2009: Email Response to Jim Cairnes

Jim,
I find it troubling that you seemed to have assumed C was telling you the truth, as you did not ask me my version, but rather wanted to know why I was not following the newly designed curriculum.
Number 1: I gave a mini lesson on fractions 2/10/09 during 4th period. We worked on the following:

- Names of the parts of fractions
- The concept of fractions and their divisibility
- How to find multiples of fractions
- How to find the lesser and greater multiples
- The concept of fraction as ratio
- How to find the common denominator

C came in from tech. We were still doing the lesson when he arrived. We finished immediately before you and Mr. Speakman came to the door of G02. The students had just gotten their personal work out when you knocked and asked to see C. It is understood that any type of game is not allowed in my class. C is the only one who seems to have violated this guideline. I have not had to reprimand anyone else concerning this matter.

- I did not give C permission to play his game; he did not ask me if he could play his game so I could not have said yes or no.
- I would not allow one student to play while the rest were required to work.
- I had completed my mini lesson for that period.
- The mini lesson consisted of material contained in the handout from the Spec Ed meeting.
- The mini lesson consisted of material included in the Math section of the PSSA.

Sallie Montanye

I asked C why he had told Mr. Cairnes I let him play the game. He told me he had not said this. He told Mr. Cairnes that I let them listen to their IPODS at the end of the period if they were done all their work. He told Cairnes that I did not let anyone play games. This was the second time a student had stated Jim Cairnes lied about what was said.

February 10, 2009: Notice of Allegations and Conference Letter
The union president came to my room at 2:00. He escorted me to the office. I was given another notice of allegations and conference letter:

- You did not send all of your emails to an administrator.
- On the day you were late you did not notify an administrator, instead you only notified the front desk receptionist.
- On Monday, February 9, 2009 in fourth period you were not teaching curriculum and you allowed a student to use an electronic gaming device.

The Loudermill hearing (#3) was to be held on February 12th. The new Superintendent, Judy Clark, signed this letter.

February 12, 2009: Third Loudermill Hearing

Chuck Herring actually attended this one. He also brought a court reporter so Michael Levin's notes would not be the only source of information. There were seven people representing the school district. What a waste of time and money!

Mr. Levin asked why I did not send all the emails to administrators. Frankly, I did not remember every time I was responding to someone. Also, I thought it was only about important communications, not banter between teachers. Of course, they had none of the emails that had been sent on to administrators, which had been the bulk of my mailings.

I also explained that when I responded to an email in which I had cc'd them, I thought it would return to them. I did not realize I had to forward each letter.

My late arrival to school. I explained to Mr. Levin I did not realize that I had to speak directly to an administrator. Mary was the person everyone called for this purpose.

Mr. Levin asked if I allowed kids to play with electronic devices. Chuck Herring took me aside and told me they had asked the kids and they had been told the children were only allowed to listen to their IPODS at the end of the period if they were finished their work. C was telling the truth. Mr. Cairnes was not. He said C told him I had let him play the game. Mr. Herring knew about this because Michael Levin had told him what C had said. He even stated it in the record:

Levin: I will tell you that after you sent your email back, it was forwarded over to me and it was determined that we would talk to other students.

In order to try to determine whether the student's statements to the administrator, as reflected in Mr. Hayes's email to you[30], are accurate or whether response is accurate, we interviewed a couple of students who, basically said that you have told them that when they are finished doing their work, they can use electronic devices.

Not quite. They could listen to their **IPods** for the last few minutes of the period. That is what C said to Jim Cairnes. Levin knew this but hoped I would say they were not allowed to use electronic devices, referring to games, and then he could jump on my "lie."

---

[30] The email was from Jim Cairnes, not Bill Hayes.

I explained I had just completed a mini lesson. Michael Levin asked what that was. He asked who told me to teach a mini lesson. I said we were told at the Spec Ed meeting. With that, Bill Hayes said that was not true, they **never** said that. To this day, the teachers are doing mini lessons in study skills class. The school board approved the concept of mini lessons and the curriculum to be taught in the mini lessons.

February 12, 2009
The union president escorted me down to the office again. I was suspended without pay pending dismissal. The president was surprised at this; he thought everything was "going along fine."

February 12, 2009: Notice of Suspension Without Pay Pending Dismissal Proceeding
This letter was from Judy Clark confirming my suspension and informing me there would be a board meeting at which I would be dismissed.

Dismissal and Notice of Charges from School Board
This was a letter that merely regurgitated all the charges in the allegations letter. There was an immorality charge added to the list. This was due to my "lying" about the mini lessons. According to the board, I was to be teaching the entire period. Again, the board of school directors **had recently passed a curriculum for "mini lessons."**

I was terminated at the board meeting.

Grievance Number Three
None of the procedures required by the contract after an unsatisfactory rating were followed. There was never an improvement plan. There was no monitoring of an improvement plan. No one mentioned any problems until they were put in an allegations letter.

May 28, 2009: Arbitration
This was postponed as per district's request.

June 2009: PSEA Filed Unfair Labor Practice Charge
The district would not give us the IEP spreadsheets they allegedly "used for all the teachers." The union filed the ULPC. I don't know what ever became of this charge because we were **never** given the spreadsheets. I assumed Herring did not pursue it.

August 12, 2009: Arbitration
The decision was made that one arbitrator would deal with all the charges that had been made. This was "track one" which dealt with the IEP charges and the termination. **Translation:** The next arbitrations would focus on whether the district had just cause to punish me for the late IEP's and to terminate me. Keep in mind I had already been suspended for these IEP's.

October 6, 2009: Arbitration
This was postponed until a later date because Mr. Herring and Mr. Levin were not in agreement as to the subject matter. After the record was set, the arbitrator and two lawyers went into the back room to talk. This was virtually where most of the discussions took place and decisions were made.

October 20, 2009: Arbitration
We spent the morning working on "stipulations" which are statements on which both sides will or will not agree. My favorite was #8:

> After a four year absence (five but who's counting) from work, Montanye returned to work at the start of the 2007-2008 school year. She was assigned as a Special Education teacher in the high school. The School District would call Jim Malley who would testify that because Montanye had been out of work, she was given a smaller caseload of students than she otherwise would have been given. He would also testify she was given additional training.

If he did so, Jim Malley would be committing perjury, which, my friends, is a felony. My caseload of IEP's was the second largest. Everyone else had three regular education classes, plus the one study skills class. I had three regular education classes, a

449

study skills class, and the Itinerant Support Room. I had the heaviest schedule of anyone.

After each charge, a school district employee was designated to testify to the truthfulness of the accusation. This never took place. No supervisors testified to anything.

The arbitrator signed an interim order reinstating me, effective for the first workweek after the New Year in January 2010. He determined there was no just cause for the termination.

November 24, 2009: Arbitration
Both sides requested a continuance.

January 4, 2010 Return to WHS
I had a meeting with the union president, Malley, and Hayes.

Bill Hayes welcomed me back with this:

I don't think you should be here. I thought you should be fired. But you prevailed, so we have to move on from here. I don't want you here but there is nothing I can do about it.

I had to go to "observe" a study skills class. I was given a calendar for my "training." I was given handouts from faculty meetings to read.

January 5, 2010
I went home for medicine at lunchtime. I asked Hayes for permission to do so. I left school at 2:55 with a debilitating headache.

January 6, 2010
I went over the IEP's in my caseload with Jim Malley. This is what I found as we reviewed them:

- No behavioral program, although IEP called for one.
- Most of the IEP's had incorrect calculations for the Penn Data information.
- Student did not have speech support, although IEP said he should.

- English as second language student had no regular English class.
- None of the goals were written as Linda had instructed me to write them.

January 2010

As directed, I went to "observe" a study skills class, so I would know "how to do it." The class spent fifteen minutes on the mini lesson i.e. going over a worksheet. The rest of the time the students were noisy: most were not working on anything. At least half the class was listening to IPods.

January 7, 2010

Meeting with Hayes, Cairnes, and Malley.

Malley explained the "mini lesson" to me. Nothing was different from before, except that the board had approved the "mini lesson." I had been terminated for following instructions and giving a board-approved lesson, and apparently, the board knew about this.

The union president was at my door fourth period. Bill Hayes wanted to see me about Monday (1/4/2010). He had a list of transgressions I had committed. I had been back three and a half days.

- I left five minutes early on Monday. They claimed I left twenty minutes early.
- I did not go with the teacher I was replacing when she went to fourth period team meeting. I asked Hayes what he meant by that? His response was "I didn't stutter did I?" I did not understand the charge because there was no team meeting period with the science teacher. The teacher I was replacing took this time to talk about her cat and cable TV. I spent that time going over manuals. Another Special Education teacher told me we did not have team meetings.

I got a new set of directives with another threat of termination.

January 2010

I went to an IEP meeting where the Special Education teacher conducting it forgot the procedural safeguards notice. The school psychologist retrieved a set from guidance.

The student was from Philadelphia. The IEP from this district was printed in portrait format. We used a landscape format. The teacher assured the parent that a difference in printing the form did not matter; it was the same content.

The teacher also commented to the parent, **"We can always do more than the IEP requires, but we can not do less."** Jim Cairnes did not correct this.

January 12, 2010
The department chair told me she had been pulled out of class in October (2009) to go to Central Office to be questioned by Michael Levin. She couldn't recall what he wanted to know. I wondered if Mr. Levin worried about the education deprivation he was causing by taking the teacher out of class.

February 4, 2010
Student without English class still did not have one. It had been one month since this was pointed out.

February 2010
The students in study skills were complaining because I would not let them use IPods or eat in the room. I explained to them that I could not because I would get in trouble. It was against school district policy. They wanted to know why they could do it in other classes.

They were also angry about a full twenty-minute mini lesson. They were used to filling out a third grade level paper and handing it in.

February 7, 2010: Email from Michael Levin to Arbitrator
Mr. Levin "reluctantly" asked for an interim hearing because the students were complaining about me. Mr. Levin "reluctantly" included statements from students "who were chosen randomly when investigating the allegations."

Here are some of the quotes.

Student 1:
> She made me feel very uncomftrbal and treated alot of the student differently due to there understanding of the material.

She went off topic...
She had alot to say about the administration...like if she
could she would change alot of things...

This was from a student who later apologized to me and
thanked me for all my help. He said he wanted to take back the note.

Yes, I did say I would change things. I was referring to IPod
use and eating in the classroom. When the students complained
about these rules, I told them I would change them if I could. By
the way, what ninth grader uses the phrase "off topic"?

Student 2:
She says she's mad at society because she doesn't have
much money...And her son was in a colma?
Mad at society comment never made.
Discussion of coma, yes.

Student 3:
Miss Mountain does not act professional at all...she said
she doesn't care about the school rules...she is off topic
all the time she bring up random things.

If I didn't care about school rules then why wouldn't I let
them eat and use IPods? This child would have no idea what "off
topic" meant.

Student 4:
It hurt my self-esteem...I also feel targeted.

Talk about giving the people what they want. He would feel
"picked on," not targeted.

February 2010
I found out that Jim Cairnes had been taking students out of study
skills class to ask questions about me. He told the students if they
had any problems with me, they should come to him. They
interpreted this as: if I didn't let them do as they pleased, they
should report it. I would ask them to do work and they would
refuse. They would threaten to go to Mr. Cairnes. When I did not
let them eat in class, some of them stormed out to go see Mr.

Cairnes. It was impossible to get this group under control as they felt the assistant principal had given them carte blanche to do as they pleased. The aide was very upset by all of this, but there was nothing either one of us could do about it.

February 17, 2010: Letter from Personnel Director

I was to be advised that the personnel office had received complaints that I was "engaging in inappropriate conduct in your class and with students." I was being "investigated." While they were "investigating" me I was to:

1. Be respectful to all students and staff. Do not make any disparaging statements or disrespectful statements.
2. Spend all of your time teaching the curriculum and assisting students with legitimate educational tasks (as opposed to illegitimate educational tasks?)
3. Do not spend time stating your opinion of the school board...or anything else having nothing to do with the curriculum of the educational needs of the students as stated in their IEP's.

My comment about the school board was they were the ones who said no IPods. I told the children if they didn't agree with this then they would have to take it up with the board. I told the students the high school administration did not want them eating in the classrooms.

February 18, 2010

I was observed by Jim Cairnes and Jim Malley. I never saw any results from this observation.

February 2010

I was out sick one day. When I returned to school, the aide informed me that some of our children were taken out of the class to be questioned by Michael Levin. No parents were notified; no permission was granted for these fourteen and fifteen year old children to be questioned by an attorney.

February 25, 2010: New Charges (Memo)
In addition to leaving early and not attending a team meeting that never took place, I was now accused of:

...calls students names, such as "retarded"[31] ...Complaints included that during class Montanye makes states that the school board is "sloopy..."

I kid you not; this was the **exact** wording and spelling of a memo written by an administrator.

I didn't call the HR office on days that I was sick. Once again, Levin got this wrong. He meant to say I did not call the administrator to leave a message that I was sick. I checked with a number of teachers; not one of them did anything but call our substitute service. How do I know this was true? Bill Hayes sent out a memo to the entire staff telling them to call the administration in addition to the agency. They got a reminder; I got a charge against me.

Also, I did not have lesson plans on file in the office. True. I had my emergency lesson plans on my desk. The aide knew where they were kept. Most teachers had their plans on their desks. When I did file my lesson plans in the main office, I noticed that the majority of file folders were empty and the alphabet on the files only went up to "S." I guess this rule didn't apply to any letter after that.

March 2, 2010
The aide was called down to answer questions posed by Michael Levin. He wanted to know "were the kids reliable?"

March 2010
I attended an IEP meeting with another Spec Ed teacher. Her cell phone rang and she left to talk to the caller. She returned ten minutes later. Jim Cairnes said nothing.

March 2010
The students were complaining about a teacher who does not help, is always late, and spends all her time on the computer. I

---

[31] This was a ludicrous assertion; however, that was the favorite slur used by the kids.

found out that this was true and some of the Special Education teachers had complained to Malley about it. She got a contract.

March 13, 2010

Bill Hayes gave a Special Education math teacher permission for his students to **listen to IPODs during class.** I was **terminated** in February for letting my students listen to IPods the last five minutes of a study hall. This teacher was told his kids could listen for an entire period while they were doing direct instruction math.

March 2010

Jim Cairnes came down to "check my emergency lesson plans." I took him up to the main office to see them. He asked me how the class was doing. I told him. The other teacher had no control over the class, and due to his supporting the students without speaking to me, I had little control. He was an assistant principal; he would know the effect his actions would have on a class, especially with a new teacher. He told me he had "a lot of bosses to answer to."

CHAPTER TWENTY-NINE

Birthday Arbitration

The world is a dangerous place, not because of those that do evil, but because of those who look on and do nothing.

Albert Einstein

When bad men combine, the good must associate; else they will fall one by one, an unpitied sacrifice in a contemptible struggle.

Edmund Burke

Character is doing the right thing when nobody's looking. There are too many people who think that the only thing that's right is to get by, and the only thing that's wrong is to get caught.

J.C. Watts, Oklahoma Congressman

March 22, 2010: Arbitration

It was my birthday and I certainly was the focus of attention. Although we had subpoenaed a number of witnesses, those previous hearings had been cancelled and Chuck Herring had not recalled these witnesses for this meeting. Herring's take on fellow teachers as witnesses was they were useless; they would say nothing for fear of losing their jobs. When I asked him if he had the resources to protect them legally, he said yes but it could take ten years to come about. In other words, there was no way a teacher had a chance of being backed up by a colleague because the intimidation factor was overwhelming.

The district's witnesses were brought in one by one. The district went all out for these. They drove two children from the study skills class in the high school, over to Central Office, to be sworn in to testify against me. The parents were **never** informed of this action. There were **no permission slips** signed to remove the children from a class, to remove them from the school building, and to subject them to being questioned by Michael Levin at a hearing. These kids were hijacked from school, forced to swear an oath and then badgered by an attorney to say what he wanted to hear. In addition, their full names were used and appeared in the record. If they had done this to my child **without any notification,** I would have been livid. How do I know the parents weren't informed? I knew the mother of one of the children. She said she had no idea any of this had taken place.

The first student was a girl from the study skills class and my inclusion science class.

Levin: Does Ms. Montanye ever tell the kids in class about her personal life?[32]

Girl: Yes.

Levin: What does she say in class about her personal life?

Girl: Her son was in a coma, how she is mad at society, stuff like that, how she doesn't like the President.

Levin: Does she say why she doesn't like the President?

Girl: No. She just says she is mad at society for some reason.

Levin: When she makes statements about these personal things...are they related at all to what she's teaching?

Girl: No she is very random.

Levin: Does she stay on topic when she teaches?

Girl: No. She just wanders off and just makes it very confusing to understand what she is talking about.

---

[32] All testimony taken directly from court reports.

Mr. Levin then asked her about another student in the class. She provided her incorrect recollection of an event that had taken place with him. Apparently, she did not remember all she had been coaxed to say:

Levin: Did you ever hear Ms. Montanye say anything to M that you thought inappropriate?

Girl: No.

Levin: You don't remember that?

Girl: No.

The testimony took on a new angle when not prodded by Mr. Levin.

Herring: Then after the mini lesson is done, then there is a study hall portion of the—

Girl: Yes. She helps us with any work we need help with.

Herring: During the study hall portion is there discussion in class?

Girl: Yes. I have to admit, yes we get off topic a lot. Which may be what upsets her.

Herring: My question is: Are people just talking about –to use your word—random things after the mini lessons are done?

Girl: After, yes.

Herring: Don't you have her for science too?

Girl: Yes. She helps me in science…If I need help, I would go ask her…she sits over on the other side of the classroom (science room) and if I need help I would go over and ask and she will help me.

Herring: You told us she said that the school board was very unorganized...Do you remember how that came up?

Girl: She was upset one day because she got mail and it didn't have a date on it...she wanted the date to be on it to be more organized...so she said it was sloppy and unorganized.

Herring: Was there any other discussion that went on with that?

Girl: No.

The next student was one of my boys.

Levin: Does Ms. Montanye ever tell the kids in class about her personal life?

Boy: No, not really.

Levin: Does she say anything about her children or her son?

Boy: She has a couple of times, yes...Relating to hockey, just some of the inside stuff.

Levin: Does she ever voice any opinions about the President?

Boy: No she has not.

Levin: (arguing) Do you remember telling me on Friday—

Boy: Saying about political stuff?

Levin: About the President?

Boy: The President? No.

Levin: Did Ms. Montanye ever send you to sit in the hallway?

At this point the witness recounted the event, forgetting to point out that he had disrupted the class a number of times, had been warned a number of times, and finally was asked to leave the room.

Now it was Herring's turn:

Herring: You and her (Ms. Montanye) cool now?

Boy: Everything's been cool for the last three, four weeks, yeah it's been good.

Herring asked about the study hall part of the period:

Herring: Is there a discussion that goes on in the second half of the period?

Boy: No we try and make it a silent study hall.

Bill Hayes was the next to testify. He provided the room with hearsay that he alleged was obtained from the teacher whose place I took. He then spoke about a meeting we had the afternoon I started (January 4th). He claimed they gave me a training schedule along with a faculty manual. He was incorrect. Jim Malley gave me the training schedule the next morning in my classroom.

Levin then questioned Hayes about my claim that he berated me. Mr. Hayes forgot his "you should have been fired speech." Levin asked Hayes if I had ever been disciplined for violating the directive of "securing approval from a building administrator for late arrival or early departure." Hayes' answer was I had not. (Yes, I had. Part of my first unsatisfactory, April 2008, was based on arriving late due to a medical emergency).

Mr. Hayes spoke of how I neglected to call the district when I was absent. Other teachers had informed me that we only had to call the sub agency.

Mr. Hayes said I did not follow procedure. When questioned by Herring:

Herring: Does every teacher do both?

Hayes: To my understanding every teacher does both.

If that were true, then explain why he sent out a memo on April 7th (two weeks after this arbitration) telling the entire faculty to call the office when they were going to be out.

Hayes reinforced his false assumption that I was the only teacher not to call in when absent: She (his secretary) "has never told me that there's been a situation where teachers have not called in." Did he ever ask her? If not, was I the only one he asked about? If all the other teachers did this, then why send out the April 7th email reminding all the teachers who called in, to call in.

Next, the man who said there was no such things as mini lessons, defined what a mini lesson was:

Hayes: Mini lessons are 20 to 25 minute long lessons that relate to a particular topic that are for the study skills class.

Mr. Hayes was asked to address the emergency lesson plans. Although I had placed them in the office, they were treating them as if they didn't exist. Jim Cairnes had checked my lesson plans. Again, in Mr. Hayes's email of April 7, 2010, he reminded the **entire faculty** to have their plans in the office in case they were absent.

Herring asked if Hayes would know whether or not I had lesson plans in the office during 2007-2008.

Hayes: No.

Herring: How frequently do you check the plans for every educator in the building?

Hayes: At the beginning of each year and then approximately midway through.

Midway through would be January 21st. If he had checked them, he said nothing to me. Funny how the email to the faculty, to submit plans, came out **right after** this hearing.

The next issue was a letter from an English teacher complaining she had not received a child's IEP. This IEP was written by the former teacher who, unknown to me, supposedly, had not sent the IEP to this English teacher. Oddly enough, all the other teachers received their copies. Instead of asking me to send a copy, this English teacher went to complain to Bill Hayes. It makes no sense that she would have asked Hayes about this, rather than me or the department chair.

Next, Mr. Hayes was appalled that I had placed a student outside of the room when he would not stop interrupting the class. He sat by the door and I kept it open to make sure he stayed put. Mr. Hayes said this was against school practice. No one did this.

Levin: Is it appropriate or inappropriate for a teacher to put a student in the hallway?

Hayes: That would be inappropriate.

Levin: Why is that?

Hayes: Inappropriate discipline consequence and they're not supervised.

This was news to me. In every regular education class I had been in, if a student became disruptive he was asked to leave and stand outside the door. I am not sure where Bill Hayes spent his time, but on any given day, there would be children standing in the hall. It was a "common practice."

Another (new) offense was that I did not fill out my grade book for two weeks. According to the principal, teachers updated their grades every two weeks. It was "common courtesy." I looked into this when I returned to school the next day. We were five weeks into the marking period. I found at least ten teachers who had not put in any grades since the last marking period. That was more than a month lapse.

The next witness was another Special Education teacher. I taught in the same room as she did. Levin asked her about a Special Education meeting that I missed, or as Michael Levin said, that I "had blown off." She was so nervous she could hardly talk. I had already said I missed the meeting. I was sick (which I was most of the year) and went back to our room after school and lay my head on the desk. I completely forgot about the meeting.

They were putting this woman through the paces just for the joy of torturing someone.

The following witness was the aide in my room. She testified that I did not call the students names. She also testified that if a child had been punished it was for disorderly behavior. She said I treated her well. The aide testified that other teachers put children in the hall for time out. Also, she stated with some conviction that I had never called the children names, and if I had, she would have reported me.

It was now my turn.

Michael Levin was barely civil. We went round and round about the data being entered for the students in study skills. We went over every entry. Then he began to attack the methodology I used for grading study skills class. Next, he criticized the content of this class:

Levin: Did you also testify that you provide no tests for the mini lessons?

Montanye: We don't use tests, no.

Levin: How do you determine if they are actually learning what you are teaching them in the mini lessons?

I explained that we used teacher observation in the study skills class and progress observations from the regular education teachers. Remember, a good deal of the work was review. After my explanation:

Levin: Are you finished? So you would agree with me that the work that is being done in the study skills class is important...So it's important to make an assessment as to whether they are actually learning the things that you are teaching, right?

Montanye: Yes.

Levin: You have been told over and over and over again that the way teachers learn or determine whether the kids are making progress and learning what they are being taught is through data, right? You do not have any data as to whether the kids are actually learning what you are trying to teach them, right?

Montanye: I have teacher observation, which is an assessment tool.

Levin: You have this teacher observation where?

Montanye: I write it down.

Levin: We're going to take a break, I'd like you to get it and bring it here.

Herring: Objection...She's not charged with not giving tests.

Levin: This goes to credibility and credibility of a party is always a relevant feature. She gave an explanation, which frankly is implausible, about her grading system. This goes to the plausibility of her testimony...She said that that's how she determines if the kids are actually learning what she's teaching...So I want to see these teacher observation data that she claims she has.

Herring: How is that in any way relevant to what was put on in their case, as to what she did or didn't do on the compliance issues?

Levin: Because one of the compliance issues is she didn't enter into the computer system data until March 3rd (this was **not part** of their compliance charges) and she also testified that she didn't even test the kids once she changed the grading system, which I haven't gotten into yet.

Herring: This program...is not a testing program. There aren't tests given out like in a regular class...The students are supported in study skills.

Levin: I'm glad Mr. Herring is such an expert on this. I don't think he's correct. We will get to that.

Arbitrator: I think it's very important that I know whether or not other teachers in similar roles to the Grievant actually give tests or do not give tests in their class.

Levin: They measure performance and they have grades and we, in fact, do have the grade reports from the other teachers for study skills.[33]

Michael Levin dragged on about the grades, what they were for, what they meant. He kept badgering me about whether an exercise was a test or quiz. He had no concept of the nature of this class.

Herring: Objection. The charge that led to the submission of SD-53 was that she didn't put stuff in (the grading program) fast enough and it didn't happen until March and (the semester) started at the end of January. She was never charged with not grading appropriately, not assessing appropriately these students. So I don't know why we are having this debate about what assessment skills or tests she used.

Levin: This all goes to the heart of credibility of the underlying testimony and not only are we finding out more and more as we are talking about things. It seems so far that she's making this stuff up, frankly.

Herring: That's not what she is charged with.

Levin: Well, she's being charged right now with that.

The arbitrator decided Levin would continue with his questioning, but the record on the testing and grading would be left open. This would give the district a "chance to provide information as to how this particular grading system is applied throughout the District and what criteria is used." Hold on! Hadn't Levin already stated he had the records of the other teachers?

---

[33] Good luck with that. We all graded the same way and we all supplied basically the same materials for the class. Levin was bluffing; he could not have had the grades because they were identical to mine.

Levin: They measure performance and they have grades and we, in fact, do have the grade reports from the other teachers for study skills.

Why then, would he need in the arbitrator's words: "a chance to provide information as to how this particular grading system is applied throughout the district and what criteria was used?" One minute before, Levin had all the evidence they needed. Was the arbitrator listening? And what was Herring doing during this exchange?

Plus, wouldn't Levin and his clients be responsible for doing this research **before** they started slinging accusations and costing the taxpayers $1500 per arbitration?

Mr. Levin then went after the fact that the students and I had a discussion about a news item as they were packing up.

Levin: There is nothing in the curriculum...dealing with people in a vegetative state, right?

Levin: There is nothing in the curriculum about talking about or teaching about a coma, right?

Levin: There is nothing in the curriculum talking about the State of the Union address that Presidents give every year, right?

Levin: There is nothing in the curriculum that you know of about talking about campaign contributions, right? There is nothing that you can identify as you sit here today in the curriculum dealing with a discussion of campaign contributions, right?

Next, Mr. Levin wanted to prove that I forced Bill Hayes' outburst when I returned in January 2010.

Levin: Isn't it true that you started to give him some lip, and you in fact, accused him that he didn't want you back? (some lip?)

Montanye: No.

Levin: You never said that?

Montanye: No.

I then explained that I had asked Mr. Hayes about the situation with the mini lessons. I was told to teach them, I did, then, I was found to be "immoral" and terminated for teaching a mini lesson. I was respectful when I asked this. What I wanted to know was how did I know if I was following instructions that I wouldn't get in more trouble for following directions.

Mr. Levin was incensed.

Levin: What did you hope to achieve by bringing all this up when he was trying to explain to you what your expectations were? (This made no sense.)

So I told him the truth:

...It's very difficult to work in a situation where if you make a mistake, rather than somebody correcting you, you are punished for it and it becomes a situation between lawyers. It's very difficult to know that you can't go to the people who are your superiors and ask a question because that could be convoluted into another reason for going after you. It's very difficult to watch somebody sit there and say "she's lying" and then to have the attorney accuse you of being immoral because you "created" a lie that wasn't a lie...even though I am a good teacher and work well with a lot of the hardest kids in the district...I'm in the constant position of digging myself out of a hole and I have nobody to turn to because everybody up the chain of command had either abandoned me or lied about me or said things that have not been exact or reported false things...I'm not the first person to miss a meeting, I didn't do that out of anger. I didn't do that out of being defiant. I was sick. I missed a meeting. I am not a perfect person; I never presented myself in that way.

Levin continued to ask questions about the meeting I missed. The arbitration concluded with the arbitrator talking about setting another date. Of one thing I was sure; they were never going to let up on me. There was no end unless I quit.

March 23, 2010: Observation Kelle Heim-McCloskey
The day after the arbitration Ms. Heim-McCloskey showed up to observe me. She sat down at a student's desk. She spent most of the period trying to clean something off her computer keyboard. Finally, I went over and asked her if she wanted some cleaner to use.

At the end of the class, she said she would talk to me within the week about her observation. I asked if there was anything wrong, and she said no, there were a few small things she would address.

I didn't hear from Kelle Heim-McCloskey for the rest of the year. She did not call me over to discuss the observation. No wonder. Her observation was deceitful and damning. Her information was incorrect. Reading this makes you wonder whom this woman was observing.

Teacher's Name: Sally Montayne (You would think by now she would know how to spell **one** of my names.)
I introduced the lesson with: "Remember our buddies the verbs; they do two things." We spent the next block of time going over action and state of being. Then we went into tenses. (Remember this is a ninth grade class.) Ms. Heim-McCloskey said the mini lesson had no introduction. She said the lesson had no content. I am not sure how she would classify the instruction concerning actions, state of being, and tense.

She was critical because I "had to pry the answers out of the students." Not so. They answered well until we got to state of being verbs. They had to be reminded what that was.

I handed out a work sheet. On the work sheet were boxes to fill in with the correct verb. Ms. Heim-McCloskey mistakenly identified this as a "crossword puzzle." It was not. There was a grid at the top of the page, which allowed the students to self-correct their answers by filling in the boxes with the correct answer.

Heim-McCloskey: Each student was given a worksheet...
at the top of the paper was a crossword puzzle. However, neither the questions nor the crossword had numbers or directional location. Students were confused with this.

Ms. Heim-McCloskey was confused. I explained to the students how to count the numbers of boxes to check their verbs. It was not a puzzle; therefore, it had no clues.

I stopped the mini-lesson after twenty minutes because the students needed to work on their other assignments. According to Ms. Heim-McCloskey, I abruptly stopped the lesson. I told the students to hand in their papers the next day. I would give extra credit if they wanted to fill in the grid at the top.

The supervisor suggested that the class started around 9:30. Then she said the lesson ended at 9:38. Hardly. I could not have gone over all that material in eight minutes. I was writing the answers to my questions on the board. As a class, we answered the twelve questions on the worksheet. In fact, when the students were giving me the past tense, I asked them to provide the present and future form, which meant they were answering thirty-six questions in total. That would take well over ten minutes, not counting the introduction of verbs, explanation of uses and examples of tense.

Heim-McCloskey: Overall, the lesson had no introduction, no lesson, content or closure. There were many opportunities for you to review and re-teach verb tense. It was obvious that several students did not understand the concept. Although it is a study skills class, it is imperative that the mini lesson has meaning.

So, by the supervisor's account, I stood in front of the class saying nothing?

How did she know the students needed review and re-teaching? Because I was asking them questions and teaching them about verbs and she was listening to the answers? How did she know the students "did not understand the concept" if no discussion was taking place? How would the lesson be meaningless if the students needed reviewing? By the way, I considered study skills to be one of the most important classes these kids had; it addressed their deficits and allowed for small group explanations they did not get in regular education classes. Finally, there is **no reason** to teach a "meaningless lesson," mini or otherwise.

A final comment was that I "under-minded" [sic] my colleagues because I allegedly stated the guidance counselors had no idea what they were doing. She missed the gist of this discussion. I was signing next year's schedules at the end of the period. I told the students they had to check off study skills or they would not get the class. I said if we don't put this down then the guidance counselors won't have any idea what **you're** doing and **you** won't get the class. Really, how dumb would you have to be to make a statement like the one alleged, in front of a hostile administrator who was waiting to jump on any perceived error?

At the bottom of the observation was a line for the observer's signature. The next line down was for the teacher's signature. Kelle signed the wrong one and then drew an arrow to indicate a switch between the two.

I told a Spec Ed co-teacher about this. She said the same thing happened to her. Kelle Heim-McCloskey wrote an observation that had no connection to what had taken place in the classroom. This teacher would not sign the sheet until she made substantial changes.

March 24, 2010: Observation Jim Malley (next day)
This was innocuous. He made a few recommendations and was very sparse with compliments. It couldn't be used for or against me.

March 25, 2010: Letter from Bill Hayes
Bill Hayes wanted the notes from my journal. I referred to the journal during the March 22nd arbitration. If I did not supply the journal, I could be disciplined or dismissed. Chuck Herring said I did not have to turn the journal over to him. Despite this, he advised me to give Hayes the few pages he wanted. I did not. There was no follow through because they had no legitimate right to my notes.

March 26, 2010
I still saw many students standing in the hallways outside the classrooms, even though it "was never done." One of our science students spent half the period outside the class that day because he would not stop talking. It was the same boy who testified at the arbitration.

April 5, 2010: Memorandum from Bill Hayes
I have reviewed your testimony about how you allegedly assess student performance in your study skills class.

Your assessment process is wholly improper and you are directed to cease and desist immediately...

In addition to your immediate termination of your inappropriate student assessment system, you are directed to prepare a proper grading system...and to provide a written description of the system to me no later than the end of the day, April 8, 2010.

Your failure or refusal to comply with these directives could lead to additional discipline, including discharge.

March 29, 2010: Charge of Unfair Labor Practice(s) Under The Public Employe [sic] Relations Act
Charles Herring filed this a week after the arbitration. His accusation was:

On January 4, 2010 immediately upon her return, the respondent's administration began a cause of conduct designed to punish, intimidate, and harass Montanye for engaging in protected activity.

Herring listed twenty-five charges against the Wissahickon School District. He pointed out that I "exercised my right to file grievances, proceed to arbitration and engage in protected union activity." It was a great write up. It was also withdrawn less than two months later.

April 5, 2010: Email from Bill Hayes
He had reviewed the grade books for study skills classes, including mine. I was to provide him with the data upon which I relied to provide the grades that were in the book from February. I was to provide him with this information by the end of Tuesday, April 6, 2010. **"Your failure or refusal to provide this information can lead to further discipline including discharge."** A familiar refrain.

April 2010
There were visitors in the school. The assistant superintendent, Kelle Heim-McCloskey, and Cathy Rossi (HR) were going to the other study skills teachers' classes and asking how they graded

their students. Considering I adopted their method, they found we used the same system.

April 7, 2010: Email from Hayes to all Faculty

1. Make sure you have emergency lesson plans on file in the office (although testimony stated this was checked and every teacher had his/her plans there.)
2. In addition to calling the substitute agency, please call into the office of the principal to whom you directly [sic] or the main office. Leaving a message is fine...(although in his testimony Hayes said every other teacher called the office.)

April 13, 2010: Special Education Meeting

I brought up what Levin said at the March 22nd arbitration, that I was not assessing children correctly because I was not using a specific test. I think at that point it finally hit Jim Cairnes. I was not the liability, Levin was. Jim Cairnes told me that I was a qualified teacher and I was able to make accurate assessments concerning the progress of my students. He looked sincerely angry, but it was not with me. He told me to continue grading as I had been.

Special Education Department Meeting Notes: April Study Skills

- Not sure what is going on with this course. Concerns: grading and assessments would like consistency with expectations, confusing, feeling like walking on eggshells.

Good job. Between what I had been accused of and the administrators crawling all over the study skills teachers, the staff was now intimidated and worried about how and what they were doing. They should have been able to focus on the students, but couldn't if they feared walking into a trap with their grading system. So now, Mr. Levin had worked his magic and totally disrupted our entire department. And the taxpayers were funding his havoc.

April 15, 2010: Email from Jim Cairnes to Spec Ed Department Chair and Study Skills Teachers

I would like to include a comment I shared yesterday addressing the uneasiness of grading the study skills class. After surveying teachers of study skills the current practice teachers employ of grading mini-lessons and independent work for participation, effort and completion of task is appropriate and acceptable.

Jim

April 20, 2010

Kelle Heim-McCloskey contacted Special Education teachers about a meeting. She did not contact me.

May 20, 2010

We were told that we **did not have** to do mini lessons for the rest of the year.

There was a "secret" meeting with Michael Levin, Chuck Herring, and the union president. I was not included. Chuck Herring agreed to drop the Charge of Unfair Practice(s) Under the Public Employe [sic] Relations Act. The district would then put me in a new situation where I would have a "clean slate." I was transferred to Stony Creek Elementary School.

I tried to explain to Chuck Herring that this was not a clean slate, but rather an impossible situation where I could be easily targeted. I had never taught elementary level children. I had no experience with the reading instruction, I had no Wilson training (phonics), and I did not know anything about elementary students. Chuck Herring, an attorney, could not see how this would be bad for me. He knew nothing about teaching, teachers, curriculum, or getting through a school day. He did not see that it was comparable to sending a psychiatrist in to do brain surgery. Both the neurologist and psychiatrist are doctors; both work with the brain and its functions. But they are not interchangeable.

May 2010

Jim Cairnes sent an email to the IEP team for which I was the case manager. I answered back within ten minutes. A few hours later, Jim Cairnes came to talk with me about the student. When he left, he said I was the only one from the team who bothered writing back to him. He said that told him a lot about me.

Over the last few weeks, I sensed a change in him. He treated me with some respect and gave me advice to avoid trouble.

June 2010

I don't know why but I wanted to talk to Bill Hayes at the end of the year. I spoke with him at length about what I had done for Kay and why I didn't think parents should bury their children. Bill Hayes had buried his niece the previous summer, when, tragically, the twenty-one year old was killed. We spoke, for the first time, with understanding and respect. We made our peace.

Hayes left the district the day before the start of the new school year. The rumor was he was let go because the high school did not make annual yearly progress on state testing.

Meanwhile, the new school year found me working at Stony Creek Elementary School.

CHAPTER THIRTY

Last Stand

PA Code for **Professional Practice:**

Section 3: Purpose
[a] Professional educators recognize their obligations to provide services and to conduct themselves in a manner which places the **highest esteem on human rights and dignity.**

[b] Professional educators recognize their primary responsibility to the student and the development of the student's potential.

Section 4: Practice:
[10] Professional educators shall exert reasonable effort to protect the student from conditions, which interfere with learning or are harmful to the student's health and safety.

Section 8: Civil Rights
The professional educator may not:
[2] interfere w/ a student's or colleague's exercise of political and civil rights and responsibilities.

Section 11: Professional Relationships
The professional educator may not:
[2] knowingly and intentionally distort evaluations of a colleague.

September 23, 2010
I sent a letter to Chuck Herring advising him that I had had a meeting with Kelle Heim-McCloskey and Gary, principal of Stony Creek. The results of the meeting were summed up in a memo from the principal:

- I was not to have contact with parents; that would be the general education teacher's responsibility.
- I was not to remove the students from the room to work with them because I was not highly qualified.
- I could not remove the students to another room for testing unless there was another teacher in the room with me, because I was not highly qualified. This directive came from Central Office.
- I was not to teach new concepts; I was to re-teach concepts.

The exact wording of this was:

Since you are not highly qualified and not elementary certified, and you operate under the former Special Education certificate, your instruction is designed to primarily reinforce and support student learning.

These dictums were quite disturbing and did not bode well for my students. Obviously, this district had a driving need to silence me. Everything they said and did had this at its core. The union president backed it up by telling me to be quiet about problems with the program.

How were my students affected?

- Sometimes it was better for learners who have difficulty shutting out external distraction to be in a more quite space for instruction. Not all the time, but there were lessons that would have been easier in a calmer environment. The only thing I could do was to teach them in the hallway. This was hardly a distraction-free environment.
- I had to give my students "probe" tests every week. This was also either done in a noisy classroom or a busy hallway. These tests were used to monitor their progress on a weekly basis. Most of my students had attention issues. Testing in the hallway or busy classroom was far from ideal.

The folks in Central Office had put me in an elementary school. If they felt I could not do what the other Special Education teachers did, because I was not highly qualified, then why did they choose to put me there? If I was operating under constrictions that hurt my kids, how was this a "fresh start"?

I called the Pennsylvania Department of Education. The representative said I was qualified to remove students from the classroom to teach or test pre-learned material. He remarked to me that it was a questionable practice and quite unusual to place a teacher with no experience in a school for which they "were not qualified" when the teacher was qualified on another level.

I told Gary that the PDE said I was qualified to test the children by myself. Gary said we could not do it because upper administration had said no. I followed directions and my students paid the price.

Keep in mind that almost all of the IEP's, under the section labeled Specially Designed Instruction stated:

The student should receive pullout for review of content areas or to reduce distractibility or to take tests.

Once again, the violation of IEP's did not seem to cause any concern. In fact, it was the administration ordering me to violate the IEP's. No parents were contacted about this change and no revisions were made to the IEP's. We just ignored the Specially Designed Instruction.

September 2010: Principal Observes Me

It was the third week of school. I was scheduled for second period for only twenty minutes, because I had to leave to assist my kindergarten student. About ten minutes before the start of class, my co-teachers decided to use a spelling program for the weekly words. I did not know how to access this program. As a result, I was not proficient according to Gary who was observing me.

When Gary met with me to discuss the observation, I felt he was supportive toward me. He gave me pointers on what to do when introducing a computer lesson to students. I had never done this before, so of course I made mistakes. He was critical of how short the lesson was, but considering I was scheduled to be elsewhere and only had half the time of the period, there was not much I could do about this. He also wanted to see my lesson plans. I had plans but they were designed for the normal word list instruction. I did not have time to rewrite them with the computer component in it because there was no time between the switch and the lesson.

Gary also said it would be awhile before I got my "timing" down, but he felt this would come with practice. He stated he was pleased at how I became a team member at Stony Creek. I felt this was a good start. After being criticized for not getting along with people, this compliment was most welcomed.

October 25, 2010: Observation Kelle Heim-McCloskey
Much like the year before, Heim-McCloskey's rendition of what took place was very different to what had actually occurred.

- I came in late to class.
  I was three minutes late. Another teacher asking me a question stopped me in the hall.
- Your classroom assistant must know what he is responsible for.
  I did not have a classroom assistant. The regular education teachers did. The classroom assistant followed a schedule made for him by the other teachers. We were never in the same room at the same time. He forgot that day where he was to go. Consequently, I became responsible for him. Heim-McCloskey did not know how the educational assistants were utilized at this school.
- My co-teacher told my students to come to the back table with their writing journals and a pencil. One of the students forgot his pencil. This was my fault. A good deal of learning time was lost because he had to walk three feet back to his desk to retrieve a pencil. As a matter of fact, according to Kelle Heim-McCloskey several students had to return for pencils and journals.
  I only had four students on Monday mornings.
- There was no evidence of my planning.
  I received the news that we were using the Egyptian vocab for spelling at 10:00 Sunday night. I did not have the vocab words at home. My lesson had been structured for my word sorting vocabulary. A lot of times teachers would change their plans on the fly. I just was too new to fake it as well as they did.

- I didn't give any lesson on digraphs. (Digraphs are two letters combined to make one sound e.g. ph = f sound). According to Ms. Heim-McCloskey, I just said the students were lucky because they could always remember a digraph because we had the **Ph**illies. No intro—no content—no ending. Gee, where have I heard that before?

  Actually, I was in luck. We had just done digraphs in the kindergarten class so I was ready. I started off by going over what "peanut butter" letters were (letters that stick together and make one sound). Then the students sorted their words.

- Heim-McCloskey gave a number of examples of what I should have done.

  Unfortunately that would have taken way too much time and my kids would have been left out of the next part of the lesson which was a rhyming exercise to be done with partners. My students needed to be back with their partners. I went over the books and made sure all the words were in order.

- Heim-McCloskey said I did not check the journals.

  I always checked their journals. Every week I did this. Suddenly, when I'm being observed, I decide to eliminate this step?

It went on in that vein. I didn't teach, I didn't assess, I didn't communicate, I didn't review, my students weren't learning, I was not providing support, I lacked clarity, I didn't have my own supply of pencils...

October 27, 2010: Post Observation Meeting
Gary and Kelle Heim-McCloskey were present, along with the new supervisor of Special Education. Kelle started lecturing me about the poor quality of my work. I started to defend myself but realized this was both futile and pathetic. I spent all of my time trying to prove myself, and they spent all of their time trying to decimate my passion and career.

I stated that I did not want to continue the meeting at that time. I would do so at another time when I had union representation. Heim-McCloskey asked me to sign the observation. I refused. She was upset. I don't know why, being as I had never signed the one the year before. I told her so. I thanked everyone and left. This may not have been the wisest move, but honestly, there was nothing I could do to ameliorate the situation. It was hopeless and I knew it. Michael Levin and the district would not stop until I was gone.

November 2010: Principal Observed my Co-teacher

My co-teacher got an excellent evaluation. In addition, Gary told her that she and I worked very well together. He was looking for us to mesh the way we did. He was very pleased with our working relationship. This of course was never told to me, I had to hear it from the teacher.

November 4, 2010

I was attending an in-service at Central Office, when I was called into the Special Education supervisor's office. This was the new supervisor for elementary schools. Guess what he had for me? Another unsatisfactory observation for an IEP meeting that had taken place a few days before. Gary was sitting in the chair next to me staring at the floor. Now here's a surprise. This supervisor found nothing but mistakes in how I conducted the IEP meeting.

- I should have stated the purpose of the meeting at the beginning. The conversation appeared to be more like a Parent/Teacher interaction.
- I let the mother talk too much.
- I had to be prompted to shut the mother up and move on.
- I did not get the signature page signed at the beginning of the meeting. In the high school and middle school we did this last.
- I did not address the student's needs. I most certainly did because I knew this mother had some strong convictions about her daughter's education.
- I did not fix an error on the anticipated duration date because I followed the old IEP's dates and the previous teacher had done this incorrectly.

This was not acceptable to the supervisor. I followed the old IEP dates because I lived in constant terror of making mistakes and getting more letters of reprimand. Additionally, Gary had checked and rechecked this IEP before the meeting. He did not catch this—or he let it go because it could be used against me. Administrators or supervisory personnel had not caught this mistake the previous year.

What I found most interesting was the supervisor had asked to see the NOREP at the IEP meeting. When he handed it back to me he said, "Most teachers miss this section but you didn't." How many teacher write-ups do you think he did on that?

Then he gave me recommendations, one of which was to make sure I got parental input for the Parental Concerns section. The only problem with this was his earlier criticism that I had let the mother talk too much **about** her concerns. I should have directed her to not speak these worries until we reached the appropriate sections. That was part of the "too much extraneous" talk. The supervisor complained that he had to "prompt" me to refocus on the IEP because the mother was stating her concerns and I was taking notes, rather than curbing her conversation.

I had approached this IEP meeting with timidity for two reasons. (1) I was scared to death to say or do anything that would get me in trouble. (2) We had most definitely violated the existing IEP and denied the child services stipulated by the document. This child was supposed to be taken to a separate room when she had a test. Kelle Heim-McCloskey told Principal Abbamont that I was not allowed to be alone with any student. Therefore, this child remained in the large classroom for testing. This was an out and out violation of the IEP and her civil rights.

The mother was upset with this situation. I had no idea what I would say to her because how could I explain that I was not allowed alone in the room with students? It was the reading teacher who pointed out this violation at the IEP meeting. The principal gave some convoluted excuse, promising that it would be remedied.

Let's look at this realistically. The supervisor was upset because I didn't muzzle the mother or the conversation, but he was not remotely concerned with the fact that we were caught in a blatant violation of federal law?

After the IEP meeting, Gary told my co-teacher that he thought the meeting went very well. Of course, he said nothing during the negative review.

There was nothing to say. This man had his orders and he was following them. I signed my name and returned to my in-service. The supervisor was gone by the end of the year. Indiscretions did him in.

Sidebar:

When we had a progress meeting with this same mother in late November, she brought up the testing situation again. I told her she would have to speak with Kelle Heim-McCloskey. The mother had some incredibly choice words for the supervisor. Mom had many dealings with Ms. Heim-McCloskey already; she had some horror stories to tell. I suddenly realized this was the mother from the Shorehaven case. One of the cases costing in the millions that Michael Levin said did not exist. She did not have much fight left in her. She had battled the district for years and was still paying off her legal debts. Sadly, her older child, who required this care, had died the past summer.

November 10, 2010

I was absent one day. I received an email from Gary. He had gone over my lesson plans and found them inadequate. I was wondering why he had said nothing about this before. I had been out for an in-service, and left plans for a substitute. I was not accustomed to the sub plan requirements on the elementary level. One of my errors was not including a floor plan of the building. In the high school, that was provided by the front office. I worked with three teachers; two of them were next to each other in the same hall as my room. I also did not list my students because the school was manic about confidentiality, and I didn't want to commit their names to a list. The lead teacher could point them out.

I wrote an apology to Gary. What I didn't understand was Gary's approach. It was not like him to rebuke someone for a first mistake. He tried to teach and set by example. It hadn't occurred to me yet that this was the plan to effect my dismissal.

The next day, I wrote up packets with a floor plan, lists of students, a complete schedule, where to find supplies in each classroom, and suggestions for working with some students who needed more encouragement or support. From that time on, I left the most comprehensive substitute lesson plans. No other teacher, regular or Special Education, left ones as in-depth as mine. When I took over for the lead teachers when they were absent, no one came in to check their plans.

November 2010: Letter from Judy Clark, Superintendent

I have been informed that you were observed October 25, 2010... According to the report and information I have been provided by the building principal and Kelle Heim-McCloskey, it is alleged that you engaged in the following wrongdoing:

The letter went on to list all the accusations contained in Kelle Heim-McCloskey's observations. In addition, it charged me with refusing to sign the observation and walking out of the meeting. There were "examples" of my "poor teaching."

You are directed to **give your side of the story** to the above allegations in writing to me …if you fail or refuse to provide a written response to these allegations, **you may be disciplined including discharged.**

The requirement of a written response was designed to provide Michael Levin with ammunition for his next letter of allegations.

November 16, 2010: Sallie Montanye/Dismissal

Not one to disappoint, Mr. Levin sent a letter to the arbitrator in record time. He was advising the WEA of additional allegations "against Mrs. Montanye." He went into the background of my numerous offenses and how the district generously reassigned me to a new school for a "fresh start." However, two months after I was assigned here the same types of performance issues arose. Levin attacked my letter to Judy Clark. He wrote to the arbitrator claiming:

Far from satisfactorily answering the allegations against her, her responses justify further allegations against her—primarily significant falsification of information. In addition to the allegations contained in Exhibit A, the school district alleges the following:

- I lied about the time I got to class.
- I falsely stated that I had asked for another meeting with a union rep.
- I falsely stated that an unknown attorney for the district (MIL) stated that signing an observation form indicated agreement.
- I falsely stated that I could only "re-teach" material.

Remember Gary's memo of September 23rd ?
Since you are not highly qualified and not elementary certified, and you operate under the former Special Education certificate, your instruction is designed to primarily reinforce and support student learning.

- I had such a high degree of incompetency that I did not even always understand the focus of an allegation and misconstrued what is alleged. (This referred to my response that I would not have an introductory lesson when the lead teacher was introducing the lesson). My statement was nonsensical.
- I didn't understand declarative sentences. I questioned Heim-McCloskey's assertion that I did not know the vocabulary.
- I lied about my group coming to the table, and what supplies to bring.
- I lied that the children did not go back to retrieve their journals and make a second trip for pencils.
- Reflective of my incompetency I stated that I did not know what a statement that Heim-McCloskey attributed to me, meant.
- I falsely stated where Heim-McCloskey sat during the observation.
- I falsely stated that I reviewed a certain concept.
- I falsely stated that we went over digraphs as a group.
- I falsely stated that Heim-McCloskey did not include all the interchange that took place.
- I falsely stated that the students made a grid in their journals.
- I falsely stated that the students wrote down the sorting rule.
- I falsely stated that there was only one boy in the group.
- I falsely stated how the children returned to their seats.
- I falsely stated that I was not given the observation report.
- I falsely stated that I wanted a union rep at the meeting.
- As further evidence of my incompetency, Mr. Levin was supplying the unsatisfactory from the Supervisor of Special Education concerning the IEP meeting.

In true accurate fashion, the letter was cc'd to **Dr.** Judith Clark. The superintendent did not and does not have a Ph.D. For people who were so particular about every breath I took, they certainly made their fair share of mistakes.

December 15, 2010: Arbitration #6

This was still track one of the arbitration. It dealt primarily with the IEP's. I had pressured Chuck Herring to ask for copies of the IEP spreadsheet that was used to track my IEP dates. I wanted to see the records kept on all the other teachers. This was first presented at Loudermill #2. Either Herring didn't ask for the correct paper or Michael Levin didn't process the request accurately. The Levin Legal Group sent over a box filled with pages upon pages of redacted names and dates for IEP's. This was not what we asked for. According to Herring, Michael Levin was angry that we were not satisfied with the box of valueless papers; it had taken a long time to copy them. I told Mr. Herring that was not our problem and I wanted the spreadsheets. I knew they didn't exist. That would point to the district singling me out. Herring said he asked for it again. He complained at the hearing that we had not received requested documents, but he was willing to proceed without this. (Why?)

Call me suspicious, but I think Mr. Levin was still harboring some resentment. In addition to including the lower court's decision in his evidence, which was totally inapplicable to this event, Mr. Levin brought up our journey through the court system during his cross:

Levin: referring to the Directives Letter of June, 2002:

Levin: Let's take the first one. The one that you went to Federal Court and complained about back in 2002. Do you remember that?

Montanye: Yes.

Levin: You never forgot about that one, you went all the way to the Third Circuit on that.
Montanye: Yes, I did.

Levin: You went up to the U.S. Supreme Court on that, right?

Montanye: Yes, I did.

His point would be…?

This next exchange was about a letter from Kelle Heim-McCloskey, which had been written for Judy Clark, listing the late IEP's in the district, along with the teachers' names.[34]

Montanye: On a document that **we received from the District**, there was a list of teachers with late IEP's and a statement that said the IEP was not considered late unless it was 30 days overdue.

Levin: Objection on the basis of hearsay.

Herring: That document from the District, was it sent to you from a District administrator?

Montanye: It had a District administrator's name on it.

Herring: Do you remember who the administrator was?

Montanye: Kelle Heim-McCloskey.

Levin: I still object on the basis of hearsay. I haven't seen it. Best evidence rule, what document?

Levin: I want to see the document.

Herring: We have the document somewhere; we would have to take a time out to find the document.

Levin: Before I cross, I would like to see the document.

Of course, we never produced the document. That was the way with these arbitrations; much ado but no follow through. In case you were wondering if Mr. Levin's objection was legitimate, it was not. He had seen the letter already; it was included as SD-31 in the **district's evidence packet.** In fact, this was noted in #27 of the stipulations. Michael Levin and his clients were the ones who produced the letter and put it into evidence.

The other absurdity of this hearing was the absence of Jim

---

[34] This was not an accurate account. There were at least three IEP's, written by other teachers that I knew about, that were over three months late. They were not on the list.

Malley. Chuck Herring had instructed me to write up questions he could ask Malley. Following my evidence packet, I addressed all the IEP's and their timeliness. I had scores of emails to back up my claims that I was not at fault for many of the late IEP's. I didn't write one question that lacked evidence as to its veracity. Before the hearing, Mr. Herring informed me that the district "might not produce Malley" because they couldn't find him. Malley had retired at the end of 2010. (Rumor was he was pushed out.) He was still doing consulting with districts. His child still went to high school and his address was still listed as local. But the district didn't know where to find him?

Herring said if they didn't produce him, he would ask me the questions I had written. Despite the fact that the man lived less than ten miles away from the district, they were "unable to locate him." I took my questions to Mr. Herring the week before the hearing. For some reason during the hearing, he never asked me any of the questions, which meant the arbitrator ignored the packet, and the district's involvement in the violations of Special Education law was once again well hidden.

Wait. It gets better. Because Malley was not there, everything I said was disregarded because it was considered "hearsay." The arbitrator used this as an excuse to ignore all the information concerning the IEP's. He also neutralized any testimony I made with the argument Mr. Malley wasn't there to dispute it.

December 2010:Opinion and Award
The arbitrator listed all the charges that had been accruing over the past two years.

> Although I find a number of the District's allegations may not warrant discipline, central to my decision in this Award, is the conclusion that the Grievant violated school district requirements and Special Education laws with respect to the development of IEP's...I am informing the parties that the facts and circumstances which led to my decision regarding "track one" (IEP's) issues will remain, where relevant, under consideration and consistent with my evaluation of "track two" issues.

Translation: Because he refused to look at the packet detailing how most of the IEP's were not late due to my negligence, and how some were not even late, although they were listed, the learned arbitrator decided to side with the district. He accepted none of my testimony as factual. In addition, he was going to decide against me in the next round. This explains why Chuck Herring came out of the backroom meeting (12/15/2010) informing me, even if I won this round, I would not win the next one. It was a done deal.

The arbitrator decided I should not have used my co-worker's name on the letter. Did he hear any testimony about this? No. The aide who was present at the letter's writing and who thanked the teacher for her support was never brought in to testify. Neither was the teacher; in fact, it was only the word of Kelle Heim-McCloskey, as **quoted** by Bill Hayes, that the teacher denied knowledge of this letter. **No one** testified to this matter.

My comment concerning the large amounts of money lost on Special Education cases was categorized thusly:

The comments made by the Grievant, regarding millions lost in special education lawsuits may have been her honest opinion or just careless gossip. On the other hand, such a comment coming from a faculty member, understandably was a singular annoyance to the school district. In my judgment, while the Grievant's comments are representative, in consideration of her position with the district, of personal immaturity, realistically, such a peccadillo is not beyond being mouthed by even the most stalwart of professional employees.

I was also guilty of altering the layout of the form. This behavior "exemplified (my) propensity to disregard legitimate directions from (my) supervisors and is worthy of discipline."

This made no sense as I followed directions immediately and destroyed the forms.

Now this is where it gets interesting. The arbitrator quoted Malley's letter of May 13, 2008. There are a few things we need to recall about this letter.

(1) The letter was never sent until July 2008. By that time, all the IEP's mentioned in the letter (other than

the two) had been completed and filed. All the re-evals and documents listed in the letter were in Central Office. Completed.

(2) Malley told my attorney at Loudermill #2 that there was information in the letter that was not true.

Showing no discernment but a boatload of bias, the arbitrator stated, "Indeed, she was the only Special Education teacher who had not completed all of her IEP's at the 2007-2008 school year." To believe this would be excessively naïve. To state it in an opinion demonstrates lack of cognitive function. I know it's not true: one of the Special Ed teachers came back from another school in the fall of 2008 to have an IEP meeting because she forgot to write the behavior plan for a spring IEP. That is not a completed IEP. Furthermore, the district submitted SD-31:

Because of concerns that IEP's were not being rewritten or completed on a timely basis, Judy Clark (who was assistant superintendent at the time, and who became Superintendent effective December 1,2008) asked one of the special education supervisors, Kelle McCloskey, to provide data as to which teachers were out of compliance and how many IEP's were late. The data is [sic] provided is contained [sic] in SD-31.

One would question why, if no other teacher was late with IEP's, this document had to be created. Did the arbitrator not read this, not understand this, or was it easier to just mouth the district's claims?

A given percentage of IEP's were late. Again, with the hundreds of IEP's written in this district, it is unfathomable that only one person had late IEP's. I personally knew of many others.

The IEP that was late due to Malley was not considered credible because the "district points out that the grievant could offer no documentation in support of her contention that Malley was the cause of the delay." I guess the fifty pages of emails back and forth to Malley wouldn't be considered "documentation." I guess the email from the guidance counselor to Malley, who said it was a disgrace that this document remained incomplete wasn't "documentation" enough.

February 1, 2011

Every spring the faculty received a paper asking if they wanted a transfer. I asked Gary if he wanted me to try and transfer. I told him I was aware that my presence was cumbersome to him; as long as I was in his school, they would be pressuring him to find something wrong. He shook his head in agreement. He then said he could not ask me to transfer. He appeared truly troubled with this discussion.

March 2011

The Friday before the next arbitration Gary requested all of my lesson plans. I had changed the format to include the information I thought he wanted. I could not provide a good deal of the previous plans because I kept changing them each week attempting to improve them. I did supply him with the week's plans, which he claimed I did not. He obviously got a call from Central Office to do this.

March 2011: Arbitration

There was another arbitration scheduled; now the topic would be my insufficient lesson plans. Today's arbitration was cancelled an hour into the meeting because Levin did not give Herring more than a weekend's forewarning of the new charges. Mr. Levin did say that it was imperative this be settled because I should not be allowed to be in the presence of children.

April 2011: Lesson Plans

Finally I just put everything in that I could think of:

- The objective or PA eligible content
- Procedure
- Differentiated Materials/Methods
- Teaching Point
- Pre-reading
- During reading
- After reading
- Follow up student tasks
- Assessments (at least two)

April 5, 2011

Gary observed me in three different classes in one day. He had nothing nice to say in his reports. One of the sessions he observed involved a "Literary Circle." This was a group of students who read the same book and had different assignments to contribute to the group discussion. My co-teachers both commented to me that they thought our discussions sounded great. I had no idea what a literary circle was. I was handed the books and the calendar to make up for the assignments. I followed the approach modeled by my co-teachers.

When Gary and I discussed the literary circle, he said there were particular techniques used to have the students control the discussion. He said he would teach them to me. He never did.

April 9, 2011

I asked Gary if I could have a meeting with him and the local union president to go over exactly what was needed in the lesson plans. No one else could help me because no one wrote plans that Gary claimed were the norm. We met and he gave me a template, which I followed religiously. Gary wrote up a memorandum reviewing the meeting and threw in the tried and true promise: **Your failure or refusal to comply with these directives may lead to discipline, including discharge.** Keep in mind this meeting was held at my request.

April 2011

I told Gary that my lesson plans were twenty pages long. He said I was including too much information. He would look them over and get back to me. An interesting point: when a teacher is not doing plans correctly, usually the principal will request a copy of the plans prior to the week they will be used. Gary never asked to see my plans in advance or to check them to make sure I was "following" his instructions. I volunteered to give him my plans.

I left him a few pages in his mailbox. A few days later, they were returned to me in my mailbox. There were no comments. Gary did not discuss them with me. Strange behavior for someone who was so concerned about the structure of my lesson plans.

Here is the template I used for each day. This is *one* lesson (one period).

MONDAY Date: Lesson: Reading 8:50—9:30	playground duty Teacher Name D1
Students	Names of Students
PA EC	**R5A.1.1.1** Identify/interp the meaning of vocabulary **R5A.2.1.1** Identify/apply word recognition [patterns] **R5A.1.2.1** Identify how meaning of word changed when affix added
Differentiation *Word Sort List/* *Individual white* *boards/Syllabication* *rules/marking vowels* **Procedure**	**Teaching Point:** Sort # Pattern: Materials: *Word Sorts for Syllables+* *Affixes Spellers;* journals; word list; white boards Before: Introduce the sort being used for the week *See expanded lesson plan #XX* During: Discuss meanings of the words Have students use them in sentences Write words on white boards—dot the vowels—syllabicate them/continue w/ words on list Follow Up student task: students make grid and put words under sort rules
Assessment	Review words/sort rules Check to make sure students have entered words under the correct sort Assessment—test Friday

No other teacher in the school had plans containing the details of my plans.

May 19, 2011: Observation

May was my observation month. I was so nervous about this because I knew no matter what I did Gary would have to find fault with it. Gary came in to social studies right after lunch.

When I walked into the room, my co-teacher informed me that she was changing the plans for the social studies lesson. I had five minutes to become acquainted with ancient Greece. The lesson went very well. The students were extremely involved and excited about the material. In fact, the speech teacher was there to observe one of the students. He needed one more good evaluation to be removed from speech. This did not happen; the student was so into the lesson he forgot to watch his speech and he failed the test. This was a bright, resistant learner; when you could get him involved you were really achieving something. The speech teacher told me it was a fantastic lesson.

Gary of course found it lacking. Let's be honest. There was nothing I could do to please Gary, because he had his orders. One of the high school teachers told me later that Stony Creek was were they sent the teachers they wanted fired. Gary was a good soldier.

May 2011

I could no longer deny that I was too sick to work. I was constantly ill or crying. I sat at one IEP meeting and the tears just streamed down my face. I was not thinking of anything other than the discussion at hand; I was having crying spells with great regularity. I had no control over them. My blood pressure was all over the place. I was so tired I could hardly move. I was having trouble seeing, and it was very difficult for me to focus for long or remember anything. My digestive system was severely responsive to my condition. Keeping food down was difficult. Processing it without extreme pain was also impossible. I suffered constant anxiety attacks. I had to leave school three times because my heart was racing and I could not stand up. Friday nights I would come home and go to bed. I would not get out of bed until Monday morning. I went nowhere. I talked to no one. I told my doctor I just wanted to dissolve into thin air.

My life was falling apart. I was in financial trouble due to all the money I had lost not working and because I was in such debt. My house went up for foreclosure. I was in a full clinical depression and had to go out on disability.

May 2011: Annual Evaluation

Shockingly, Gary gave me an unsatisfactory. A blind man could see that coming. There are a few things to note about Gary and his behavior toward me. Whenever I asked for help or to talk to him, Gary was attentive and kind. He was well liked at the school and for the most part he treated his teachers with respect. Unless he was following orders, he was equally kind and considerate to me. He was concerned when I went home with panic attacks. He always had the secretary call to see that I made it home. He helped me write my personal yearly goals. We had an enjoyable relationship except for his instructions to find fault. I am not saying he wouldn't have found me lacking; of course, there would be a gap. It would take a few years to learn the techniques and curriculum. Most of the time I was operating in the dark. The teachers did not have time to show me all the materials or explain how to do the lessons. I followed the script and did the best I could. Strangely enough I genuinely liked the elementary school. The fifth grade class was a very nice group of kids. I liked their enthusiasm and youthful wonder. And I loved my little kindergartener.

September 7, 2011: Notice of Allegations and Conference

I received another letter from Judy Clark. It included all the charges from the previous year. In addition, the observation of Kelle Heim-McCloskey was included along with my "falsification of information" response to Judy Clark about the observation. Additionally, Gary's memo concerning the substitute plans and all his unfavorable reviews of my teaching, including the final observation and unsatisfactory evaluation, were present.

Also included was the "testimony" of one of my co-teachers. According to Mr. Levin, this teacher had said I did little more than an aide. Remember, according to Gary's memo that's all I was allowed to do.

What I enjoyed the most was this comment from my fifth grade co-teacher: According to her I had referred to a child as "retarded" and that made her "feel sick and awful."

Here's the real story. We had a student who was very low academically. This teacher kept telling me she felt she wasn't able to help him because he could not do much work even with support. What I said was, she was doing a good job and we would give him all the support we could. However, he was in the wrong placement. I said, "In years past, he would have been considered educable retarded and would not be forced into regular education classes, but would be given math and reading instruction in a support room where his needs could be fully met." The next year he was placed in a self-contained room, which is what I referred to in my statement.

It was also alleged that I said I was going "after Gary." I did not say this. For that matter, I don't know if the teacher ever made this remark. Mr. Levin had a habit of crediting his thoughts to others. I will point out that this was the same teacher who changed the lesson plans five minutes before my observation. She knew Gary was observing me.

I was to have another Loudermill hearing so I could explain my side of the story. By this point, I was too sick to tell my side of the story.

September 28, 2011 Re: Statement of Charges and Notice of a Right to Hearing

I was charged with: persistent negligence in the performance of duties, willful neglect of duties, and persistent and willful violation of or failure to comply with school laws of the Commonwealth (including official directives and established policy of the board of directors) and **immorality.**

Charge number one was left over from the high school: not going to the team meeting that never was and leaving five minutes early because I was sick.

Charge number two dealt with the lesson plans, Kelle Heim-McCloskey's observation, the Spec Ed supervisor's observation, not informing my classroom assistant of his responsibilities (even though I did not have a classroom assistant), my first set of substitute plans, failing to provide time in my lesson to monitor what my students were recording in their packets. The immorality charges came with my response to Judith Clark concerning my observation meeting.

September 28, 2011: Second Termination Letter from School Board

STATEMENT OF CHARGES AND NOTICE OF RIGHT TO HEARING

It was an identical reproduction of Michael Levin's nasty letter of November 2010. The letter reiterated all the accusations of the letter from Judy Clark. The supervisor's critical observation was also included, although it had been conspicuously altered. There was a long list of accusations from Gary, all of which centered around the lesson plans. This was followed by the explanation for the immorality charges:

You have provided false information in response to allegations of wrongdoing. You were asked to respond to the allegations contained in the letter (from Judy Clark, November 3, 2010). Far from satisfactorily answering the allegations against you, your answers justified further allegations against you— primarily falsification of information.

Here was another "lie." When I left the room on the day of the observation meeting, I said thank you and walked out. The letter said I walked out without saying thank you. Now that's just ridiculous. How do I know? Because at Stony Creek everyone *always* says thank you at the end of a meeting. That's the way we rolled at Stony.

This venomous missive was signed by Young K. Park, head of the school board. Mr. Park was on the original school board that I sued back in 2002. Mr. Park was one of the board members who paid Michael Levin money to perpetuate Wissahickon School District's argument that a child's emotional troubles were of no importance to the community. Mr. Park was offended that I allegedly didn't say thank you when I left the room, but he stuffed the pockets of the man who said a suicidal kid was of no importance.

I did not attend this hearing; it would be an exercise in meaninglessness. Although I was on disability, according to the district I had been terminated yet again. This is how they claimed they were not responsible to fulfill the contractual obligations for disability pay and retirement supplementation.

In a letter dated September 12, 2011 from Judy Clark:

> As a result having given you the opportunity to give **your side of the story** and you having waived that right, I have considered the allegations against you and the evidence available to me. Based on the nature of the allegations and the available evidence, I have determined to suspend you without pay pending dismissal proceedings.

This would affect my retirement and money due me.

According to the contract anyone who retired after sixty-two was given $10,000 per year to provide for health care until she was eligible for Medicare. However, the district considered me fired, even though I was on disability. They would not give me this benefit.

According to the contract, any person who goes on disability is entitled to one hundred days pay from the district before the disability kicks in. The district did not give me that. Initially,

Michael Levin told PSEA I would not get this. Then, although I went out on disability in May 2011, they claimed I had been terminated. This termination would have taken place in September of 2011 after the district's insurance company had granted me disability. Terminating me was illegal.

Chuck Herring's response to this was we could go ahead with the last arbitration. Of course, the PSEA lawyer was well aware that was a wasted effort.

2011

Once again, I foolishly hired an attorney to make the district live up to the contract. This was a waste of money and time. The claim was filed with the Pennsylvania Human Relations Commission. My attorney said we had to file a discrimination charge. A year and a half later, the PHRC sided with the district. My lawyer then informed me that ninety-nine percent of all decisions went against the employee. She said that although I obviously was the target of retaliation, the courts were notoriously reluctant to grant this to the employee. Also, a school district is looked on with favor because no one wants to take taxpayer money for a legal award.

My lawyers said the union was basically disinterested. They then advised me that I could give them $10,000 and we could sue the district. I was done shoveling money into a system that disregarded the truth, and black and white evidence. I had had it with stoking the financial fires of the legal institution where a judge felt that ejecting a battered child from school and sending her home to die was exemplary of a superintendent who "protected the children." My husband had always claimed, "the fix was in." I don't know about that; however, I do know that precedential law was not applied, that manufactured law was accepted, and that the district was allowed to get away with the extensive infringement of civil rights that could affect every student and teacher in this country.

August 2013: Email from Michael Levin

I have reviewed this matter with my client and in exchange for a full and complete release of all claims and a withdrawal of all grievances/arbitration using our standard release and settlement agreement, the District is willing to pay Ms. Montanye Two Thousand, Five Hundred Dollars ($2,500). The claims against the district **have no** *value*. Ms. Montanye and her army of attorneys who represented her in her first federal case against the district did not believe me when I told them that the case **had no** *value*, but they got nothing and Ms. Montanye ended up paying costs to the district. This offer is being made on a take it or leave it basis...

Michael Levin, Esquire

"I told them the case had no value, but they got **nothing**..."

Mr. Levin and his clients **never** got it. It was about a child, struggling to survive. It was about a teacher fighting to be allowed to help this child. In the end, a frightened girl lived through her tribulations and grew into a healthy, beautiful young woman.

"They got nothing..."

Only in the Wissahickon School District and Michael Levin's world, would the survival of a battered, suicidal child be judged as "getting nothing." Only in the morally bankrupt environment of this district would saving a child's life hold no value.

What about Kay? What about the girl whose life held no significance to those who were charged with educating her and making her into a "good citizen."? The years after ninth grade were still fraught with issues. However, through her efforts, her family's support, and outside help she was able to cast off the pall of death and to develop into a successful woman. Other children may not be so lucky, especially if the Wissahickon School District's belief that *one child's problems are of no importance to the community* remains the guiding beacon of administrative concern.

EPILOGUE

I submit that never has a teacher been given so many chances. The time has come to issue an order affirming her dismissal.

Michael Ira Levin, Esquire   Letter March 26, 2011

It was time for me to retire. I was too tired and too sick to continue fighting the district. When I sent in my letter for retirement, I received an extensive communication from Chuck Herring, PSEA attorney. He wanted to know if I had been provided with medical benefits, why I was no longer on disability, and what I thought the district owed me. His unusual interest was bewildering.

True to form, Herring denied a conversation that had taken place in May of 2011. That's why I had taken a witness with me. My witness, who took notes, remembered the conversation and Chuck's assurances for resolution. Herring's words in his new communications were contradictory to his original statements. He denied the assurances he made.

The attorney sent me letters asking me what I felt the district owed me. This would be followed by union action if deemed appropriate. Where was this enthusiasm when Michael Levin sent letters from the district stating I would get nothing from them? It was too little, too late. Chuck Herring's newfound interest in my case would have been welcomed years before. I sent him a letter telling him I would not go through another arbitration. I had enough experience with them and with Herring's nebulous support. When I needed the union, Herring was not overly concerned with presenting evidence or my case. This change in his focus was sudden and unprecedented.

Mr. Herring once told me that at one time he a had passion for what he did, but he learned that "no one cared." His work would be wasted. (Conversation at PSEA 3/22/2003, with witness) Maybe this was his reason for doing a job with as little effort as possible for other cases, but it certainly was not applicable to my case. I was passionate, tenacious, and fighting for a rock-solid cause: the freedom to help a child as a private citizen. I should have been his dream case. I was an annoyance. That's a sad commentary on the union and what it now represents. Much like the district, empty rhetoric is all they have to offer. You can't be concerned with the good of the children if you allow the teachers to be crushed when they advocate for their students. What does that say about our society?

Speaking of sad commentaries, not one person thought to question the expense and message being sent by the Wissahickon School District. No one had the grit to stop the macabre madness of a school district advocating for letting a child die? No one even bothered to find out the truth concerning Kay?

The lawyer was driven by greed and ego, the WIN team by jealous pettiness, and the administration and school board by indifference. Through their collective stupidity, they went along with deadly and inane arguments that cost thousands in taxpayer's dollars, and conceivably some other child's life.

Think about it. A vindictive woman writes a letter; and rather than analyze what was really going on, the administrators couldn't throw away public money fast enough to pay an odious lawyer to represent them with the argument that a dead kid didn't matter to the community. This horrendous claim was put forth and financed by a SCHOOL DISTRICT!

If Stanley Durtan had been concerned about my actions, he could have spoken to me and told me not to do it again. No lawyer. No phony Loudermill. No Directives Letter.

Instead, the legacy of Stanley Durtan, Jr., Judith Clark, Maria Salvucci, Imelda Kormos, Thomas Speakman, Kelle Heim-McCloskey and the rest of the group is this: when confronted with a bullied, suicidal child, it is both professional and an indicator of good judgment to ignore the child. After all, that's what **all of these people did.**

What about me? My marriage ended: the constant strain was too much for it to bear. I almost lost my house twice; I still don't know if I will be able to keep it. My credit rating is in the negative numbers. I owe a lot of people a lot of money. I was forced out of the profession I excelled in and truly loved. I was betrayed by the union and eviscerated by the monsters who said letting a kid die was the preferable option. I still get sick if I have contact with the district or for that matter, PSEA.

Conversely, I have unfailing support from friends and family. My attorneys, Anita, Sarah, and Catherine, believed in me completely and went beyond the call of duty in the name of saving a kid's life.

The serious repercussions of the WIN team letter were forthcoming, but not in the manner threatened. Kay's parents did not sue the district for intervening to save her life. The district that "feared" the serious repercussions was the malevolent catalyst for them. They turned my world upside down. With methodical deliberation and malicious intent, these people devised ways to torture me. Their constant persecutions resulted in illness and clinical depression. They destroyed my reputation and ended my career. They made no bones about it—helping a bullied, suicidal child would cost a teacher her livelihood. The Wissahickon School District said a dead child was not important to the community. Judge Jan DuBois of the Eastern division court said that was so. The Third Appellate Court agreed. The implications of these are staggering.

Knowing what would be forthcoming, how my life would be affected, and some of the grim consequences that would result, would I do it over again?

In a New York minute.

ACKNOWLEDGMENTS

My life did not turn out exactly as I thought it would. Yes, I was married, had two children, three cats, and a steady teaching job. Everything was going along as usual; then suddenly it wasn't. It seemed life had decided that I was not going down the mundane road. I was set on a course that twisted my life, convulsed my future, and challenged every belief I held dear. It was rough at some points, terrifying at others. Like all great challenges, you come out stronger or you never recover. I consider myself lucky to have weathered this storm and been transformed into a better person. This I owe to many of the wonderful people who were in my life.

My family: my husband who worked tirelessly to provide money for the fight he so deeply believed in. It was also his future going up in smoke.

My children who believed in the values I fought for.

My friends who listened to what could be considered the longest rendition of legal thought in modern history. They were loyal and extremely self-sacrificing when suffering through stories rehashed over ten years.

My attorneys: Anita who made the case come alive; Sarah who dedicated every ounce of her strength giving it life and form; Catherine who worked tirelessly to do justice to a case she felt was "extremely important."

At every point of need, the divine provided. I was supplied with Judi, my formatter, who walked me (at least once a week) through the steps to make this a real book.

The one who put in more than anyone should have to is my wonderful editor, Mary Beth. This woman did not sit over the final edition putting in her commas and changing tenses. God bless her, she slugged through at least three other writings before this version came into being. Her stamina alone is noteworthy; because, believe me, those other editions were like pushing your way through hundreds of wet blankets. And about as interesting. Once I mastered the art of not writing down every idea that passed through my mind, MB could tighten up the story, fathom all the legalese, take out the snarky, put in the semi- colons and make sure I stayed on track (and in proper tense.)

This book is a tribute to all who helped and all who believe in the value of a child's life.